RICHARD LINGEMAN

The Nation Guide to the Nation

RICHARD LINGEMAN, a senior editor of *The Nation,* was for many years the magazine's executive editor. His books include *Small Town America: A Narrative History, 1620–Present*; *Don't You Know There's a War On?: The American Home Front, 1941–1945*; *Theodore Dreiser: An American Journey*; *Sinclair Lewis: Rebel from Main Street* and, most recently, *Double Lives: American Writers' Friendships.*

The Nation
GUIDE TO THE NATION

The Nation
GUIDE TO THE NATION

BY RICHARD LINGEMAN

Introduction by **VICTOR NAVASKY** and **KATRINA** vanden **HEUVEL**

Original Drawings by **ED KOREN**

VINTAGE BOOKS

A Division of Random House, Inc.

NEW YORK

A VINTAGE BOOKS ORIGINAL, JANUARY 2009

LIBRARY OF CONGRESS CATALOGING-IN-PUBLICATION DATA
Lingeman, Richard R.
    The Nation guide to the Nation / by Richard Lingeman and the editors of The Nation ; introduction by Victor Navasky and Katrina Vanden Heuvel ; illustrations by Ed Koren.
        p. cm.
    Includes index.
    ISBN 978-0-307-38728-8
    1. Nation (New York) 2. United States—Civilization—1945– I. Nation (New York) II. Title.
    E169.12.L548 2009
    973.91—dc22   2008032189

Cover and book design by BTDNYC

www.vintagebooks.com

Printed in the United States of America
10 9 8 7 6 5 4 3 2 1

TO THE MEMORY OF

Daniel Singer and Andrew Kopkind

Contents

The Nation
GUIDE TO THE NATION

Introduction

VICTOR NAVASKY AND KATRINA VANDEN HEUVEL

One day not long ago we returned to *The Nation*'s office just a block east of New York's Union Square and found this message on our voice mail from an individual with a soft Southern accent who identified herself as a sixty-eight-year-old widow:

> "I need to ask a favor of you. I'm stuck in Abbeyville, Louisiana, and I want to move, but I want to move to somewhere where I can see a Democrat before I die. It occurs to me that you might be able to rummage up a place where people are actually subscribers to *The Nation*, where I'd have somebody to talk to. I don't want their names or anything. I just want a town where there are a few kindred souls." And then she added, "If you could call around noon I'd be grateful. I'm about to cut the grass."

Caller, this book is for you and all the other people who want to connect. People of the left-liberal-radical persuasion (the kind of people who read *The Nation*) who find themselves in some red state backwater hungering for kindred spirits, for community, for folks who'll help them organize an antiwar rally or a fund-raiser or a peace march or a discussion group or a food co-op.

The Nation Guide to the Nation is for and about a community of committed, passionate people who have active consciences and a lively sense of social justice. It's a mixture of the *Whole Earth Catalog, 1000 Places to See Before You Die* and *The Old Farmer's Almanac*. It's a kind of collage of the Left; it's a Sears Roebuck catalog of tools and ideas for people who want (with help from their friends) to change the world (or at least the neighborhood); who want to shop their values and hash out their attitudes and who also want to know a good slow food restaurant (not too pricey) that serves only natural, locally grown ingredients—if possible. They may not be full-blooded locavores, but they share with Alice Waters—the California chef, doyenne of locally grown food and radical food reformer—a political concern with the link between the foods they eat and protecting the environment. (See page 276.)

They might be looking for a good salon with bright subversive talk or (like the nationwide group Drinking Liberally) a good saloon that serves drinks with a political twist, a home away in which to relax, drink and talk politics. Rather than the newest thing or the latest link in a corporate chain, they want the *real* thing; say, a place with local roots that's become a hangout with its own body of legend. A landmark place like Scholz Garten in Austin, where the state pols and cynical liberals congregate. Or Manuel's in Atlanta. Or the weary traveler in Madison.

The Nation Guide tells you about those kinds of places, but it's not set up to be a Zagat. As the title says, it's *The Nation Guide,* which means it's selective, even arbitrary. As the poet Allen Ginsberg once said, "Always be just, but if you can't be just, be arbitrary."

Like a Soviet dam, this book is a Mighty Collective Effort of the People! (We threw that line in to bait the right-wing reviewers.) More accurately, this guide represents the input of time and knowledge from Our People. The primary writer was *Nation* senior editor Richard Lingeman, but he received considerable help from smart assistants (all former *Nation* interns, a smart group in itself) named Max Fraser (who stayed with it to the end), Molly Bennet and Thaddeus Kromellis. They have contributed greatly, finding and providing obscure arts groups or small-town cafés or exotic blogs, and writing them up for the editor's final touch. The summer 2007 intern cohort contributed collectively at a crucial moment: Sara Abbas, Peter Baker, Michael Gould-Wartofsky, Bob Hammond, Rashi Kesarwani, William Pentland, Florencia Soto-Martinez and Jayati Vora. Beyond them came the editors, columnists, writers and friends of the magazine who sent us all manner of suggestions about hot or cool spots or political groups or favorite American places. Also helping were the Nation Associates, 27,000 loyal and true *Nation* readers who reported preferred places in their necks of the woods. And last but not least there were *Nation* readers and friends of friends from the great amorphous greater *Nation* community who sent in suggestions or just radiated support.

With all this input from all over, *The Nation Guide* could serve as an anthropological study with the impressive title *The Culture, Manners and Mores of the American Left, as Evidenced by Their Patterns of Culture, Codes of Consumption, Tastes in Food and Drink, Styles of Political Activism, Haunts and Meeting Places and Mating Habits.* The footnotes would cite a core sample of 180,000 *Nation* readers, a heterogeneous group of people who hold in common certain political, social and moral beliefs.

We used to hear a lot of buzz about "identity politics," which refers to political movements structured around racial or ethnic or religious identity. The trouble with identity politics was that identity sometimes transcends politics. This guide is less about a left identity or philosophy than about a way of life. It is not intended only for true believers; it is aimed at liberal-minded, freethinking people everywhere from liberals to compassionate libertarians, nonviolent anarchists, recovered SDSers and decent Republicans.

One section of *The Nation Guide* covers a lot of political organizations, associations, think tanks, nonprofits, advocacy groups and other bunches of people seeking common objectives, whether through research and thought or solidarity and action. Their number is legion, too numerous for more than limited coverage in a single book. But in their numbers lie strength. No doubt Alexis de Tocqueville would be as amazed by the number of associations progressive Americans form today as he was by those he wrote about in *Democracy in America*.

This sociopolitical culture of the Left has its proud history, one that can be claimed by all Americans. It is steeped in a revolutionary tradition of ordinary people fighting for a place in the sun denied them by the powerful. The narrative of this struggle courses through American history, as Howard Zinn teaches us in his *People's History of the United States*. It is traced in the Left Heritage Trail that runs through the book, a road lined by markers commemorating where people fought and died for their rights, winning, losing but always struggling.

Finally, *The Nation Guide* makes no bones about its provenance. It is clearly the product of a money-losing, troublemaking, dissenting, establishment-questioning magazine that, as one of its founders once said, has "the faculty of seeing through the tribe."

Like *The Nation,* this book is quirky and eclectic and quite contrarian, unique, improbable, impractical, handy, cheap at the price and priceless. As we said at the outset, the book doesn't know if it's a catalog or a guide or an almanac. Actually, it's all those things. Instead of directing you to the faces on Mount Rushmore (which we know you already know about), it seeks the whereabouts of Joe Hill's ashes, starting with his "Last Will" composed on death row: "let the merry breezes blow / my dust to where some flowers grow / Perhaps some fading flower then / will come to life and bloom again." (See page 251.)

Instead of listing motels to stay at when you visit Graceland (nothing wrong with going there), *The Nation Guide* takes you to Woody Guthrie's hometown of Okemah, Oklahoma, which is still trying to live up to Woody's description of it as "one of the singiest, square-dancingest, drinkingest, preachingest, walkingest, talkingest, laughingest, cryingest, shootingest, fistfightingest, bleedingest, gamblingest, gun, club and razor carryingest . . . towns."

Instead of routing you to the Bellingrath Gardens near Mobile (nothing wrong with that), *The Nation Guide* tells you about a community garden on Chicago's South Side. And Studs Terkel tells you why Chicago (surprise!) is his favorite American place.

If we have omitted or overlooked your favorite funeral home, no-sweat sweater shop, ecofriendly spa, Spanish Civil War Song, slow food joint or coffeehouse, just give us a holler or send us an e-mail (at guide@thenation.com) and we'll see you in the next edition.

Prologue: The Past

LEFT HERITAGE TRAIL: A VIRTUAL HISTORY TOUR

This Heritage Trail is a virtual tour proceeding from East Coast to West Coast. It memorializes selected sites of importance to the history of this country. Some sites are negative—in the "lest we forget" category. Overhanging it is the notion that the Battle of Homestead is in its way as worthy of being commemorated as the Battle of Bull Run. Note: Filmmaker John Gianvito made a film showing, silently, places mentioned in Howard Zinn's People's History *(some of them on our Trail). It's called* Profit Motive and the Whispering Wind, *and Gianvito makes it available at john.gianvito@verizon.net.*

THE PEOPLE'S PLACES

I think the preservation of historic sites is important, where those sites represent events in history overlooked or minimized in the orthodox telling of history or where they look at a historical event from a different point of view. For instance, the monument in Colorado representing the Ludlow Massacre (see page 111) of striking mine workers and their families in 1914 cannot help but stun anyone who comes across it and remind him or her of the brutality of class conflict in our nation. And I remember how surprised and gladdened I was to visit a small town in western Massachusetts and find a memorial to the soldiers of World War I that was not the usual paean to military heroism but a bitter comment on the futility of war.

—HOWARD ZINN, author of *A People's History of the United States.*

Massachusetts

Heritage Trails. Step off! Pass go! Go off the tourist-beaten path. Go to the Black Heritage Trail in Boston. See the Robert Gould Shaw Fifty-fourth Black Regiment Memorial, by August Saint-Gaudens, the Museum of African American History and African Meeting House. Go to the Women's Heritage Trail. See places associated with Phillis Wheatley, Anne Hutchison, Dorothea Dix, the offices of the Women's Trade Union League (see Triangle Shirtwaist Factory, page 12).

Women's Heritage Trail. Begin at the Boston Common Visitor Information Booth, Boston, MA (617) 522-2872, www.bwht.org; Black Heritage Trail, Boston Common, Shaw Memorial, Boston, MA.

Sacco-Vanzetti Trail. In death two Italian immigrants became heroes of the working people. Nicola Sacco and Bartolomeo Vanzetti's funeral procession along Boston's Hanover Street on August 29, 1927, drew thousands of mourners from urban intellectuals to North End paisanos. The Save Sacco and Vanzetti Committee (membership in which caused some of its members to be considered security risks in the Red Scare times) had its headquarters at 256 Hanover Street. The two men, a fishmonger and a cobbler, had been convicted at an Alice in Wonderlandish trial before a prejudiced judge on mostly hearsay testimony and little real evidence, of two robbery-murders. There was abundant evidence that the Massachusetts courts were prejudiced against two Italian immigrants and anarchists. (Presiding judge Webster Thayer: "I'm gonna get those anarchist bastards good and proper.") The case split Boston along class and ethnic divides; it radicalized writers like Dorothy Parker, John Dos Passos, Robert Benchley, Donald Ogden Stuart, Katherine Anne Porter and Edna St. Vincent Millay, who hobnobbed with real, shabby Reds on the picket lines. Sacco and Vanzetti's ashes, death masks, death certificates (cause of death: "Electric shock. Judicial homicide"), box of bullets and other items repose at the Boston Public Library, 700 Boylston Street (www.bpl.org). On August 25, 2007, the eightieth anniversary of their deaths, the Sacco and Vanzetti Commemoration Society (SVSC) held a parade from Stony Brook Park to the Forest Hills Cemetery, where the two were cremated.

SVSC, 33 Harrison Avenue, Boston, MA 02111, www.saccoandvanzetti.org

Walden Pond. The environmental movement starts here, near Concord, where in 1845 eccentric Concord resident Henry David Thoreau built a cabin at Walden Pond costing a total of twenty-eight dollars and eleven and a half cents, with his own hands. His deep-diving memoir of life in the woods, *Walden*, is an American classic. Walden Pond, threatened by developers in the 1990s, is now protected by the Commonwealth of Massachusetts. The site, which comprises 333 wooded acres surrounding the 102-foot-deep pond, draws large crowds. There's a replica of Thoreau's cabin and a statue of him at the original site.

Walden Pond State Reservation, 915 Walden Street, Concord, MA 01742, (978) 369-3254, www.mass.gov/dcr/parks/walden/

Shays's Rebellion. This early uprising at the U.S. armory in Springfield inspired Thomas Jefferson to write: "God forbid we should ever be twenty years without such a rebellion . . . What country can preserve its liberties, if its rulers are not warned from time to time, that this people preserve the spirit of resistance?" In 1787 a regiment of angry farmers led by Daniel Shays, a decorated captain in the Revolutionary War, marched on the armory. Known as "Regulators," their fury was fueled by corrupt officialdom and higher taxes levied to pay off Revolutionary War debts, resulting in bankruptcy sales of their farms to Eastern speculators. The Regulators were met by a force of 1,200 mercenaries hired as a state militia, who put them to flight with a close-in cannonade. The uprising so disturbed George Washington that he leant his magisterial blessing to the Constitutional Convention of 1787, which James Madison and other Nationalists were pushing.

Springfield Armory NHS, 1 Armory Square, Suite 2, Springfield, MA 01105, (413) 734-8551, www.nps.gov/spar/

Bread and Roses Strike. The 1912 Massachusetts textile workers' strike at the Lawrence mills was named after strikers' signs demanding "Bread but roses too." The city of Lawrence now sponsors a Bread and Roses Heritage

NEW ENGLAND MILL TOWNS

If New England was the cradle of the American Revolution, its textile mills were the maternity ward of the American Industrial Revolution. The industrialization of America started here; the deindustrialization of America did as well.

Festival on Labor Day, with bands and singers. Stroll along the Merrimack River for views of the massive American Woolen Company, the largest textile mill in the world when built in 1903, and the Great Stone Dam, a 943-foot-long, 32-foot-high reminder of Lawrence's leading role in the textile industry's early history. In the Lawrence courthouse the IWW organizers Joseph Ettor (poet) and Arturo Giovannitti (editor of *Il Proletario*) were tried on trumped-up murder charges and held without bail for eight months and then acquitted. At the railroad station, striking mothers who had come to send their hungry children to temporary foster homes in New York; Barre, Vermont (see also page 10) and other cities were beaten up by police for unlawful assembly.

Lawrence Heritage State Park, 1 Jackson Street, Lawrence, MA 01840, (978) 794-1655, Breadandroses99@hotmail.com www.mass.gov/dcr/parks/northeast/whp/htm

Jack Kerouac Park. Tucked into the Lowell Mills Historical District (see below) is a vest-pocket park commemorating native son Jack Kerouac, with a trail symbolizing the warring Catholic and Buddhist streams in his religious quest. Kerouac's *On the Road* foretold the cultural revolt of the sixties. He is buried under a flat stone in Edson Cemetery, and the grave is now a shrine for latter-day hipsters, who adorn it with flowers, hash pipes, joints, bottles of wine. Buried beside Kerouac is his third wife, Stella Sampas, a Lowell girl and sister of his best boyhood friend, Sammy Sampas.

Jack Kerouac Park, Lowell National Historical Park, Lowell, MA 01853, (978) 970-5000, www.nps.gov/archive/lowe; Edson Cemetery, 1375 Gorham Street, Lowell, MA 01852

Lowell Mills. The former Boott Cotton Mills, open to visitors, has working looms that ear-splittingly demonstrate what workers' lives were like. The "Lowell girls," young women recruited from nearby farms, were exploited under a model of Christian paternalism. In 1836, a pay cut provoked them to go out on one of the earliest strikes in America. The farm daughters were replaced by immigrant women, more easily exploited.

Lowell National Historical Park, Lowell, MA 01852, (978) 970-5000, www.nps.gov/lowe

Charles River Museum of Industry. The museum chronicles Waltham's textile industry and its rise as America's watchmaking capital. It displays an array of early machinery.

154 Moody Street, Waltham, MA 02453, (781) 893-5410, www.crmi.org

New Hampshire

Amoskeag Mills. The Amoskeag Mills lasted nearly a century. Their history recapitulates that of the New England textile industry. Born in 1839, Amoskeag grew to be the largest textile plant in the world, encompassing thirty major mills. It prospered through World War I, and then cheaper labor in the South and new styles dragged it down into bankruptcy in 1936.

Millyard Museum, 200 Bedford Street, Manchester, NH 03101, (603) 625-2821, www.amoskeagfalls.com/history

Rhode Island

Slater Mill Museum. The very first water-powered looms in America were introduced here by Samuel Slater, a British immigrant who had worked on the looms invented by Richard Arkwright.

67 Roosevelt Avenue, Pawtucket, RI 02860, (401) 725-8638, www.slatermill.org

Vermont

Italian Socialist Labor Party Hall. This is a monument to the thousands of skilled stonecutters who immigrated from Italy to Barre's granite quarries in the late nineteenth century. In 1900, after raising $2,000, the stonecutters built the Socialist Labor Party Hall, which served as a combined meeting place and social hall. Above the front entrance is a granite slab carved with the letters SLP and the party's arm-and-hammer emblem. From 1900 through 1935, political rallies, speeches and debates and community gatherings were held here. The Socialist Labor Party advocated an eight-hour day, a pay raise, free schooling for all children under eighteen and workmen's compensation. The hall served as the headquarters of the now-extinct Granite Cutters International Association, once a large, energetic union that drew to Barre speakers like Mary

"Mother" Jones, Eugene Debs, Samuel Gompers and Norman Thomas. Thirty-five children whose parents were in the Bread and Roses Strike (see page 8) were sent here in 1912. The building also housed a worker-owned cooperative store—the opposite of the company stores of the era, selling fair-priced produce, groceries, dry goods, and coal and operating a bottling works and a bakery; it used special scrip with the SLP logo on it. Sold in 1936 for use as a fruit warehouse, the hall fell into decay and precious papers stored there were tossed away. In 1994, the people of Barre rallied behind restoring it; and it was reclaimed for use as a social center and reopened (in 2000) as a National Historic Landmark.

46 Granite Street, Barre, VT 05641, (802) 658-6647, www.nps.gov/nr/travel/cen/vermon/

Hope Cemetery. The talents of Barre's stone carvers, not to mention a certain irreverence in the face of death, are on display at this cemetery, which opened in 1896. One headstone is a stuffed armchair; others are airplanes and automobiles. A lucky Donati is immortalized on his grave marker with a burning cigar in hand, his wife, wraithlike, floating in the smoke. Even old sectarian divides persist in the hereafter, as ties and cravats differentiate the graves of anarchists and socialists.

262 East Montpelier Road, Barre, VT 05641, (802) 478-6245

New York

Susan B. Anthony House. Susan B. Anthony, abolitionist, suffragist, temperance advocate, women's rights agitator, moved to Rochester in 1845 with her Quaker parents. The red brick house was her home from 1866 until her death forty years later. On the third floor Anthony labored with her friends Elizabeth Cady Stanton and Matilda Joslyn Gage on their groundbreaking tome *The History of Woman Suffrage.* From this base she launched redoubtable crusades for women's rights and published a feminist paper called *The Revolution*. She was arrested in Rochester in 1872 for the crime of voting while female, tried in an adjacent county and fined $100, a verdict directed by the judge. Ultimately, her belief that woman's political power started with the ballot prevailed.

17 Madison Street, Rochester, NY 14608, (585) 235-6124, www.susanbanthonyhouse.org

Women's Rights National Historical Park. The park commemorates a single historical event, the First Women's Rights Convention, held in Seneca Falls, July 1848. More than 300 men and women gathered in the

Wesleyan Chapel to discuss remedying the inferior status of women. At the end, they issued a Declaration of Sentiments, patterned after the Declaration of Independence, calling for full gender equality. In the visitors center are statues of the five women behind the 1848 conclave (Elizabeth Cady Stanton, Lucretia Mott, Mary Ann M'Clintock, Martha Wright and Jane Hunt) and a water wall with the names of the declaration signers. The shell of the chapel stands.

Visitor Center, 36 Fall Street, Seneca Falls, NY 13148, (315) 568-0024, www.nps.gov/wori

John Brown Farm and Gravesite. Near Lake Placid in upstate New York lies John Brown's body, "a-moldering in the grave." In the 1850s the abolitionist hero lived on a farm here, part of a vast tract of land purchased by Garrit Smith, a wealthy patron of the antislavery movement, to provide farms for freed slaves. Brown at first peaceably worked his land and helped black farmers cultivate their plots. But he departed to stir up violence in Kansas Territory and in due course was tried and hanged

in 1859 for leading the failed raid on Harpers Ferry. His wife had his body brought back for burial with two of their sons who had died with him. Twelve of his followers at Harpers Ferry also lie here. Brown's admirers added an iron fence and a boulder carved with his name. There is also a statue of a paternal Brown, with his arm around the shoulder of a young black farmer, striding confidently into the future.

115 John Brown Road (south of the intersection with Old Military Road), Lake Placid, NY 12946, (518) 523-3900, www.history.com/gerritsmith/nelba.htm

Robert Green Ingersoll Birthplace Museum. Located in Dresden on the west shore of Seneca Lake, southeast of Rochester, this site marks the birthplace of America's most famous agnostic in the nineteenth century. The meticulously restored home is crammed with memorabilia of Ingersoll's life from Civil War hero to lawyer to free thought crusader. Ingersoll was a peerless orator; Mark Twain not only sympathized with his sermons against religion but also considered Ingersoll a master of the English language.

Off State Route 14 between Geneva and Watkins Glen, Dresden, NY, www.secularhumanism.org/ingersoll

Stonewall Inn. It was a sweaty steamy night in June 1969; Judy Garland's funeral had taken place earlier that day. The police made one of their routine raids on the Stonewall Inn, a clandestine Greenwich Village gay bar reputedly run by the Mafia. They made the usual homophobic slurs and arrested the usual flamboyant queens. Usually, a day or so later, Stonewall would reopen, but

I'm a New Yorker, born and bred, and there are so many places I love in the city I can't even count them. But if I had to choose my favorite place, it would have to be Grand Central Station. To me, its main concourse ranks with the Parthenon, the nave of Chartres Cathedral, and the courtyards of the Forbidden City in Beijing, as one of the great man-made spaces in the world (and one of the few made for entirely secular purposes). Flanked by anonymous skyscrapers and crowded streets, it's a huge surprise in the city. A half million people pass through it every day, yet its majestic height and its perfect proportions give it an extraordinary serenity. People hurrying to work or rushing to their trains rarely look up, but we all feel its influence because, though our paths cross from every angle, we don't collide or exchange angry words, as we might in the subways or the streets. The space can't be photographed, much as tourists try. It's a presence. And when I look up, I feel a sense of elation.

—FRANCES FITZGERALD, author of the Pulitzer Prize–winning *Fire in the Lake, Cities on a Hill, America Revised* and other books.

not this time. The embattled gays and lesbians fought back with such vehemence that the cops had to lock themselves in the bar until a SWAT team freed them. The protest electrified Greenwich Village's gay community, which turned out for nightly rallies on Christopher Street in increasingly larger numbers. A month later, the Gay Liberation Front was formed and the gay rights movement stepped out of the closet, borne by the momentum of sixties militancy and the civil rights movement. The Stonewall Inn epitomized the shadowy homosexual demimonde of that day, closeted by shame

and prejudice, purged by the rebellion that erupted there. It would be designated a National Historic Landmark. Toto, we're not in Kansas anymore.

53 Christopher Street, New York, NY 10014, (212) 488-2705

Judson Memorial Church. This landmark house of worship might irreverently be dubbed the First Church of bohemians, hippies, immigrants, sodomites, fallen women and NYU students. Designed by Sanford White, it has since its consecration in 1891 stood for everything the Fundamentalists warn will send you to hell. Located in the heart of Greenwich Village, it has provided services to immigrants, promoted civil rights activism, sponsored political art shows, catalyzed demonstrations against the Vietnam War and for gay rights, referred women to abortionists before New York State legalized the procedure, counseled prostitutes and much more. Under activist ministers like Bob Spike, Howard Moody and Donna Schaper, Judson has been both a nerve center of the Village's political counterculture and a religious sanctuary for political activists in New York. Typically, it was home to the creation of the anti–Iraq War movement. On November 8, 2002, an ad hoc group of seventy anti–Iraq War activists met at the church to "Take back the future." They sought to formulate a coherent, unvengeful response to the ominous post–September 11 world. Their efforts—and those of people like them—go on. And Judson stands unscarred by divine lightning.

55 Washington Square South, New York, NY 10012, (212) 477-0351, www.judson.org

Triangle Shirtwaist Factory. This building, now owned by New York University, was once the home of the Triangle Shirtwaist Company. On March 25, 1911, a fire raged in the upper three floors trapping many of the 400 workers, most of them young women. Exits had been locked to reduce alleged pilferage and the fire escape collapsed. In all, 146 were killed. Many of them jumped to their deaths, their bodies piling up on the sidewalk like broken dolls. The factory owners, acquitted of criminal guilt, settled twenty-three civil lawsuits brought by families for an average of $75 per life lost. Future labor secretary Frances Perkins, who witnessed the fire, said it had awakened her and the people of New York to "the individual worth and value of each of those 146 people who fell or were burned in that great fire. . . ." Out of the tragedy came stricter safety laws.

Brown Building (former Asch Building), 23–29 Washington Place, New York, NY 10003

Union Square Park. The name does not refer to labor unions but to the junction of Fourth Avenue and Broadway at Fourteenth Street. Nevertheless, this park has a long radical labor pedigree. In 1882, under the aegis of the Central Labor Union, 25,000 marchers stepped off for the nation's first Labor Day parade. On May 1, 1886, the American Federation of Labor called a Worker's Day parade, which drew 30,000 and was associated with labor's campaign for an eight-hour day (see Bay View Massacre, page 187). The funeral procession for the Triangle workers started in the square. Communist Party–sponsored rallies were held here during the Great Depression; one drawing 35,000 was so brutally suppressed that it stirred up popular sympathy, assuring Union Square's reputation (if not inviolability) as a free speech zone. On nearby streets were the headquarters of the Communist Party and the office of the *Daily Worker*; of the Socialist Party and its organ, the *Call*; of several trade unions and, representing the old order, of Tammany Hall. (Now the offices of *The Nation* are a short block east at 33 Irving Place.) Speakers held forth from the pavillion at the north end. Crowds raised massed voices against the Ludlow Massacre in 1914 (see page 111), against the executions of Sacco and Vanzetti (see page 8) in 1927 (police machine guns were trained on them from the roof of nearby S. Klein's department store) and against the execution of the Rosenbergs in 1953. After September 11, nightly candlelight vigils were held; pathetic homemade signs affixed to trees and walls appealed for help in finding missing loved ones. Anti–Iraq War marches often terminate here.

Tompkins Square Park. This pleasant patch rests atop a social geology striated by the upheavals generated by successive waves of immigrants that populated Manhattan's Lower East Side: German and Irish, then Italians, Eastern Europeans and Orthodox Jews and Puerto Ricans, Dominicans and Colombians, hippies and yuppies. Starting in the 1960s, after the Lower East Side became the East Village but before it became the Latino Loisaida, the park was rocked by clashes between hippies, radicals and squatters and cops over issues of lifestyle, gentrification and homelessness (as it had in earlier times been rocked by cops beating up unemployed workers). Now iron fences gird the winding paths; and the band shell, where Jimi Hendrix, the Fugs and the Grateful Dead once played, is gone. A decade before the youthquake, revolutionary saxophonist Charlie "Yardbird" Parker lived at 151 Avenue B from 1950 through 1954. Look for his name inscribed, along with a family memorial to monologist Spalding Gray (presumed drowned in the churning wake of a Staten Island ferry, a suicide) and to other departed neighborhood folk, on the composition asphalt tiles surrounding the base of a statue to Temperance, which was fatally not practiced by Bird.

500 E. 9th Street (Between Avenues A and B and 7th and 10th Streets), New York, NY 10009, (212) 387-7685

African Burial Ground. This cleared block in one of the busiest and most congested quarters of New York City was once a cemetery for the city's slaves. Forgotten for two centuries, its original purpose was discovered when an archaeological dig unearthed human remains. How many are buried here is unknown, but analysis of the 400 recovered skeletons has already revealed much more than any other source about the lives of New York slaves—what they ate, what diseases they suffered, how they died. If these bones could talk . . . A monument was dedicated in September 2007.

Corners of Duane and Elk Streets adjacent to the Ted Weiss Federal Building at 290 Broadway, New York, NY 10017, www.africanburialground.gov

23 Wall Street. Once the House of Morgan (J. P. Morgan & Company), this glum gray stone building, as cheerful as a balance sheet, is being converted into apartments for rich hedge fund traders—the first luxury condominiums to be located in the financial quarter. Buyers beware! On September 16, 1920, at the height of the noon-hour swarm, a huge explosion near the subtreasury building shook the canyons of Wall Street, taking the lives of more than thirty people and injuring four hundred. It left the facade at 23 Wall Street permanently pocked and cratered. Although the perpetrators were never caught, a note discovered in a mailbox suggested anarchists were behind it.

Corner of Nassau and Wall Streets, New York, NY 10005

New Jersey

Greenwich Village, Paterson Pageant of 1913. The cataclysmic 1913 silk strike in Paterson, New Jersey, radi-

calized bohemians in Greenwich Village. It was precipitated by new machines and a mill owners' speedup. John Reed reported it for the radical Village publication *The Masses,* and he and other artists staged a fund-raising pageant at Madison Square Garden that starred a thousand real-life Paterson workers and figures like IWW leader William D. "Big Bill" Haywood, Elizabeth Gurley "Rebel Girl" Flynn and anarchist Carlo Tresca. As a fund-raising device, if not as theater, it flopped. The penniless strikers were starved out, proving bread and roses are fine but you can't eat flowers. The Paterson pageant represented the high-water mark of Greenwich Village bohemian radicalism before World War I.

2 Market Street, Paterson, NJ 07501, (973) 321-1260, www.thepatersonmuseum.com

Part I.

"Ars gratia politicus"

COLLECTIVES

Beehive Design Collective. Members of the busy Beehive Design Collective refer to themselves as "culture workers" or "pollinators"; individuals use "bee" as a surname. The group is based in an old Grange hall and identifies with the Grange's nineteenth-century Populist fight against Wall Street. They oppose transnational corporations, free trade, biotechnology, industrialization; they believe that art (design, graphics, cartoons and caricatures) can play a pivotal part in conveying political ideas. They conceive their role in the fight to be designing elaborate, historically accurate posters; touring universities with graphic presentations on the issues; discussing same with other activists at the grass roots and giving away their posters.

3 Elm Street, Machias, ME 04654, (207) 255-6737, www.beehivecollective.org

The Bubble Project. Artist Ji Lee cut out 30,000 blank white bubbles and plastered them on ad posters all over New York City. People responded by filling the bubbles with caustic, antiadvertising quips. Lee slapped the funniest bubbles on his website, which received 50,000 hits and crashed. In 2006 he collected some of the all-time great quips in a book called *Talk Back: The Bubble Project.* In late 2007 Ji Lee told us: "The BP is still going strong. The website has been visited by over two million people. The bubbling has spread to hundreds of countries. I receive e-mails every day from different bubblers around the world, from India, Australia, China to Turkey. Now Italy has a Bubble Project website (www.progettobolla.com) as does Argentina (www.proyectoburbuja.com). The BP has taken on a life of its own, and it will keep going as long as there are ads on the streets!" Recently sighted on the Bubble Project website: "What country would Jesus bomb?"

www.thebubbleproject.com

The Busycle. A bicycle built for fifteen, a pedal-powered traveling art piece, this contraption sits on the stripped-down chassis of a van. Fourteen pedalers sit seven to a side, facing out, a set of pedals in front of each of them. The driver up front guides the Busycle as they pedal in unison. Their leg power is transmitted to a central gear shaft that turns the wheels. The Busycle travels to different cities on cross-country story-collecting tours. During stops, the crew invites locals to climb aboard, work the pedals and experience the purposeful joy of pulling together, of being cogs in a larger effort. Then they assemble around a virtual campfire to tell their stories, which are videotaped and shared with people at the next stop. The Busycle was created by Boston-based artists Heather Clark and Matthew Mazzotta while they were in residence at the Berwick Research Institute's Public Art Satellite Program.

www.buscycle.com

Center for Tactical Magic. CTM believes in opening creative lines of communication, spreading information and bringing people together. Over the past eight years they've mobilized more than 200 people on projects in cities across the United States as well as internationally. For example, they have a Tactical Ice Cream Unit (TICU) that distributes free ice cream and political literature from a truck, which "is familiar but different—

it's a fully armored car that's an ice cream truck." It displays two menus: "treats for the streets" and "food for thought." The truck carries audiovisual equipment and is available as the centerpiece at rallies, providing the sound system, stage, music and refreshments.

1460 Madison Avenue, Memphis, TN 32104, (901) 722-3001, www.tacticalmagic.org

Critical Art Ensemble. CAE is a collective of five "tactical media artists"—Steve Kurtz, Robert Ferrell, Steve Barnes, Dorian Burr and Beverly Schlee, who are variously trained in computer graphics and web art, film/video, photography, text art, book art, performance art and science. They formed CAE in Tallahassee, Florida, in 1987, because they wanted a public voice and chose collective activity. "The idea is to look for cracks in the system and exploit them," says Kurtz. His 1994 book *The Electronic Disturbance* attacked the Internet and urged "digital disobedience." One CAE project in Halifax, Nova Scotia, invented a cultural tour of the city. CAE produced glossy brochures, icons and LCD displays of what was wrong with the city, such as its sewage-

---

ART OR BIOTERRORISM?

Two members of the Critical Art Ensemble have been investigated by the Department of Justice for mail fraud, a stand-in for the Feds' real but unprovable allegation: bioterrorism. In its biotech reenactments, CAE uses nontoxic bacteria, obtained legally from reputable pharmaceutical companies. Steve Kurtz, an associate professor at the State University of New York at Buffalo, employed such bacteria in creating Marching Plague. He had been working on this project on January 25, 2004, when he found his wife, Hope, dead of a heart attack. He immediately called the police. Upon arrival, the officers spied the home laboratory equipment used for growing the bacteria and suspected Kurtz was a bioterrorist. They impounded his wife's body, cordoned off the house and called in the FBI. The upshot was that Kurtz and his CAE collaborator Robert Ferrell, former chair of the Department of Genetics at the University of Pittsburgh Graduate School of Public Health, were prosecuted for mail and wire fraud, which carry a possible twenty-year sentence (the same as for bioterrorism). According to CAE: "As it is, mail fraud law is already the most broadly written law on the books—and one that's been used against political dissidents since Marcus Garvey—so the government's power of selective persecution would become almost unthinkable." The accused have formed a defense fund (www.caedefensefund.org). A documentary film about the case, *Strange Science,* was shown at the 2006 Sundance Film Festival. Kurtz and Ferrell were expected to stand trial in summer 2008.

filled harbor. Marching Plague (see box), illustrated a 1952 British Army experiment, in which the spread of bubonic plague was studied by infecting guinea pigs. The installation was displayed at the Whitney Biennial in 2006.

www.critical-art.net

Ron English. Call him English the Highwayman. He hijacks billboards. It all began back in the 1980s while he was a student in northern Texas. His MO was and is covering a billboard with his own message. Of course, this requires fast hands, and English has trained himself so that he can paste over a billboard in seven minutes flat. His messages have included: cigarettes kill, fast food makes you fat, right-wing talk show hosts are nuts, Jesus would not have driven a large SUV, and Apple Computer does not have the right to say what companies Albert Einstein would have endorsed (in its "Think Different" campaign). Since his first boardjacking, Ron English has covered more than 900 of them. Notable ones include: *The Poor: What Good Are They?*

www.popaganda.com

GUERRILLA GIRLS: A RECENT CAPER

Blake Gopnik, chief art critic of the *Washington Post,* asked us to create a full page in the newspaper as part of a special section on feminism and art, published April 22, 2007. America's favorite feminist masked avengers (and creative complainers) designed a tabloid, *NOT OK! The Guerrilla Girls' Scandal Rag,* to reveal the shocking truth about the low, low number of women and artists of color in our national art museums. Plus, with the help of Brangelina (no tabloid is complete without them), we show the Smithsonian how to atone for its bad behavior. We got all our statistics from the museums themselves or from their websites, but when the *Post* called to fact-check, the institutions went bananas! The National Gallery hurriedly installed a sculpture by an artist of color, and the Hirshhorn suddenly found works by women and artists of color it never knew it owned! Who knows how many works they're scrambling to install right now? Let's all keep up the pressure!

—GUERRILLA GIRLS WEBSITE

Guerrilla Girls. The Guerrilla Girls are five or maybe thirty or twenty-five (the number is secret) artists, who take aliases of famous women artists, such as Frida Kahlo or Georgia O'Keeffe. Their objective is to rag the art establishment for what they see as its systematic exclusion of women. Their means are humorous, because humor gets through to people. First, of course, are those gorilla masks they don before invading an exclusive art site (inspired by one of their members' misspelling their name as "Gorilla Girls"). Second, they create a lot of alternative art, for example, posters that have become collectors' items, been sold in galleries and hung in museums. These were published in a book, *Confessions of the Guerrilla Girls.* See also *The Guerrilla Girls' Bedside Companion to the History of Western Art* and *Bitches, Bimbos and Ballbreakers.* The GGs contributed an illustration to a special issue of *The Nation* on the movies called *The Anatomically Correct Oscar*—a drawing of a statuette of a fat white guy with his hands modestly covering the family jewels. This was enlarged and appeared on a billboard in Hollywood at Academy Awards time with the legend "He's white & male, just like the guys who win!"

www.guerrillagirls.com

Preemptive Media. This collective, born at cutting-edge Carnegie Mellon University in Pittsburgh, was the brainchild of Beatriz da Costa, Jamie Schulte and Brooke Singer. Its vision is making works of art that subvert actual technologies used by the government and companies to mine data and amass information on all of us. An example of their creations was the project Zapped! that focused on radio frequency identification (RFID) tags used by companies like Wal-Mart to track products and sales. Preemptive Media has held workshops that have instructed people on how to build detection devices to tell them they're being monitored. Still another work is called Swipe, created to blow the whistle on the way merchants lift data encoded in the magnetic stripe on drivers' licenses. PM sets up a real bar serving drinks at social functions with a real driver's license scanner. After reading his receipt, the customer can down a stiff drink to numb the knowledge that Big Brother, Inc., is watching—for profit or worse.

www.preemptivemedia.net

Speculative Archive. This two-person collective, comprising the Los Angeles–based artists Julia Meltzer and David Thorne, has been creating videos, photographs, installations and published texts exploring intersections of politics and life since 1999. One of their preoccupations is classified documents. They started with a twenty-five-minute video called *It's not my memory of it: three recollected documents.* The film includes interviews with CIA officials. Their work has been shown at various museums, galleries and at the California Biennial.

www.speculativearchive.org

subRosa. This feminist art collective calls itself "a reproducible cyberfeminist cell of cultural researchers committed to combining art, activism, and politics to explore and critique the effects of the intersections of the new information and biotechnologies on women's bodies, lives, and work." It grew out of a reading club on the Carnegie Mellon campus in Pittsburgh in the late 1990s. Its central concern has been the effect of technology on the female body as well as on what it means to be feminine. The name honors feminist pioneers Rosa Bonheur, Rosa Luxemburg, Rosie the Riveter, Rosa Parks and Rosie Franklin.

www.cyberfeminism.net

Your Art Here. A nonprofit public art project founded "on the belief that everyone has the right to 'be the media,' " Your Art Here was born in September 2002. Since then, they have put together three community-run art billboards in Bloomington and Indianapolis. (They've since expanded into rented spaces and art on buses.) Perhaps their most gutsy campaign took place during the 2004 presidential election in very red Indiana. That was the Patriotic Art Series of four billboards, in which "each piece took a unique look at the media's influence on the mainstream perception of 'patriotism.'" It included a billboard depicting President Bush and shouting "Lies, Lies, Lies!" Another, called *#2,* evaded censorship by showing Bush next to the words "eats #2."

1419 S. Washington Street, Bloomington, IN 47401, www.yourarthere.org

GRAPHIC DESIGN STUDIOS

Avenging Angels. A New York atelier that takes liberal losers as its clients. "Winning isn't everything, but incessant losing deadens the soul, and, besides, when liberals lose, too many innocent people get hurt. If you choose to lose no longer, heed the Bible at Romans 12:19 (slightly amended): 'Justice is mine' saith the Lord; 'I will repay, but in the meantime, call these guys.'" Avenging Angels caught the media eye back in 2003 when it teamed up with Ben & Jerry's founder Ben Cohen, who started Business Leaders for Sensible Priorities. AA produced television and print ads for the antiwar group opposing the invasion of Iraq. The television spots starred, among others, Susan Sarandon and Janeane Garofalo. AA counts *The Nation* among its clients and has worked for various liberal causes, such as the Brady Campaign to Prevent Gun Violence, True-Majority, Peace Action, United for a Fair Economy, John Kerry for President and Riverkeeper.

10 W. 18th Street, New York, NY 10011, (212) 243-8100, www.avengingangels.org

Design Action Collective. Inkworks Press (see page 24), a mainstay of progressive-cause printing in Berkeley, spawned this Oakland-based group of designers, who do work for social change organizations in the Bay Area. DAC is a worker-owned union shop (CWA).

1110 Franklin Street, #300, Oakland, CA 94612, (510) 452-1912, www.designaction.org

Point Five Design. This atelier specializes in design "with an educational, cultural or political focus." It has served a long list of clients on the left, including *Columbia Journalism Review, The American Prospect,* Drum Major Institute for Public Policy (see page 198), Catholics for a Free Choice and Feminist Majority Foundation.

118 E. 25th Street, 10th floor, New York, NY 10010, (212) 414-4309, www.point5.com

WBMG. Milton Glaser/Walter Bernard. Milton Glaser cofounded Pushpin Studio, considered the Tiffany of New York graphic design for more than forty years, with many advertising accounts. Glaser wears his liberal politics on his sleeve on occasion. For the 2004 GOP convention in NYC he concocted the Light Up the Sky demonstration that called on New Yorkers opposed to Bush and the war to hold silent vigils with a lighted candle, flashlight or light in their windows. Glaser founded Pushpin Studio with Seymour Chwast, Reynolds Ruffins and Edward Sorel in 1954 at a time when photography and television were radically changing graphic design. Pushpin was on the cutting edge in creating a new design vocabulary, working in various media from record and book jackets to posters and websites. In 1974, Glaser created the famed "I ❤ New York" logo. With Walter Bernard, former art director at *Time* magazine, he founded WBMG in 1983, which was and is dedicated to magazine and newspaper redesign (its clients have included *The Nation*).

207 E. 32nd Street, New York, NY 10016, (212) 889-3161, www.miltonglaser.com

TUMIS. A design firm that "has participated in hundreds of progressive projects challenging racism, classism, homophobia, sexism, and corporate irresponsibility." Tumis is a member of the East Oakland–based EastSide Arts Alliance, a Third World artist collective. The shop is owned by women and has an ethnically diverse staff comprising designers, techies, artists, activists and youth advocates, according to the website.

2289 International Boulevard, Oakland, CA 94606, (510) 532-8267, (877) 738-8647, http://tumis.com

PRINT SHOPS

One by-product of the political ferment of the early 1970s was the Progressive Printers Network (PPN), set up by several print or copy shops whose employees had fought for the right to join a union and set up cooperatively owned ventures. They vended their sympathies and services to progressive groups that needed pamphlets, handbills, posters and other message materials. To recognize their historic role, in 1994 PPN with the Center for the Study of Political Graphics (see page 28) mounted a show called Freedom of the Press that celebrated the role of public printers in getting out the message.

Collective Copies. Back in 1983 this copy shop was called Gnomon Copies. The employees, fed up with low pay, decrepit machines and cramped quarters, organized themselves into a union and struck. Some in the community rallied behind them, boycotting the shop and honoring the picket line. The local media kept the strikers' cause in the public eye. By the end of the year negotiations were successfully concluded, but the landlord evicted the owners and the shop closed, apparently for good. The former employees then launched a new copying business that has thrived, added two branches, and moved to larger quarters with triple the staff and state-of-the-art digital equipment.

71 S. Pleasant Street, Amherst, MA 01002, (413) 256-6425, www.collectivecopies.com

Community Printers. 1827 Soquel Avenue, Santa Cruz, CA 95062, (831) 426-4682, www.comprinters.com

Grass Roots Press. 401½ W. Peace Street, Raleigh, NC 27603, (919) 828-2364, www.grassrootspress.net

Inkworks Press. 2827 7th Street, Berkeley, CA 94710, (510) 845-7111, www.inkworkspress.org

Red Sun Press. 94 Green Street, Boston, MA 02130, (617) 524-6822, www.redsunpress.com

Urban Press. 1226 S. Bailey Street, Seattle, WA 98108, (206) 325-4060, www.urbanpressseattle.com

ART AND HUMANITIES EDUCATION

The Center for Urban Pedagogy. CUP's in the business of making educational projects "about places and how they change." Their projects unite artists, graphic designers, architects and urban planners with community-based activists and advocates, organizers, government officials, academics and policy makers to work with CUP staffers to create educational services, exhibitions, community partnerships, public programs and media projects. In 1997 CUP—then a small, informal group—assembled a booklet titled "A How-To Guidebook for Urban Objects." CUP now works with teachers to develop a curriculum that teaches kids about urban planning and their neighborhoods. At an alternative school, called City-as-School High School in lower Manhattan, students studied how New York disposes of garbage. They visited dump sites, interviewed sanitation department officials and created a documentary film and posters telling what they had learned. CUP has also put together programs that look at issues like public housing, toxic waste sites and poverty. They enter into partnerships with myriad community-based organizations; for example, with residents on the Lower East Side of Manhattan to create Public Housing Television, a series of videos that ventilate issues of concern to people in public housing.

232 3rd Street, B402B, Brooklyn, NY 11215, (718) 596-7721, www.anothercupdevelopment.org

The Clemente Course. A course in the *humanities* for working people? The original idea for the Bard College Clemente Course in the Humanities came from Earl Shorris, a writer of novels and histories and a long-time contributing editor of *The Nation.* Why not, Earl asked, offer blue-collar people a full-course humanities menu of college-level philosophy, literature, art history and American history? In other words, redistribute the fruits of civilization to hungry and deprived minds? He started experimenting with his curriculum at the Roberto Clemente Family Guidance Center on East 13th Street in Manhattan, aided by some volunteer teachers who knew their subjects practically if not always academically. Shorris enlisted Bard College's help in setting up a national Clemente Course. Bard administers it, working through local organizations. The courses are free; even books, carfare and child care are gratis. Students meet with college-level instructors two evenings a week for eight months, logging a total of 110 hours of class time. Bard awards a certificate to students who complete the course. Those who score above a certain grade level receive six college credits. Bard helps them enroll in a college of their choice, should they decide to continue their education, which about half do. This immersion in the humanities improved their work lives, their home lives and their citizens' lives.

Bard College, PO Box 5000, Annandale-on-Hudson, NY 12504, (845) 758-7066, http://clementecourse.bard.edu

SCRAP (School and Community Reuse Action Project). This nonprofit aims to "promote creative reuse and environmentally sustainable behavior by providing educational programs and affordable materials to the community." The SCRAP store offers "so many great bargains and thousands of items to meet all your education and creative needs"; provides space to local artists who use found objects in their art and organizes monthly showings and community events; offers workshops for the public and in local schools that educate about the value of reuse.

Creative Reuse Center, 3901A N. Williams Avenue, Portland, OR 97227, (503) 294-0769, www.scrapaction.org

Side Street Projects. A community art-teaching group in Pasadena, with offices in two vintage trailers, which claims to serve more than 1,000 kids from diverse communities. Side Street provides assistance to nearly 200 amateur adult artists each year, offering classes to help them get their act together. Actually, one of the most popular courses is called Get Your Sh*t Together, which teaches artists to hone their business skills, make things happen through "bare-knuckled, practical strategies for negotiating the baffling terrain of the contemporary art world." After getting your sh*t together, you can enroll in Get Your Grant Together or Get Your Website Together. Still another Side Street project is Alternative Routes: Education on Wheels, a wood shop in a bus that goes from neighborhood to neighborhood. The bus houses ten woodworking stations, each equipped with tools, adjustable workbenches, supplies and materials. The kids learn to be creative and artistic.

Armory Northwest, 965 N. Fair Oaks Avenue, Pasadena, CA 91109, (626) 798-7774, www.sidestreet.org

MONEY FOR ART'S SAKE AND SPACES AVAILABLE

Creative Capital. Creative Capital was founded in 1999 in response to budget cuts for the NEA designed to eliminate grants by the government-funded organization to individual artists. Creative Capital is there to fill the gap. It has distributed more than $5 million to some 250 artists. The basic thrust of the organization is helping emerging artists get over the hump by giving them the tools to see their projects through. In some instances, the grant money they award has been called an IPO, an investment in an artist who will grow into an established contributor to the arts. Aside from just giving money, they also run programs that teach artists how to create a five-year budget, how to manage art as business and how to make sure they'll keep producing art even during the slow times. According to an article in the *Los Angeles Times,* "Creative Capital targets 'catalytic' moments in artists' careers, then signs on as a combination guidance counselor and business partner." Notable grantees include Sam Green and Bill Siegel, whose documentary *The Weather Underground* was nominated for an Academy Award in 2003 and included in the 2004 Whitney Biennial.

65 Bleecker Street, 7th floor, New York, NY 10012, (212) 598-9900, www.creative-capital.org

Experimental Station. This center is home to publications, artists, activists and community projects. In the 1990s the building, fondly known as "the Building," located on the edge of the run-down Woodlawn neighborhood not far from the University of Chicago, was owned by the artist Dan Peterman, creator of internationally renowned sculptures. Before Peterman, the trapezoidal structure was a recycling center. During his tenancy it evolved into a kind of ramshackle hippie haven, honeycombed with odd-size spaces, in which lived and worked diverse inhabitants. All of that went up in smoke in the fire of 2001. The walls of the building survived, and Peterman raised money, kindled support and the Experimental Station rose phoenix-like. The new station's occupants get help in the form of below-market rents, and they share technical facilities and meeting places. In exchange, they stage exhibitions, programs, lectures and whatever. Recent tenants include *The Baffler* (see page 126); the Invisible Institute ("we work to keep visible fellow citizens and fundamental questions threatened with invisibility") and the Woodlawn Buying Club, which brings organic food to South Side residents. Peterman also maintains his studio in the building.

6100 S. Blackstone Avenue, Chicago, IL 60637, www.experimentalstation.org

ART CENTERS, MUSEUMS AND GALLERIES

Elizabeth A. Sackler Center for Feminist Art. Feminist art and artists have a room of their own in the Brooklyn Museum, thanks to the generosity of Elizabeth A. Sackler, a wealthy art collector, political activist and feminist. She became a friend and patron of the artist Judy Chicago, and when the latter's historic work, *The Dinner Party,* created with the help of 400 volunteers, ended up homeless, Sackler endowed a permanent refuge for it at the Brooklyn Museum. When the monumental installation was unveiled in 1979, many critics dismissed it as propaganda, though women critics recognized it as a major work akin to the heroic paintings of the Renaissance on mythical, historical or religious themes. The public came in droves to see it in San Francisco: 90,000 over three months. The huge triangular table combines art and crafts; it displays thirty-nine ornate place settings, each emblematic of the life of a great woman. The settings consist of embroidered runners, gold chalices and utensils and china-painted porcelain plates with raised central motifs. On the tiled floor space inside the triangular table the names of 999 notable women are inscribed in gold script. In an adjoining gallery feminist art is hung. The opening show in 2007, Global Feminisms, mingled the shocking with the politically provocative.

Brooklyn Museum, 200 Eastern Parkway, Brooklyn, NY 11238, (718) 638-5000, www.brooklynmuseum.org

Gallery 1199. If you wanted to imagine the opposite of the typical upscale Manhattan art gallery, you might come up with something like Gallery 1199. This space was established by Local 1199 Service Employees International Union's Bread and Roses Project that was sparked by the great union lefty Moe Foner in 1978. Programs include lunch-hour plays, street fairs, films, concerts and art and photography exhibits. In April through May 2007, Gallery 1199 mounted a show titled Unseen America, consisting of photographs taken by workers. First, they learned how to use the donated 35mm point-and-shoot cameras in classes taught by professional photographers, then they were set free to click away. Cameras were given to homeless people (who took photos of homes and apartment buildings). Sweatshop workers, fearing the boss but feeling a strong urge to record what they did all day, secretly snapped views of their workplace. A Mexican woman, who worked all day standing up, took a lot of photos of chairs. Each of the photos on exhibit included a caption that seemed an inextricable, almost poetic part of it. Samuel Contreras summed up the humanity inspiring the exhibition: "There's a second soul to everybody here that nobody seems to know. Unfortunately a lot of people will assume that you are what your job is. Taking out garbage or fixing plumbing. They don't realize that there's an artful soul to everybody."

310 W. 43rd Street, New York, NY 10036, www.bread-and-roses.com

POLITICAL POSTERS

Every war has its emblematic poster(s). World War I's was James Montgomery Flagg's Uncle Sam "I Want You." World War II left us Rosie the Riveter, most famously in Norman Rockwell's Saturday Evening Post *cover. (Rockwell was the iconic artist of World War II as Flagg was of World War I.) The dominant graphics of the Vietnam War were photos of a South Vietnamese policeman shooting a suspected member of the Vietcong and a little girl whose clothes were burned off by napalm. (A dearth of patriotic posters seems to be the sign of an unpopular war.) Is there an iconic Iraq War poster? Answer: Yes. The Abu Ghraib hooded man with wires attached transformed into a silhouette as in an iPod ad.*

Center for the Study of Political Graphics. Scholars will deconstruct the Abu Ghraib poster at this central repository for the study, history and dissemination of political poster art. Carol Wells is in charge and says it's the only political poster archive in the world. Started in 1988 with some 3,000 posters, the center now has a collection of more than 50,000. The center is not a gallery; nothing is on display—the art travels. The staff curates roughly one show a year in a space provided by a host institution. The center provides posters, mounts the pictures, includes translations of foreign text and so on. As many as twenty-five traveling shows might be out on the road at any specific time. Given the political nature of the posters, shows can stir up censorship issues. At a USC show commemorating the five hundredth anniversary of Columbus's landing in America, posters critical of America's colonial conquests and racism displayed in the large windows of the college bookstore were found offensive and removed. Wells recalled some small victories as well, such as the show of women's rights posters at a Catholic college whose students told Wells no pro-choice posters, but she sent one anyway, the tamest one she had. It showed in childish handwriting the words: "My mom had an illegal abortion and I don't miss the baby but I do miss her." That passed muster with a liberal nun on the faculty and the show went on.

8124 W. 3rd Street, Suite 211, Los Angeles, CA 90048, (323) 653-4662, www.politicalgraphics.org

Museum of Comic and Cartoon Art. "What does the art tell us about the time period it was created in? How does it stand the test of time? What First Amendment issues regarding content come into play? How does censorship determine what is (and isn't) published?" asks the MoCCA website. Cartoons are not usually considered the loftiest medium or most sophisticated form of political dialogue, but MoCCA is doing its part to change that snobbish view by presenting comics, cartoons and drawings—political, editorial and so forth—as products of their time, shaped by the society they comment on or lampoon. MoCCA stitches together shows like Cartoons Against the Axis, She Draws Comics and Infinite Canvas: The Art of Webcomics.

594 Broadway, Suite 401, New York, NY 10012, (212) 254-3511, www.moccany.com

Northland Poster Collective. Since 1979 this artist collective has been linking art and activism. Northland does mostly labor-related (but also antiwar, environmental and immigrant rights) posters, T-shirts, bumper stickers and buttons. Its posters hang on many a union hall's walls and those of the AFL-CIO headquarters in Washington, D.C. The collective went through a period of financial crisis, but after a fund-raising campaign brought in $200,000 it seems to be afloat again.

PO Box 7096, Minneapolis, MN 55407, (800) 627-3082, www.northlandposter.com

PUBLIC ART

During the Great Depression, the Federal Arts Project (FAP) emerged as the main agency devoted to helping artists. State administrators of the program commissioned artists to cover a school, municipal building or post office wall with an inspiring mural of American scenes. Inevitably, many of the works were bland, stodgy or jingoistic (saintly frontiersmen converting tribes of grateful Native Americans or idyllic farms and small towns). Pastoral realism was the favorite style because rural subjects were noncontroversial. The violent labor organizing drives going on and the wretched conditions among the unemployed, made urban settings, scenes of factories, workers or poor people prima facie controversial, and few muralists tackled them. Those who did found their work removed or hidden or painted over by community art vigilantes. In 1934, the predecessor to FAP was accused of "Communist tendencies" because murals it sponsored in San Francisco's Coit Tower included pictures of Das Kapital *and the* Daily Worker. *Congress passed a loyalty oath requirement for FAP artists and banned Communist Party members. August Henkel refused to sign the loyalty oath and his murals at Brooklyn's Floyd Bennett Field were destroyed. In the private sector, Diego Rivera's mural for Rockefeller Center,* Man at the Crossroads, *was painted over because it contained the figure of Lenin. Technically speaking, WPA murals were a far cry from the great revolutionary mural work being done by the Mexican artists Rivera and José Orozco. Nevertheless, the FAP did bring art to the people and the people to art. It also brightened up a lot of gray public spaces and put food on the tables of some great artists (as well as worthy unemployed house painters). Among those who drew federal paychecks: Ben Shahn, Jackson Pollock, Arshile Gorky, Charles Alston, Willem de Kooning, Stuart Davis and many others. The program even produced some stunning art, such as Arshile Gorky's murals at Newark Airport and the works of Thomas Hart Benton and Rudolph Weisenborn discussed below.*

Thomas Hart Benton. Benton was born in Missouri, named after his great uncle, the famed senator. He once taught Jackson Pollock at the Art Students League of New York, though by then he had abandoned nonrepresentational art. He would gain a

bit of fame or notoriety from the so-called Indiana murals, which he was commissioned to do for the state pavilion at the 1933 Chicago World's Fair. His controversial mural *Parks, the Circus, the Klan, the Press* was supposed to show the history of Indiana, and Benton did so truthfully—with images of the Ku Klux Klan burning a cross amid images of circus performers, laborers and farmers. The mural is now displayed in Woodburn Hall on the Indiana University campus in Bloomington and may be viewed when the building is open.

Indiana University, Bloomington, IN 47405, (812) 855-6494, www.indiana.edu

Philadelphia Mural Arts Program. In an interesting experiment in redemption through art, the city of Philadelphia, suffering a graffiti plague, hired muralist Jane Golden in 1984 to find the graffiti makers and harness their natural creativity to produce legitimate art. She found the underground graphologists to be a talented bunch and was able to turn their hands to mural making. Her effort evolved into the Mural Arts Program. The MAP has thrived, employing an average of 300 artists a year to complete more than 2,700 murals, making Philly Mural City.

Thomas Eakins House, 1729 Mount Vernon Street, Philadelphia, PA 19130, (215) 685-0750, www.muralarts.org

Diego Rivera. *Detroit Industry* fresco. The famous Mexican muralist painted this in 1933. It consists of three sets of images, depicting the races and ethnic stocks that came together in Detroit and made up the workforce of the auto and other industries. At the bottom of the mural are small panels that show the daily life of workers at the River Rouge plant. Art historians consider this to be one of the finest Rivera works in America today. It was commissioned by Edsel Ford, and Rivera received a handsome paycheck of $20,289, considerably more on an hourly basis than the average Ford worker was making at the time.

Detroit Institute of Arts, 5200 Woodward Avenue, Detroit, MI 48202, (313) 833-7900, www.dia.org

Ben Shahn. Shahn was among the many artists succored by the WPA. He was a radical, and among his best-known political works is *The Passion of Sacco and Vanzetti*, painted in 1932. It shows the funeral of the martyred anarchists. The painting is owned by New York's Whitney Museum of American Art. At Syracuse University there is a giant mosaic mural of this painting. Unveiled in 1967, it is twelve feet tall and sixty feet long. It was assembled in Chartres from bits of glass and stone under Shahn's supervision. Shahn—a Lithuanian-born painter, illustrator, photographer, designer and teacher—immigrated to America in 1906. He assisted Diego Rivera on his notorious Rockefeller Center murals. He photographed and painted rural poverty for the Farm Security Administration, designed posters for the Office of War Information during World War II and served as the Charles Eliot Norton professor of Poetry at Harvard during the 1956–57 academic year. His deliberately crude, caustic cartoons and paintings effectively etched the sufferings of the poor, oppressed by the rich and powerful.

East wall of Huntington Beard Crouse Hall, Syracuse University, Syracuse, NY 13244.

The Social and Public Art Resource Center (SPARC). The most notable piece SPARC completed was called the *Great Wall of Los Angeles,* which Judy Báca started painting the same year as SPARC came into being, 1974. A mural a half mile in length, the work of many hands, it is located in the San Fernando Valley, surrounded by a park and bike trails. The mural depicts the history of the peoples of California from prehistoric times to the 1950s. It was completed over five summers employing more than 400 youths and their families, working with "artists, oral historians, ethnologists, scholars, and hundreds of community members." After the *Great Wall,* the organization sponsored a program called Great Walls Unlimited: Neighborhood Pride that since 1988 has produced 105 murals in neighborhoods all over Los Angeles. SPARC was recently forced to defend *Danzas Indigenas,* a monument designed by Judy Báca, at a metro station, which was attacked by anti-immigrant groups demanding the city remove it.

685 Venice Boulevard, Venice, CA 90291, (310) 822-9560, www.sparcmurals.org

Rudolph Weisenborn. His mural *Contemporary Chicago* is unlike the great majority of WPA murals: Weisenborn rendered it in the cubist style. Abstract painting was generally forbidden on WPA projects, but a few slipped past the congressional watchdogs. Weisenborn's picture is also noteworthy for the images of workers and industry that are woven into the fabric of abstractions. *Contemporary Chicago* is sited in the Nettelhorst elementary school.

3252 N. Broadway, Chicago, IL 60657, (773) 534-5810, www.nettelhorst.org

CARNIVAL OF THE ANIMALS: A SHORT HISTORY OF ART CENSORSHIP IN OUR TIME

Our thanks to Svetlana Mintcheva, director, Arts Program, National Coalition Against Censorship, 275 7th Avenue, 15th floor, New York, NY 10001, (212) 807-6222.

1989

Al Is Really, Really Pissed

Rev. Donald Wildmon, director of the American Family Association, attacks Andres Serrano's photograph *Piss Christ,* which won an NEH-supported grant. Wildmon claims tax dollars were being spent to support "pornographic, anti-Christian 'works of art.' " Senator Al D'Amato demands a review of NEA grants, insisting it was "a question of taxpayers' money," not artistic freedom.

A Mighty Armey of the Lord

Rep. Dick Armey and more than one hundred other members of Congress, who also worry about taxpayers' money going to spread homoeroticism and other evil things they can't spell, criticize NEA support for a Robert Mapplethorpe retrospective at the Corcoran Gallery of Art in Washington, D.C. The Corcoran cancels the exhibition.

Don't Tread on It

Veterans' organizations fire off a lawsuit at a student exhibition at the Art Institute of Chicago. It features Dred Scott Tyler's installation with an American flag laid on the floor. Visitors are invited to write their answers to the question "What is the proper way to display a U.S. flag?" in a book positioned so they have to walk on the flag to do so. The suit is dismissed but the city cuts the Art Institute's funding from $70,000 to $1 and many benefactors withdraw support.

1990

The NEA Four

NEA's John Frohnmayer vetoes a grant to chocolate-covered performance artist Karen Finley, along with grants to Tim Miller, John Fleck and Holly Hughes. Three are gay, one a radical feminist. They sue and win compensation greater than the original grants.

Subway Kiss-Off

The Chicago Transit Authority delays displaying an anti-AIDS poster by Gran Fury, *Kissing Doesn't Kill: Greed and Indifference Do,* showing a same-sex couple kissing, until city and state legislators can pass ordinances banning "same sex affection" in CTA advertisements. Whew! That was close!

Cincinnati Reds

Robert Mapplethorpe's show The Perfect Moment opens at the Contemporary Arts Center of Cincinnati. Thanks to smart police work the arts center director is nabbed for pandering to obscenity. But a jury of bleeding hearts acquits him.

1991

Babes in Birmingham

The public library removes six "improper" drawings by Teresa and Jean Campbell of a woman breast-feeding her baby. An angry public rises up against the library! The pictures are returned!

1995

NEA Defunds Smut

The National Endowment for the Arts eliminates all grants to individual artists because they "might do things [to] offend . . . mainstream America," explains Senator Kay Bailey Hutchinson.

1996

Next They'll Want to Marry Our Sisters

An Amherst, Massachusetts, citizen sues to stop the exhibit Love Makes a Family: Living in Lesbian and Gay Families from being shown in public schools. U.S. District Judge Frank Freedman refuses to halt the exhibit.

1997

Hopeless in San Antonio

Saying that the Esperanza Center (see below and page 366), a community arts organization, is "pro-homosexual," "pro-abortion" and "anti–family values," the San Antonio city council withholds funding. A federal judge rules that the city violated alleged First Amendment rights of the Esperanza Center.

1999

Who Flung the Dung?

New York City Mayor Rudolph Giuliani orders the Brooklyn Museum to remove Chris Ofili's elephant-dung-spattered painting *The Holy Virgin Mary,* cuts off funding to the museum, threatens eviction. The museum sues, wins $5.8 million to help repair its entry hall.

2001

War Jitters

The Los Angeles City Cultural Affairs Department cancels War, an exhibition by Los Angeles–based artist Alex Donis at the Watts Towers Arts Center, claiming it might provoke violence.

2002

Boobs on the Tube

Attorney General John Ashcroft orders drapes to cover two bare-breasted Art Deco statues in the Great Hall of the Department of Justice because they're visible on TV when he holds press conferences there.

We Know What We Don't Like

Afraid of offending city officials, the Willits Center for the Arts in Mendocino County, California, nixes two panels from Evan Johnson's photographic work, which criticize American foreign policy.

2004

Don't Monkey with W

Chris Savido's Bush Monkeys,

which looks like a portrait of President George W. Bush but at close range shows monkeys swimming in a marsh, is so objectionable to the manager of Chelsea Market, an upscale, covered food market and exhibition space in Manhattan, that he closes the whole sixty-piece show.

2005

Stamped Out

Secret Service agents turn up before the public opening of Axis of Evil, the Secret History of Sin, at Columbia College in Chicago and take pictures of some of the art pieces— including Al Brandtner's Patriot Act, a sheet of mock 37-cent stamps showing President Bush with a revolver pointed at his head. The agents order the museum director to turn over artists' names and phone numbers. Later, at the University of Wisconsin–Green Bay, the chancellor orders Patriot Act removed from the show.

Southern Fried

The director of the Customs House Museum in Clarksville, Tennessee, removes an art installation for fear that the deep-fried flags in it would offend community sensitivities

and imperil the museum's public funding.

2007

No Thought Please, We're Texan

State Representative Boris Miles removes two works from an exhibit about the death penalty at the Texas Capitol Building in Austin on the ground that they were "questionable, offensive or simply thought provoking."

So It's Come to This

The Bush Library orders, then cancels, a portrait of the president by the well-known British painter Jonathan Yeo. Miffed, Yeo creates a portrait that consists of a collage of pornographic images. A Republican Party spokesman in Texas calls the picture "very distasteful. Why would anyone want to make a picture of our president from pornographic material?"

Books

PUBLISHERS: OTHER VOICES

Akashic Books. Brooklyn-based Akashic (Sanskrit for "giant library") was founded in 1997 by rocker Johnny Temple, bassist for the band Girls Against Boys. He told the *New York Times* he wants to sell books to "more of the population . . . there's no gentrification of the music world. I feel that the books we're publishing are just as exciting and dynamic as the music in my band." Such as? "African Diaspora" writers like Nigerian activist and novelist Chris Abani and ex–New Jersey State poet laureate Amiri Baraka. There's also a novel by Joe Meno, *Hairstyles of the Damned,* that reads like Holden Caulfield on drugs, according to the *Times.* Akashic teamed up with the rock fanzine *Punk Planet* to create Punk Planet Books. It's published some political nonfiction and even a mystery novel cowritten by Zapatista leader Subcomandante Marcos, which segues us into Temple's most successful titles, a series of short noir crime fictions. The first was *Brooklyn Noir,* which begat *Chicago Noir* which begat *San Francisco Noir, Dublin Noir, Delhi Noir, Istanbul Noir* and *Wall Street Noir.*

PO Box 1456, New York, NY 10009, (718) 643-9193, www.akashicbooks.com

AK Press. This is the American branch of AKA Books Co-Operative, Ltd., a British anarchist collective owned by its members. In 2007 AK Press America published *End*

Times: The Death of the Fourth Estate by Alexander Cockburn and Jeffrey St. Clair. The firm is strenuously antichain and anticonglomerate; its website proclaims: "We urge you to support your local independent booksellers and infoshops. Join campaigns to keep corporate chains out of your town. Mail order or web order from independent stores or distros. Better yet, become an independent distro. If you and your comrades sell books or other stuff at tables, through your newsletter or zine, via your website, or any other way, contact us about discounts available."

674-A 23rd Street, Oakland, CA 94612, (510) 208-1700, www.akpress.org

Beacon Press. In 1971 Beacon published the complete *Pentagon Papers,* a huge project that probably won it more fame or notoriety than any other of the hundreds of books it has published in more than a century and a half on Beacon Hill. Daniel Ellsberg, the Pentagon analyst who first leaked the papers to the *New York Times,* got a separate set to Alaskan Senator Mike Gravel, a vocal foe of the Vietnam War. Gravel read

a section of them into his subcommittee's record and sought publication in book form. Thirty-five publishers turned him down, fearing likely government prosecution and financial loss. As a Unitarian, Gravel turned to Beacon Press, which had already issued a number of antiwar books. Ideologically in tune with

Gravel's intentions, Beacon shouldered the task despite a threatening personal phone call from President Nixon to the press's director, Gobin Stair; despite the possibility of jail time and despite the onerous burden of the project's costs for a small press, Beacon went ahead with the papers. The publisher lost money but set an example for others, who had kowtowed to political pressure and abdicated editorial responsibility. Recent books include: Rashid Khalidi's *The Iron Cage: The Story of the Palestinian Struggle for Statehood*; Mary Oliver's Pulitzer Prize–winning poems; Sasha Abramsky's *American Furies*, on the U.S. prison archipelago.

25 Beacon Street, Boston, MA 02108, (617) 742-2110, www.beacon.org

Archie Green,
David Roediger, Franklin Rosemont,
Salvatore Salerno, *editors*

The
BIG RED
SONGBOOK
250-plus IWW Songs!

Charles H. Kerr Publishing Company. As its jaunty motto—"Subversive literature for the whole family since 1886"—would suggest, Charles H. Kerr is the granddaddy of radical publishers. Started by the eponymous Charles Hope Kerr, the press has been publishing texts on radical labor and socialist history and theory since before the turn of the twentieth century. Kerr published the first three-volume English translation of Marx's *Das Kapital,* as well as the Second International's journal *International Socialist Review.* Kerr is now run as a "worker-owned co-operative not-for-profit educational association." It reprints Socialist classics like the works of C.L.R. James, Mary Marcy, Edward Bellamy, Eugene V. Debs, Clarence Darrow, Isadora Duncan and Vachel Lindsay, as well as books by living authors like Staughton Lynd, H. L. Mitchell, Warren Leming and Carlos Cortez, to name a few. Kerr continues to be the leading source of histories (recent and past) of the I.W.W. by the prolific Franklin Rosemont (author, most recently, of *Jacques Vache and the Roots of Surrealism*) and others, and offers various historical series, including the Sixties Series (which published the original text of the *Port Huron Statement*), the Lost Utopias Series and the Bughouse Square Series. Kerr has a long tradition of publishing leftist songbooks, including *The Big Red Songbook,* edited by folklorist Archie Green, David Roediger, Franklin Rosemont and Salvatore Salerno, with an Afterword by Utah Phillips. It contains some 250 Wobbly songs, plus essays, history and interpretations. Kerr keeps alive the cocky, irreverent Wobbly spirit (with a sixties' twist) with new titles like "Dancin' in the Streets! Anarchists, IWWs, Surrealists, Situationists & Provos in the 1960s."

1726 W. Jarvis, Chicago, IL 60620, (773) 465-7774, www.charleshkerr.net

Chelsea Green Publishing. Since its founding in 1984 Vermont-bred Chelsea Green has had a good income from books on sustainable living, with a backlist of some 400 titles. Chelsea Green's vegan-and-potatoes subjects have been "green building, organic growing, and renewable energy—the practical aspects of sustainability." As the alarm about global warming spread, Chelsea Green broadened its vision, promoting books with an activist orientation toward developing sustainable, ecofriendly communities and economies. Recent books in this vein include *Crashing the Gate: Netroots, Grassroots, and the Rise of People-Powered Politics* by Jerome Armstrong and Markos Moulitsas. George Lakoff's *Don't Think of an Elephant! Know Your Values and Frame the Debate* and Jean Giono's *The Man Who Planted Trees* ("an ecological fable") both sold between 100,000 and 200,000 copies.

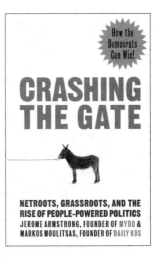

85 N. Main Street, Suite 120, White River Junction, VT 05001, (802) 295-6300, www.chelseagreen.com

Fantagraphics Books. Times were tough in 2003 for Fantagraphics; the Seattle publisher of comics and graphic literature needed $100,000 fast. So it sent out a web mailing asking people to buy Fantagraphics books immediately. According to co-owner Gary Groth, "The response totally exceeded our expectations." In less than two weeks, the appeal raised $150,000. With that boost, Fantagraphics was able to go on publishing well-known writers and artists like R. Crumb, Gilbert and Jaime Hernandez, Peter Bagge, Chris Ware, Dan Clowes and Joe Sacco. Having already issued the complete *Krazy Kat*, Fantagraphics had the commercial sense to ink a deal with Charles M. Schulz's estate to publish the complete *Peanuts* cartoons. That project will take twelve and a half years and twenty-four volumes. The first volume was issued in 2004; it sold 150,000 copies and made the *NYT* best-seller list. Usually, though, this firm specializes in cutting-edge work reflecting the subversive spirit of the underground artists who flowered in the sixties. And it not only publishes 'em, it sells 'em at its own store, 1201 South Vale Street, Seattle, WA 98108, (206) 658-0110.

7563 Lake City Way NE, Seattle, WA 98115, (800) 657-1100, www.fantagraphics.com

Haymarket Books. The name of this Chicago-based nonprofit publisher-distributor honors the anarchist massacre. Its philosophy calls for publishing books that are weapons in the struggle for change. No question where its politics lie: Haymarket is

PAUL BUHLE ON RADICAL COMICS

Yes, there are radical comics, though recognition of them was an awfully long time in coming. Actually, it arrived in the years after the appearance of the underground comix in the late sixties. I was publisher of *Radical America Komiks,* which appeared in 1969. It was the third in this political genre, edited by Gilbert Shelton, and the first title from Rip Off Press. As anticapitalist as the counterculture, with most of its limitations, the undergrounds lasted less than a decade. Head shops, a prime outlet, closed, production costs went up and other factors kicked in; most of the artists just quit. Thirty or so years later, comic art is at last getting some respect. Perhaps a dozen politically minded artists on this side of the ocean are making a living. The *New York Times Book Review* gave a front page review to a Harvey Pekar book, and the *New York Times Magazine* now runs a weekly strip by different artists. Graphic novels are fast-moving items in the chain stores. Pantheon and the Roaring Brook Press division of Holt are bringing out illustrated fiction, Hill and Wang has placed itself in front in nonfiction and there's a whole lot in the pipeline.

The picture is too furiously in motion for any easy assessment. Didactic radical comics have faded in the past for want of sales. But *World War 3 Illustrated* (see page 137), a satirical annual, is a survivor. Its crew of artists includes Peter Kuper, who drew the *Spy vs. Spy* page in *Mad* magazine; they continue to make progress with interesting new books, such as Sharon Rudahl's biography *Dangerous Woman: The Graphic Biography of Emma Goldman.* My view is that, despite past disappointments, the well-scripted, well-drawn political-minded book has a grand future.

PAUL BUHLE coedited *Wobblies!: A Graphic History of the Industrial Workers of the World, Students for a Democratic Society: A Graphic History* and *A People's History of American Empire: A Graphic Adaptation,* an adaptation of Howard Zinn's *People's History of the United States* by Zinn and Buhle with drawings by Mike Konopacki. He is currently toiling on *The Beats* and *Working,* an adaptation of Studs Terkel's oral history, both with the artist Harvey Pekar.

a nonprofit project of the International Socialist Organization and the Center for Economic Research and Social Change. That said, it offers a good variety of titles. A recent list contained something in the celebrity-newsmaker genre, in this case, Italian journalist Giuliana Sgrena's account of her kidnapping by Iraqi fighters (*Friendly Fire: The Remarkable Story of a Journalist Kidnapped in Iraq, Rescued by an Italian Secret Service Agent, and Shot by U.S. Forces*); a young adult novel about a Palestinian boy under the Israeli occupation (*A Little Piece of Ground,* by Elizabeth Laird); a debunking of right-wing anti-immigrant propaganda (*No One Is Illegal: Fighting*

Racism and State Violence on the U.S.–Mexico Border, by Mike Davis and Justin Akers Chacon); *Welcome to the Terrordome: The Pain, Politics, and Promise of Sports*, by *Nation* sportswriter Dave Zirin.

PO Box 180165, Chicago, IL 60618, (773) 583-7884, www.haymarketbooks.org

Monthly Review Press. This is the book wing of *Monthly Review* (see page 124). A sampling of recent titles: *Cheap Motels and a Hot Plate* by Michael D. Yates (an economics prof's adventures on the road after retiring and setting off with his wife in their van); *The Cold War and the New Imperialism: A Global History, 1945–2005* by Henry Heller and *Build It Now: Socialism for the Twenty-first Century* by Michael A. Lebowitz.

146 W. 29th Street, 6W, New York, NY 10001, (212) 691-2555, www.monthlyreview.org/mrpress.htm

Nation Books. In 2000 Nation Books was founded as a copublishing venture between the Nation Institute and Avalon Books. The imprint's mission was to "publish arresting titles on the social and cultural forces that shape our lives today." In just seven years, Nation Books has published more than 200 titles. Its eclectic catalog covers politics and current events, with topics ranging from human rights to art and culture to the environment. Highlights include *Pity the Nation: The Abduction of Lebanon*, by Robert Fisk; *Imperial America*, by Gore Vidal; *Iraq Confidential*, by Scott Ritter; *Hope in the Dark*, by Rebecca Solnit; *The Impeachment of George W. Bush*, by Elizabeth Holtzman and Cynthia L. Cooper;

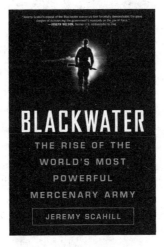

Life Out of Context, by Walter Mosley; *A People's History of Science*, by Clifford D. Connor; and *Blackwater: The Rise of the World's Most Powerful Mercenary Army*, by Jeremy Scahill, which made the *New York Times* best seller list. Building on the success of recent years, Nation Books was repositioned in spring 2007 as a stand-alone imprint at Basic Books, one of the leading nonfiction imprints in the country and a member of the Perseus Books Group. In fall 2007 Nation Books published an account of the prisoners held at Guantanamo Bay by human rights lawyer Clive Stafford Smith, who represents over fifty detainees. Other listings: *Lords of the Land*, the definitive history of Israeli settlements by historian Idith Zertal, Ph.D., and journalist Akiva Eldar; *The Man Who Pushed America to War: The Extraordinary Life Adventures and Obsessions of Ahmed Chalabi* by NBC investigative journalist Aram Roston; *A Quiet Revolution*, Mary Elizabeth King's history of the first Palestinian Intifada revealing nonviolent strategies that were employed by large segments of the Palestinian community in response to occupation.

116 E. 16th Street, New York, NY 10003, (212) 822-0250, www.nationbooks.org

The New Press. One of the best known of the small independent, nonprofit publishers, the New Press was founded by André Schiffrin, a distinguished editor who had been chief of the Pantheon Books division of Random House. In *The Business of Books,* he recalls coming up with a vision of a new kind of nonprofit publishing house that would be freed from the pressure to make the two-figure percentages such conglomerate-owned houses demand their subsidiaries produce, which creates pressure to avoid radical or demanding or ahead-of-their-time books. Since its first title in 1992, the New Press has grown into an operation turning out some eighty titles a year on a variety of social, historical and political themes, as well as books on art, criticism and the law (no fiction or poetry, however). Past lists have included works by Studs Terkel (whom Schiffrin first edited at Pantheon), Margaret Duras and Noam Chomsky. Several *Nation* contributors have appeared on its lists: John Leonard (*When the Kissing Had to Stop*), John Nichols (*The Genius of Impeachment*), David Cole (*Enemy Aliens*), Mike Davis (*Dead Cities*), Tom Hayden (*Street Wars*), Doug Henwood (*After the New Economy*), Esther Kaplan (*With God on Their Side*), Lewis Lapham (*Pretensions to Empire*). The New Press also takes pride in presenting its volumes in innovative designs, and published a graphic biography of Emma Goldman. It expanded into audio and video works, such as slave narratives recorded by the WPA in the 1930s.

38 Greene Street, 4th floor, New York, NY 10013, (212) 629-8802, www.thenewpress.com

Red Letter Press. Here's the straight story from managing editor Helen Gilbert: "Red Letter Press publishes radical books and feminist writing in English and Spanish on socialist theory, race liberation, queer activism, and grassroots organizing. . . . Our mission, as a nonprofit small press, is to create attractive, readable, and low-cost publications that can change the world!" The very first book the firm brought into the world, back in 1990, was *Woman Sitting at the Machine, Thinking,* a collection of feminist working-class poetry by Karen Brodine. According to Gilbert, the book met "unexpected resistance from the printer . . . who said he objected to the content of the work. Was it the poet's description of union organizing at the print shop where she worked, the sweet lesbian love poem, the backdrop of joyful activism or all those combined that made the manager reject the job? He never would tell us. But it was a good object lesson in the power of the printed word to rock the establishment. May all Red Letter Press books be as subversive!" Other popular Red Letter Press titles: *The Radical*

Women Manifesto, Socialism for Skeptics, Voices of Color, Gay Resistance and *Revolutionary Integration.*

4710 University Way NE, #100, Seattle, WA 98105, (206) 985-4621, www.redletterpress.org

Seven Stories Press. Website: "In response to the political crisis triggered by the attacks on September 11, 2001, Seven Stories has stepped up its publishing on issues regarding U.S. foreign policy, civil liberties, human rights and social justice." Shortly after the World Trade Center attack, the press rushed out *9-11* by Noam Chomsky, a radical critique of U.S. policy that sold more than 300,000 copies. Seven Stories has made a point of publishing censored books in recent years, including Gary Webb's *Dark Alliance,* about the CIA and ghetto crack; Carol Felsenthal's critical biography of media tycoon Si Newhouse, *Citizen Newhouse* (originally under contract to a large house but killed because of its unflattering portrayals of some boldface names in the media and publishing industries); a collection of essays by the death-row journalist Mumia Abu-Jamal, *All Things Censored,* and an anthology of Project Censored's top twenty-five censored stories of the year. In 2006 Seven Stories published Elizabeth de la Vega's *U.S. v. George W. Bush et al.,* a mock impeachment proceeding on grounds of misleading and defrauding Congress. Seven Stories also publishes fiction and poetry. Alan Dugan's *Poems Seven: New and Complete Poetry* won the National Book Award for Poetry in 2001.

140 Watts Street, New York, NY 10013, (212) 226-8760, www.sevenstories.com

Soft Skull Press. This small, radical publishing outfit was launched in 1992 by Sander Hicks, punk musician (former lead singer of White Collar Crime), writer, activist, 9/11 truther, candidate for the Green Party nomination for the 2006 New York Senate race (lost to Howie Hawkins) and all-around provocateur. Soft Skull has the distinction of starting life as a "guerrilla operation" in a Manhattan Kinko's copy shop, where Hicks was working the graveyard shift and assembling chapbooks written by friends. Success followed, and Soft Skull was incorporated in 1996. Hicks was soon publishing poetry by Lee Ranaldo of Sonic Youth and, notably, William Upski Wimsatt's *Bomb the Suburbs,* which gained a cult following. In 2000, Soft Skull decided to republish James Hatfield's biography of George W. Bush, *Fortunate Son,* with a new foreword in which Hatfield discussed his own criminal record. Hicks neglected to have the book vetted by lawyers. Big mistake. It drew a libel suit (*not* from the president) resulting in an out-of-court settlement that nearly bankrupted Soft Skull. In 2001, paralyzed by this and other financial difficulties, the house chose board member Richard Nash to put it on a business footing and Hicks departed. His most recent project is Vox Pop (see page 332), a radical coffee shop, bookstore and event space in the Ditmas Park neighborhood of Brooklyn. Nash rescued the press from near insolvency, though Soft Skull has continued to publish radical or controversial books, including a new edition of *Arming*

America, Michael A. Bellesiles's revisionist history of American gun culture, which in its initial appearance caused a scandal when historians discovered it was riddled with inaccuracies and invented citations. On top of that, it took withering fire from the gun lobby, doubly underscoring the need for left publishers to get their facts straight. But Soft Skull came up with a hit in *Get Your War On,* David Rees's foulmouthed, satiric comic strip about the war on terror.

19 W. 21st Street, Suite 1101, New York, NY 10010, (718) 643-1599, www.softskull.com

South End Press. This Bostonian wheelhorse in the left-independent team originated as the project of a six-person living and working collective that incorporated in 1977 as a nonprofit, called the Institute for Social and Cultural Change, with South End as a subsidiary. Since then it has published more than 250 books consonant with its motto "Read. Write. Revolt." Authors have included Arundhati Roy, bell hooks, Winona LaDuke, Manning Marable, Ward Churchill, Howard Zinn, Jeremy Brecher and many others. None of the founders—most of them grad students—knew anything about publishing. They drew up a charter organizing them into a truly nonhierarchical, cooperative workplace in which all had an equal voice and equal salaries with assistance to those with special needs or dependents. They vowed the press would dedicate itself to fighting "oppressions in the United States, especially those based on race, sex, class." Then they learned the publishing business by trial and error. According to cofounder Lydia Sargent: "Our first book came out in January 1978. We produced six to ten books every year after that. We almost went bankrupt in 1978, 1979, 1980, 1981, 1982, 1983, 1984, 1985, etc." Now the staff is majority female and over 50 percent people of color. In 1990, South End Press helped launch Speak Out, a speakers' bureau designed to showcase South End authors. Today, South End Press, *Z Magazine* (see page 123), Speak Out and *Alternative Radio*—a weekly progressive radio program—comprise the Institute for Social and Cultural Change.

7 Brookline Street, #1, Cambridge, MA 02139, (617) 547-4002, www.southendpress.org

Verso. Verso's website brags that "with global sales approaching $3 million per year and over 350 titles in print, Verso can justifiably claim to be the largest radical publisher in the English-language world." London-based, Verso (as in "left hand page") was founded in 1970 by the important sixties organ *New Left Review*. In 1995 it opened a New York office. Though North American sales account for roughly two-thirds of Verso's business, the main editorial functions are carried on at the London office, with the New York people handling marketing and publicity. Along with British writers, Verso publishes many of the better-known North American left authors (and more than a few past or present *Nation* contributors).

6 Meard Street, London W1F OEG UK; 180 Varick Street, 10th floor, New York, NY 10014, (212) 807-9680, www.versobooks.com

West End Press. This moveable feast of books ended up in Albuquerque after a journey that started in New York at Columbia University. Its first incarnation in 1971 was as a magazine founded by doctoral candidate John F. Crawford. He took the name from the West End bar, hangout of Columbia University students, poets and writers. The West End became the informal headquarters of Crawford and his magazine. In 1976 Crawford tired of the magazine and vowed to create "something less ephemeral." That something turned out to be West End Press. It now specializes in "multicultural and working class poetry, drama, and fiction" and books that are oriented toward stirring up social change. One of its earliest and most regularly published authors is the Minnesota-born Meridel Le Sueur, whose writing and radical thinking inspired Crawford's vision of a literary "people's culture." "I hopped a bus to meet [Le Sueur] in Minneapolis in December 1976," Crawford recalled, "and moved to the Middle West a year later." In its thirty years, West End has published more than one hundred titles, including five books by Le Sueur, who died in 1996, as well as authors like Pablo Neruda, Thomas McGrath, Sharon Doubiago, Cherríe Moraga, Luci Tapahonso, Laura Tohe and Joseph Bruchac. Says Crawford: "We believe not only that the personal is political, but the political is personal—that progressive art must be brought to individual awareness. We believe that all people should be able to develop their own cultures in freedom, with tolerance for others and consideration for the natural world around them."

PO Box 27334, Albuquerque, NM, 87125, (505) 345-5729, www.westendpress.org

BRIEFLY NOTED

Clarity Press (globalization, human rights), 3277 Roswell Road NE, Suite 469, Atlanta, GA 30305, (877) 613-1495, www.bookmasters.com/clarity

Common Courage Press (social justice, "informed dissent"), PO Box 702, Monroe, ME 04951, (207) 525-0900, www.commoncouragepress.com

The Feminist Press at CUNY (feminism, women's studies), 365 5th Avenue, Suite 5406, New York, NY 10016, (212) 817-7925, www.feministpress.org

Firebrand Books (feminist/lesbian titles, gender studies; recipient of LGBT book awards), 2232 S. Main Street, #272, Ann Arbor, MI 48103, (248) 738-8202, www.firebrandbooks.com

International Publishers (Marxism/socialism), 235 W. 23rd Street, 7th floor, New York, NY 10011, (212) 366-9816, www.intpubnyc.com

Paradigm Publishers (left politics/current affairs), 3360 Mitchell Lane, Suite E, Boulder, CO 80301, (303) 245-9054, www.paradigmpublishers.com

PoliPointPress (mainstream progressive politics), PO Box 3008, Sausalito, CA 94966, (415) 339-4100, www.p3books.com

WRITERS' RETREATS

Kopkind Colony. Andrew Kopkind, who died in 1994, was one of the Left's finest journalists. He ended his career at *The Nation*, after writing for *Time, The New York Review of Books* and various radical publications. His complete body of work (the best of it collected in *The Thirty Years' Wars: Dispatches and Diversions of a Radical Journalist, 1965–1994*, edited by JoAnn Wypijewski) would be legacy enough for most writers on the Left. He covered just about every important story from the 1960s through the 1990s with shrewd intelligence in prose that had panache and wit and with a broadly radical and humane worldview. Andy Kopkind's friends created a second "living" legacy in his name at Tree Frog Farm in southern Vermont, where he spent summers with his longtime partner, John Scagliotti, director of the definitive gay history documentaries *Before Stonewall* and *After Stonewall* and cocreator of the television series *In the Life*. The Kopkind Colony is a kind of living memorial to Andy, devoted to bringing activists and journalists together. Seven or eight young writers and activists come for a ten-day session. The visitors stay in cabins on the grounds and meet in daily seminars with four mature journalists and activists serving as their mentors. Each session features a movie night and a speaker's night, which are open to the surrounding community. Speakers and mentors to the colony have included Tariq Ali, Patricia J. Williams, Rabab Abdul Hadi, Robin D. G. Kelley, Grace Paley, Robert Pollin, Makani Themba-Nixon, Ron Nixon, Mandy Carter, Doug Lummis, Kevin Alexander Gray, Margaret Cerullo, Alisa Klein, Mike Marqusee, Nabil Abraham, Victor Navasky and Alexander Cockburn. The colony cosponsors, with the Center for Independent Documentary (see www.documentaries.org), the Annual Kopkind Grassroots Film Festival ("Lights, camera, take action!") in nearby Brattleboro.

158 Kopkind Road, Guilford, VT 05301, (802) 254-4859

The Mesa Refuge. The refuge sits on a bluff overlooking Tomales Bay near Point Reyes Station. This literary Eden is underwritten by Peter Barnes, a journalist and author of the influential *Capitalism 3.0: A Guide to Reclaiming the Commons.* He moonlighted rather successfully as a businessman and set up Working Assets (see page 307), the liberal-inclined purveyor of credit cards and long distance service. Barnes runs Mesa under the auspices of Oakland's Common Counsel Foundation, a consortium of family foundations and individual donors that are committed to funding economic, environmental and social justice initiatives. A former resident reports: "Hummingbirds and other small representatives of the wildlife kingdom might come up to inspect you as you read in a chair outside the refuge house. You must travel a few miles through an unspoiled beautiful national seashore to walk along the shores of majestic, empty beaches but there are few other distractions or demerits, leaving it to visiting writers to supply their own bad moods, writer's block, and failed chapters. And occasionally, successes!"

c/o Common Counsel Foundation, 678 13th Street, Suite 101, Oakland, CA 94612, (510) 834-2995, www.commoncounsel.org/pages/mesa.html

LITERARY SERVICES

Creative Writing MFA Program. Some say writing can't be taught. To which we say, yes, but it can be learned. Anyhow, the communal experience of writing courses can be helpful to new writers, looking for a jump start, and to old writers, looking to recharge their batteries. There are scores of excellent creative writing programs at universities, with the oldest and best known being the Iowa Writers' Workshop (University of Iowa, Iowa City) and Stanford University (Palo Alto, CA). But the MFA in creative writing at Florida International University in Miami stands out as a "blue collar" program, attracting not just fresh-out-of-college kids but also men and women of all ages who joined the working world (some still hold jobs) and went back to school to study writing seriously. Results: more than fifty books published by graduates of the program in its seventeen years of existence, including novels, short-story collections, nonfiction and poetry. There have been best sellers by Dennis Lehane and Barbara Parker, plus poetry prizewinners John Evans and Richard Blanco (his first published poem, "Last Night in Havana," appeared in *The Nation*). Faculty includes best-selling crime writer James B. Hall and *Nation* veteran Dan Wakefield.

Florida International University, Biscayne Bay Campus, North Miami, FL 33181, (305) 919-5857, http://w3.fiu.edu/crwriting/

Frances Goldin Literary Agency. The standard advice to neophytes with a manuscript in their backpack is "Get an agent." Progressive authors might try Fran Goldin, whose stable includes notorieties like death-row journalist Mumia Abu-Jamal, as well as literary writers and social commentators like Adrienne Rich, Susan Brownmiller, Frances Fox Piven, Sasha Abramsky, Jacob Hacker, Tom Tomorrow, Ian Williams, Juan Gonzales, Dorothy Allison and Barbara Kingsolver. Goldin only handles writers and work that she finds politically and morally compatible. She lays out the boundaries in her *Literary Market Place* entry: "No racist, sexual, ageist, homophobic or pornographic material considered. Adult literary fiction and serious progressive nonfiction our specialty." A veteran activist herself, she's a former member of the CP who quit because she didn't like them commanding her to work on this or that cause; also, they weren't revolutionary enough. She was then toiling for a literary agent and growing increasingly unhappy with representing clients like Harold Robbins. So she rounded up $5,000 and hung out her shingle at her one-bedroom apartment on Manhattan's Lower East Side. She's since moved on and up to Greenwich Village and to handling best sellers like Kingsolver. Her clients swear by her devoted attention to their interests and her straight-shooting manner. Now in her early eighties, she admits her small agency seems an anomaly in an industry dominated by mergers: "The world's going to hell in a handbasket and here we are thriving," she told *In These Times*. She has no plans to retire but would like to cut back on her six-day workweek to four. "I could spend the fifth day getting arrested."

57 E. 11th Street, Suite 5B, New York, NY 10003, (212) 777-0047, www.goldenlit.com

Gail Leondar Public Relations. Don't say "PR" like it is a dirty word. Depends on what you're publicizing—right? Gail Leondar-Wright devotes herself and her company to talking up the books solely by progressive authors, which are, she told us, the kind of books she believes in. Her job, she continued, is introducing them to "thoughtful, well-informed media people and their audiences across the country." Gail prefers books on "politics, peace, justice, anti-racism, environmental protection, human rights, criminal justice and public policy topics, feminism, gay and lesbian concerns, and progressive spirituality and religion." She has represented *Nation* contributors Sasha Abramsky, Laura Flanders, Robert McChesney and many other left-inclined authors. One of her most satisfying projects, she said, was Kate Bornstein's *Gender*

Outlaw, published in 1994, a book on transgender theory by a transgender author. At that time such a subject-author combo was taboo to the gatekeepers on the media circuit. But Leondar-Wright kept plugging. She says she takes pride that the book and her own work on it were "instrumental in fostering a movement that sprang up around transgender rights."

www.glprbooks.com

BOOKSTORES FOR LEFT-BRAINED PEOPLE

What the following bookshops have in common is that they are independently owned and minded and very much politically involved in their neighborhood, community and world. Bookstores these days (and that includes the Barnes & Nobles and the Waldens) not only sell books but also serve as gathering places and free-speech forums where authors talk and sign, reading groups meet and talk, books are read, ideas are generated, actions contemplated. As they say at Internationalist Books in Chapel Hill: "This is more than a place to buy information. It's a place to get involved." The proceedings may even be fueled by fresh-brewed coffee. Some of the most successful indies function as community centers (see also Bookshop Cafés).

Vermont

Black Sheep Books. This small store has a big customer base and a selection of titles relevant to left causes as broad as all outdoors. Worker owned, it specializes in radical and scholarly used books. It's located on the second floor of the Langdon Street Café with organic eats, live music and art shows and potent coffee.

4 Langdon Street, Montpelier, VT 05602, (802) 225-8906, http://blacksheepbooks.org

New York

Autumn Leaves Used Books. Owner Joe Westmore says this used book-cum-record store in Ithaca is "an extension of me and my politics." He serves up a basic diet of "Chomsky, Zinn, Ehrenreich, Doug Henwood, etc." but mixes in plenty of mainstream literature. "They may come in to get a Stephen King novel, but they may also walk out with an Emma Goldman book." Westmore self-publishes a pamphlet series promoting progressive viewpoints not found in the local paper. He says, "The store is so regularly the outlet for bus tickets for rallies in NYC and DC that folks come to it looking for tickets before buses are organized." There's also a café, music and records from the Bop Shop.

115 the Commons, Ithaca, NY 14850, (607) 273-8239, www.mediastudy.com

Bluestockings Books. At the beginning of the 1990s, feminist bookstores had their flowering. At the peak there were something like 120 of them in the United States. Now there are, by one count, fewer than twenty. One of the casualties was Bluestockings Books in New York's Greenwich Village. Then Brooke Lehman and Hitomi Matarese resuscitated it with a new business model, calling for a broader focus, encompassing books covering the spectrum of left issues. Bluestockings still carries lots of women's stuff and gender studies but also more tomes on other issues. Progressives of all genders and sexes praise the place, including its hosting of groups like Dyke Knitting Circle, Radical Cheerleaders and Books Through Bars (books donated to prisoners).

172 Allen Street, New York, NY 10002, (212) 777-6028, www.bluestockings.com

---

HARLEM, USA: A TALE OF TWO STORES

When we last visited Liberation Bookstore, it was padlocked and heavy metal screens covered the windows. It was like seeing a good friend turned suddenly old and ill. Peering through the screen, past the says-it-all sign reading, "If you don't know, learn. If you know, teach," we made out in the dusty gloom books on black and African history and culture still on the shelves, as though caught in a time warp. Una Mulzac, daughter of a merchant marine officer, a union leader who was blacklisted by HUAC during the McCarthy troubles, founded Liberation Books in 1967. In its heyday the store served as a radical black power center, but in recent years business slowed, as did Una, who couldn't keep it open competitive hours. She battled her landlord's rent increases and eviction notices but was felled by a stroke in 2007. The neighborhood people and her old customers turned out to picket and show support. On one such occasion, some protesters told *Harlem Live* what the store meant to them. "If this store does close, then our history will die and our children will have one less place to go to research on their culture," said Grant Maire, a resident of Harlem. Elombe Brath, who has lived in Harlem since 1962, recollected: "These types of bookstores turned Negroes into Africans."

Meanwhile, since 2002, a successful new store called Hue-Man has represented the gentrifying face of Harlem. It doesn't have Liberation's radical chops, but it is bright and black owned and friendly and shelves a respectable selection of African-American history, biography, culture and politics. Senator Barack Obama's books flew off the shelves when he announced his candidacy for the presidency. Bill Clinton, whose office is a couple of blocks over on 125th Street, dropped by in 2002 to sign his autobiography, *My Life*. They sold 1,000 copies that day.

Liberation Bookstore, 421 Malcolm X Boulevard, New York, NY, 10027 (closed); Hue-Man Bookstore & Café, 2319 Frederick Douglass Boulevard, New York, NY 10027, (212) 665-7400, www.huemanbookstore.com

The Strand Bookstore. The *Village Voice* called it "The best 18 miles in Manhattan." The Strand is the place to go for the largest selection of reviewers' copies and like-new remainders. Rare books are on a separate floor. This New York institution has a pedigree stretching back to Book Row on Fourth Avenue below Fourteenth Street. Benjamin Bass opened a store there and transplanted it to its present location in the 1950s. Now it occupies five of the building's eleven floors and has been handsomely refurbished in design as well as spirit since the old days of groaning shelves, creaky stairs and ponytailed clerks (male). It has broadened its community outreach, keying in with C-SPAN book events, hosting author appearances and panel discussions, where you might catch an occasional *Nation* and Nation Books author among the provocative guests.

828 Broadway, New York, NY 10003, (212) 473-1452, www.strandbooks.com

Three Lives & Company. The secret password (a friend confided) is: "Ask for Carol." Carol's the lady whose in-your-face e-mail address "screwtheright" contrasts with her subtle taste in left-wing literature. She's a mine of suggestions on authors from all over the world with either covert or overt left sensibilities. A visit to Three Lives can turn into an encounter with authors, critics or opinionated readers. "It's the last true literary hangout left in the Village," says our scout.

154 W. 10th Street, New York, NY 10014, (212) 741-2069, www.threelives.com

Pennsylvania

The Big Idea. Pittsburgh's only lefty store runs itself like a nonprofit without legal nonprofit status. It gets by on regular fund-raisers and an unpaid staff of about twenty young volunteers. The shop offers a range of nonfiction titles not on display elsewhere in Pittsburgh: small press titles of feminist, gay and lesbian, prounion, or antiwar slant; books about alternatives to capitalism, labor issues or environmental debates, periodicals and zines. The Big Idea works with Book 'Em to keep prisoners supplied with reading, and it's also tied in with the Thomas Merton Center.

504 Millvale Avenue, Pittsburgh, PA 15224, (412) 687-4323, www.thebigideapgh.org

Wooden Shoe Books. Opened in Philly in 1976 and going strong, Shoe is owned by the Philadelphia Solidarity collective. The name echoes the French workers' wooden shoe (*sabot*), from which "sabotage" is derived. It sells books, music, pamphlets, zines, T-shirts, buttons and so on. According to *Philadelphia City Paper* there are some forty-five active members in the collective, which received federal nonprofit status. The spirit of the place is suggested by the portraits displayed on the walls: Ward Churchill (radical professor); Kuwasi Balagoon (slain Black Panther); Dolores Ibárruri (Spanish Communist—"They shall not pass!"); Sylvia Rae Rivera (early transgender activist); Ben Fletcher (black IWW leader) and Voltairine de Cleyre (nineteenth-century feminist-anarchist).

508 S. 5th Street, Philadelphia, PA 19147, (215) 413-0999, www.woodenshoebooks.com

Maryland

Red Emma's Bookstore Coffeehouse. Though situated in family-friendly Baltimore, this place is not for your aunt Emma. It's owned and operated by the workers and they're out to "subvert the logic of capitalism" and bring on the revolution. Says Baltimore *IndyMedia*, "Red Emma's offers well-stocked book sections on Surrealism, Philosophy, Situationalism, and Marxism alongside Labor History, American Politics, Gender, Fiction, Globalization, and several other topics." *Baltimore CityPaper* called Red Emma's the town's "best nonbar hangout," and they seem to have found the right mix of socializing and socialism.

800 St. Paul Street, Baltimore, MD 21202, (410) 230-0450, www.redemmas.org

District of Columbia

Busboys and Poets. In the nation's capital, an alternative left culture quickly crystallized around the multicultural facilities of artist and peace activist Andy Shallal's Busboys and Poets. Primarily a restaurant, performance space and coffeehouse in the Langston Hughes condominium, it also stocks a respectable selection of poetry and literature. (See also page 329).

2021 14th Street NW, Washington, DC 20009, (202) 387-7638, www.busboysandpoets.com

Politics and Prose. There's a saying among D.C. realtors that "walking distance to Politics and Prose can sell a house in Washington." A neighborhood regular (and *Nation* reader) fondly recalled how it grew from a "hole in the wall" twenty years ago to a book emporium patronized by policy wonks, inside-the-Beltway types, movers and shakers, a straggling of literati and, well, neighborhood regulars. "Every night and some afternoons," reported our source, "there are top speakers and authors who feel honored to be there. The originators of this enterprise, Carla Cohen and Barbara Meade, have created a real community. A wonderful, vibrant, alive place." And of course there's a coffee shop.

5015 Connecticut Avenue NW, Washington, DC 20008, (202) 364-1919, www.politics-prose.com

Virginia

Chop Suey Books. "The funkiest bookstore in the Fan," says *WorkMagazine*, referring to the hip neighborhood in Richmond harboring Virginia Commonwealth University. Ward Tefft, a VCU graduate, opened Chop Suey in 2002 in a converted fraternity house. He's made the place into a multimedia center with books for sure but also regular events like the twenty-four-hour bookman parties and the bring-your-own-chair nights when locally produced movies and feature films are projected on the backyard wall. All that and the flea market that irregularly sprouts nearby, where people purvey crafts and semiprecious objects and junk of local provenance.

1317 W. Cary Street, Richmond, VA 23220, (804) 497-4705, www.chopsueybooks.com

North Carolina

Internationalist Books & Community Center. Being a radical in Chapel Hill isn't easy. It got Bob Sheldon, the founder of this store, shot. Sheldon was a peace activist and a ex–Revolutionary Communist Party zealot who had turned from Red to a gentler shade of Green. He opposed the first Gulf War heart and soul and let everyone know it. His friends and associates theorize that someone angry at his antiwar views shot Sheldon inside his store in 1991. The killer was never caught, although the incident received much attention in the alternative media. The Internationalist, now run as a worker-owned collective, continues to play an important political role in the Chapel Hill/Triangle community. The chairman of Internationalist's board, Ethan Clauset, told the *Daily Tar Heel*, "We are a focal point for organizing protests. We house groups outside of the mainstream. This is more than a place to buy information. It's a place to get involved."

405 W. Franklin Street, Chapel Hill, NC 27516, (919) 942-1740, www.internationalistbooks.org

Regulator Bookshop. The Regulator Bookshop prides itself on adhering to a "strong American tradition of truth-seeking and independent thinking." That's why it was the first place south of the Mason-Dixon line to carry cutting-edge magazines like *Spy, New York Rocker, Raw, Wet* and *Wired.* Opened in 1976 by co-owners Tom Campbell and John Valentine, who "grew up in the shadow of the counterculture of Duke University," Regulator has become a key player in this college town's cultural life.

720 9th Street, Durham, NC 27705, (919) 286-2700, www.regbook.com

Georgia

A Cappella Books. Like Charis, A Cappella's located in Little Five Points. "The smartest bookstore in town," declares *Creative Loafing,* an Atlanta alternative weekly. In the neighborhood since 1989, A Cappella sells new and used books. There's an active monthly discussion group that mulls over timely books on current issues. Acoustic music happens on Thursday nights and author events are held in the store or at the nearby Carter Center.

484-C Moreland Avenue NE, Atlanta, GA 30307, (404) 681-5128, www.acappellabooks.com

Charis Books & More. More than thirty years in business, Charis in Atlanta still calls itself a feminist bookstore, and the largest one in the South to boot. In 2006 three new owners—Amanda Hill, Sara Look and Angela Gabriel—took over a faltering enterprise. Look is in the renovation business and gave the place a face-lift, including a lavender paint job and a new patio. They draw oxygen from the bohemian atmosphere of their Little Five Points neighborhood.

1189 Euclid Avenue, Atlanta, GA 30307, (404) 524-0304, www.charis.booksense.com

Alabama

Jim Reed Books. Jim Reed's place is an object lesson in what will happen to you if you let your library get out of hand. "A pack rat's dream . . . a junkyard of hardbound and paperbound treasures—a time capsule, crammed floor to ceiling with history, culture, and a fetching collection of twentieth-century pinup girls," marveled *Black & White,* a Birmingham alternative weekly. Reed insists he knows exactly where everything is in his hoard, which now stands (teeters?) at 40,000 "books, magazines, newspapers and movie posters" and assorted memorabilia. In 2007 Reed moved the place to a more upscale neighborhood. Ensconced in his new store, he shook his head at the thought of being "in the middle of the lawyers and bankers."

2021 3rd Avenue N., Birmingham, AL 35203, (205) 326-4460, www.jimreedbooks.com

Florida

Books & Books. Our correspondent calls this shop "one of the last great independent bookstores, run by local hero Mitchell Kaplan, who invented the Miami Book Fair, one of the country's largest and most varied. Known as a supporter of writers and writing programs, Kaplan is a true friend to authors, no matter how large or small in size of sales or literary stature. Complete with a wine bar, terrace, and lunch or dinner dining."

265 Aragon Avenue, Coral Gables, FL 33134, (305) 442-4408, www.booksandbooks.com

Key West Island Bookstore. A literary haven based in the jumping-off place, a far-out town that was and is peopled by many writers. Hemingway, Tennessee Williams, Elizabeth Bishop, John Hersey and James Merrill had homes here. Alison Lurie, Joy Williams, Richard Wilbur and Annie Dillard are more recent residents. Key West Bookstore promotes local writers and holds signings; it sells current, used and rare books.

513 Fleming Street, Key West, FL 33040, (305) 294-2904

Wild Iris Books. If you're in Gainesville and thinking of shopping here, you'd better first read the store's profile of its ideal customer: "a free and independent thinker," "a feminist or believer in a non-sexist society," "lesbian, gay, bisexual, transgendered, or queer," "part of a cultural minority group," "pro-peace and have liberal political or religious views." If you made the cut, you may enter Wild Iris, which stocks books and authors fitting those descriptions.

802 W. University Avenue, Gainesville, FL 32601, (352) 375-7477, www.wildirisbooks.com

Mississippi

Square Books. If Oxford, William Faulkner's home-town, has indeed shed the redneck image acquired during the Ole Miss riots of 1962 over the admission of the school's first black student, James Meredith, *Mother Jones* wrote, "that would be in some measure due to that store, Square Books, and its owner, Richard Howorth." Opened in 1979 by Richard and Lisa Howorth using $10,000 in savings and another $10,000 in loans, Square Books was soon hosting events with Willie Morris (who lived and worked in Oxford) and his friend William Styron; organizing the Oxford Conference for the Book with William Ferris, who ran the Center for the Study of Southern Culture at Ole Miss; and anchoring the revitalization of Courthouse Square. Square Books has been such a success that it's hatched two offspring, Square Books, Jr. (children's books) and Off Square Books (used and remaindered books), from

LOCAL WRITERS' FAVORITES

There are two great bookstores in Mississippi, as good as or better than the best literary bookstores anywhere. One is John Evans's Lemuria Books in Banner Hall on I-55 North in Jackson, with a great many old and new first editions as well as a huge selection of general interest, literary and political titles and an extensive children's books collection. Lemuria also sponsors an elaborate readings series, bringing interesting writers to town on a regular basis.

The second is Square Books, on the Square in Oxford, with an equally extensive range of books and its own fancy readings series. Both stores are a great comfort to anyone who loves books, and both are justly well known.

—STEVEN BARTHELME

which in 1997 Richard Howorth and some local musicians began broadcasting a weekly music and literature radio show called *Thacker Mountain Radio*. The show, carried on PBS, offers live bluegrass, folk, jazz and blues music by well-known and local musicians, and readings by prominent writers. Howorth has served two terms as Oxford's mayor.

160 Courthouse Square, Oxford, MS 38655, (662) 236-2262, www.squarebooks.com

Left Bank Books. Not to be confused with the anarchist collective shop of the same name in Seattle—though we seriously doubt you would confuse Seattle's anarchist collective's LBB with more traditional St. Louis's LBB or vice versa. Anyhow, this is a sturdy, independent bookseller that has been located in the city's Central West End since 1969. The three veteran owners and staff are dedicated to reading (one described her job as "book pimp"). The store sponsors reading groups (including a Lesbian and Gay Men's groups), book clubs and other kinds of community outreach. It's opening a new store downtown under an agreement with a local developer. Meanwhile, it fights the big guys and sells to its local base, and mail orders are accepted.

399 N Euclid Avenue, St. Louis, MO 63108, (314) 367-6731, www.leftbank.com

Illinois

57th Street Books. Our usually reliable operative calls 57th Street Books "Chicago's all-around biggest and best left-of-center bookstore." It's a spin-off of the larger Seminary Co-op Bookstore, which is located in the basement of the University of Chicago Theological Seminary. The sister store, started more than twenty years ago, carries a bigger mix of nonacademic, general interest titles.

1301 E. 57th Street, Chicago, IL 60637, (773) 684-1300, http://semcoop.booksense.com

New World Resource Center. Chicago's longest-running left-labor-independent bookstore (founded in 1972), New World is operated by an all-volunteer collective and offers a wide-ranging selection of left-wing nonfiction, much of it low-print-run books published by academic or small independent presses. As they describe it, their titles run from "'A' to Zinn: Anarchism, Anti-Racism . . . Feminism, Geo-Politics, Labor Struggles, Leftist History, Marxism, Philosophy, Socialism, Sociology and much, much more." They sell both new and used books, T-shirts, buttons, bumper stickers, magazines and newspapers; they also offer meeting space for a "nominal donation."

1300 N. Western Avenue, Chicago, IL 60622, (773) 227-4011, www.newworldresourcecenter.com

Quimby's Bookstore. Quimby's shares its name and mascot with a comic book character named Quimby the Mouse, created by Chris Ware, who is a friend of the store, but both parties state that any resemblance between the store name and mascot and Ware's character is "a weird coincidence." A sign hanging in the store explains all: "Specialists in the importation, distribution, and sale of unusual publications, aberrant periodicals, saucy comic booklets and assorted fancies as well as a comprehensive miscellany of the latest independent zines that all the kids have been talking about." *Frommer's Irreverent Guide to Chicago* calls it "the ultimate alternative newsstand" with obscure periodicals, cutting-edge comics and zines. Categories for books run from "fiction" and "biography" to "conspiracy," "erotica & fetish," "lowbrow art," "mayhem," "outer limits," and (ta-da!) "politics & revolution."

1854 W. North Avenue, Chicago, IL 60622, (773) 342-0910, www.quimbys.com

Women & Children First. This lesbian-feminist shop proclaims it's strategically planted in a North Side neighborhood "known for its diversity, lesbian-friendliness, women-owned businesses and community spirit." Opened in 1979, Women & Children First is one of the largest and best-known feminist bookstores in the country, specializing in titles "by and about women, children's books for all ages, and the best of lesbian and gay fiction and non-fiction," as well as music, movies, magazines and "pride products." (They have books by men, too.) The Women's Voices Fund underwrites feminist programming at the store.

5233 N. Clark Street, Chicago, IL 60640, (773) 769-9299, www.womenandchildrenfirst.com

Wisconsin

Broad Vocabulary. The founding "broads," three women who matriculated at the University of Wisconsin-Milwaukee, started this independent bookstore in Milwaukee in 2005. They offer feminist literature, "subculture studies, progressive politics, cultural movements, and non-sexist young adult/children's books . . . magazines, T-shirts, bumper stickers, magnets, buttons, soy candles, homemade books and journals, pepper-spray, cards, pride-gear, local art, stationery, zines and more." They sponsor a distinguished speakers series that presents speakers on topics like Islamic feminism and gender issues in Islam.

2241 S. Kinnickinnic Avenue, Milwaukee, WI 53207, (414) 744-8384, www.broadvocabulary.com

Rainbow Bookstore Cooperative. Like Rick's Café Americain in *Casablanca*, all of progressive Madison will show up here later or sooner. The store calls itself the "politically conscious alternative." *Nation* Washington correspondent John Nichols, a Wisconsin native, gave this quote: "George W. Bush, Dick Cheney and Donald Rumsfeld do not want you to shop at Rainbow Bookstore Cooperative. Noam Chomsky, Howard Zinn and Alice Walker do want you to shop at Rainbow Bookstore Cooperative. Pick a side." Run as a cooperative, Rainbow is staffed by thirty volunteers and four paid employees. Even the topics under which the books are cataloged are subliminally ideological: "activism," "empire," "media studies." Go!

426 W. Gilman Street, Madison, WI 53703, (608) 257-6050, www.rainbowbookstore.org

Minnesota

Amazon Bookstore Cooperative. Amazon Bookstore Cooperative claims to be the oldest independent feminist bookstore in North America (it opened in 1970). These Minneapolis women fought amazon.com to a draw over the exclusive right to use the name. The suit ended in an out-of-court settlement under which Amazon (the bookstore) agreed to use only its full legal name (Amazon Bookstore Cooperative), while Amazon (the dot-com) pledged to "give a license back to Amazon Bookstore Cooperative for use of the Amazon name."

4755 Chicago Avenue S., Minneapolis, MN 55407, (612) 821-9630, www.amazonfembks.com

Arkansas

That Bookstore in Blytheville. Owner Mary Gay Shipley has a nose for literary novels with legs. Malcolm Gladwell, of best-selling *Blink* fame, wrote a 1999 article about Shipley in the *New Yorker* called "The Science of the Sleeper." Among Shipley's dark horse picks that took the Roses: Rebecca Wells's *Divine Secrets of the Ya-Ya Sisterhood* and David Guterson's *Snow Falling on Cedars*. No science involved; she talks up books she likes to people who come into her store, and they buy them because they trust her judgment and the word keeps spreading. The shop, founded in 1976, pretty well defines what a small-town (pop. 18,272) independent bookstore should do: serve the community as a cultural oasis (this has become a must stop on the national book tour route) and serve as a lynchpin of local retailing. Shipley was lead plaintiff in a class action suit challenging amendments to the Arkansas State Constitution that required retailers and libraries to physically segregate material deemed inappropriate for minors. Shipley observed: "Under this law, I would be required to create an 'adults only' section in my store to display some of the greatest novels and most important works of serious fiction and nonfiction such as *Of Mice and Men* and *The Joy of Sex*."

316 W. Main Street, Blytheville, AR 72315, (870) 763-3333, www.tbib.com

Colorado

Left Hand Books. This "all volunteer, not-for-profit, progressive bookstore" has its political-cultural antenna in a constant state of arousal. Kathy Partridge, who was one of the early collective members, explained: "At first we sold a lot of safe energy and solar energy books. . . . Then when the Central America solidarity movement was getting going, we phased into more books about Central America and sold lots of fair exchange crafts and a lot of Nicaraguan coffee. . . . Now we have more books on Green issues and what a better society would look like." One thing doesn't change: Howard Zinn's *People's History* is the store's "bestselling book of all time."

1200 Pearl Street, #10, Boulder, CO 80302, (303) 443-8252, www.lefthandbooks.org

Tattered Cover. This big, well-known independent bookstore in Denver has sprouted two offshoots since its debut in 1971. The main venue on Colfax Avenue carries more than 150,000 titles, provides armchairs and reading lamps for browsers and donates 1 percent of all purchases to progressive charities. Joyce Meskis, who has run Tattered Cover since 1974, opened media eyeballs when she successfully fought a court order demanding a list of books purchased by a customer who'd been accused of running a meth lab. The police search warrant was validated by a lower court decision, but Meskis and Tattered Cover appealed with help from the American Booksellers Foundation for Free Expression. In April 2002, the Colorado Supreme Court overturned the lower court's decision, finding: "Had it not been for the Tattered Cover's steadfast stance, the zealousness of the City would have led to the disclosure of information that we ultimately conclude is constitutionally protected." In stopping the cops, Meskin inadvertently provided an early warning of the next assault on bookstore customers' privacy: the U.S. Patriot Act.

2526 E. Colfax Avenue, Denver, CO 80206, (303) 322-7727, www.tatteredcover.com

Arizona

Changing Hands Bookstore. In Tempe stands a large and well-known independent bookstore that's been irrigating Southwestern culture since 1974. It stocks 100,000 new and used books and shares space with Wildflower Bread Company, a neighborhood bakery-café chain. Cindy Dach, marketing manager for Changing Hands, is a cofounder of a small and locally owned business coalition called Arizona Chain Reaction, set up to combat the chain stores' negative impact on local economies. Dach is also on the board of the National Council on Bookstore Tourism, a group devoted to a "type of 'cultural tourism' that promotes independent bookstores as a group travel destination."

6428 S. McClintock Drive, Tempe, AZ 85283, (480) 730-0205, www.changinghands.com

Alaska

Fireside Books. This independent bookstore sells new and used books under the slogan "Good books, bad coffee." In keeping with the store's decidedly local, anticorporate ethos, they sell a lot of anti–Wal-Mart paraphernalia. As for the coffee, they stock Real Alaskan Ugly Coffee, which is roasted right here in Palmer. On December 3, 2006, Fireside Books held a reading of *Howl* to celebrate the fiftieth anniversary of its publication. Fireside co-owner David Cheezem said of the event: "You don't measure the success by the amount of people, but the passion they bring to it." The reading won Fireside an award for the best *Howl* celebration in a contest sponsored by City Lights Books (see page 59).

720 S. Alaska Street, Palmer, AK 99645, (907) 745-2665, www.goodbooksbadcoffee.com

Old Harbor Books. "This is not a neutral sort of place," says Don Muller, owner and manager of this bookstore on the coast of Alaska's Inside Passage. Miller, trained as a chemist, is very unneutral on environmental issues. He moved to Sitka to work for a pulp mill but left to fight the mill's despoliation of the local environment. In 2004, protesters gathered outside the store to demonstrate against a state-sponsored plan to kill wolves, calling the event a howl-in. Sitka also hosts an annual summer symposium, having writers fly or sail in to talk about books, community issues, writing and other matters.

201 Lincoln Street, Sitka, AK 99835, (907) 747-8808

Washington

Left Bank Books. "As an anarchist collective, Left Bank has no bosses or managers." And the customer is always left. This Seattle collective started in 1973, operating out of a kiosk in Pike Place Market, where it sold mostly political paraphernalia. In its present digs it carries all the usual range of books and stuff. It also sponsors and supplies matter for the Books to Prisoners group that sends free books to inmates of U.S. prisons. Given its political base, it's no surprise Left Bank was deeply involved in the WTO protests of November 1999.

92 Pike Street, Seattle, WA 98101, (206) 622-0195, www.leftbankbooks.com

Oregon

Powell's City of Books. The flagship store of the Powell's empire, City of Books is a 68,000-square-foot book lover's paradise that claims to be "the largest used and new bookstore in the world." Powell's makes it onto any list of left-minded stores because it is also the largest *unionized* bookstore. Local 5 of the International Longshore and Warehouse Union represents the workforce at Powell's six Portland-area stores, as well as its warehouses and even its website. If you can't get to Portland to have the Powell's experience firsthand, order from the nation's largest unionized online bookstore!

1005 W. Burnside Street, Portland, OR 97209, (503) 228-4651, www.powells.com

Reading Frenzy. Powell's is not the only game in Portland. Reading Frenzy, a big, well-known zine store, sits just down the street and deals in "independent and alternative media. . . . queer notions, and quality smut." Chloe Eudaly, the longtime owner, helped found the Independent Publishing Resource Center that makes available work space and workshops to those who would add even more books to the great river of literacy.

921 SW Oak Street, Portland, OR 97205, (503) 274-1449, www.readingfrenzy.com

California

City Lights. This historic store became the intellectual epicenter of the Beat movement and the San Francisco counterculture of the 1950s and 1960s. Poet Lawrence Ferlinghetti opened it in 1953. Three years later his small press published Allen Ginsberg's *Howl and Other Poems.* In 1957, Ferlinghetti and store manager Shigeyoshi Murao were arrested on obscenity charges for publishing and selling *Howl* and *Miscellaneous Man* magazine. Ferlinghetti, who faced six months in jail and a $500 fine, fought back. In his store window he placed stacks of great works of literature that had been suppressed in other days, by other bluenoses. Above the books he hung a defiant banner reading: "Banned books

---

MY FAVORITE AMERICAN PLACE

When I visit big American cities, I like Portland, Oregon, the best. It has the greatest bookstore in the United States, Powell's, and a lively, somewhat raw feeling in the streets.

My favorite place is where I live [Dunhill, New Hampshire]. This is an old farmhouse, nothing fancy whatsoever, with floors that undulate. My great-grandparents lived here, and it stopped being a farm in 1950, when my grandfather had a heart attack. My grandmother lived on until she was ninety-seven and Jane and I moved in the year she died in 1975.

The original Cape was built in 1803. When my great-grandfather moved in, in 1865, he had a big family and extended the house back into Ragged Mountain and built a barn on the upward slope. Early on we added bookshelves and a usable bathroom, then, after ten years of woodstoves, central heating. I love the natural world around me, and spend a lot of time enjoying it. I am a solitary and I like the sparse population. I can see one house from where I live— and my assistant lives there. My telephone seldom rings and there are few callers. I work here all alone— my wife, Jane Kenyon, died in 1995—and read and watch the Boston Red Sox in season.

Doing poetry readings, I do travel all over the country and during this coming year will visit literary festivals in Mexico, Spain and Ireland. Maybe these travels make possible my pleasure in solitude.

—DONALD HALL was Poet Laureate of the United States in 2006. His most recent book is *White Apples and the Taste of Stone: Selected Poems, 1946–2006. The One Day* won a National Book Critics Circle Award and *The Happy Man* won a Lenore Marshall Poetry Prize.

for sale." At the trial a star-studded cast of literary critics and scholars ridiculed the state's claims of obscenity (that is, filthy language one heard every day) and hailed *Howl* as a conceivably great and prophetic work of art. The result was a landmark holding for artistic freedom, proclaiming that the only permissible censorship of a work of literature was by the readers who exercise their freedom not to buy or read what they find offensive.

261 Columbus Avenue, San Francisco, CA 94133, (415) 362-8193, www.citylights.com

Modern Times Bookstore. Collectively owned Modern Times assumes a clear political mission: "We came to realize that maintaining a strong and viable independent bookstore was in many ways the most politically effective thing we could do." The store touts its wide-ranging selection of books on globalization, politics, media and sexuality and gender. Since 9/11 it has sponsored an ongoing reading group on the war on terrorism. Its members read histories of the Middle East, Afghanistan and neighboring states and study histories of U.S. foreign policy in these regions. The store holds an annual zine and book arts fair that features the products of local independent and self-publishers. It also features a different small, indie press every month, with displays, window space, parties, sales and so forth.

888 Valencia Street, San Francisco, CA 94110, (415) 282-9246, www.mtbs.com

Walden Pond Books. Walden Pond is left coast Oakland's oldest independent bookstore. Although it stocks all categories and genres, it's a "nice store for the radical Bay Area reader," said the *Oakland Tribune*. It's solidly centered in the local left community, selling tickets to events like a talk by the veteran journalist Robert Fisk or the World Can't Wait anti-Bush fund-raiser in Oakland. They buy and trade old books daily.

3316 Grand Avenue, Oakland, CA 94610, (510) 832-4438, www.waldenpondbooks.com

Book Club

Progressive Book Club. Launched in 2008, the Progressive Book Club aims, in the words of founder Elizabeth Wagley, "to create a powerful tool to showcase the ideas of the left," taking a leaf from conservative clubs already in operation. Other such operations have tried in the past, with varying success, to reach the left demographic. PBC hopes to knit together a community of progressive authors, publishers and readers and offers social networking and discussion groups. As the spate of exposé books on the war in Iraq demonstrated, well-reported books on contemporary issues can have an impact on public opinion, especially when the media are slow to penetrate the fog of war or have not organized the scattered facts into a coherent narrative. To entice new members, PBC offers three books for $3 (plus shipping and handling). Members pledge to purchase four books over two years of monthly offerings, chosen by a board that includes Erica Jong, Barbara Kingsolver, Katrina vanden Heuvel and Todd Gitlin. at prices of up to 30 percent off the cover price. PBC also contributes a percentage of the price to a political group of the member's choice.

www.progressivebookclub.com

A LEFT MYSTERY TOUR BY PHILIP GREEN

On the whole, the detective story is a conservative literary genre: a law is broken, the truth is uncovered and the legal and moral order is restored. Contrarily, tales of conspiracy in high places, police power as a police state, corporate corruption on a national or global scale and systemic injustices of the kind that progressive readers are alert to fit more easily into the thriller genre. There are exceptions, though, most often in subgenres featuring a private eye, a defense lawyer or (less frequently) a minority or female character. The brief list that follows contains some favorite explicitly or implicitly left whodunits listed in chronological order from the 1930s to today. It is intended to spark further investigations by readers.

Red Harvest, by Dashiell Hammett (1929)

Hammett, the founder of the hard-boiled school of fiction, was one of the most influential crime writers in American history. André Gide called *Red Harvest* "the greatest American novel." *Red Harvest* was certainly a seminal novel of the private eye genre. It's a story about union busting (with which Hammett the ex-Pinkerton was all too familiar) in Montana's copper country. It's the most politically conscious of American detective novels, at least until Sara Paretsky came along. But even V. I. Warshawski isn't as tough as the Continental Op.

The Big Sleep, by Raymond Chandler (1939)

Chandler was not overtly political and neither was his private eye Philip Marlowe. But Marlowe's combination of worldly cynicism, boyish romanticism and razor-sharp irony in the tradition of classical American humor makes him an entertaining and incisive observer of the corruption of the rich and powerful in their Southern California habitats—not to mention the nastiness of the LAPD. The pleasure of reading Chandler never dies. *The Big Sleep* was his first full-length mystery; read them all after that, though I'd especially recommend *Farewell, My Lovely* (1940), *The Lady in the Lake* (1943) and *The Long Goodbye* (1953).

The Doorbell Rang, by Rex Stout (1965)

Nero Wolfe versus the FBI! A young woman claims she is being harassed by the Feds, and Wolfe and Archie Goodwin decide to take on her case. The plot turns on revelations about FBI boss J. Edgar Hoover in a *Nation* article by Fred Cook. No doubt about it—the best civil liberties mystery of all time.

Cotton Comes to Harlem, by Chester Himes (1965)

An ex-convict and prolific novelist who was an expatriate in Paris during the 1950s and 1960s, Himes wrote a series of eight wild, delirious detective stories featuring two black cops, Coffin Ed Johnson and Gravedigger Jones. His books are noteworthy less as racial protest—though that's always at least implicit—than as sheer anarchy: the streets of New York City and especially Harlem envisioned as nightmare, but a nightmare embraced as much as repudiated. There's nothing quite like them.

Death in a Tenured Position, by Amanda Cross (pseudonym of Carolyn G. Heilbrun) (1981)

Heilbrun, who taught English at Columbia for more than three decades, wrote fourteen pseudonymous academic mysteries with Kate Fansler, an English professor, as private eye. Throughout the series Fansler battles male chauvinism, academic pettiness and conservative political ideology generally. This one takes place at Harvard, where the first tenured woman ever in the English Department is murdered. "Quiet rage" best describes its literary mood.

Briarpatch, by Ross Thomas (1984)

In movies (*Bad Day at Black Rock, High Noon*) and especially on television, left-wing politics during the 1960s and 1970s was often implied rather than stated in what might be called the "corrupt town" genre. A man (usually) lives in or comes into a small town where the inhabitants, including business leaders and law officers, are covering up some terrible secret. Usually this involves the dispossession of property—the "loot" that Marx called "the secret of primitive accumulation." *Briarpatch,* a satisfying mystery as well as small town thriller, is a rare literary entry in this genre.

Blood Shot and *Burn Marks,* by Sara Paretsky (1988, 1990)

Paretsky has said that Philip Marlowe was the chief inspiration for her female private eye, V. I. Warshawski, but her take on the sociology and politics of Chicago is much more complex and politicized than Chandler's on Los Angeles; and Marlowe wouldn't be caught dead with even a hint of V. I.'s feminism. But they'd get along, and probably become lovers. In *Burn Marks,* as in all Paretsky's books, a seemingly minor case of arson leads Warshawski to uncover corporate scandal and municipal corruption and puts her life in danger. *Blood Shot,* in which V. I. sets out in search of a friend's missing father, explores the same milieu. Between them, the two novels take on the seamy side of American society in the Reagan era.

Devil in a Blue Dress, by Walter Mosley (1990)

Nation readers will be familiar with contributor Mosley's trenchant analyses of class and race in the contemporary United States. His ten Easy Rawlins novels, featuring an African-American private investigator, are noirish thrillers set in the period beginning in the postwar years and continuing through the 1960s. Much more explicitly than Chandler or even Paretsky, Mosley exposes the brutality of racism and police power. *Devil* is the first of the ten, and the most like a true detective story.

The Rainmaker, by John Grisham (1995)

This is my favorite courtroom novel ever though, like *Briarpatch,* it really borders on the thriller genre and is about civil rather than criminal law. A neophyte lawyer takes on a giant insurance company that has been defrauding poor and black policyholders by systematically denying their claims. What's so compelling about it is how various social outcasts come together to aid him in his case and bring out the truth. Rarely if ever has underdog solidarity been so central to an American mystery story.

The Raggedy Man, by Lillian O'Donnell (1995)

An excellent mystery, in which P.I. Gwenn Ramadge befriends a policewoman who's been framed by her colleagues, and uncovers a tangle of misogyny and corruption in the NYPD. O'Donnell also writes feminist police procedurals about policewoman Norah Mulcahaney, in many of which the woman-in-peril genre is reconstituted as the woman cop in peril from male chauvinism (or worse). *Lockout* (1994) is perhaps the best of these.

Apparition Alley, by Katherine V. Forrest (1997)

Lesbian detective Kate Delafield of the LAPD investigates a shooting (her own) for which a homophobic cop is being framed, while another cop, who was on the verge of outing gay and lesbian LAPD officers, is murdered. Reader alert: Forrest interrupts the action on several occasions for bouts of hard-core sexual coupling, à la contemporary romance fiction (think Nora Roberts); those scenes are narratively irrelevant (and can easily be skipped). Still, this is a topflight mystery—especially for those who dislike the LAPD. And who doesn't? Though a cop, Delafield has the personality, world-weary toughness and romanticism of a classic private eye.

No Defense, by Kate Wilhelm (2000)

Kate Wilhelm is my nominee as the all-time number one author of courtroom dramas. In this, one of her (so far) nine cases, "death qualified" Oregon attorney Barbara Holloway fights the political establishment, the legal powers that be and a dangerous crime lord to save the life of an innocent defendant: a typical day's work for her. Her cross-examinations are brilliant, without Perry Mason's histrionics, and her out-of-court maneuverings tough and adventurous. In an earlier incarnation, Wilhelm was a topflight writer of science fiction and intriguing novels of what might (or might not) be the occult.

Theater, Puppets, Dance, Circuses, Satire

AND OTHER FORMS OF POLITICAL ACTING OUT

Appalshop. Appalshop is a nonprofit multimedia, multidisciplinary arts and education complex in Appalachia where people get together to produce original films, video, theater, music and spoken-word recordings, radio, photographs and books. The emphasis is on preserving the local cultural heritage, particularly disseminating and revitalizing the traditions and creativity of the Appalachian people. Various units turn out films (*Stranger with a Camera*), radio (*Real People Radio* on WMMT) and theater (see Roadside Theater, page 71).

91 Madison Avenue, Whitesburg, KY 41858, (606) 633-0108, www.appalshop.org

Bill T. Jones/Arnie Zane Dance Company. Jones, a highly regarded dancer-choreographer, has not dropped the name of his deceased partner in life and in dance during the 1970s and 1980s. Race, identity and multiculturalism are still leitmotifs in Jones's dance, but sexual tolerance also plays an important role (he has been HIV positive for more than twenty years). Jones, who still performs, resists attempts to politicize his work. "Political is an exhausted term," he says. Instead, he describes his dances as "concerned with moral choice" and "right action." Yet his 2005 production *Blind Date* is considered a reflection on the presidential election of the previous year, the war, urban poor and conservative sexual morality. About a recent Jones's production *Chapel/Chapter*, staged at the Gatehouse, an old water-pumping station in Harlem, the *New York Times*'s John Rockwell said, "Rarely has he been better able to sublimate his wide-ranging political, social and moral concerns into art. Rarely has the strength of that art made his vision express itself more purely."

27 W. 120th Street, #1, New York, NY 10027, (212) 426-6655, www.billtjones.org

Bread & Puppet Theater. Hardly an antiwar parade goes by without the towering, colorful, larger-than-life effigies made by Bread & Puppet. One of the best-known American puppet theaters, it was born in the turbulent early sixties on the Lower East Side, the offspring of Silesian Peter Schumann and his American wife, Elka. A historian writes that "the concerns of the first productions were rents, rats, police, and other problems of the neighborhood." During the Vietnam era, Bread & Puppet staged elaborate antiwar street performances. In the 1970s, Schumann fled the Lower East Side to settle on a peaceful farm in Glover, Vermont, a countercultural magnet. There, Schumann baked his coarse corn and rye bread, made puppets and turned the old hay barn into the Museum of the Art of Impermanence, as Schumann calls his craft, and presented outdoor productions large and small, such as the two-day Domestic Resurrection Circus. A *New York Times* critic recalled one he'd attended in 1982 as "the single most beautiful sight I've ever seen in the theater." They drew Woodstock-size crowds of 30,000 camping out in the hills around the farm. But in 1998, Woodstock shaded into Altamont; an excess of drinking and argument resulted in a fatal shooting, and the pageants stopped. Today, Bread & Puppet produces small circuses at the farm for audi-

ences of 200 or so. It also sends out circuses with a message on national and global tours. Schumann created the Cheap Art philosophy in 1982 as a protest against corporate big-bucks co-optation of fine art. Cheap Art makes art "political whether you like it or not. . . ." The idea, Bread & Puppet avers, is to share with all the experience of art and the joy of creating. The company gives lessons in street theater to aspiring puppet-provocateurs. "If you are interested, please feel free to contact us and we will try to come to your group with a subversive lesson or two," they promise.

753 Heights Road, Glover, VT 05839, (802) 525-3031, www.breadandpuppet.org

The Brecht Forum. Since 1975, the Brecht Forum has been among the premier New York City venues for left cultural and educational programs. It offers a regular schedule of classes, lectures, seminars, workshops, art exhibitions and dramatic performances, often in conjunction with a variety of social movements and organizations. Brecht Forum projects include: the New York Marxist School, which "uses Marx's uniquely valuable contributions, along with others within and outside of the Marxist tradition, to study conditions today and possibilities for transcending capitalism and building an emancipatory society"; the Institute for Popular Education, which builds on "popular education traditions developed in Latin America"; and Arts at the Brecht, which offers "visual arts exhibits pertaining to topics of political and cultural interest." In 2000, the *Village Voice* named the Brecht Forum the "Best place to start thinking about the revolution."

451 West Street, New York, NY 10014, (212) 242-4201, www.brechtforum.org

Broom Street Theater. Madison, Wisconsin, is Progressive City so you might expect extreme liberalism on its stages. The Broom Street Theater certainly fulfills that expectation. Madison's reigning experimental theater since 1969, producing seven original works a year, Broom Street flaunts the credo "no censorship—no restrictions—no limits." Emerging from the 1960s counterculture, BST has traditionally been dedicated to what Rod Clark, board member and longtime associate of the theater, describes as "cheap, curtainless theater." Its artistic director, Joel Gersmann, died in 2005. A *Nation* reader assures us: "The theater has continued on, honoring Joel's vision and continuing to operate just barely in the black, thanks to a loyal audience who must endure horrible bleachers, sometimes for several hours with intermission, but who are rewarded with some of the best new theater in the country."

1119 Williamson Street, Madison, WI 53703, (608) 244-8338, www.broomstreet.org

Circus Amok. From the verdant fields of Van Cortlandt Park in the Bronx to the sloping hills of Prospect Park in Brooklyn, a free-range flock of clowns, acrobats, jugglers, tightrope walkers, puppeteers and pranksters known as Circus Amok goes its merry way, presenting instructive entertainment—not to mention entertaining instruction—that addresses "contemporary issues of social justice." Circus Amok was assembled in 1989 by founder and leading bearded lady Jennifer Miller, and has been putting on "funny, queer, caustic and sexy political one-ring spectacles" ever since. Current performers include Mme. Miller, Michelle Matlock, Ashley Brockington and acts like the Swiss Misses, Basil Twist and MC Carmelita Tropicana, plus the Circus Amok Band. Circus Amok is well versed in the higher arts—dance, experimental theater, life-size puppetry, transgender performance, improvisation, dramatic monologues and music of all kinds. Annual themes give some coherence to the troupe's productions (recent ones: "Home Land Security," "Citizen Ship"). There's a political twist in most everything they do, as well as a distinctive gay sensibility (message: tolerance of those who are "different"): Clowns break into a hula-hoop routine to decry tax loopholes. We watch a soaring acrobatic treatise against entitlement cuts called the "Disappearing Safety Net Act." Guerrilla gardeners vault over and overrun the developers.

www.circusamok.org

Dance Brigade. The Dance Brigade descended from the Wallflower Order, a pioneering politically engaged women's dance theater collective founded in the 1970s by Krissy Keefer. The Dance Brigade follows in its steps. Of the interplay of dance and politics, Keefer told the LGBT weekly *San Francisco Bay Times*: "Telling the truth is the most massive act of defiance you can make. Dancers don't usually speak, so maybe it's even harder for us to tell the truth. What all dancers struggle with is to find the truth in their own bodies, and then there's some of us who want to bring words to that." Many of her dances incorporate text. The brigade's response to 9/11 was a piece called *Women Against War: A Vision for Peace*. Following the 2004 elections, the brigade declared war on the Bush administration with *Spell, or 13 Invocations for Regime Change*. Dance Brigade regularly performs at antiwar rallies and has danced in places ranging from San Francisco's Civic Center to Lincoln Center to flatbed trucks in Nicaragua to federal building sidewalks at demonstrations. In 2006 Keefer ran for Congress on the Green Party ticket, receiving 8 percent of the vote against the organization-backed candidate, Nancy Pelosi.

Dance Mission Theater, 3316 24th Street, San Francisco, CA 94110, (415) 826-4441,
www.dancemission.com

Culture Clash. San Francisco–based Culture Clash is a three-man troupe, founded and directly descended from Luis Valdez's El Teatro Campesino. Since its emergence in the Mission District on Cinco de Mayo in 1984—led by Richard Montoya, Ric Salinas and Herbert Siguenza—Culture Clash has performed everything from sketch comedy to Aristophanes. It also creates theater by weaving together interviews with neighborhood people and dramatizing their stories. They have created full-length plays, notably *Chavez Ravine,* about the traumatic destruction of a Mexican neighborhood in Los Angeles to build Dodger Stadium. In a 2001 interview Richard Montoya recalled that "Reaganomics were right over our shoulder. It was 1984. The arts were getting blows left and right. And that's what fueled us. We went out and protested with our humor." They're strongly left in politics but not predictably so. Recalled Montoya: "One guy told me the other day that with Culture Clash you never know whether you're talking about Karl Marx or Groucho Marx." By 2007 Culture Clash was so deeply embedded in the California scene that UCLA offered a course on its complete works.

www.cultureclash.com

Corpus Delicti. In the big peace march in LA on February 15, 2003, appeared twenty-five ghostly figures, in white and red flowing robes, who were covered with white body makeup and contorting and walking silently. Some viewers took them to be spirits of the dead, others to be angels. They were Corpus Delicti, a dance and street theater troupe that was founded by two performance artists, Carla Melo and Joe Talkington. Their work is adapted from the Japanese dance form *butoh* (from *antkoku butoh*—dance of darkness) that emerged in postwar Japan with seeming psychological roots in mourning for the war dead, especially those incinerated in Nagasaki and Hiroshima. Talkington has said, "The Latin phrase *corpus delicti* literally means 'body of evidence.' Our performances symbolically embody the evidence of U.S. crimes through our ghostlike presence on the multicultural body of Los Angeles." Among its antiwar performances, Corpus Delicti organized a Butoh Surge to end the war. It also sponsored a silent march through the streets of Hollywood.

www.corpusbutoh.org

Democracy Burlesque. The slogan of this monthly cabaret and variety show is "Only the politics are naked." Fans of the Jon Stewart/Stephen Colbert school of put-on humor are sure to enjoy the antics of Chicago's Democracy Burlesque as they send up Bush conservatism and Chicago machine politics. Each Democracy Burlesque show features a particular progressive organization whose work the group supports, such as Code Pink, Amnesty International and Chicago Legal Advocacy for Incarcerated Mothers. Shows are staged on the second Tuesday of every month at the No Exit Café, an old Beat Generation hangout.

No Exit Café, 6970 N. Glenwood Avenue, Chicago, IL 60626, (773) 743-3355, www.democracyburlesque.com

HartBeat Ensemble. When three former members of the San Francisco Mime Troupe decided to set up an activist theater company in Hartford, Connecticut, in 2001, they did so because they believed the economic contradictions in a city that was both the second poorest and the capital of the richest-per-capita state in the nation made it ripe for political theater. Combining staged productions with brash street theater send-ups, and drawing inspiration from Augusto Baol's Theater of the Oppressed, HartBeat's often-comic performances have won a wide following. A locally staged production called *News to Me* took aim at the failures of Bush's No Child Left Behind Act; another, *Graves*, set *The Grapes of Wrath* in the twenty-first-century economy of corporate globalization; at Yuletide, *Ebeneeza, a Hartford Christmas Carol*. In 2005, the Service Employees International Union commissioned HartBeat to develop a play based on stories by unionized nurses. In early 2007, HartBeat put on a mock State of the Union address, called *Running Bush Out of Town*, in front of the West Hartford war memorial, which culminated in "Bush" being chased by the actors and audience into a neighboring parking lot. The ensemble runs a workshop program on creative organizing for labor unions that trains union members in street theater techniques.

555 Asylum Avenue, Studio 101, Hartford, CT 06105, (888) 548-9144, www.hartbeatensemble.org

The I-10 Witness Project. A community-based story collective made up of Louisiana artists, educators and community organizers, I-10 documents the aftermath of Hurricane Katrina through the stories of the people who experienced it. They have talked to a broad cross-section of people, including displaced citizens in shelters, relief workers, community organizers, neighborhood leaders, artists, medical staff, city planners and government officials. The interviews are available on their website as well as through partnerships with local colleges, public radio and the national oral history archives. They have collaborated with Mourning Line Productions and the 78th Street Theater in New York on an installation based on the stories.

916 2nd Street, Apt. B, New Orleans, LA 70130, www.i10witness.org

In the Heart of the Beast Puppet and Mask Theatre. This much-loved puppet theater has been pulling strings since 1973. The troupe now makes its home in the old Avalon movie theater. HOTB mounts original plays and touring productions, along with workshops on puppetry and pageantry for children, teachers and communities. The name of the theater comes from a line by the Cuban patriot/poet José Martí describing people of El Norte as "in the heart of the beast." The company has been organizing a popular May Day Parade and Festival since 1975, starting out with fifty or sixty people and a few puppets to celebrate the end of the Vietnam War. That march has grown into a major, community-wide event that draws tens of thousands of people to Powderhorn Park in south Minneapolis on the first Sunday of May. Anyone whose message is peaceful may join the march.

1500 E. Lake Street, Minneapolis, MN 55407, (612) 721-2535, www.hobt.org

In the Street Theatre Festival. This San Francisco troupe, produced by the 509 Cultural Center, draws together some 200 unpaid artists to perform in the Tenderloin neighborhood. "Street theatre is a reclamation of our public spaces and our community," the group says. The annual festival offers two days of theater, plus a sculpture garden and other attractions. The participating groups are multiethnic in keeping with their city. Among them: Los Payasos Mendigos, the Vietnamese Youth Development Center, Pearl Ubungen Dancers and Musicians, Mr. Lu Yi's Young Chinese Acrobats, CORE, High Risk Group and the Prescott Clowns. The festival staff encourages the troupes to work with neighborhoods to tailor their productions to local issues.

c/o 509 Cultural Center, 509 Ellis Street, San Francisco, CA, (415) 255-5971, www.luggagestoregallery.org

Labor Heritage Foundation. Labor Heritage Foundation has been working since 1984 to encourage artistic expression of, by and for the union movement and to stimulate the study of labor history. The roots of the foundation trace back to an event organized by union troubadour Joe Glazer in 1979, the first of what has become the annual Great Labor Arts Exchange. That year, over the course of three days at the George Meany Center for Labor Studies in Silver Spring, Maryland, fourteen labor musicians and artists gathered to discuss ways of joining art with justice and workers' rights (see DC Labor FilmFest). The Labor Heritage Foundation picked up the torch and continues to mingle union members with artists and teachers. Since the early days, the festival has attracted artists such as Pete Seeger, Hazel Dickens, Bernice Johnson Reagon, Ralph Fasanella, Gary Huck and Mike Konopacki. The foundation also gives support to regional labor festivals, produces labor art of various forms, organizes concerts and consults with unions on how to incorporate art and music into their rallies and other events.

815 16th Street NW, Washington, DC 20006, (202) 637-3963, www.laborheritage.org

Pangea World Theater. "Pangea" refers to the primal landmass that existed before the continents split apart. Since 1996 this theater's goal has been to stage plays with an international perspective. It has presented old and new plays—from works by the South African playwright Athol Fugard to an original production of *Rashômon* and Sophocles' *Ajax*. They also do original pieces such as *Bearing Witness,* which evoked the dislocations and carnage of war in Bosnia. Pangea employs multiethnic casts and aims to attract a diverse audience. Minnesota's population comprises 9 percent people of color; Pangea's audiences are regularly made up of more than 30 percent people of color. A 2005 production called *Truth Serum Blues* looked at the detention and mistreatment of Muslim American men in the war on terror. Pangea sponsors community-oriented events and workshops and holds discussions after performances such as "The War on Terror: From Israel-Palestine to Iraq and Guantánamo." In 2004, the theater collaborated with the Minnesota Advocates for Human Rights on a project called Building Immigrant Awareness and Support. The company sponsored an Asian American theater conference in 2007 and 2008.

711 W. Lake Street, Suite 101, Minneapolis, MN 55408, (612) 822-0015,

www.pangeaworldtheater.org

Paperhand Puppet Intervention. Paperhand Puppet Intervention was cofounded by Jan Burger, who interned with Bread & Puppet Theater, and Donovan Zimmerman. Zimmerman has said that the use of "intervention" in the group's title signifies "an intervention into the deadly silence of apathy, into business as usual, and into commonplace injustice that plagues the planet in many forms." Their tools are like those of Bread & Puppet Theater: giant puppets, masks, stilt dancing, rod puppets, shadows or silhouettes used in puppet theater productions and street demonstrations. The troupe has journeyed as far as Seattle for WTO protests and attended the last Bush inauguration.

6350 Whitney Road, Graham, NC 27250, (919) 923-1857, www.paperhand.org

Roadside Theater. This award-winning company is part of the Appalshop (see page 64) complex. Since 1975 it has produced some fifty-five plays, molding them from local history, oral histories, traditional ballads, folktales, church services and traditions. Roadside's productions have toured Appalachia, forty-three states and Europe. It has collaborated with African-American artists in various states; Puerto Rican and Dominican actors and musicians in the Bronx; Mexican and Mien artists in Richmond, California; and Native American storytellers, singers and dancers in Zuni Pueblo, New Mexico, according to the theater's director, Dudley Cocke. It recently mounted a musical called *Betsy*, telling the story of a middle-aged woman of African and Scots-Irish descent searching for her roots in America. The piece had a national tour in 2007–2008. Another popular production is *Music from Home*, a review made up of twenty-one original songs, ranging in style from Appalachian gospel to Southern soul, linked by dramas based on the lives of Appalachian people. *Voices from the Battlefront*, a docudrama-cum-workshop on domestic violence, travels to various cities.

PO Box 771, Norton, VA 24273, (276) 679-3116, www.roadside.org

Rhythm Workers Union. "There are drums beyond the mountain and they're getting mighty near," goes an old Peter La Farge song. The Washington, D.C.–based Rhythm Workers Union tries to sound the drumbeat of change in the capital. It was formed in spring 2001 by a group of percussionists with a shared interest in noisemaking and political protest. Since then, the RWU has participated in hundreds of events, from the biggest antiwar marches in Washington and New York to local demonstrations (and celebrations) in neighborhoods and communities throughout D.C. Sometimes leading these forays is the MotherDrumShip, a homemade contraption "built up from the bottom portion of an antique baby carriage found in a Dumpster. A four-foot tower was attached, and a pulling mechanism was created out of a pair of used crutches. Holes on the sides of the tower hold bells, and rigged up to the back of the tower with bungee cords are three Djuns (large African drums)." When not serving as drummer boys to the Armies of the Night, RWU members meet for monthly potluck jam sessions, honing their skills for rallies to come. Some groups in the union add woodwinds to the mix; still others sing.

(202) 330-5117, www.rhythmworkersunion.org

Soul Invictus Gallery & Cabaret. "There's something raw, uninhibited and uncensored taking place in the anemic cultural wasteland of Phoenix, Arizona," boasts this all-in-one art gallery, music venue, performance space and boundary-defying hot spot in downtown Phoenix. Soul Invictus has won accolades from the *Phoenix New Times* as "Best place to catch a queer-friendly show," for such recent events as the Genderfuct Film Festival, stage productions like *Psycho Beach Party* and *Die, Mommy, Die!*, poetry slams, body painting and even nude fire spinning with a distinct LGBT 'tude. Soul Invictus is something of an exotic plant in Phoenix, but it seems to thrive in the desert air. As one Arizona college paper puts it, "If you're looking for edgy arts in Phoenix, there's one place you absolutely have to go: Soul Invictus Gallery and Cabaret. . . . a collaborative effort to fight the evil overlords of censorship."

1022 NW Grand Avenue, Phoenix, AZ 85007, www.soulinvictus.com

Spiral Q Puppet Theater. When Spiral Q founder Matthew Hart visited the Bread & Puppet Theater (see page 65) farm he judged its pastoral base as "too divorced from the urban environment," so he returned to Philadelphia resolved to work in the city. Spiral Q started out doing gigs at local events, but working with the surrounding community became and has remained central to Spiral Q's mission. The theater has collaborated with more than one hundred school and community groups in the Philadelphia area, presenting Bread & Puppet–style social pageantry in an urban setting created and presented by neighborhood residents themselves. Spiral Q's most notable work is the annual Peoplehood: An All-City Parade and Pageant, which emerged out of community workshops to unite more than 3,000 people "to celebrate community, diversity and the challenges and triumphs of life in Philadelphia and its neighborhoods." The parade begins at the Paul Robeson House in West Philadelphia and straggles to Clark Park, where Spiral Q stages the Peoplehood Pageant.

3114 Spring Garden Street, 2nd floor, Philadelphia, PA 19104, (215) 222-6979, www.spiralq.org

El Teatro Campesino. As the Spanish name has it, this is *farmworkers* theater, literally born in the fields amid struggle. Founder Luis Valdez, son of migrant workers who had dramatic training, joined César Chávez and the United Farm Workers during the turning point 1965 strike and produced workers theater in the fields. A story in *High Performance* describes El Teatro as "somewhere between Brecht and Cantinflas." After working for the UFW, Valdez struck out on his own in 1967 and became a founding father of Chicano theater. Under his guidance, El Teatro dramatized conditions beyond the farmworkers' struggle—including race and Chicano identity, the Vietnam War and police brutality. Two of its best-known works, both written by Valdez, are *Corridos!! Ballads of the Borderlands* and *Zoot Suit*, about the LA riots during World War II, when Chicanos were attacked by soldiers and sailors because of their far-out clothing but really because of their ethnicity. Valdez and El Teatro Campesino are trying to create "a popular art with 21st century tools that presents a more just and accurate account of human history, while encouraging the young women and men of a new generation to take control of their own destiny. . . ."

705 4th Street, San Juan Bautista, CA 95045, (831) 623-2444, www.elteatrocampesino.com

Ten Thousand Things Theater. Among Minneapolis's lively theater groups, community outreach is traditional, but Ten Thousand Things trumps them. It brings theater to money-poor, health-poor, art-poor citizens. Why? "Because theater is richer when everyone is in the audience." Ten Thousand Things got its start in LA in 1990, with a production of Brecht's *The Good Person of Szechwan* at a homeless shelter in Santa Monica. The company's founder and artistic director, Michelle Hensley, moved it to Minneapolis in 1993, where it has won strong support. The intensity of that support can be assayed in this notice posted by the Twin Cities' *City Pages* critic: "We wish everyone could experience the immediacy of a Ten Thousand Things performance in Hennepin County Women's Prison. The troupe performed Aphra Behn and Shakespeare in a small cafeteria, surrounded by inmates sitting on the edge of their seats, talking back to the actors, screaming with laughter." The project of sharing the theatrical wealth has taken the company to homeless shelters, prisons and low-income community centers, where they give uncondescending performances of Euripides, Aeschylus, Shakespeare, Lorca, Beckett, Brecht and Albee. These productions attract uptown theater lovers as well. Ten Thousand Things may seem apolitical, but Hensley insists that "choosing to go to places where there are people who don't go to the big institutional theatres, by making it available to low-income people or people with really different life experiences—that in itself is a political act."

3153 36th Avenue S., Minneapolis, MN 55406, (612) 724-4494, www.tenthousandthings.org

Theater of the Oppressed Laboratory. A favorite choice among radical theater groups are the works of the Theater of the Oppressed, based on the theory and praxis of Augusto Boal in Rio de Janeiro in the 1970s. Boal worked with denizens of the streets and slums of Rio to create "a form of participatory theater . . . rooted in the Latin American popular education movements" and coaching the people to write and develop plays dramatizing their own stories and proposing solutions to the desperate problems plaguing their daily existence. TOPLAB in New York was founded in 1990 as a collective of theater artists and educators devoted to disseminating Boal's techniques and ideas. As a member of the Institute for Popular Education at the Brecht Forum (see page 66), TOPLAB runs workshops for a broad array of groups of working people, union organizers and community activists on how to use theater as an organizing tool. TOPLAB has staged an evening of women's voices on immigration, featuring performances by two of its members, and also staged a play on housing by the immigrant rights group Make the Road by Walking.

451 W. Street, 10th floor, New York, NY 10014, (212) 924-1858, www.toplab.org

Urban Bush Women. Based in the gentrifying Fort Greene neighborhood of Brooklyn, this African-American company was founded in 1984 by Jawole Willa Jo Zollar, who is dedicated to using dance and performance for social change. By dancing the stories of the voiceless poor, it believes it can contribute "to a more equitable balance of power in the dance world and beyond." The *New York Times* has described Zollar's work as dealing "with black female experience, spiritualism and black urban and African cultures." Although it plays mostly in New York, UBW has toured the country and the world. Zollar's 2006 work *Walking with Pearl . . . Southern Diaries*, a dance inspired by the late dancer-choreographer and activist Pearl Primus, won a New York Dance and Performance Award. In keeping with the company's activist spirit, UBW established the Summer Dance Institute as a place where professionals and amateurs can work together using the arts to express political and civic engagement.

138 S. Oxford Street, 4B, Brooklyn, NY 11217, (718) 398-4537, www.urbanbushwomen.org

Vox Feminista. For the better part of two decades, this "performance tribe of radical womyn bent on social change through cultural revolution" has been a welcome player on the Boulder, Colorado, indie arts scene. Activist theater at its liveliest, Vox Feminista's semiannual multimedia productions engage audiences with a smorgasbord of timely topics, from white supremacy (*White Lies*) to industrial food processing (*The Last Supper to Go*) and oil wars (*Global Warning! Burning the Midnight Oil*). "Even though we are a local troupe, we also want to discuss global issues," says founder Joy Boston, who's not afraid to "step on toes."

www.voxfeminista.org

Wise Fool Puppet Intervention. This West Coast troupe, connected with In the Street Theatre (see page 70), offers some of the best street puppetry in beautiful downtown

Berkeley. It covers the puppetry landscape—giant puppets, mask stilt dancing, music and theater—while serving the community with workshops and educational programs. They relate their history as follows, yea verily: "Wise Fool evolved out of an effort to heighten the visual impact of the Hiroshima Day Action at Lawrence Livermore Laboratories in July 1989. The organization was officially birthed in the Spring of 1990" and became a nonprofit known as Wise Fool Community Arts. Its agenda includes staging original outdoor theatrical pieces as well as site-specific presentations and annual processions. It is available for ceremonial occasions such as weddings, and holds workshops and school demonstrations and gives stilt walking lessons. ("In a culture where so many of us are disappeared, stilt walking gives us a chance to be seen.") There are also training programs for political activists—and the group often dedicates its art to stimulating social and political change and has a long antiwar pedigree.

Wise Fool Community Arts, 2633 Etna Street, Berkeley, CA 94704, (415) 905-5958,

www.zeitgeist.net/wfca/wisefool.htm

The Working Theater. Since 1985 this New York–based theater company has been reviving the ancient storytelling tradition that dramatizes the stories of obscure folk. They have created works on such themes as the Memphis sanitation workers strike of 1968, the debilitating effects of pesticides on migrant farmworkers, the planning and construction of New York City's third water tunnel and retired women feeding their pensions to the slots in Atlantic City. In its stellar career the company's work has won it the New York theater critics' Drama Desk Award and grants from the Kennedy Center, NEA, Rockefeller and Ford foundations. The troupe has also premiered work by playwrights who've gone on to wider fame, among them Israel Horovitz, Cherrie Moraga, Romulus Linney, Suzan-Lori Parks, John Sayles and Michael Henry Brown. The productions are staged at borrowed venues like the Theater at Riverside Church, the Public Theater and Culture Project.

128 E. Broadway, Box 892, New York, NY 10002, (212) 539-5675, www.theworkingtheater.org

WOW Café Theater. A recent slogan of this theater collective based on Manhattan's Lower East Side was "26 years of vulva rockin' theater!" WOW started at a women's theater festival in October 1980. The theater's predominantly a lesbian/transgender space, but the collective, which meets every Tuesday at 6:30, is open "to all sexualities and spiritualities," languages, ages, races. WOW is bent on challenging "classism, ableism, sexism, ageism, and sizeism." Regular shows include a weekly cabaret featuring women and "trans artists" of color and monthly queer burlesque shows. In keeping with its political bent, WOW is also a member of Theaters Against War, an international organization of theaters and theater artists against the war on terror.

59–61 E. 4th Street, New York, NY 10003, (212) 277-4280, www.wow.cafe.org

CULTURE JAMMERS AND MERRY PRANKSTERS

Billionaires for Bush. "For much of the 20th century, democratic notions like 'opportunity for all' and 'public services' dominated American public policy, seriously threatening the privileges of wealth all Billionaires depend on. Government taxed the rich, regulated corporations, protected the environment and the average person felt increasingly entitled to share in America's prosperity. Ordinary people were educated for free and over 50 media companies helped give them a balanced picture of what the government and corporations were up to. They were dark days." Who but the satirists at Billionaires for Bush could tap out such irony-rich prose? These comedians work in the streets rather than on stage. Wherever the wealthy are partying, there the Billionaires

will be, dressed to kill their joy. When we asked Monet Oliver D'Place (pseudonym) about the post-Bush future of the organization, he predicted that it will concentrate on croissant-and-butter economic issues such as repealing the estate tax. It has started hitting environmental issues, too; for example, demonstrating in support of TXU, the Texas-based utility that wants to build eleven new coal-smoke-belching power plants. Be assured: they'll keep puttin' on the rich.

PO Box 20280, Tompkins Square Station, New York, NY 10009, (646) 219-4607, www.billionairesforbush.com

Reverend Billy and the Church of Stop Shopping. Reverend Billy is actually Minnesota-born Bill Talen. In San Francisco he started the Life on the Water theater, which produced monologist Spalding Gray's early work. He moved to New York City in 1994; three years later he donned a collar bought from a clerical-supply shop and a white tuxedo jacket left over from a catering job and became the Reverend Billy as a protest against the Disneyfication of Times Square. Reverend Billy uses street performance to awaken shopaholics from their credit-card comas in an attempt to get people to think about not buying stuff they don't need or to act locally and think globally. The rev likes to walk into a store accompanied by the Stop Shopping choir and exorcise demons from cash registers with shouts of "change—hallelujah!" The rev and his followers travel around the country fighting large transcontinental corporations, especially Wal-

Mart and its ilk, in hopes of preserving communities and neighborhoods. The Stop Shopping Choir includes professional singers, actors and even some former Starbucks employees. Reverend Billy was arrested in Union Square Park, New York, under the following circumstances: "On June 29, 2007, Bill Talen—a street performer known as Reverend Billy—was in Union Square Park, in support of the Critical Mass bike riders—and repeatedly recited with the aid of a nonbattery megaphone the forty-four words of the First Amendment to the Constitution of the United States, in the presence of several NYC Police Department employees. He was arrested and held approximately twenty hours." On November 3, 2007, the Manhattan DA's office quietly dropped its prosecution. Other achievements: Preaching against Victoria's Secret's tree-wasting clear-cutting catalogues (365 million mailed a year) at a tent "crusade" at the South Street Seaport Mall in New York City. A 2000 memo circulated among Manhattan Starbucks with the question: "What should I do if Reverend Billy is in my store?" A court order in California enjoined him from coming within 250 yards of any of the 1,481 Starbucks franchises there. A documentary on him titled *What Would Jesus Buy* and a book with the same title were produced.

PO Box 1556, Canal Street Station, New York, NY 10013, www.revbilly.com

Joey Skaggs. Claiming to be "America's most notorious socio-political satirist, media activist, culture jammer, hoaxer, and dedicated proponent of independent thinking and media literacy," this Renaissance hombre is a New York–based artist who gained his first burst of notoriety when he erected a large, slightly grotesque crucified corpse in Tompkins Square. In 1968, inspired by bus tours through the bohemian quarter of the Lower East Side, Joey Skaggs arranged tours for hippies through middle-class neighborhoods in Queens. Over the years he has arranged such press events as a Celebrity Sperm Bank auction (offering prime stuff from Jagger and Dylan, "vintage Hendrix"), a Wall Street Shoe Shine, a dog brothel, and in 1986 the first annual April Fools' Day Parade in Greenwich Village. The parade features a king and queen, the supreme fools, you might say. For the 2007 parade Skaggs featured live music, food, concessions and entertainment and "a 100-yard drug-enhanced sprint between track star Marion Jones on foot and Tour de France winner/loser Floyd Landis on a bicycle."

www.joeyskaggs.com

The Yes Men. Back in 1999, with the Seattle world trade meetings looming, Mike Bonanno and Andy Bichlbaum constructed a website for the WTO (GATT.org), which powerful people mistook for the real PR. The Yes Men were invited to appear on CNBC, at industry events and schools and were assumed to be legit representatives of the WTO. They gleefully crashed the party in their new thrift store suits and shocked unsuspecting audiences with dark, satirical inventions about the worst aspects of global free trade. They have since assumed the identities of Dow Chemical and Cargill spokespersons. One of the Yes Men appeared on the BBC to promise that Dow would clean up the toxic mess it left at Bhopal, India, caused by a massive leak of MIC gas at its subsidiary Union Carbide in 1984. But then, in a Yes Men cooked-up press release, Dow "explained" that while the company "understood the anger and hurt" of those who suffered after the explosion, it could not acknowledge responsibility because doing so would open the floodgates to compensation by such poor but honorable companies as Amoco, BP, Shell and Exxon. You can book the Yes Men through Evil Twin Booking, which handles lefty acts, to speak at your school, church group, quilting bee or Greenpeace demo.

www.theyesmen.org

Film

THE POLITICAL LENS: DOCUMENTARIES AND DOCUMENTARIANS

In recent years the political documentary has become a powerful organizing and fund-raising tool on the Left, as well as an art. Robert Greenwald's guerrilla DVDs, viewed in living rooms and church basements; Michael Moore's Fahrenheit 9/11, *as seen in your local multiplex;*

Al Gore's An Inconvenient Truth, *which won him an Academy Award and the Nobel Peace Prize, and many docs on the Iraq War, including Charles Ferguson's* No End in Sight: *the political advocacy, muckraking documentary has developed new scope, range and technical versatility.*

Brave New Films. Robert Greenwald founded this documentary company with Jim Gilliam in 2004. Greenwald makes low-budget, high-concept, eye-opening exposés with input and financial backing from activists, both individuals and groups; for example, $267,892 was raised in ten days to wrap up *Iraq for Sale: The War Profiteers,* which linked Halliburton

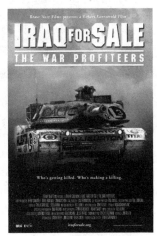

REEL POLITICS: POV SCHECHTER

Danny Schechter is a veteran filmmaker who paid his dues working for network news shows on ABC and CNN. He has made more than twenty award-winning documentary films for the independent company Globalvision, which he cofounded with Rory O'Connor. He is a passionately political person, an activist and a media critic, renowned as the "News Dissector." His *WMD: Weapons of Mass Deception* (2004) dissected the mainstream media's cheerleading for the Iraq War, as did a later companion book, *When News Lies*.

SCHECHTER: Today there are tremendous market pressures on filmmakers. Public television has grown more fearful. The MacArthur Foundation, which used to be the biggest funder of documentaries on PBS, has cut back funding.

Another pressure on filmmakers is the need to raise big money in order to market your film—if you want it to be seen in theaters. Michael Moore is a prime example of what it takes. He raised $62 million for *Fahrenheit 9/11* from Miramax. Only $6 million of that went into the cost of making the film; the rest went for marketing. That film was a big hit at the box office. I spent $30,000 marketing *Weapons of Mass Deception*. It ended up being seen in thirty-seven countries, which was good but nothing like the audience Moore reached.

Today it's much harder to get funding for films analyzing or describing a social problem. Take my film *In Debt We Trust* [about predatory credit card loans in America]. I had a hard time getting it chosen by a film festival. The director of one told me: "I'm sorry, your film isn't right for us." Later I saw the festival was funded by American Express. Obviously, a film about credit card debt wasn't "right" for AMEX.

Now there's a great opportunity for a new breed of citizen filmmakers to come forward with all this new cheap equipment enabling and empowering them. I tell young would-be filmmakers to go in with a sense of mission or a political point of view. Maybe there'll be more of them who do this. I hope so.

575 8th Avenue, Suite 2200, New York, NY 10018, (212) 246-0202, www.globalvision.org

and others to the Bush administration. He made *Outfoxed: Rupert Murdoch's War on Journalism*, for MoveOn and the Center for American Progress, which anted up $80,000 with Greenwald providing the rest. He enlists groups to help sponsor a film by getting members to buy at least one $10 DVD; he also asks the people to send him material, such as reports on Wal-Mart's pricing practices in their towns. When the film is completed the organizations sponsor screenings for their members, friends or sympathizers. Greenwald, who makes nonpolitical movies as well, says he is out "to create change, not just movies." During the election he made films for YouTube.

10510 Culver Boulevard, Culver City, CA 90232, (800) 525-8212, www.bravenewfilms.org

Bullfrog Films. This company was formed in 1973 by John Hoskyns-Abrahall and Winifred Scherrer, who had been working for the Rodale Press's short-lived film division where they made six films. The two decided to go on distributing films and eventually formed Bullfrog Films, which handles films about globalization and social issues. In 1995 they won a ten-year court battle over censorship, which started when the U.S. Information Agency's head, a friend of President Reagan, ordered his people to stop issuing certificates of educational content to Bullfrog's films, meaning they were no longer exempt from customs duties in other countries. The USIA claimed Bullfrog's proenvironmental films were biased and threatened national security. Represented by the Center for Constitutional Rights, Bullfrog won an appeals court ruling that the USIA regulations violated its First Amendment rights.

PO Box 149, Oley, PA 19547, (800) 543-3764, www.bullfrogfilms.com

Cabin Creek Films. This is the home base of Barbara Kopple, one of America's best-known documentary makers. She landed on the scene in 1976 with *Harlan County U.S.A.*, the Academy Award–winning saga of the efforts of Miners for Democracy to reform their union. "I learned what life and death was all about," she later recalled. "We were machine-gunned with semiautomatic weapons. A miner was killed by a company foreman. Women took over the picket lines." Reviewing the movie in *The Nation*, Robert Hatch wrote: "It is a shock to discover that these expendable, burrowing creatures are in fact as splendid a people as the country can show." Kopple repeated in 1990 with *American Dream*, about the pain and betrayal felt by workers in an Austin, Minnesota, Hormel plant when their wages were cut. Other films, both theatrical and made for television, have focused on celebrities enduring public backlash (including *Shut Up & Sing*, about the right-wing retribution against the Dixie Chicks for criticizing President Bush). She made an Iraq War film, *Bearing Witness*, the stories of five women war correspondents covering Iraq and earlier wars.

270 Lafayette Street, Suite 710, New York, NY 10012, (212) 343-2545, www.cabincreekfilms.com

Carnivalesque Films. Ashley Sabin and David Redmon teamed up to form this company in Brooklyn in 2004 to make films evoking large social issues through individual lives. David Redmon's first film, *Mardi Gras: Made in China*, juxtaposes scenes of bare-breasted bacchanalians in New Orleans with an investigation of the lot of Chinese factory workers who work sixteen-hour days for ten cents an hour to make Mardi Gras beads. Other films from this shop are *Kamp Katrina*, about an eccentric New Orleans woman bent on providing shelter for displaced citizens, and *Intimidad*, depicting the impact of globalization on the lives of a Mexican family on the Texas border.

2316 Charleston Drive, Mansfield, TX 76063, (203) 417-3136, www.carnivalesquefilms.com

Daylight Factory. James Longley, who, with two major films under his belt, has emerged as one of the promising younger filmmakers, formed this. Though he claims to have no political take on the Iraq War or the Israeli-Palestinian conflict, he shot two well-received documentaries dealing with those subjects: *Gaza Strip* (2002) and most recently *Iraq in Fragments* (2006). He spent two years on location filming the latter, which won a fistful of awards at Sundance and a Grand Jury Award at Full Frame Documentary Film Festival. His approach is multivoiced cinema verité rather than single-voice advocacy. Culling from 300 hours of film, he evokes a fragmented Iraq through the stories of three sets of individuals: a pushed-around little boy and the older mechanic he works for; the fanatical followers of Shiite leader Mogtada Al-Sadr enforcing religious morality at gunpoint, and pro-American Kurdish farmers participating in their first, chaotic election.

www.daylightfactory.com

Displaced Films. Founding filmmaker David Zeigler includes in his oeuvre generational themes such as *Senior Year, The Band,* about his son's generation, and *Funny Old Guys,* about his father's friends. As a member of the sixties generation he was involved in the antiwar coffeehouse movement. Out of those experiences came *Sir! No Sir!* that unearths the near-forgotten history of the anti–Vietnam War resistance among the military, which took multifarious forms including desertions, demonstrations and "fragging" and gave rise to a dissident subculture of antiwar rock music, underground papers and off-base coffeehouses where disaffected soldiers gathered. Zeigler has also made a film about immigrants, *Displaced in the New South,* and *A Night of Ferocious Joy,* about the 2002 ArtSpeaks! Not in Our Name concert, one of the earliest mass protests against the invasion of Iraq.

3421 Fernwood Avenue, Los Angeles, CA 90039, (323) 906-9249, www.displacedfilms.com

High Plains Films. This nonprofit company specializes in nature and environmental films set in the West. Its work does not broadcast its political convictions, but films about the environment hit hard at government and corporate neglect. *End of the Road,* for example, shows how the increasing number of roads in national forests, encouraged by the Bush administration, threatens animal habitats. *Libby, Montana* tells the story of a town where hundreds of people fell sick or died from asbestos exposure.

PO Box 8796, Missoula, MT 59807, (406) 728-0753, www.highplainsfilms.org

Kartemquin Films. A nonprofit, Chicago-based Kartemquin has been producing films for more than forty years. It issued its first documentary in 1966, *Home for Life,* a moving account of two people's first month in an old-age home. According to the company, this documentary "established the direction the organization would take over the next four decades," that is, to make "documentaries that examine and critique society through the stories of real people." Since then, Kartemquin has tackled such topics as immigration (*The New Americans*), labor, stay-at-home mothers, gender issues, the stem cell debate, Vietnam vets (*Vietnam, Long Time Coming*) and others. Its best-known work is *Hoop Dreams* (1994), a feature-length exposé of the shattered dreams of black high school athletes (see "Klawans's List," page 92). In 2007 Kartemquin reported a record number of films in production, including Steve James and Peter Gilbert's *At the Death House Door* (with the *Chicago Tribune*), about a wrongly executed man.

1901 W. Wellington Avenue, Chicago, IL 60657, www.kartemquin.com

Anne Lewis. She got her start as the editor of Barbara Kopple's Academy Award–winning documentary *Harlan County U.S.A.* While she was in Kentucky she met and married a union organizer and stayed down there to make films with labor themes, including *Fast Food Women*, about speedups for McDonald's workers. Lewis's most recent documentary is *Morristown: In the Air and Sun* (2007), about how globalization, the loss of jobs and the importation of foreign workers affected a Tennessee town and the response of a successful unionization drive. Others include *Texas Majority Minority*, about the fight to register Latino and black voters, and *High Stakes*, on the effect of testing on Latino students. Some think that her finest film is *On Our Own Land* (1989), about a type of contract that allowed people to keep their land but gave mining companies the rights to all minerals beneath the surface. Lewis's films are shown regularly on Kentucky Public Television. This one was scheduled, but it was suddenly rescheduled until after the vote on a proposition to invalidate the contracts. After protests, the ban was lifted, the film was aired and the referendum passed with 82 percent of the vote.

400 Post Road Drive, Austin, TX 78704, www.annelewis.org

Maysles Films. Albert and his brother, David Maysles, were considered two of the most influential innovators in the American documentary film movement that emerged in the 1960s. Albert started his career behind the camera with Drew Associates, the company founded by *Life* photographer Robert Drew, who pioneered the technique called direct cinema, or cinema verité. This form liberated documentaries from narrators, scripts and story lines, freeing the camera to spontaneously see and record reality as it was happening, rather than rearranging the greenery and then filming it. Documentaries converged with the "nonfiction novel" techniques that contemporary New Journalists were infusing into magazine articles. Maysles's first film for Drew was *Primary* (1960), which documented the 1960 Wisconsin primary between Hubert H. Humphrey and John F. Kennedy. In 1962 Albert founded his own company and was joined by David, a soundman, along with a brilliant editor, Charlotte Zwerin. They made a number of acutely observant films, most notably *Salesman* (1968), about a group of burned-out Bible salesmen; *Gimme Shelter* (1970), the epical crash of the love generation at Altamont; and *Grey Gardens* (1976), the gothic lives of a reclusive mother and daughter in a crumbling East Hampton mansion. Albert Maysles's films inspired filmmakers like Michael Moore in *Roger and Me* and Barbara Kopple in *Harlan County U.S.A.* The Maysles Institute offers instruction and workshops to underprivileged young people. It operates the Harlem Cinematheque, a center for the regular screening of films by the African-American, African, Caribbean and other world communities, and their distribution to other screening sites.

343 Lenox Avenue, New York, NY 10027, (212) 582-6050, www.mayslesfilms.com

Moxie Firecracker Films. Cofounded in 1998 by Liz Garbus and Rory Kennedy, this company has turned out a number of documentaries that probe social issues like AIDS and violence against women. Garbus was thrust into prominence when she received an Academy Award nomination for her film *The Farm: Angola, USA.* Kennedy gained fame with her 1999 film about an Appalachian family, *American Hollow,* which garnered several festival awards and was broadcast on HBO. Kennedy's most recent film, *Ghosts of Abu Ghraib,* graphically refuted right-wing whitewash that the hellish prisoner tableaus at the U.S. prison were the product of high-spirited hazing.

39 Lincoln Place, Brooklyn, NY 11217, (718) 730-5111, www.moxiefirecracker.com

Women Make Movies. Founded in 1972 "to address the under representation and misrepresentation of women in the media industry," Women Make Movies boasts that it now sponsors more than 200 projects in its production assistance program run by experienced filmmakers and has helped filmmakers raise close to $4 million in funding over the last five years. More than half the films were made by women of foreign cultures. It funds films by both experienced and new filmmakers. Its production assistance program trains women in the techniques of filmmaking, generating some provocative films, but the good work would never be seen unless WMF involved itself in distribution as well. Hence it set up its distribution program, which currently has an inventory of more than 500 titles, ranging from documentary to experimental. More than half of these were produced by women of diverse cultures.

462 Broadway, Suite 500WS, New York, NY 10013, (212) 925-0606, www.wmm.com

FILM CLIPS

Magnolia Films distributes some of the best political documentaries around: *The Smartest Guys in the Room,* probing the Enron debacle; *No End in Sight,* by Charles

Ferguson, a painstaking investigation of the blunders in the Iraq War and *Taxi to the Dark Side,* Alex Gibney's documentary on torture. *On the Media: Orwell Rolls in His Grave,* Robert Kane Pappas's essential report on how the media conglomerates distort and censor the news, features the *Nation*'s famous chart of the Big Ten media conglomerates and also interviews with media analysts like Charles Lewis, Robert McChesney, Mark Crispin Miller and Senator Bernie Sanders (www.orwellrollsinhisgrave.com). Media critic and executive director of the Institute for Public Accuracy (see page 147) Norman Solomon takes his message to film in *War Made Easy,* directed by Loretta

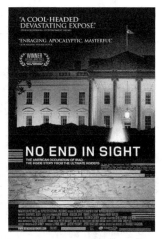

Alper and Jeremy Earp, an analysis of the strategies used by administrations, both Democratic and Republican, to promote their agendas for war, from Vietnam to Iraq.

www.fair.org

FESTIVALS

The more successful a film festival becomes, the more it is castigated by True Cineastes for being about deals rather than ideals. Herewith a boiled-down roster of truly alternative, authentically indie festivals. Their backstories all contain a heartening subtext: you don't have to be Robert Redford to start your own film festival (not that there's anything wrong with being Robert Redford).

Bicknell International Film Festival. The people in Bicknell decided to build their own film festival—and if nobody came, well, heck, it'd still give them something to do on a hot Saturday night in summertime. The Bicknell people hold theirs in the Wayne Theater, a cinema palazzo that seats 306, which is six more seats than the town has people. Each year they choose a theme and select a trio of movies by the criterion "Better Living Through Bad Movies." In 2006, for example, the judges chose "three of the best bad B movies ever made about the circus," leading off with *Charlie Chan at the Circus.* In 2008, three of the best bad B movies ever made about Christmas. Everybody gets to dress up in costumes appropriate to that year's theme. Seminars/discussions follow each screening—or maybe not. The highlight of the weekend is the Wrap Party at Rim Rock Inn and Restaurant in nearby Torrey. Another prominent happening is "the world's fastest parade," in which drivers zoom down Main Street at 55 miles per hour.

Wayne Theatre, 11 E. Main Street, Bicknell, UT 84715, (435) 425-3554, www.waynetheatre.com

Birmingham Shout. This was a new venture of the Alabama Moving Image Association, which gave Birminghamians the Sidewalk Moving Picture Festival (so named because it was and is held in theaters downtown and the audience strolls from venue to venue discussing what they've just seen). Anyhow, Catherine Pfitzer, executive director, told us she and her coconspirators decided the time was ripe for a roundup of lesbian gay bisexual transgender flicks for Birmingham's growing LGBT community. All has gone smoothly: no denunciations of godless sodomites from the pulpit. Screenings are at the WorkPlay Theater. Social events inevitably transpire.

2312 1st Avenue N., Birmingham, AL 35203, (205) 324-0888, www.bhamshout.com

DC Labor FilmFest. This one, held every September, showcases some thirty films about work and workers. Its professed goal is to bring "directors, stars, workers, and activists together in an annual celebration of the struggle for economic and social justice." It screens both old films and new ones. Sponsors include the Metro Washington Council, the AFL-CIO, the Debs-Jones-Douglass Institute and the American Film Institute.

AFI Silver Theatre and Cultural Institute, 8633 Colesville Road, Silver Spring, MD 20910, (301) 495-6720, www.afi.com

Environmental Film Festival. This crusading screen forum celebrated its fifteenth anniversary in March 2007. Michael Gottwald of Wesleyan University checked it out:

Most were documentaries, including a miniretrospective by George Butler (the director of *The Endurance: Shackleton's Legendary Antarctic Expedition* and *Pumping Iron,* among others); nature films about subjects like the tulip and the American buffalo; arts and architecture pieces like *Building the Gherkin* and obligatory multiple screenings of *An Inconvenient Truth.* There were features as well, such as a just-released environmental horror film called *The Last Winter,* the French modernist classic *Playtime* and, of course, the token movie about a boy and a cheetah, this one entitled *Duma*. In addition there were animated series, student films and movies for kids—all held at venues all over the city, from the embassy of the Czech Republic to the National Geographic Society to the American Film Institute in Silver Spring, Maryland.

1228½ 31st Street NW, Washington, DC 20007, (202) 342-2564, www.dcenvironmentalfilmfest.org

Full Frame Documentary Film Festival. A Durham rite of April since 1996, it draws a huge number of submissions. In 2006, for example, Full Frame chose seventy-three films from among 1,100 entries, an all-time record number of documentary submissions to a single film festival, including Sundance. The documentaries hailed from fourteen countries, and twenty-three of them were world premieres. The theme was Class in America with a sidebar of nine films on our society's response to Katrina and its aftermath. The panel discussing the latter included jazz musicians Branford and Ellis Marsalis. Past festivals have screened the oeuvre of a single artist: Martin Scorsese, Ken Burns, Ric Burns, Errol Morris, Iranian Abbas Kiarostami and Michael Moore. Themes in past years have reflected the festival's ongoing political concerns: "Why War?" "Leadership Through a Camera Lens" and "Tolerance."

Carolina Theatre, 309 W. Morgan Street, Durham, NC 27701, (919) 687-4100, www.fullframefest.org

Global Peace Film Festival. Dig this premise: boy meets girl. It's 2003. He's a wealthy Moroccan Muslim businessman named A. T. Alishtari, a conservative Republican who wants to do something to promote peace. She's Nina Streich, a Jewish liberal Democrat. Bells ring. Fast forward four years: Executive Director Streich says A.T.'s moved on, but the Global Peace Film Festival, held in September, is thriving in Orlando, even though it's a conservative town. She says the festival aims to educate the community, not only by showing films but also through outreach programs like bringing in antiwar groups to speak and circulate literature and petitions. They've sponsored traveling festivals in New York, Cyprus, Japan, Los Angeles and Israel and Jordan. Typical screenings: Dutch film *Schnitzel Paradise* (Moroccan immigrant dishwasher falls in love with the restaurant owner's daughter); *A Peck on the Cheek* (girl searches for birth mother in war-torn Sri Lanka); *Criminalizing Dissent* (antiwar demonstrators try to be heard at the G8 summit in Georgia).

1000 Universal Studios Plaza, Building 22A, Orlando, FL 32819, (407) 224-6625, www.peacefilmfest.org

Human Rights Watch International Film Festival. The main idea here is to "showcase the heroic stories of activists and survivors from all over the world." The core concept is human rights in all their permutations. The first festival was held in 1988, with then *Nation* publisher Hamilton Fish the driving force, in the basement of the Angelika

Film Center in New York. Humans Right Watch people were skeptical at first, but Fish persevered with Robert Bernstein, then publisher of Random House. The festival's programming committee nominates the films to be shown each June and Human Rights Watch representatives vet them for factual accuracy. The rules say films may be barred for inaccuracy but not for point of view. The 2006 festival featured several anti–Iraq War docs: *The Camden 28* (a group of objectors to the draft), *The Road to Guantánamo* (three Pakistanis who ended up in the U.S. prison) and *Iraq in Fragments* (scenes of a war). In 2007 features included *Carla's List*, *The Devil Came on Horseback* and others. HRW also spins off a traveling film festival of the year's best.

Walter Reade Theater, 165 W. 65th Street, New York, NY 10023, (212) 290-4000, www.hrw.org/iff

Media That Matters Film Festival. Showcases short films—very short, eight minutes or less. The entries are screened by a jury. Many of the first-time filmmakers are under twenty-one; their products range through documentaries, music videos, animations and experimental work. Each year a jury selects sixteen winning films that are screened at the International Film Center theater in Manhattan, and then they appear on HBO. They are also circulated as DVDs to private groups for screenings in schools, town halls and other venues and during a fifty-city tour. DVDs are available from Netflix or Amazon. The online streamings can be accessed on www.mediathatmattersfest.org. The Media That Matters Festival is produced by Arts Engine, a foundation devoted to encouraging independent media.

104 W. 14th Street, 4th floor, New York, NY 10011, (646) 230-8368, www.artsengine.net

MIX NYC. Founded in 1987 by writer Sarah Schulman and filmmaker/archivist Jim Hubbard, MIX NYC claims to be the longest-running LGBT festival in New York City. Held in November, a typical one will offer more than 200 short films, videos, digital media, installations and performances, the majority of them by directors making their debuts. Among commercially distributed films that have premiered here is *Me and You and Everyone We Know*. Festivals run for five days and are held in November. MIX also holds free community screenings, sponsors a cable access TV show, helps disadvantaged LGBT youth and fosters film preservation. MIX prides itself on being an "artist-driven" film festival, rather than a showcase for celebs.

79 Pine Street, #132, New York, NY 10005, (212) 742-8880, www.mixnyc.org

Reel Work May Day Labor Film Festival. This conclave's left-wing purity is matched by its organizational savvy. It's the real social change deal. To give you an idea: in 2006, the festival, held from April 20 through May Day, featured the world premiere of *Sir! No Sir!* Weavers member Ronnie Gilbert did an impersonation of Mother Jones and filmmaker Renee Tajima-Peña discussed her new doc *Labor Women*. Cosponsors include the Monterey Bay Labor Council, UCSC Community Studies Department and many unions. In 2007 the bill included *The Motherland Manifesto, The Devil's Miner* and *Morristown: In the Air and Sun.*

170 Hagemann Avenue, Santa Cruz, CA 95062, www.reelwork.org

Rooftop Film Festival. In 1997 Mark Elijah Rosenberg started showing films on his apartment rooftop until the landlord evicted him. He moved the action to a converted warehouse roof in Brooklyn. Now he's got staff and volunteers and shows films through the summer atop the old American Can Factory on a twenty-one-by-fourteen-foot permanent screen. His organization funds indie filmmakers and provides free equipment, distribution and school outreach.

232 3rd Street, Studio E103, Brooklyn, NY 11215, (718) 417-7362, www.rooftopfilms.com

San Francisco International LGBT Film Festival. Known as "the gay Sundance," the festival is produced by Frameline, a nonprofit group dedicated to the "funding, exhibition, distribution, and promotion of lesbian, gay, bisexual and transgender media arts." The festival goes back to 1977, and Frameline Distribution was started in 1981 to handle LGBT films and video for U.S. circulation. There is also the Frameline Film & Video Completion Fund that gives strapped filmmakers that final financial push. It has helped bring nearly one hundred films and videos to parturition. Attendance is now around 70,000 people. Marvelous!

145 9th Street, #300, San Francisco, CA 94103, (415) 703-8650, www.frameline.org

Slamdance Film Festival. Shunned by Sundance, Peter Baxter and three friends started Slamdance in Park City, Utah, just down the road a piece and held in January, the same

month as Sundance. It was embraced by the rejected-indie community and has burgeoned into a ten-day cinemathon drawing upwards of 20,000 reel people. More than 3,000 entries are received. The festival tries to highlight new films by first-time writers and directors on limited budgets. It also previews video games, declaring them a new art form.

Slamdance, Inc., 5634 Melrose Ave., Los Angeles, CA 90038, (323) 466-1786, www.slamdance.com

True/False Film Festival. Convinced that the general run of fests had grown boringly formulaic, David Wilson and Paul Sturtz, who run the Ragtag Cinema in Columbia, Missouri, decided to start a documentary film festival. They put a premium on controversy and discussion, chose edgy nonfiction films and lined up panels that would pulse with interesting views and arguments. One panel, for example, was called Me and My Shadow—the relationship between nosy documentary filmers and the subjects they follow around. Add to the mix pleasurable things like live music—young buskers or traveling bands with banjos play before screenings—and gala dinners and evening programs. That recipe has gone down well in this college town. Attendance has climbed from 4,400 in 2004 to around 13,000 in 2007.

PO Box 1102, Columbia, MO 65205, (573) 442-TRUE, www.truefalse.org

Vermont International Film Festival. This October fest has been around since 1985 and claims to be one of the oldest human rights film showings (see Human Rights Watch International Film Festival, p. 88). It's the brainchild of George and Sonia Cullinen, and was inspired by the reception of their 1981 pro–nuclear freeze documentary called *From Washington to Moscow*, which chronicled a walk for peace. Its success led them to endow the Vermont International Film Foundation, which makes awards in three categories: War and Peace, Human Rights and the Environment.

One Main Street, Suite 307, Burlington, VT 05401, (802) 660-2600, www.vtiff.org

Wild and Scenic Environmental Film Festival. In the beginning, in 1983, a group of environmentally conscious residents of Nevada City, California, created the South Yuba River Citizens League (SYRCL). The object was to unite the community in the cause of protecting the Yuba, turning back proposals to dam the river. The festival concept started as a fund-raiser, but they quickly decided to inspire local activists to fight the green fight in their own communities. At festival time they take over the entire town for meetings, panels and events designed to inspire action, art shows, wine tastings and an awards ceremony. They have some 500 volunteers and a handful of paid staff to run all this. SYRCL decided to take the show on the road. It now visits some fifty towns and cities, talking up environmentalism, teaching the hosts how to put on their own film festival.

216 Main Street, Nevada City, CA 95959, (530) 265-5961, www.wildandscenicfilmfestival.org

STUART KLAWANS'S 25 GREATEST POLITICAL FILMS, *OR, NOTES TOWARD A FILMOGRAPHY OF THE LEFT*

Stewart Klawans is film critic of The Nation. *He won the 2007 National Magazine Award for criticism.*

The Battleship Potemkin. **1925.**

Directed by Sergei Eisenstein. The first international hit of Soviet filmmaking—more popular in export than it was at home—*The Battleship Potemkin* was a landmark in the arts of both the propagandists and the avant-garde. Nowadays, people watch it for the sake of Eisenstein's editing, then discover that his electrifying, endlessly imitated technique can't easily be separated from its message.

The Man with a Movie Camera. **1929.**

Directed by Dziga Vertov. If classic Marxism had at its heart a faith in the creative power of working people, coupled with an optimism about the new technology in their hands, then *The Man with a Movie Camera* is the classic Marxist thrill ride. Dynamic, inventive, mind-boggling and eye-popping, this masterpiece of nonfiction filmmaking is cinema's greatest celebration of city life and industrial production—including the heroic production of movies.

Gold Diggers of 1933. **1933.**

Directed by Mervyn LeRoy. Outstanding musical entertainment from the director and studio that brought you *I Am a Fugitive from a Chain Gang.* A story about backstage workers' solidarity meshes perfectly with Busby Berkeley's choreography, which recognizes no differences in the rhythms of industrial production and sex. The climax: an all-singing, all-dancing phantasmagoria of Depression-era joblessness, "Remember My Forgotten Man."

Fury. **1936.**

Directed by Fritz Lang. After fleeing Nazi Germany, where Goebbels had given him the unwanted opportunity to oversee the Reich's film production, Fritz Lang began his Hollywood career with a picture about a subject he understood: blind hatred and mob violence. It took a great immigrant director to make the first studio movie dramatizing America's culture of lynching—even though the mob's victim, played by Spencer Tracy, had to be a white man.

The Crime of Monsieur Lange. **1936.**

Directed by Jean Renoir. The crime is murder, the victim is the boss and the unofficial verdict is "not guilty" in this delightful comedy of worker empowerment, set in a pulp-fiction publishing house in Paris. The supreme master of French filmmakers, Jean Renoir, collaborated with the so-called October Group collective to make this masterpiece of European Popular Front culture.

Modern Times. **1936.**

Directed by Charles Chaplin. The world's most famous movie star, if not simply the most famous man in the world, responded to the Depression by refashioning his Little Tramp. No longer just a plucky wanderer who picked up odd jobs in restaurants or the circus, or who drifted into the army or to the Alaskan gold fields, the Little Tramp now became a machine-tending member of the industrial proletariat—in other words, eventually unemployed and subject to arrest.

The Grapes of Wrath. **1940.**

Directed by John Ford. Many people have applied seven- and twelve-letter epithets to John Ford, but no one ever called him a man of the Left. Nevertheless, the films of this bullying, sentimental, paternalistic, magniloquent, intermittently racist boozer are the epitome of classic American moviemaking—and among the highest peaks is this, the archetypal story of struggling, displaced families in the Great Depression.

Citizen Kane. **1941.**

Directed by Orson Welles. Perpetually in contention for the title of greatest film of all time, *Citizen Kane* is also the undisputed pinnacle of American Popular Front culture—a rousing review of contemporary public affairs not unlike the Federal Theatre Project's Living Newspaper. The difference: *Kane* brilliantly uses the resources of one mass medium, film, to challenge the masters of another. Its targets are press barons who opposed the New Deal—not only William Randolph Hearst but also Colonel Robert McCormick of Welles's hometown paper, the *Chicago Tribune*.

The Bicycle Thief. 1948.

Directed by Vittorio De Sica. Not just a movie but the rallying point for a movement, *The Bicycle Thief* astonished and exhilarated contemporary viewers by seeming to eliminate actors, sets and plot contrivances and show reality itself. Of course this wasn't true. De Sica prepared meticulously, and his screenwriter, Cesare Zavattini, was almost too elegantly crafty. But the impulse was there: to strip away affectation and focus on the problems of ordinary, contemporary life. Filmmakers everywhere are feeling the effects to this day.

The Day the Earth Stood Still. 1951.

Directed by Robert Wise. Antiwar activists from outer space warn earthlings to be careful with those nuclear weapons—or else! When the Cold War was at its hottest, and the blacklisting of filmmakers at its most intense, Robert Wise still managed to protest the arms race in the guise of a science fiction thriller. Sam Jaffe, though recently accused of Communist sympathies by *Red Channels,* nevertheless escaped blacklisting to portray the smartest man in the world.

Salt of the Earth. 1954.

Directed by Herbert J. Biberman. Everything that people said about *The Bicycle Thief* is actually true of this dramatic feature, which tells the story of Latino workers on strike in the Southwest. The locations are authentic; the actors are mostly nonprofessionals, playing people much like themselves; the situations are real. The filmmakers—blacklisted Communists—overcame intense opposition to complete the picture, the most moving and credible that any of them had done.

Johnny Guitar. 1954.

Directed by Nicholas Ray. Because a steely, imperious Joan Crawford faces off against the furious Mercedes McCambridge, *Johnny Guitar* has become known as a pathbreaking feminist Western. But it is also an allegory of the blacklist, in which demands for incriminating testimony are focused on the title character, played by Sterling Hayden, an actor who had named names before HUAC. An entire generation of cinephiles used this film, and Nicholas Ray, to argue that genre movies could becomes vehicles of individual expression.

Vidas Secas. 1963.

Directed by Nelson Pereira dos Santos. A defining work of the Cinema Novo movement, and therefore crucial for a generation of Latin American filmmakers, *Vidas Secas* was Pereira dos Santos's adaptation of a novel about peasants struggling against landowners in the parched northeast of Brazil. The film is uncompromising in portraying poverty, unblinking in registering the landscape's harsh light, uncanny in conveying the inner lives of its inarticulate people.

Dr. Strangelove, or: How I Learned to Stop Worrying and Love the Bomb. 1964.

Directed by Stanley Kubrick. Only months after the Cuban missile crisis, Kubrick and screenwriters Terry Southern and Peter George sprang on the world a gloriously dirty-minded, gleefully morbid picture about bumbling political leaders and blustering generals taking the whole planet to doomsday. The fact that half these people were Peter Sellers made the madness seem that much more inescapable.

Point of Order. 1964.

Directed by Emile de Antonio. One of the earliest and most influential examples of the clip documentary, *Point of Order* created a damning portrait of Senator Joseph McCarthy in the most coolly effective way possible: by putting together actual footage of the man without commentary. Artfully reassembled from television coverage of the Army-McCarthy hearings, the footage reawakened alarming recent memories, yet seemed to emerge from a strange, distant era.

Memories of Underdevelopment. 1968.

Directed by Tomás Gutiérrez Alea. When Castro took power, Havana had one of the world's most vibrant moviegoing cultures; but film production was nil, and beyond the cities people rarely got to see a movie. Could anyone make a work with integrity in this situation, responding to the imperatives of art, of an impossibly divided audience and of the revolution? Gutiérrez Alea did, with droll brilliance, taking this very dilemma as his theme.

High School. 1968.

Directed by Frederick Wiseman. Although it was his scandalous, banned *Titicut Follies* (1967) that made Wiseman famous, his great career arguably began with his second film, an institutional portrait of a school in Philadelphia. There is no editorializing: just broadness of vision, density of detail, a palpable sense of time and an unobtrusive structuring of events. But out of this emerges an indictment of a system of public education that is deadening, and even deadly.

Burn! 1969.

Directed by Gillo Pontecorvo. Not half as famous as Pontecorvo's *The Battle of Algiers,* and arguably not half as good, *Burn!* nevertheless has the distinction of being the only costume drama made during the Vietnam War era to lay out a coherent analysis of colonialism. With lace at his throat, Marlon Brando tells his horse to "Giddyap, you fool," then goes back to scheming: overturning the feudalists on a Caribbean sugar island, installing commerce-friendly liberals, then putting down the freed workers when they get too troublesome.

Sweet Sweetback's Baadasssss Song. 1971.

Directed by Melvin Van Peebles. Its visual style is lurid, its dramaturgy outrageous and its sexual politics verged on the unforgivable even in 1971, but *Sweet Sweetback* remains a milestone, not only in the history of African-American cinema but in independent filmmaking as a whole. Whatever its faults, it

still has the greatest of all redeeming features for a movie: it pops off the screen.

The Resolution. 1972.

Directed by Judit Ember and Gyula Gazdag. Essential viewing for all Western leftists, this documentary from Hungary was never released in the United States and is not generally available on video, so people who want to be honest in their politics will have to make an effort to find it: a rare, remarkable and damning record of Communist Party practice, which is all the more devastating for being about the handling of a petty matter in a small town.

Soylent Green. 1973.

Directed by Richard Fleischer. A dystopian vision of the future, an environmentalist polemic and a tender story of the love between Charlton Heston and Edward G. Robinson, *Soylent Green* is above all one of the screen's most corrosive satires about corporate power. Death can be a blessed release in the world of this film, but feeding yourself is a horror.

Hearts and Minds. 1974.

Directed by Peter Davis. Made while the Vietnam War was still raging, Davis's documentary is a three-part wonder. It captures the actions and attitudes of soldiers in the field (and in the Saigon brothels), provides a lucid narrative history of the conflict and explores a specifically American form of enthusiasm for busting heads. Amazingly, it does all these things well, and at the same time.

Xala. 1975.

Directed by Ousmane Sembene. Novelist, dockworker and Communist militant, Ousmane Sembene turned to filmmaking in order to reach the widest possible audience in his native Senegal, and in so doing became the father of African cinema. *Xala* was one of his earliest features and is one of the most invigorating: a harsh, vivid satire about corruption and paternalism among Africa's new class of native rulers.

Jeanne Dielman, 23 Quai du Commerce, 1080 Bruxelles. 1976.

Directed by Chantal Akerman. The crucial masterpiece for feminist filmmakers and theorists everywhere, *Jeanne Dielman* was also a key work in the development of a new international style of observational filmmaking. Using long, distanced, meticulously detailed takes, Akerman slowly built a portrait of her protagonist (played by the incomparable Delphine Seyrig) and her cramped, drab, parsimonious, utterly typical world.

Harlan County U.S.A. 1976.

Directed by Barbara Kopple. Documentarians who go into the field (rather than work in the editing room) need persistence and courage—and no one ever had more of those qualities than Kopple and her crew. While making this revelatory film about a 1973 coal miners' strike, they not only recorded attacks by armed goons but also were beaten up and shot at themselves. It's a mark of Kopple's integrity that her encounter with a shotgun is only a small part of this very big picture.

Insiang. 1976.

Directed by Lino Brocka. As direct as a punch to the stomach—or a knife to the throat, as in the slaughterhouse scene that opens the film—*Insiang* is a tale of duplicity, rape and revenge, set in the garbage-choked slums of Manila. Unseen in the background, yet always palpable, is a regime that fosters such brutality. *Insiang* is not the most politically explicit film by Brocka—a brave opponent of the Marcos dictatorship—but it ranks as one of his strongest.

A Grin Without a Cat (Le Fond de l'air est rouge). 1977.

Directed by Chris Marker. If you want to know the global meaning of the year 1968, there is no better guide than Chris Marker. Collecting, mixing, analyzing and interrogating a world's worth of documentary footage—from the years leading up to the great date to those dribbling after it—Marker assembles a history of the Left that might be called comprehensive if it weren't also so brilliantly teasing.

Man of Marble (1977) and Man of Iron (1981).

Directed by Andrzej Wajda. These twin fiction films, made immediately before and after the founding of Poland's Solidarity movement, are invaluable both as historical drama and as history itself. Spanning the years from the 1950s to the strike at the Gdansk shipyards, they explored the image and the reality of Polish workers' lives, contrasted propaganda with honest filmmaking and played a role of their own in the fitful demise of Soviet authority.

Born in Flames. 1983.

Directed by Lizzie Borden. Soon after Chantal Akerman, in Belgium, gave feminism the gift of her observational cinema, Lizzie Borden in the United States burst out with a quick-cut, rock-and-roll feminist action thriller. Women in New York are banding together in bicycle brigades, guerrilla radio stations, commando units. Many still hold firm to nonviolence; but by the end of the movie, something's got to go boom.

High Hopes. 1988.

Directed by Mike Leigh. A visit to Marx's grave is one of many lovely diversions in *High Hopes,* Mike Leigh's free-flowing dramatic excursion through London in the cold winter of Thatcherism. A scuffling left-wing couple tries to hold on to what's left of their spirits as the sleek and ambitious celebrate themselves. Meanwhile, a sweet, lost soul comes wandering through, looking as wonder struck and heartbroken as the movie itself.

Riff-Raff. 1990.

Directed by Ken Loach. The most consistently and explicitly political of the filmmakers who trained in British television, Ken Loach teamed up with screenwriter Bill Jesse to make this ensemble film about construction workers on a London building site. While risking their necks to renovate vintage housing stock for the wealthy, the workers themselves live in squats and use crowbars as their door keys. Their lives are tough; but their garrulous camaraderie—perfectly captured by Jesse, who was himself a construction worker—often gives *Riff-Raff* a buoyant, comic tone.

Hoop Dreams. 1994.

Directed by Steve James. Made by three white guys from Chicago from a screenplay by God, *Hoop Dreams* is a monumental documentary about two African-American high school kids, their families, their neighborhoods and the society that offers few hopes or rewards to these young men outside the context of their striving to play basketball. This is documentary filmmaking at its deepest—and, given the reversals in the subjects' lives, at its most astonishing, too.

Lamerica. 1994.

Directed by Gianni Amelio. Impeccably controlled in style, yet as wrenching as any classic neorealist film, *Lamerica* is a road movie from hell, a buddy picture for the insane. It is also a thorough, responsible, semidocumentary report on the migration of masses of people through post-Communist Europe. An up-to-date, predatory capitalist comes from Italy to the ruins of Hoxha's Albania, intending to skim as much as he can, but soon finds himself sharing the fate of his prey.

Life Is to Whistle. 1998.

Directed by Fernando Pérez. An enthusiastic young woman from the United States comes to Havana and meets a scuffling, disillusioned son of the revolution, under the watchful eyes of a young Saint Barbara. Meanwhile, beautiful women are abandoning love, and people are fainting dead at the sound of certain words, such as "truth." Poetic, fanciful and deeply mournful, Pérez's beautiful film is both a love song to Cuba and an elegy for a generation's hopes.

The Music Scene

ROOTS

The Arhoolie Foundation. The foundation, whose mission is to "document, present, and disseminate authentic traditional and regional vernacular music," is directly descended from Arhoolie Records, a folk label started in 1960. (The name comes from Mississippi vernacular for a field holler.) Arhoolie specialized in recording a broad array of regional musical genres—blues, roots and country mainly (but reflective of a number of distinct dialects within those broad categories, such as Mississippi Delta, Texas, Southern, etc.), Cajun, zydeco, gospel, Native American, jazz, Tejano, world music. In 1995 Chris Strachwitz set up the Arhoolie Foundation to educate the public about roots music. Its assignments include issuing relevant books and pamphlets, collecting memorabilia and maintaining an archive for scholars and the general public.

10341 San Pablo Avenue, El Cerrito, CA 94530, (510) 525-7471, www.arhoolie.com/arhoolie_foundation

Old Town School of Folk Music. Folk musician Win Stracke, a friend of Studs Terkel and veteran of the labor movement, along with Frank Hamilton, founded the Old Town School in December 1957 to encourage "the study of folk music and folk instruments." Along with guitar and banjo classes, folk dances and sing-alongs, Old Town staged concerts by Pete Seeger, Mahalia Jackson, Big Bill Broonzy, Josh White and other artists of top stature. In the early 1990s, Chicago recognized the school's cultural significance, giving it new quarters and $2.2 million toward renovations. Now in two facilities (plus some smaller venues around the city), the school teaches 6,600 students per week, more than one third of whom are children. It also organizes performances featuring touring stars, Chicago artists and talented staff and students; it holds free concerts on most Wednesday nights. Branches of the Different Strummer music store opened at each of the school's two locations, offer a big selection of guitars, banjos, mandolins, violins, ukuleles and other traditional stringed instruments, as well as more exotic instruments like ouds, charangos, djembes and darbukas, sitars, vihuelas and many others.

4454 N. Lincoln Avenue, Chicago, IL 60625; 909 W. Armitage Avenue, Chicago, IL 60614; www.oldtownschool.org

Smithsonian Folkways. Folkways Records, the legendary company founded by Moses Asch in 1948 to document authentic folk music, was acquired by the Smithsonian Institution Center for Folklife and Cultural Heritage in 1987. Asch's heirs stipulated that the Smithsonian keep the label's entire catalog in print in perpetuity. So eclectic was Asch's taste that the Folkways catalog reads like a history of American folk music celebrating singers from Woody Guthrie and Brownie McGhee to Cisco Houston and Texas Gladden. There is also world music, including arcane titles like *Bedouin Music of Southern Sinai*, *Temiar Dream Songs from Malaya* and *Lappish Joik Songs from Northern Norway*. Smithsonian director anthropologist Anthony Seeger strove to preserve this heritage in digital format.

600 Maryland Avenue SW, Suite 2001, Washington, DC 20024, (888) 365-5299, (202) 633-6450, www.folkways.si.edu/

RECORD LABELS

Alternative Tentacles. This label was founded in 1979 by Dead Kennedys' frontman Jello Biafra to produce the band's debut single, "California Über Alles," an irony-rich attack on Governor Jerry Brown. Since then, Alternative Tentacles' four-person staff has produced some 350 albums and provided a home for a diverse group of nonmainstream musicians, punk and otherwise. Biafra, the self-described "absentee thoughtlord" of the company, has been an outspoken lefty and political provocateur since the early days of the Dead Kennedys. In 1979 he ran for mayor of San Francisco against Dianne Feinstein, coming in fourth out of ten candidates. He stumped for the Green Party presidential nomination in 2000 with death row inmate Mumia Abu-Jamal as his running mate, dropping out to support Ralph Nader. He remains an active Green, telling *The Progressive* in 2002 that he wants to "bring the spirit of punk rock and roll into the Greens—make the party rock." He has been a loud supporter of First Amendment rights for decades, going to court in 1987 to fight a ban on a Dead Kennedys' album on the ground that it constituted "distribution of harmful matter to minors," i.e., an accompanying poster with pictures of penises. He vociferously opposed Tipper Gore's campaign to require parental advisory labels on album covers.

PO Box 419092, San Francisco, CA 94141, (510) 596-8981, www.alternativetentacles.com

AK Press Audio. The audio wing of the worker-run anarchist independent publisher AK Press (see page 34) offers a smorgasbord of radical recordings: audio versions of AK Press books; old Phil Ochs, Woody Guthrie and Pete Seeger albums; lectures by Howard Zinn, Noam Chomsky and Arundhati Roy; audio pamphlets like *When Fucking the System Isn't Enough,* by Ramsey Kanaan (on anarchist and community organizing in Edinburgh); *Al Gore: A User's Manual,* a scathing critique by Alexander Cockburn; *Emma Goldman—The American Years* and *Colonialism, Imperialism and Globalization*; anarcho-punk compilation albums; songs from the Spanish Civil War and the Lincoln Brigade; Bertolt Brecht songs and so on. First-stop shopping for those out to upend the system.

674-A 23rd Street, Oakland, CA 94612, (510) 208-1700, www.akpress.org

Earthology Records. Based on an organic farm in northern Minnesota, Earthology is the self-created label of indie band Cloud Cult and bandleader Craig Minowa. They call themselves a record-company-cum-activist organization and are dedicated to influencing the music industry "into operating in an ecologically sustainable manner." Earthology claims to be "the only nonprofit Record Company in existence to offer environmentally and socially friendly CD replication services at reduced rates for struggling artists"; and also "100% recycled/reclaimed jewel cases" and biodegradable shrink wrap for its CDs; "the highest recycled content papers on the market, with nontoxic soy inks," for its album covers and inserts. It even packs CDs in dried leaves for shipping instead of bubble wrap or Styrofoam. Earthology's studio is located on an organic herb and vegetable farm with a geothermal heating and cooling system, and electricity via wind power. According to Minowa, the band's name, Cloud Cult, derives from a Hopi word connoting a sustainable and harmonious human relationship with the planet.

46970 Tenquist Lane, Hinckley, MN 55037, (320) 237-0432, www.earthology.net

Empowerment Records. Empowerment Records is an offshoot of Project: Think Different, a Boston-based nonprofit that aims to use music, film and video to stimulate change. The label's founder and president Scherazade Daruvalla King says the project stemmed from her frustration with the mostly misogynistic, negative and boring messages spewed by the media. She's bent on reaching people with positive examples of social change, such as a 2006 mixtape called *Empowerment: The Power to Break You Free*, in which Boston-area hip-hop stars rap about the dreary state of commercial music and the entertainment industry.

18 Wenham Street, Boston, MA 02130, (617) 320-6433, www.empowermentrecords.com

Guerilla Funk Recordings. This hip-hop label belongs to the outspokenly political rapper-stockbroker-independent–record producer Paris. He launched it post–September 11, 2001, as a response to the increasingly repressive political climate. Also, Paris was angry because no other label would take *Sonic Jihad*, an album on which, according to Paris, "We were indicting the Bush administration's involvement with September 11," which may or may not be a recommendation, depending on which 9/11 conspiracy you believe in. Since then, Paris has produced music by political hip-hop artists like Public Enemy, Dead Prez, Immortal Technique and The Coup. Paris is committed to loosening "the corporate stranglehold of censorship" in music.

PO Box 2317, Danville, CA 94526, www.guerillafunk.com

Hard Knock Records. This Oakland-based label, which features hip-hop artists from the yeasty Bay Area underground scene, got its start in 2003 with the album *What About Us?* a musical outcry against the war in Iraq, emphasizing its effects on poor and minority communities. The label is an offshoot of *Hard Knock Radio*, the hip-hop talk show on Pacifica Radio, hosted by Davey D, a politically outspoken journalist, critic and community activist. In advance of the 2004 election, Hard Knock Records released *Slam Bush: The Official Mixtape*, featuring twenty-nine relentlessly anti-Bush tracks. As rapper Huff put it at the time, "Sending Bush home to Texas is the least Hip Hop Nation could do."

www.hardknockrecords.com

Righteous Babe Records. This independent record label was started by the folkie and activist musician Ani DiFranco in her hometown of Buffalo, New York. It is housed in an old Gothic Revival church that DiFranco bought, restored and turned into a concert hall, arts center and cultural venue ("The Church"), as part of the broader mission to revitalize the city's decaying downtown area and provide an anchor for the local artistic community. Righteous Babe generally records music that is in harmony with DiFranco's taste for politically or socially conscious folk or indie rock.

341 Delaware Avenue, Buffalo, NY 14202, www.righteousbabe.com

Riot-Folk. Riot-Folk reflects the combined enterprise of eight politically minded folk music acts (Adhamh Roland, Brenna Sahatjian, Evan Greer, Kate Boverman and Ethan Miller, Mark Gunnery, Ryan Harvey, Shannon Murray and Tom Frampton), who came together in 2004 to form a "radical music collective" with the goal of sharing resources, funds, equipment and tour gigs. As the group's website defiantly proclaims: "Riot-Folk was founded as and remains an anti-profit music collective working from the principles of anti-oppression and anti-capitalism. We do not wish to capitalize on our music, but use it as a tool or weapon against capitalism." Riot on, folks. They travel and perform together as a band, keeping separate identities like circus performers and earning money by making CDs on their own label. Shared profits, sliding scale prices for CDs, free downloads and uncopyrighted songs are the ways the groups tries to socialize its music. The website sells CDs, enables MP3 downloads, provides tour information, profiles members of Riot-Folk and disseminates news of the collective.

c/o Ethan Miller, 217 South Mountain Road, Green, ME 04236, www.riotfolk.org

The RPM Challenge. The RPM (Record Production Month) Challenge combines an independent, D.I.Y., anticorporate aesthetic with a time-tested artistic exercise meant to get aspiring musicians over the hump. The concept is simple: participants must record an album in one month (and that month February!) using whatever recording devices they have on hand. As the RPM website puts it, "Do your best. Use the limitations of time and gear as an opportunity to explore things you might not try otherwise." In 2006, the first year the challenge was held, 165 bands were able to meet the one-month deadline, writing more than 1,600 songs in all forms from rock and roll to jazz to soundtracks for children's books. In 2007, there were more than 600 submissions from around the country and globe. There are no winners in the challenge; the point is to nurture a creative community that thrives on the interchange of ideas. Submissions are posted on the website, and listening parties are organized after the challenge is over.

10 Vaughan Mall, Suite 1, Portsmouth, NH 03801, (603) 427-0403, www.rpmchallenge.com

THE CLUB SCENE

Mutual Musicians Foundation. Originally home to the Black Musicians Protective Union, Local 627 of the American Federation of Musicians, the foundation is strategically located in the 18th and Vine district, the heart of Kansas City's storied jazz tradition that flowered in the 1930s and 1940s with touring greats like Count Basie and Charlie Parker. A rehearsal space by day, the club became famous for its late-night/early-morning jam sessions on Fridays and Saturdays, at which local stars and visiting big-time jazz musicians would play. Though the club had no liquor license, the after-hours action was tolerated and went on for decades. Then, late one night in September 2006, the unthinkable happened. Two vice squad detectives showed up and politely informed club manager Betty Crow that this was an, uh, raid, ma'am, and she needed to stop serving alcohol without a license. The foundation was caught in a double bind. Since the law had announced it would no longer look the other way, the club couldn't continue to host the after-hours action. But neither could it do so if it applied for a license because liquor regulations commanded a 1:30 A.M. curfew. Fortunately, jazz buffs raised a row, and in May 2007 the state legislature passed a bill allowing the Mutual Musicians Foundation to serve alcohol until 6 A.M. So once again they were operating on musicians' rather than squares' time.

1823 Highland Avenue, Kansas City, MO 64108, (816) 471-5212, www.thefoundationjamson.org

Tipitina's. This neighborhood joint started jumping in 1977 as a place where New Orleans rhythm and blues pianist Professor Longhair could play out his later years (the club's name is the title of one of Longhair's best-known songs). More than a quarter century later, it has expanded into a 1,000-seat auditorium, recording studio and record label. The place features both local artists and major national musical acts and is cherished as an important New Orleans cultural institution—an honor it tries to live up to. In 1997, the Tipitina's Foundation was established, and began organizing benefit concerts like Injuns A Comin' and Instruments A Comin' to raise money for the Mardi Gras Indian Council and to purchase instruments for two high school bands, respectively, and providing rehearsal space as well as business equipment and services for local bands. After the hurricanes in 2005, the Tipitina's Foundation and the club began playing an even more central role in the rejuvenation of the New Orleans music scene. Drawing on profits from the club, fund-raisers and donations, the foundation supports local musicians, providing everything from housing and clothing to legal and accounting services and instruments. It donated $500,000 worth of instruments to eleven high schools on the one-year anniversary of Katrina. Tipitina's offers free Sunday afternoon workshops to students, giving them an opportunity to watch and sit in with professional musicians.

501 Napoleon Avenue, New Orleans, LA 70115, (504) 895-TIPS, www.tipitinas.com, www.tipitinasfoundation.org

Cain's Ballroom is a legendary music venue in Tulsa. It was built in 1924 to serve as a garage for one of Tulsa's founders, then was named Cain's Dance Academy in 1930 and dance lessons were given for ten cents an hour. The academy was the site of the Texas Playboys' first regular radio broadcast; they continued to play there regularly. In 1976

Larry Schaeffer purchased the building, refurbished it and reopened it as Cain's Ballroom. In 1978, it was one of a few venues to host the Sex Pistols in their first American tour. Cain's Ballroom was listed in the National Register of Historic Places on September 4, 2003. Cain's has experienced an impressive increase in bookings of cross-genre hubbin' and has housed a vast array of our modern age of musical subversion and experimentation artists. It's also become a hospitable venue for progressive political events.

423 N. Main Street, Tulsa, OK 74103, (918) 584-2306, www.cainsballroom.com

RAISE YOUR VOICES!

Fisk Jubilee Singers. Fisk University opened its doors in 1866 as the first American university to offer a liberal arts education to "young men and women irrespective of color." With little capital behind it the school was soon in financial straits, but hard times made the idealists in charge buckle down to practicalities, such as thinking up ways to raise money. One idea was to form an all-black, nine-member choral ensemble made up of students (all but two of the original members were former slaves) that would tour and return the proceeds to the university. The Jubilee Singers, as they came to be called, were among the first real black musicians (as opposed to white minstrels in blackface) to gain support from white audiences. Their repertoire consisted mainly of spirituals and slave songs, and their performances generated a wave of popular and critical jubilation. At the end of 1872, the Jubilee Singers performed at the White House for President Ulysses S. Grant; the following year they toured Europe. The funds they raised went to the construction of the first permanent building on the Fisk campus, Jubilee Hall, which was named a National Historic Landmark in 1975. In their long history, the Jubilee Singers have performed at the United Nations, the Kennedy Center and the Smithsonian, as well as the funerals of Al Gore, Sr., and Johnny Cash.

Fisk University, 1000 17th Avenue N., Nashville, TN 37208, (615) 329-8744,
www.fiskjubileesingers.org

Fruit of Labor Singing Ensemble. As the cultural arm of Black Workers for Justice, which was founded in 1981 to fight for worker rights and social justice for black people in North Carolina and throughout the South, the Fruit of Labor Singing Ensemble devotes itself to performing for and raising money for a wide range of workers' causes. Songs the group has created include "The Story of Shiloh," which celebrates an African-American community near the Durham Research Triangle Park that fought "toxic terrorism"; "Organize, Organize, Organize," an inspirational solidarity anthem; "Never Again," a tribute to the twenty-five workers killed in a 1991 fire at a poultry plant in rural North Carolina. The ensemble is composed of up to a dozen voices; the core consists of Nathanette Mayo, her husband, Anganza Lauginghouse, and fellow activist Rick Scott. The group is headquartered in a combination library, civic center and church fellowship hall.

Fruit of Labor World Cultural Center, PO Box 5574, Raleigh, NC 27650, (919) 876-7187, www.fruitoflabor.org

New York City Labor Chorus. If you've spent any time on a picket line, at a labor demo or a union rally in New York City since 1991, chances are you've heard the New York City Labor Chorus. With seventy-five members from more than twenty local unions and district councils, the chorus promotes union solidarity by singing the grand old anthems of social justice. They join "the power and culture of union music with the great gospel, jazz, classical and folk traditions." The singers have performed at Carnegie Hall as part of a 1998 tribute to Paul Robeson and on the picket line with striking NYU grad students. They sang at a 2006 ceremony hosted by UNITE, commemorating those who died in the Triangle Shirtwaist Fire (see page 12), and all over the world. The chorus is available for union conventions, rallies and shop steward meetings, as well as community, church, college and school events. The ensemble's leader is Peter Schlosser, a former conductor of the Jewish People's Philharmonic Chorus and a professor at the CUNY Center for Worker Education.

275 7th Avenue, 18th floor, New York, NY 10001, (212) 929-3232, www.nyclc.org

FESTIVALS

The HONK! Festival. If you're a honk band (or a fan of this unique folk art form) your destination of choice next Columbus Day weekend should be Davis Square in Somerville, Massachusetts. That's when an eclectic group of street musicians from around the country will converge on the small city to give public performances. What's a honk band? We'll defer to the festival website: "a new type of street band. . . . Acoustic and mobile, borrowing repertoire and inspiration from a diverse set of folk music traditions—New Orleans second line brass bands, European Klezmer, Balkan and Romani (Gypsy) music, Brazilian Afro Bloc and Frevo traditions, as well as the passion and spirit of Mardi Gras and Carnivale—these 'honkers' all share a commitment to several core principles. Metaphorically speaking, they honk their horns for the same reasons motorists honk theirs: to arouse fellow travelers, to warn of danger, to celebrate milestones, and to just plain have fun." Honk groups go by names like the Leftist Marching Band, the Revolutionary Snake Ensemble, the Hungry March Band, Environmental Encroachment and the Brass Liberation Orchestra. The inaugural 2006 Honk Festival featured 150 musicians in twelve bands. They parade with dancers, stiltwalkers, jugglers and other motley folk. The festival has become a regular part of the lively Davis Square scene.

Davis Square, Somerville, MA, www.honkfest.org

MUSICAL ACTION COMMITTEES

Hip Hop Caucus and Hip Hop Caucus Institute. The Hip Hop Caucus was set up to coordinate political action by progressives within the hip-hop community. Its parallel body, the Hip Hop Caucus Institute, formulates an agenda for these communities. The caucus, a nonpartisan, nonprofit political education organization founded on September 11, 2004, sees itself as a "grassroots movement institution for the Hip Hop generation." The institute provides research and policy thinking to guide the caucus and maintains links to the grass roots, the hip-hop community, scholars and elected officials. The Institute for Policy Studies sponsors the Hip Hop Caucus Institute, which has organized: **the Hip Hop Vote 2008 program,** which tries to inspire more political participation by the "Hip Hop generation" (the cohort born after 1964); **Gulf Coast Renewal Campaign (GCRC),** an ad hoc coalition of organizations and individuals "fighting for the rights of those displaced by Hurricane Katrina"; **Hip Hop Helping the Homeless,** which encourages young people to participate in campaigns against hunger and homelessness; **Southern Progressive Leadership Conference,** which coordinates and facilitates connections among young leaders throughout the country who are organizing in their own communities for racial, social and economic justice; **Cities for Progress,** a joint project of the Institute for Policy Studies (see page 199) and the Hip Hop Caucus Institute.

1112 16th Street NW, Suite 600, Washington, DC 20036, (202) 787-5256, www.hiphopcaucus.org

Music Row Democrats. Music Row Democrats, born in Nashville in late 2003, was the creation of a group of Nashville music industry bigs who were bent on countering the stereotype that country music people were all Okies from Muskogee like the Merle

PROTEST ON MUSIC ROW

James McMurtry, son of the novelist Larry McMurtry and a successful Nashville song-writer, wrote in *Billboard* in 2006: "Sadly, most of us so-called artists are afraid to use our voices, afraid to take a stand for fear of committing career suicide. We have to get over that fear, because in succumbing to it we become invisible, and invisibility, for an artist, is true career death. We cannot please everybody, and we should not bother trying. It is not our job to be loved. It is our job to be remembered." Music Row Democrats started a campaign to encourage political country songs with the slogan "Use your own voice." Many artists responded with the following songs and messages:

Nanci Griffith, "Big Blue Ball of War" (If women were in charge wars wouldn't happen)

Darrell Scott, "Goodle, U.S.A." ("Joe McCarthy is our acting president")

Ed Pettersen, "Gather the Family 'Round" (Power to the people)

Scott B. Bomar, "Two Paper Town" (Anti–media monopolies)

Honky Tonkers for Truth, "I'm Takin' My Country Back" (Singing the Music Row Democrats party line on the budget, the war, exporting jobs and so on)

Monkey Bowl, "Al Gore" (How Al wuz robbed in 2000)

James McMurtry, "We Can't Make It Here" (America's social ills starkly stated against ominous background music)

Tim O'Brien, "Republican Blues" ("Vote away those blues, Republican blues," the MRD theme song)

The Mavericks, "I Want to Know" (Why do Republicans lie—and when have you had enough?)

Beth Nielsen Chapman, "Yes Sir, No Sir" (Covering inner-city poverty, poisoned environment, global warming)

Derek Webb, "Rich Young Ruler" (Our faith-based president gives to the rich and takes from the poor)

Bobby Braddock, "Thou Shalt Not Kill" (Abortion versus wartime killing and poisoning the environment)

Sean Locke, "Just an Old Soldier" (War is hell)

Todd Snider, "Conservative Christian Right-Wing Republican Straight White American Male" (Satire of religious Right beliefs)

Dan Tyler, "Left Wing, Right Wing" (The eagle needs two wings to fly)

Shawn Camp, "You Let the Fox Run the Henhouse" (Spoof of a prez "with a bushy tail")

Matt King, "Before It's Gone" ("The poor go to prison and the rich ones walk")

Haggard song. Many were Democrats well before Haggard switched in 2007 and wrote "Hillary," a tribute to the senator. By 2007 MRD's ranks had swelled to 1,500 members—producers, songwriters, musicians, managers, agents, promoters, publicists, video directors and producers, editors and journalists. The organization supported John Kerry's presidential campaign in 2004 by launching a "Kerry-oke" fund-raising initiative that enlisted big-time Nashville country musicians. The MRD jumped into the 2006 congressional election with both feet, and during the long run-up to the 2008 presidential campaign it released a compilation of country songs critical of the Bush administration and the war.

900 Division Street, Nashville, TN 37203, www.musicrowdemocrats.com

WOBBLY ANTHEMS

The Big Red Songbook. The Industrial Workers of the World was by far the most fertile source of proletarian anthems of its day. Starting in 1909, the songs that members like Joe Hill, Ralph Chaplin, Jane Street, T-Bone Slim and others, known or anonymous, wrote and set to popular melodies, were collected through many editions of the *Little Red Song Book.* In 2007 the Socialist publisher Charles H. Kerr issued *The Big Red Songbook,* a kind of All-Time Hit Parade of Wobbly Songs, containing the words to more than 250 of them, including classics like "Hallelujah I'm a Bum," "The Preacher and the Slave" ("Pie in the Sky") and "Solidarity Forever." Other lesser-known songs in the book often had their bygone day as rallying points in earlier struggles, or were resurrected and updated to energize modern strikes, civil rights protests or environmental actions. The book includes essays, analyses, recollections by the original songwriters and illustrations comprising Wobbly publications, posters, handbills, comic strips and other ephemera.

Chicago: Charles H. Kerr. 2007. $24. www.charleshkerr.net

EVERYBODY'S PROTEST SONG

The singer, songwriter and poet John Handcox gave as good a definition as any of the role of the protest song: "Singing to me is the most inspirational thing that you can do to organize labor. If you're making a speech, that's just you doing it. But when you get all of them singing, they have a different feeling. They have a feeling that they're part of what's going on."

ANTHEMS OF THE LEFT

EDITOR'S NOTE. *We wanted to publish a list of the Top Ten Protest Songs but couldn't agree on how to go about it. So we turned the thankless task over to Eric Alterman and Danny Goldberg. Alterman, a* Nation *columnist and professor of English and journalism at Brooklyn College, also wrote a book about Bruce Springsteen. Goldberg is a long-time record company executive and producer who wrote* Dispatches from the Culture Wars: How the Left Lost Teen Spirit. *They hammered out a Top Ten but included an even longer list of songs they disagreed on. In the great* Nation *magazine tradition of inclusion, we include them as well. If you don't agree with their list, draw up your personal ten best. In the next edition of this book we plan on publishing "The Ten Best Ten Best Protest Songs Lists."*

NOTE: *The Vietnam War generated great protest songs. The Iraq War songs you don't hear as much about.* —**EDITOR**

The Ten Anthems Upon Which Eric and Danny Agree

Patti Smith, "People Have the Power"

Marvin Gaye, "What's Going On?"

Bob Marley and the Wailers, "Get Up, Stand Up"

The Rascals, "People Got to Be Free"

Sam Cooke, "A Change Is Gonna Come"

U2, "Pride (In the Name of Love)"

Jefferson Airplane, "Volunteers"

Peter LaFarge, "The Ballad of Ira Hayes"

Jackson Browne, "Before the Deluge"

James Brown, "Say It Loud, I'm Black and I'm Proud"

Eric's Choices with Which Danny Does Not Agree

The Clash, "The Call Up"

Crosby, Stills, Nash and Young, "Chicago"

Pete Seeger, "Bring Them Home"

Bruce Springsteen, "The Promised Land"

The Special AKA, "Free Nelson Mandela"

Thunderclap Newman, "Something in the Air"

The Rolling Stones, "Salt of the Earth"

Gil Scott-Heron, "What's the Word?"

Bob Dylan, "Like a Rolling Stone"

Steve Van Zandt, "I Ain't Gonna Play Sun City"

Bobby Fuller Four, "I Fought the Law"

John Lennon, "Working Class Hero"

Jerry Jeff Walker, "Up Against the Wall, Redneck Mothers . . ."

Randy Newman, "Mr. President (Have Pity on the Working Man)"

Iris Dement, "Wasteland of the Free"

Jimmy Cliff, "The Harder They Come"

Pink Floyd, "Another Brick in the Wall, Part II"

Peter Gabriel, "Biko"

The Who, "Won't Get Fooled Again"

Sly and the Family Stone, "Stand!"

Creedence Clearwater Revival, "Fortunate Son"

Merle Haggard, "Okie from Muskogee"

Billie Holiday, "Strange Fruit"

Edwin Starr, "War"

The O'Jays, "Love Train"

Danny's Choices with Which Eric Does Not Agree

Billy Bragg, "There Is Power in a Union"

Country Joe and the Fish, "Feel Like I'm Fixin' to Die Rag"

Crosby, Stills, Nash and Young, "Ohio"

Dixie Chicks, "Not Ready to Make Nice"

John Lennon, "Power to the People"

The Clash, "London Calling"

Bob Dylan, "A Hard Rain's A-Gonna Fall"

Steve Earle, "Fuck the FCC"

Green Day, "American Idiot"

Nick Lowe, "(What's So Funny 'Bout) Peace, Love and Understanding?"

John Hall, "Power"

Gil Scott-Heron, "The Revolution Will Not Be Televised"

Michael Jackson and many others, "We Are the World"

John Lennon, "Give Peace a Chance"

Curtis Mayfield, "People Get Ready"

MC5, "Kick Out the Jams"

Midnight Oil, "Beds Are Burning"

Holly Near, "We Are Gentle, Angry People"

Phil Ochs, "I Ain't Marchin' Anymore"

Public Enemy, "Fight the Power"

Tom Robinson, "Glad to Be Gay"

Bruce Springsteen, "Born in the U.S.A."

Twisted Sister, "We're Not Gonna Take it"

Steve Van Zandt, "I Am a Patriot"

Neil Young, "Lookin' for a Leader"

Left Heritage Trail

BATTLES IN THE LABOR WARS

Homestead Strike. On July 5, 1892, two barge loads of Pinkerton detectives touched land near Pittsburgh on the south bank of the Monongahela River at the 400-acre Homestead Works of the gigantic Carnegie Steel Company. A crowd of locked-out workers fired back when the detectives fired at them. Nine strikers and five Pinkertons were killed in the exchange. The governor dispatched 8,000 state militia to Homestead, and the occupying strikers went home. It would be many years before the steelworkers had a union. The cause of labor suffered a further setback a few months later when anarchist Alexander Berkman, Emma Goldman's lover, attempted to assassinate Henry Frick.

Pullman Strike. George Pullman lowered wages at his sleeping car company by 33 to 50 percent but did not lower deductions for rent and so on at his company town near Chicago. On May 11, 1894, the Pullman workers

GREAT BATTLE OF HOMESTEAD.
Defeat and Capture of the
PINKERTON INVADERS
July 6th 1892.

struck, and the recently founded American Railway Union, led by Eugene V. Debs, joined them in boycotting trains with the sleeping cars. At its peak 260,000 workers were out. The railway corporations rallied behind Pullman through their General Managers Association, which was set up to destroy the ARU. In solidarity, President Cleveland sent in 2,000 federal troops and 5,000 marshals. With the power of the federal government, the press and the courts behind the owners, their leaders imprisoned and the AFL sitting it out, the railway workers were licked. Most strikers were fired under an industry-wide blacklist.

Lattimer Massacre. On September 10, 1897, 400 coal miners marched into this coal patch town in western Pennsylvania in a show of solidarity with the Lattimer miners. They were confronted by 150 heavily armed sheriffs. It's unclear who started shooting, but the miners turned and ran. The deputies continued firing at their backs, leaving nineteen miners dead and some thirty wounded.

Lattimer Massacre Monument, Route 940, Lattimer Mines, PA 18234

Paint Creek and Cabin Creek. Some of the deadliest organization fights in the struggle by coal miners to unionize took place in West Virginia during the teens

and twenties. In 1912 7,500 miners in the Paint and Cabin Creeks area in Kanahwa County walked out to protest the owners' refusal to raise their wages. The owners, in a preview of future tactics, hired detectives ("gun thugs") from the Baldwin-Felts Detective Agency to evict the strikers from company housing. The eighty-four-year-old, foulmouthed UMWA organizer Mary "Mother" Jones barreled in and tongue-lashed the men. They picked up their guns and battled the mine guards until the governor declared martial law, ending the unrest. Jones was tried by a military court and convicted of attempted murder and conspiracy to incite a riot.

Mingo and Logan Counties, West Virginia. After World War I, UMWA organizing accelerated in the coal-mining regions; mine owners (who ran the state) declared the southern part, including Mingo and Logan counties, off-limits to the union. Mine owners in Matewan locked out their men and imported a contingent of Baldwin-Felts operatives, led by Albert Felts, to evict them from company houses. On May 19, 1920, shooting broke out; Felts, his brother Lee and five other detectives were shot dead. Two miners and the mayor of Matewan were slain. Police chief Sid Hatfield was tried in the detective shootings; he'd sided with the miners. He was murdered at the courthouse, touching off a new miners' war. The mine security men and their civilian allies dug in at Blair Mountain, and 4,000 armed miners marched in to chase them. At least eighteen miners were killed in ensuing firefights and many detectives as well. President Harding sent in 2,200 troops with machine guns and air support, and the miner army headed for the hills. More than 900 miners were later indicted for conspiracy to commit murder and treason against the state. Most were acquitted for lack of evidence but a few were locked up, some for up to twenty years.

Matewan Memorial, Matewan, WV, (304) 426-4239, www. matewan.com. Blair Mountain Battle Site, Route 17 between Blair and Ethel, WV

Ludlow Massacre. During a 1914 strike of Colorado miners, a firefight broke out between miners and state militia at a tent city. The militia set the tents on fire, and two women and thirteen children hiding under a wooden floor were asphyxiated. John D. Rockefeller, Jr., who controlled one of the mining companies, drew bad press, forcing him to hire pioneering PR man Ivy Lee, to burnish his image.

Ludlow Massacre Memorial, between Walsenburg and Trinidad, three quarters of a mile west of I-25, Ludlow, CO

PENNSYLVANIA

Rachel Carson Homestead. The author of *Silent Spring* was born in 1907 and grew up in this old-fashioned farmhouse near Pittsburgh. With a view of the Allegheny River, the house sits amid suburbia but offers an organic garden stocked with native plants, a short nature trail and tours. Recently, conservatives have sought to discredit Carson's work in exposing the harm to wildlife and the environment caused by indiscriminate spraying of DDT. The charges simply reprise those made in the 1950s by chemical company flacks, blaming Carson for malaria deaths in the Third World, for example. Carson never called for a total ban on DDT, and it has been used to kill malaria-bearing mosquitoes to this day. Also, overuse of agricultural DDT resulted in some malaria mosquitoes developing immunity to it.

Rachel Carson Homestead, 613 Marion Avenue, Springdale, PA 15144, (724) 274-5459; www.rachelcarsonhomestead.org

St. Nicholas Croatian Catholic Church. Because of its powerful labor murals, this Pittsburgh church has been dubbed "the Sistine Chapel of the American working class." The Rev. Albert Zagar commissioned the Croatian-born artist Maximilian (Maxo) Vanka to paint twenty politically charged murals in the tiny Romanesque house of worship. The murals, painted between 1937 and 1947,

meld religious iconography with antiwar and anticapital-ism scenes illustrated in Croatian immigrants' lives. In one the Virgin Mary is separating two soldiers, fending off one's bayonet. In another a Croatian mother weeps over the body of her son, killed in a mining accident. Another mural shows a capitalist reading the stock tables while being waited on by black servants; a judge peers at scales on which a pile of gold outweighs a loaf of bread.

24 Maryland Avenue, Pittsburgh, PA 15209, (412) 821-3438, www.stnicholascroatian.com

DISTRICT OF COLUMBIA

Lincoln Memorial, the Mall, Washington Monument, Lafayette Park, Capitol steps, White House and other demonstration sites. "Congress shall make no law respecting . . . the right of the people peaceably to assemble, and to petition the government for a redress of grievances."

MARCHES ON WASHINGTON

APRIL 30, 1894: COXEY'S ARMY—Unemployed workers demanding jobs.

MARCH 3, 1913: VOTES FOR WOMEN—5,000 march to support women's suffrage.

JUNE 17, 1932: BONUS ARMY—Some 31,000 jobless World War I veterans and their families camp out in Washington while petitioning for advance payment of the bonus promised them after World War I.

AUGUST 28, 1963: MARCH ON WASHINGTON FOR JOBS AND FREEDOM—Led by the Rev. Martin Luther King and other civil rights movement figures, more than 250,000 march to the Mall.

APRIL 17, 1965: One of the first mass protest rallies against the Vietnam War sparked by Students for a Democratic Society—25,000 attend.

NOVEMBER 27, 1965: March against the Vietnam War.

Washington, D.C., has been my home for the better part of the last forty-five years. When I came here as a quivering thirty-year-old to join the administration of John F. Kennedy, I could never pass within the sight of the Capitol or the White House without gawking.

Now as a seventy-five-year-old who has experienced the Nixon, Reagan and Bush II presidencies, who remembers Eastland of Mississippi, Ellender of Louisiana, Talmadge of Georgia and Duke Cunningham and Robert Ney, formerly of the House of Representatives, and Jack Abramoff, formerly of K Street, I still look at iconic Washington with a substantial dollop of awe in my soul.

I don't see the buildings and monuments as symbols of civics-book democracy but rather of the stumbling efforts of a substantial number of decent human beings to govern themselves honorably. I remember great moments, of course—the Cuban Missile Crisis, managed brilliantly out of the White House while all of the chips were on the table; Kennedy sending a civil rights bill to Congress in one of the last months of his life, and Lyndon Johnson driving that bill and the Voting Rights Act through the Congress—along with antipoverty legislation—even as he was smearing his legacy with Vietnam.

But mainly I think of the young people who come each and every year to bring their ideals to this city and throw themselves into the churning stew of America's aspirational politics. I find it thrilling when a former student of mine does it and ecstasy when—as in two instances—my children do it.

—ROGER WILKINS is professor of history, George Mason University; former editor at the *New York Times* and the *Washington Post,* where he shared the Pulitzer Prize for Watergate reporting. He was chairman and publisher of the NAACP's journal *Crisis* and is author of *Jefferson's Pillow: The Founding Fathers and the Dilemma of Black Patriotism.*

MAY 16, 1966: March against the Vietnam War.

OCTOBER 22, 1967: Exorcise the Pentagon demonstration to protest the Vietnam War.

NOVEMBER 15, 1969: NATIONAL MOBILIZATION TO END THE WAR IN VIETNAM—600,000 march.

MAY 9, 1970: KENT STATE/CAMBODIA INCURSION PROTEST—More than 100,000 demonstrators protest Ohio National Guardsmen's killings of four Kent State students and Nixon's "wider war" invasion of Cambodia.

APRIL 19, 1971: OPERATION DEWEY CANYON THREE BY THE VIETNAM VETERANS AGAINST THE WAR—More than 2,000 antiwar veterans camp on the Mall.

APRIL 24, 1971: VIETNAM WAR OUT NOW RALLY—500,000 call for end to Vietnam War.

MAY 3, 1971: Protests by Vietnam antiwar militants to shut down the federal government.

JANUARY 20, 1973: ANTIWAR PROTEST DEMONSTRATION—Includes the Yippie-Zippie RAT float and SDS "March Against Racism & the War" contingent.

JULY 9, 1978: 100,000 feminists march up Constitution Avenue supporting extension of the deadline for states' ratification of the Equal Rights Amendment.

OCTOBER 14, 1979: NATIONAL MARCH ON WASHINGTON FOR LESBIAN AND GAY RIGHTS—First such mobilization in which 100,000 gay men and lesbians protested discrimination on the basis of sexuality.

SEPTEMBER 19, 1981: SOLIDARITY DAY MARCH— AFL-CIO organized march to protest the Reagan administration's antilabor policies; 260,000 march.

MARCH 1 TO NOVEMBER 15, 1986: The Great Peace March for Global Nuclear Disarmament.

APRIL 10, 1988, AND NOVEMBER 1988: Mobilize for Women's Lives rally draws 600,000; 350,000 supporters of reproductive rights march to the Lincoln Memorial.

APRIL 5, 1992: Third March for Women's Lives attracts 750,000 protesters against restrictions on abortion rights.

OCTOBER 12, 1996: IMMIGRANT RIGHTS MARCH— First national march for equal rights for immigrants.

APRIL 16, 2000: Supporting march for blockades of an IMF/World Bank meeting.

MAY 14, 2000: Million Mom March for gun control.

SEPTEMBER 29, 2001: Anti-Capitalist Convergence against planned World Bank and IMF meetings. When these are cancelled, rally changes course to oppose the invasion of Afghanistan— the first major action of the post–September 11 antiwar movement.

OCTOBER 26, 2002: 100,000 people converge on their representatives to oppose war in Iraq.

JANUARY 18, 2003: Antiwar demonstration on the National Mall attended by between 100,000 and 200,000.

APRIL 25, 2004: March for Women's Lives.

OCTOBER 17, 2004: Million Worker March.

JANUARY 20, 2005: Rally against George W. Bush's second inauguration.

SEPTEMBER 24, 2005: Anti–Iraq War protest.

JANUARY 27, 2007: United for Peace and Justice (see page 212)—anti–Iraq War march.

MARCH 17, 2007: ANSWER Coalition anti–Iraq War march.

SEPTEMBER 15, 2007: National March and Die-In against the Iraq War sponsored by ANSWER Coalition, Iraq Veterans Against the War, Veterans for Peace and Families.

OCTOBER 19–20, 2007: World Bank and International Monetary Fund protests.

"The Little Red House." The red brick Victorian mansion in Georgetown, once rented by Ulysses Grant before he became president, gained its nickname when it was rented by Thomas G. "Tommy the Cork" Corcoran, a protégé of Felix Frankfurter and speechwriter-adviser–back channel operator for FDR during the mid-1930s. Corcoran lived there with Benjamin Cohen, another member of FDR's inner circle, and the house became a gathering spot for the architects of New Deal legislation. In 1934, Illinois Republican Representative Frederick Albert Britten complained on the House floor about the nightly meetings where a dozen or so young men drafted "communistic legislation" in a "little red house in Georgetown." The name stuck. Historian Cabell Phillips once referred to the house as "sort of a semiautonomous fourth level of government." (This is not to be confused with **the Little Green House** at 1625 K Street, where the original K Street lobbyists— known as the "Ohio Gang"—operated a 24/7 speakeasy, gambling den, whorehouse and political-favor mart during the Harding Administration.)

3238 R Street NW, Washington, DC 20007

MARYLAND

Knights of Columbus. The Catonsville chapter of the Knights of Columbus housed the local selective service

draft board. On May 17, 1968, radical Catholic priests and antiwar activists Philip and Daniel Berrigan, with seven other members of what became known as the "Catonsville Nine," walked into the building, stole several hundred draft cards and burned them with napalm to protest the Vietnam War. The nine were severely punished with three-year prison sentences.

1010 Frederick Road, Catonsville, MD 21228

WHITTAKER CHAMBERS'S FARM

Pipe Creek Farm, near Westminster, Maryland, is where Whittaker Chambers claimed he had hidden in a pumpkin classified documents received from Alger Hiss. It was named a National Landmark in 1988. Don't bother, even at Halloween. It's privately owned and closed to the public.

WEST VIRGINIA

John Henry Monument. Atop the Big Bend Tunnel near Talcott stands a giant statue of John Henry, the steel-drivin' man whose superhuman strength enabled him to defeat a machine in an epic battle that is the stuff of song and legend. But maybe not so legendary. Historian Scott Reynolds Nelson, in his 2006 book *Steel Drivin' Man,* presents evidence that a real John Henry worked for the railroad at the time of the great duel in 1872. John Henry's story dramatized workers' fears that machines would encroach on their jobs or work them to death.

Big Bend Tunnel, Big Bend Mountain, Talcott, WV

TENNESSEE

National Civil Rights Museum. When mostly black Memphis municipal sanitation workers seeking a living wage launched a long and bitter strike here in February 1968, the Rev. Martin Luther King, Jr., brought his Poor People's Campaign to the racially polarized city in support of the strikers. Their slogan, "I am a man," came to symbolize African Americans' aspirations for equal rights. At a rally on April 3, he called for a worldwide "human rights revolution" and prophesied, "I may not get there with you, but I want you to know tonight that we as a people will get to the promised land." At 6:01 P.M. the following day he was assassinated on the balcony of his room at the Lorraine Motel.

Stained by King's murder, the Lorraine Motel went out of business. A foundation purchased it for conversion into the National Civil Rights Museum. The facility has since been remodeled, and additional money was raised for an expansion that added 12,800 square feet of exhibition space and connected the main museum to the Young and Morrow building and the Main Street Rooming House, where James Earl Ray skulked and allegedly fired the fatal shot.

450 Mulberry Street, Memphis, TN 38103, (901) 521-9699, www.civilrightsmuseum.org

NORTH CAROLINA

Fontana Dam and Fontana Village. One of the great achievements of the New Deal was the Fontana Dam located in the Great Smoky Mountains. Between December 1941 and November 1944, in a remote area accessible only by a single dirt road through deep forest, the Tennessee Valley Authority built a dam that towered 465 feet high and created Fontana Lake, 29 miles long with 280 miles of shoreline. The dam provided hydroelectric power to Alcoa Aluminum plants, which had moved to the area when U.S. involvement in the war seemed more imminent, and to the Oak Ridge atomic laboratories. At the project's peak, some 5,000 construction workers (including 350 women) lived in a specially created village. In 1946 Fontana Village was expanded to become Fontana Village Resort. In addition to the dam and lake, the area includes Joyce Kilmer Memorial Forest, Slickrock Creek Wilderness Area, the Nantahala National Forest and the Great Smoky Mountains National Park.

PO Box 68, Highway 28, North Fontana Dam, NC 28733, (800) 849-2258, www.fontanavillage.com

---

REMEMBER THE NEW DEAL

The seventy-fifth anniversary of Franklin D. Roosevelt's New Deal occurred in 2008. The National New Deal Preservation Association designated March 4, 2008, the anniversary of FDR's inauguration, as the kickoff of year-long observations. The New Deal spawned a host of governmental programs to ease the severe economic depression that gripped the country. Many of these programs—like Social Security, TVA, Federal Deposit Insurance—are with us today.

GEORGIA

Atlanta White Race Riot Tour. Deep South race riots in the nineteenth and twentieth centuries were much fewer and are less well known than those in the North, but they happened—mainly in the form of white raids on black neighborhoods, provoking their residents to fight back. One of the worst of these took place in Atlanta, on the night of September 22, 1906, when gangs of whites, egged on by heated rhetoric about a black crime wave, attacked African-American neighborhoods, burning, looting and killing. The final toll was fifteen blacks dead and two whites. The tour visits places associated with the riot, permanently etched in local black memory.

(770) 423-6069, www.1906atlantaraceriot.org

United States Penitentiary, Atlanta. On June 16, 1918, Socialist Party leader Eugene Victor Debs was indicted under the Espionage Act for sedition and obstructing the draft, and then immured in the high-security federal penitentiary in Atlanta, known as a hellhole. In November 1920 he ran for president on the Socialist Party ticket and received nearly 1,000,000 votes. In stir he counseled inmates but was kept isolated from comrades outside and sank into deeper and deeper depression. But when he was offered amnesty in exchange for his promise to stop agitating, Debs refused, saying, "I either go out a man as I came in or I serve my term to the last day." President Harding commuted his sentence to time served as of Christmas Day, 1921. As Debs walked out the prison gates all the inmates assembled at the front of the prison and cheered him. Debs spread out his arms and wept. Later he donated the $5 he was given for a new suit to the newly formed Save Sacco and Vanzetti committee (see page 8).

601 McDonough Boulevard SE, Atlanta, GA 30315, (404) 635-5100, www.bop.gov/locations/institutions/atl/

Part II.

THE MEDIA GALLERY

Print

THE DISESTABLISHMENT

The Nation. America's oldest continuously published liberal political weekly—founded in 1865 by a group of New York abolitionists and reformers—has always been a

"liberal" magazine, but it depends on what you mean by "liberal." Over a century and a half *The Nation* has followed the description through all its transmogrifications, under such editors as E. L. Godkin, a brilliant Irish émigré who was a free enterprise liberal as well as pro–Negro rights. Oswald Garrison Villard, who took over in 1919, was more like it—a pacifist, socialist and civil libertarian; Freda Kirchwey supported the New Deal and World War II; and Cary McWilliams carried the magazine through the dark 1950s, when it was smeared as a communist publication by the McCarthyites and circulation slumped. McWilliams, incidentally, attributed the

magazine's longevity to its never having to make a profit—thanks to support from readers and wealthy capitalists who shared its values. Victor Navasky, who became editor in 1978 and later publisher as well, describes how to keep a chronically underfunded political journal alive in his memoir *A Matter of Opinion.* Under Katrina vanden Heuvel, current editor and publisher, the magazine continues its mission of conducting a dialogue between the radical and the liberal Left. Under her (and the unpopular George W. Bush), circulation soared to 190,000, the largest in the magazine's history and more than any other political weekly left or right.

33 Irving Place, New York, NY 10003, (212) 209-5400, www.thenation.com

In These Times. "I am a man without a country, except for the librarians and a Chicago paper called *In These Times,*" wrote the late Kurt Vonnegut, who was a senior editor and contributor. In 1976 James Weinstein came to Chicago, a city with a socialist and Wobbly tradition, bent on founding an independent socialist weekly. In a time of hope for a revived New Left, buoyed by a successful antiwar movement, the election of a Democratic president and energetic progressive organizing, Weinstein believed such a publication could succeed; more important, he believed such a publication was needed. *ITT* was dogged by the financial problems chronic on the Left and especially severe in the 1980s under the Reagan counterrevolution. Its circulation stabilized at around 17,000, and it survived in part on the generosity of friends and loyal readers who added a donation to their subscription renewal checks. Yet Weinstein created a resoundingly successful publication in terms of the respect it won for its integrity, news sense, courageous coverage and strong critical voice. The magazine has been ahead of the curve in its stories of global warming, the Iran-Contra scandal and genocide in Darfur, as well as its reporting about challenges by various groups on the Left to the status quo that the major media had ignored. *ITT* has recruited a stable of able regulars and distinguished outside contributors.

2040 N. Milwaukee Avenue, Chicago, IL 60647, (773) 772-0100, www.inthesetimes.com

Mother Jones. Named after the inspirational old labor organizer Mary Harris "Mother" Jones (see page 110), this magazine was a kind of summer of love child, born in San Francisco in 1974 in a small office over a McDonald's restaurant. Its longtime financial backer Adam Hochschild has written that to him and the original crew, "It seemed as if the '60s were still going on, with new strains of activism in the air and political earthquakes to come." Financed by Hochschild's considerable fortune (and other sources), it spurned the sober look traditional to Old Left periodicals and the funky makeup of the counterculture papers. The idea has been to attract a broad readership by melding bright design with good writing and kick-ass investigative reporting. It has fairly well stuck to that concept ever since. It debuted in 1976 and made a splash in 1977, with an investigative article by Mark Dowie about the Ford Pinto's lethal tendency to catch fire, which won a National Magazine Award. *Mother Jones* received another NMA in 1980 for Dowie's "The Corporate Crime of the Century," which exposed U.S. manufacturers' practice, abetted by the State Department, of dumping toxic products, banned in the United States, in underdeveloped countries that lacked adequate regulatory defenses. *Mother Jones* probed the rotting system of campaign funding. It became the first general interest magazine to publish on the Internet in 1993. It's now a nonprofit, comes out bimonthly, sponsors a website with original material and continues its investigative reporting tradition.

222 Sutter Street, 6th Floor, San Francisco, CA 94108, (415) 321-1700, www.motherjones.com

The Progressive. This low-budget stalwart in the Left journalism lineup traces its roots back to the original Progressive Era. It was founded as *La Follette's Weekly* in 1909 by Wisconsin Senator Robert M. "Fighting Bob" La Follette, Sr., the patriarch of Progressivism. The agenda of the old Progressive Party—antimilitarism, antimonopoly, prodemocracy—lives on in its pages, adapted to the exigencies of modern times. As the home state paper of Senator Joseph McCarthy, *The Progressive* was among the first journals with the guts to denounce his demagoguery. One of the most notable fights in a long history of standing up to the powers that be came about in 1979 when *The Progressive* published an article by Howard Morland blazoned on the cover, "The H-Bomb

Secret: How We Got It—Why We're Telling It" (see box). The magazine, a monthly, sponsors the weekly half-hour interview *Progressive Radio Show,* conducted by Matthew Rothschild, the editor. In an effort to add balance to opinion pages in the national press, the Progressive Media Project commissions and edits op-ed pieces confected by a range of progressive experts, activists, nonprofit advocates and regular people, and distributes them via the McClatchy-Tribune News Service to papers around the nation.

409 E. Main Street, Madison, WI 53703, (608) 257-4626, www.progressive.org

ERWIN KNOLL AND THE SECRET OF THE H-BOMB

One of *The Progressive*'s greatest editors, Erwin Knoll, is little known today, except in those chanceries of journalism where the cause of freedom of the press is venerated above all others. Knoll was born in Austria in 1931 to Jewish parents; he barely escaped the Holocaust to America, losing many family members. He became a journalist, reporting for the *Washington Post* among other papers, and in 1973 was appointed editor of *The Progressive.* His criticisms of the Nixon administration earned him a spot on Nixon's infamous "enemies list," which Knoll took as a mark of distinction: "To be secure in the knowledge that your government counts you among its enemies [is] a grand feeling," he said. A staunch foe of the Vietnam War, Knoll was once accosted by a woman brandishing her umbrella and shouting, "I hold you and your magazine responsible for my son's refusal to register for the draft." Knoll told her: "I hope you are as proud of him as I am." In 1979 Howard Morland, a former Air Force pilot with no scientific training, submitted a story revealing the "secret" of the H-bomb. He had "discovered" it by dint of research in the open shelves of public libraries. As Knoll was about to go to press with Morland's revelations, he was visited by a delegation of Washington national security types. Somehow the government had gotten wind that Morland's piece was in the works. The visitors warned Knoll he had better make a number of cuts or he would be charged with publishing classified information. Knoll refused to alter the article. He saw the real issues as defending the press against prior restraint and challenging a secrecy system that sought to limit access to information about the bomb to a cabal of government officials. As Knoll said, "So long as we have that [secrecy] mystique, it is possible for a tight little group—the guardians of secrets—to exclude the rest of us from having a say." Left periodicals like *The Nation* jumped to *The Progressive*'s defense, but the mainstream media grumbled about a reckless "socialist magazine" risking Armageddon by revealing the Greatest Secret Never Told. The case went to trial and the redactions in the defendant's brief made at the government's behest were revealing: most of the deletions were of citations to published articles and textbooks containing the same information that was in Morland's article. Eventually, the imbroglio became so embarrassing to the government that it dropped prosecution. *The Progressive* had won; even more the Bill of Rights.

The American Prospect. *The American Prospect* emerged from the Boston-Washington academic-government corridor as a quarterly in 1990 and immediately established itself as a sharp, authoritative voice. The founders were Robert Kuttner, a present coeditor, former Labor Secretary Robert Reich and Paul Starr. The editors organized a stable of contributors from academe, journalism and think tanks and went monthly as circulation rose to a very respectable 55,000 by 2007. The editors regard their mission as seeking "a just society" and opposing the "massive propaganda apparatus" of contemporary conservatism.

2000 L Street NW, Suite 717, Washington, DC 20036, www.prospect.org

Z Magazine. *Z* is considered harder left than its coevals, prone to cut the American imperium less slack. It was founded in Boston in 1977 by Lydia Sargent and Michael Albert, both members of the original collective that started South End Press (see page 42). The pair had grown impatient with the long publishing lead time of books and wanted to bring more timely information to the Left. Sargent explained: "We also felt that there was a need for a magazine that included coverage of activism as well as vision and strategy. *The Progressive, The Nation, In These Times,* etc. were pretty much social democratic at best, often uncritically supporting the Democratic Party, and rarely criticizing the institutions—such as patriarchy, capitalism, etc." They called the new magazine *Z* after Costa-Gavras's film. (In the movie the letter stands for the resistance against a military junta.) In 1987, with money from South End Press (repayment of a loan Sargent had made to the press) and a mailing list of subscribers, which Victor Navasky of *The Nation* gave them, they sent out a prospectus describing the new radical publication they envisioned. This mailing raised $40,000, and *Z* was launched with an editorial staff of Sargent and Albert, until 1990, when Sargent's son Eric joined them. Now a staff of five (and two office parakeets, Zeek and Zaak) produces the magazine. Under the umbrella of Z Communications, they run ZNet, an informative international website; Z Media Institute, a summer course in radical politics; and Z Video Productions. With about 10,000 print and 6,000 online subscribers, *Z* survives on subscriptions, donations, occasional emergency fund-raisers and a $30,000 per month Sustainer Program that covers deficits (more or less). Sargent frets: "We can no longer solicit print subscribers through the mail as mailings are too costly and returns are barely 1 percent. The sixties left is dying or not buying left magazines; the younger generation prefers the Internet."

18 Millfield Street, Woods Hole, MA 02543, (508) 548-9063, www.zmag.org

THE OLD LEFT

Dissent. "When intellectuals cannot do anything else, they start a magazine," said *Dissent* founding editor Irving Howe. Howe and two confreres, all of them hardened veterans of the factional strife of the 1930s, founded *Dissent* in 1954. Ideologically, they were Trotskyists—embittered defectors from the Communist Party USA. *Dissent* distanced itself from the ideological certitudes of the Communist Party while holding to a more flexible, pragmatic socialism. The editors fiercely denounced McCarthyism, unlike old comrades at *Partisan Review* and *Commentary,* who defected to or drifted into the enemy camp. In the 1960s *Dissent* clashed with its would-be heirs in the New Left even while sharing their causes, such as opposition to the Vietnam War. Eventually, aging new lefties who had matured into respectable academics were contributing to the magazine at its traditional zero rates and joining *Dissent*'s editorial board. *Dissent*'s articles remain left-centrist-inclined—though the coeditors were split over the Iraq invasion—analytic yet readable. Some of the standout issues (such as one on New York City) benefited from an infusion of journalistic energy. The magazine, issued quarterly, also provides solid coverage of the arts, in line with its early associations with critics like Harold Rosenberg and Meyer Schapiro.

310 Riverside Drive, Suite 2008, New York, NY 10025, (212) 316-3120, www.dissentmagazine.org

Monthly Review. The small, influential socialist monthly with a circulation of 7,000 was founded in 1949 by Paul M. Sweezy and Leo Huberman. When Huberman died in 1968, Harry Magdoff stepped in. The lead article in the debut issue was "Why Socialism?" by Albert Einstein. During the McCarthy bad times and the Reagan counterrevolution, the magazine was buffeted by hostile economic winds and endured the untimely deaths of its early editors. But it came through—continuing to pour the straight stuff, no chaser: factual, scholarly, no frills. The magazine treads a pragmatic anti-imperialist, prosocialist path but also makes a "heartfelt attempt to frame the issues of the day with one set of interests foremost in mind: those of the great majority of humankind, the propertyless." The rising concern about global warming has added new impetus to the socialist project, on the theory that capitalism, trapped in the relentless cycle of ever-greater production and consumption, will always be the problem, not the solution. *Monthly Review* has developed a global reach, using intellectual power to reach and teach Third World socialists.

146 W. 29th Street, 6W, New York, NY 10011, (212) 691-2555, www.monthlyreview.org

THE YOUNG LEFT

Fifth Estate. Perhaps *Fifth Estate* is too old to be classified as Young Left. Harvey Ovshinsky started it in 1965 in Detroit. Ovshinsky was certainly young at the time—only seventeen. *Fifth Estate* (meaning an alternative to the Fourth Estate, the mainstream press) was a child of the sixties, one of the earliest examples of the underground press. It had a successful antiestablishmentarian run, but by 1975 its staff was burned out. Just as they were about to write their last "30," a collective with the improbable name of the Eat the Rich Gang took over and revived it as an anarchist publication with the credo "All isms are was-isms." They steered the magazine on a Luddite course—antitechnology, anticapitalism, neo-countercultural—though actually, the Eat the Rich Gang was pretty much against any kind of authority or dogma and open to a variety of views. Converting to a quarterly magazine format, they continued to publish *Fifth Estate* more or less quarterly in Michigan. They've published Fall 2006, Winter 2006–7, Spring 2007 and Spring 2008 issues, offering articles like: "Abolish Restaurants: A Worker's Critique of the Food Service Industry," "Learn from Appalachia: On Primitism, Participation and Tactical Retreat," "The End of the World?" (special issue) and "Police Terrorize Earth Firster Mary Mason: Powerlessness and the Power of Prank."

PO Box 201016, Ferndale, MI 48220, (615) 536-5999, www.fifthestate.org

The Indypendent. In the fall of 2000, buoyed by a $500 grant, the paper set sail. A New York *Independent* editor, John Tarleton, recounted, "We aren't an anarchist paper but we have been strongly influenced by the DIY ethos that is central to most anarchist organizing; i.e., don't wait for the politicians or mainstream NGOs to change the world but get together with other like-minded people and start making the change you want to see. Indymedia, of which we are an offshoot, was a DIY-media project founded during the 1999 WTO protests. Its open-publishing newswire theoretically makes it possible for anyone to 'be the media.' We sought to fuse the 'be the media' ideal with a rigorous, structured editorial process. It hasn't always been an easy marriage but it has certainly been a creative one!" Written, edited and produced by a sixty-member volunteer collective, with two full-time employees, *The Indypendent* is distributed free in stores, libraries, bookstores and other walk-ins that agree to carry it. It's also fully available online (the website takes 144,000 hits a month) and by subscription. Through its community reporting workshop series, *The Indypendent* mentors young journalists and has helped launch grassroots media projects, including the youth-run *Rise Up Radio* show on WBAI, New York's left indie radio station; *IndyKids,* with a progressive take on the news for eight- to twelve-year-olds; *NYU Inc.,* an alternative student web publication at New York University; *El Independiente,* a free Spanish-language publication, and others. In October 2002 it ran a special issue blasting the Bush administration's unadmitted plans to invade Iraq. It has expanded its cultural coverage and runs more first-person stories. It comes out seventeen times a year, on Fridays.

4 W. 43rd Street, Suite 311, New York, NY 10036, (212) 221-0521, www.indypendent.org

Left Turn. *Left Turn* was born amid the energy unleashed by the 1999 Seattle protests against predatory global capitalism. Run by the Left Turn Collective, the paper subtitles itself "Notes from the Global Intifada," a voice of the radical anticapitalist movement in America. Of course, the editors' ultimate objective is revolution, but they admit they have no clear vision of the form that revolution would take. Nor do they possess any road map showing how to get there, though they rule out both the Old Left (i.e., Communist) idea of a vanguard party leading the way and the liberal notion of progress via electoral politics. *Left Turn*, a quarterly, publishes both essays and reportage. The Middle East leads its foreign affairs coverage, with emphasis on Israel-Palestine and Iraq. A recent issue featured articles on "Palestine and 60 Years of Occupation" and the "Prison Industrial Complex."

PO Box 445, New York, NY 10154, www.leftturn.org

SPECIALTY ACTS

The Baffler. *The Baffler* reports on "the culture of business" and "the business of culture," commenting on the economic substructure of the arts in America. It was cofounded in 1988 by students at the University of Chicago led by Tom Frank, a gifted essayist in the Marx-Mencken tradition. *The Baffler* group's fresh perspectives quickly won attention, and Frank went on to contribute to *The Nation* and other magazines, adding a book, *Commodify Your Dissent: Salvos from the Baffler*, which argued revolution was being co-opted by Mad Ave. In 2004 he published the best seller *What's the Matter with Kansas?* which dusted off the question asked in a famous article in the 1890s by the old-time, small-town Kansas editor William Allen White. Frank turned White's point (that wild-eyed Kansas Populists were hurting the business interests of small towns and cities) upside down. His book wondered why so many middle- and working-class blue-collar people in his home state voted the GOP-Bush religious nationalism ticket to the neglect of their economic interests. When you subscribe to *The Baffler* you're betting that all the issues you signed up for will arrive in your lifetime rather than the magazine's. So far seventeen *Bafflers* have made it out—three since a fire destroyed the magazine's offices in 2001. Frank since moved to Washington and wrote another bestseller on the corrupt culture of the capital: *The Wrecking Crew*.

Tom Frank, PO Box 5912, Washington, DC 20016, www.tcfrank.com

Black Commentator. This premier black radical web-only weekly was founded in 2002 by Peter Gamble and Glen Ford, friends and veteran journalists who in 1974 had created *America's Black Forum*, a nationally syndicated interview show, the first of its kind on commercial television. Then came *Black Commentator*, aimed at "African Americans and their allies in the quest for social and economic justice." It offered strong, hard-hitting analysis and opinion on black issues. *BC* didn't pull racial punches, criticizing black leaders like Al Sharpton, Condoleezza Rice and Barack Obama, always in the context of their contributions (or lack of them) to the larger struggle for equality. The publication maintained a high level of sharp, punchy analysis, but in August 2006 Ford and Gamble split up. Ford said it wasn't personal; they had "philosophical" differences over the "business model." That is, he opposed Gamble's new policy of charging $50 for website subscriptions. He said the fee slammed the doors of enlightenment on teachers, students and others who couldn't afford the price of admission. Ford walked, accompanied by several *BC* associates, then founded a website called BlackAgendaReport.com, which does all that *Black Commentator* did in content but is free to all. He serves as executive editor. Gamble riposted that *Black Commentator* would issue a complimentary subscription to anyone who couldn't afford the $50 fee. After the publication of *BC*'s two hundredth issue, Gamble, serving as publisher, announced the formation of a new editorial board, which would write for the publication and provide editorial advice. At last look, both websites were offering hard-hitting coverage of national issues.

127 Bridgeton Pike Unit B, Suite 254, Mullica Hill, NJ 08062, (202) 318-4032, www.black commentator.com; www.blackagendareport.com

Utne Reader. Eric Utne conceived *Utne Reader* in 1984 as a kind of New Age *Reader's Digest.* The first version failed, but the second incarnation caught on. Utne, who had been a literary agent and editor of *New Age Journal,* selected the best articles on timely themes of interest to a growing community of "yuppies who care." By 1989 *Utne Reader* was in the black with a circulation of 150,000 and lots of ads. Eric Utne stepped down in 1999, leaving his wife, Nina Rothschild Utne, in charge. The publication he founded changed its name to *Utne Magazine* in 2004, when its circulation had soared to 225,000, then changed it back to *Reader* after being purchased by Ogden Publications, which owns *Mother Earth News* and *Natural House.* The annual Utne Independent Press Awards, which have gone to alternative magazines, are much coveted and prove that the *Utne* stays in close touch with the people who grow the grain for its mill. The magazine, now bimonthly, also runs an active website with much original content.

12 N. 12th Street, Suite 400, Minneapolis, MN 55403, (612) 338-5040, www.utne.com

TAKING CARE OF BUSINESS

Dollars & Sense. A publication calling itself "the magazine of economic justice" (as opposed to, say, "the magazine that will make you a million") gets off on the left foot. Since start-up in 1974, Boston-based *Dollars & Sense,* a bimonthly, has steadily trained a progressive perspective on economic issues. An aftershock of the radical upheavals of the 1960s, the publication was founded by a collective of leftist academics associated with the Union for Radical Political Economics. *Dollars & Sense* is no longer affiliated with URPE, but it has continued to energize economics with a passion for social justice and is still edited by a collective, with five staffers attending to the logistics. The articles are crafted in layman's language and not averse to showing outrage when describing, say, the fall in real wages from 1979 to 2004. But there's no ranting and no effort to oversimplify complex subjects. The treatment is often comprehensive to a fault, larded with statistics and charts. But if you're a conscientious citizen who likes to be among the earliest to hear about new economic issues like how subprime loans bilk the poor—with facts and figures from reliable sources—or wants a fully documented treatise on how the widening income gap undermines the U.S. economy and social cohesion, *Dollars & Sense* is essential reading. What the journal lacks in pizzazz it makes up for in straight talk and plain writing.

29 Winter Street, Boston, MA 02108, (617) 447-2177, www.dollarsandsense.org

Left Business Observer. Doug Henwood founded *LBO* in 1986 not as a leveraged buyout but as an antidote to Reaganomics. One of the most literate lefties writing on economics today, Henwood's style reflects his studies in English and American literature before he switched to economics after finding John Maynard Keynes more fascinating than Percy Bysshe Shelley. For twenty-odd years now he has written lucidly and insightfully on dry political-economic issues, including income distribution, the IMF and World Bank, the national debt, trade deficits, globalization and Third World debt. He is a contributing editor at *The Nation*, where he publishes editorials and articles. Adept at creating computer charts and other visual aids, he wrote and illustrated a graphic social atlas called *The State of the USA Atlas*. He is also the author of *Wall Street* and *After the New Economy*. He has a weekly radio program on WBAI called *Behind the News*. *LBO* aspires to be a monthly "but can't quite make it."

38 Greene Street, 4th floor, New York, NY 10013, (212) 219-0010, www.leftbusinessobserver.com

Multinational Monitor. This bimonthly publication is an offshoot of Ralph Nader's nonprofit group Essential Information (see page 198), which was formed to generate projects that encouraged citizen involvement in issues of the day. Back in the early 1980s when EI was founded, a publication reporting on the abuses of economic power by the transnationals was a novelty. Enter *Multinational Monitor*, which probed into the hitherto overlooked doings of global giants like ExxonMobil and Merck. Since its inception *MM* has ventilated such issues as international labor, threats to the environment and global warming, corporate crime, international banking and Third World development. The *Monitor* confines itself to reporting and analysis, no opinion pieces. However, each issue features an editorial note commenting on, praising or deploring some recent flare-up on the business economic horizon. One of the *Monitor*'s best-known features is its annual list the "ten worst corporations," which it keeps fresh by avoiding nominating the same offender for two years running (there is no shortage of world-class offenders). Each year's hall of shame is prefaced by an update detailing the recent sins of last year's dishonorees.

PO Box 19405, Washington, DC 20036, (202) 387-8034, www.multinationalmonitor.org

REGIONAL VOICES

The Lone Star Iconoclast. This good ol' populist weekly rag, named after a nineteenth-century sheet called *Brann's Iconoclast,* flaunts a Crawford, Texas, zip code. In addition to expansive coverage of state peace initiatives, *The Iconoclast* regularly slams neighbor Bush and the Iraq War and has dabbled in 9/11 conspiracy theories. It also comments on state politics and issues like education by means of a stable of regular columnists who denounce the latest injustice, sometimes in one-sentence paragraphs. The paper claims a national readership and has a colorful website.

PO Box 420, Crawford, TX 76638, (254) 675-3634, www.lonestaricon.com

Mountain Eagle. While visiting Kentucky to research a story, Barbara Garson, a New York–based writer, became addicted to reading the weekly small-town gossip in the *Mountain Eagle*—also, its political slant on life. After police had broken a sit-in strike at a coal mine in nearby Pittston, the *Eagle* commented, alluding to the recent Tiananmen Square crackdown in Beijing: "We understand there were some divisions of the Chinese Army that refused to fire on the students. Where is the unit of the West Virginia National Guard that refused to go into Pittston?" Garson writes: "This kind of editorial is part of an amazing mix that includes pickups from Pacific News Service, liberal syndicated columnists and cartoonists, stories on local crime and elections and some investigative reporting. They also publicize the best of mountain culture and history. Over the years the office has been firebombed and the paper shut down more than once. In a couple of cases, before elections, all copies disappeared. The *Mountain Eagle* is owned by the Gish family (husband, wife and two sons), who promote dignity, solidarity, egalitarianism, decency, trade unions and wit both in print and in the life of their community. It's a great read once you get to know the local cast of characters."

357B Hazard Road, Parkway Plaza, PO Box 808, Whitesburg, KY 41858, (606) 633-2252, bengish@bellsouth.net, bengish@mac.com

The New Hampshire Gazette. Our NH correspondent Mike Dater writes: "*The New Hampshire Gazette* is a sort of under-the-radar gadfly, published fortnightly. It is quite small both in size (sixteen pages) and circulation (I don't have any figures, but I think there are around 1,000 paid subscribers. Otherwise, it's free and is sustained by advertisers). [Website reported a 5,500-copy press run and 700-plus subscribers.] It has a loyal following among those of the lefty persuasion. The editor, Steven Fowle—who refers to himself as the 'alleged editor'—does 90 percent of the paper, including layout and design. His primary writing input each issue is a front-page observation on the ironies, contradictions and outrages that are so commonplace these days. His opening salvo is always under the rubric of 'The Fortnightly Rant.' . . . I draw the political cartoons for the paper. I mention this not to blow my horn but to let you know that I am, however tangentially, associated with the paper, also paid (also not much—in fact most contributors are volunteers). The cartoons usually have some relationship to Steve's aforementioned fortnightly rant. . . . A small section called 'Vintage News' ('Better old news than new lies') culls whimsical tidbits from old *Gazette* editions. . . . The *Gazette*, incidentally, is 'the nation's oldest newspaper,' established in 1756. Yes, the *Hartford Courant* is the oldest *daily*, but not the oldest paper. Some people dispute our claim, but we give them no mind. . . ."

PO Box 756, Portsmouth, NH 03802, www.nhgazette.com

Texas Observer. For many years this biweekly broadsheet has covered Austin, the state legislature and government like a saddle blanket. Because Texas is such a hyper-American state, the *Observer*'s muckrake frequently turns up stories that raise a national stink, such as its investigations into the favored financial dealings of the Bush siblings while Poppy was in the White House. More recently the *Observer* was first to lift the rock hiding House Majority Leader Tom DeLay's PAC that laundered illegal corporate donations to Republican candidates for the state legislature. It also revealed conservative guru Grover Norquist's palship with superlobbyist Jack Abramoff. *The Observer*'s digging has provided leads for stories in the *New York Times* and on *60 Minutes, 20/20* and other national media. It's served as a journalistic residency for liberal Texas writers, with the state legislature as their clinic. Through these portals have passed some of the state's all-time great reporters: Ronnie Dugger (the *Observer*'s founding editor and publisher), Molly Ivins, Billy Lee Brammer (author of *The Gay Place*, the definitive LBJ novel), Robert Sherrill (latter-day muckraker who became corporate correspondent to *The Nation*), Jim Hightower (see Hightower Lowdown, page 138), Willie Morris (legendary editor of *Harper's* in the 1960s) and others. It's garnered a shelf full of awards since its founding in 1954 by a Houston lumber heir. (The Texas Democracy Foundation, a nonprofit, now owns it.) The paper's back of the book attends to Texas literature and culture. "I love Texas," Molly Ivins wrote in her very first column in the *Observer*. "It's a harmless perversion." These Texas observers love their state tough as hell.

307 W. 7th Street, Austin, TX 78701, (512) 477-0746, www.texasobserver.org

LITERARY POLITICS

Boston Review. This tabloid-size, liberal bimonthly divides its space between politics and current affairs (front) and literature and the arts (back). The beating heart of the front is a permanent floating symposium that features several—often three—authoritative writers discussing a topic of the day, sometimes leading to the impression that there are three sides to every question, but *Review* readers can handle it. As *Boston Review* coeditor Joshua Cohen describes it, the publication is "a left-center-of-gravity magazine" whose main aims are to facilitate political debate and create "greater space for political initiatives guided by egalitarian, radically democratic, and culturally plural-ist values." The forums are followed by essays. In the back of the book, respected New Fiction Forum editor Neil Gordon presides over a parallel universe of art and ideas, dollops of fiction, good poetry and film reviews.

35 Medford Street, Suite 302, Somerville, MA 02143, (617) 591-0505, www.bostonreview.net

The New York Review of Books. Behold Parnassus! It has taken over the New York intel-lectual higher criticism franchise once shared by *Partisan Review* and other politico-cultural organs born in the 1930s. Coming out twenty times a year, *NYRB* mainly publishes credentialed academics and critically approved novelists, journalists, critics and assorted public intellectuals. Until his retirement, the caricatures by the great David Levine graced its pages. The *Review* was founded in the early sixties by Robert Silvers, Barbara Epstein and Elizabeth Hardwick, the feudal barons of New York's intellectual establishment (Epstein in the dual status of wife of Random House editor Jason Epstein and editor in her own right). They productively coedited the *Review* until Epstein's untimely death in 2006. The founders took advantage of a window of opportunity that opened when the *New York Times Book Review* was out on strike in 1963. *NYRB* mainly covers the effusions of university presses and the more serious products of the commercial mills. (Academic publishers are a major source of advertis-ing revenue.) It delves into other aspects of culture: art, architecture, photography, cin-ema, TV, music. Most contributors bring a liberal perspective to their critiques of the Bush administration and the Iraq War (as their predecessors had to the Vietnam War). The *Review* has featured some epic literary battles on its letters page, such as the Edmund Wilson–Vladimir Nabokov feud over the former's criticism of the latter's translation of Pushkin. The letters pages still ring with swordplay between authors protesting a bad review (or even a good one) and riposting reviewers. The critical form nurtured by *NYRB* is the essay review, a long article ostensibly on a number of books clustered around a person, subject or topic. For company or amusement the reader can turn to the Personals column, a preserve for mating dances in the groves of academe.

1755 Broadway, 5th floor, New York, NY 10019, (212) 757-8070, www.nybooks.com

POSITIVE THINKERS

Ode. Cofounder and chief editor Jurriaan Kamp and his wife, Hélène de Puy, were Dutch journalists who felt the need for a publication reporting stories "that give reasons to hope." *Ode*'s contents run to the New Agey, environmentalism, natural living and grassroots power. Optimism reigns; stories have hopeful conclusions. An article on Latin American banana workers poisoned by pesticides ends by pointing out where fair-trade, organic bananas are successfully being farmed. The magazine's articles deal with topics like nonviolence (it works), free immigration (creates economic opportunities and jobs for natives) and the joys of geotourism ("good" tourism sensitive to local culture, geography, history, heritage and environment). American editor Jay Walljasper says: "The editorial philosophy of *Ode* is to emphasize positive developments in global issues, since all that's going wrong is well covered in the major media. That does not mean we ignore or gloss over the myriad problems in the world. Indeed, exposure of what's wrong is often the first step to making things better." The magazine, issued ten times a year, tries to inspire a demand for change and inform readers about alternatives.

35 Miller Avenue, Suite 330, Mill Valley, CA 94941, www.odemagazine.com

Yes! Another upbeat quarterly, *Yes!* lives up to the exclamation point by offering a determinedly positive take on national and international problems. It has featured departments like "People We Love," profiling "inspiring individuals who are making valuable contributions to improving our world," and an advice column that describes "practical ways to live sustainably," dealing with issues such as wax stains on fabric, obsolete textbooks, extending the life of clothing. In a typical theme issue on standing up to corporate power, there's an article headed "7 Cool Companies." An article like "Project Censored's 10 Most Neglected Stories of the Year" is typically headed "10 Signs of Hope," Stories of Action and Change. *Yes!* editors are not Dr. Panglosses; they don't overlook the world's hard cases, such as Iraq, Guantánamo or Darfur. They advocate seceding from the global economy, alternative energy and turning work into play.

284 Madrona Way NE, Suite 116, Bainbridge Island, WA 98110, (206) 842-0216, www.yesmagazine.org

SHADES OF GREEN

Grist. Considered by some enviros to be a must read on the green list, *Grist* has migrated to the Internet (see page 151). It continues to be one of the freshest voices around—smart, funny, hospitably laid out, with a strong youth pull. The home page billboards the week's lead stories, regularly updated; the "Gristmill Blog" (comments from readers) and a list of departments: the "Daily Grist" (short news items), "Muckraker" ("the dirt on environmental politics and policy"), "InterActivist" (people taking action), "Victual Reality" ("The ecopolitics behind your food"), "Dispatches" ("Firsthand accounts from the field") and "Ask Umbra" (a charming enviro advice column). To a man who wanted to know which was better, environmentally speaking, peeing on the beach or in the ocean, the unflappable Umbra replied: "When urinating on land, it's best to target less sensitive sandy or rocky areas. Which sounds just like a dune— but wait. Dunes are notoriously sensitive, and let's also keep in mind avoiding social contacts, i.e., being careful not to leave a stinky location for fellow beachgoers to encounter. Given all this, I think ocean water would be the preference. If the water is too cold or you are too wimpy, just make sure you go below the high-tide line (though still out of sight of your fellow beachgoers) then nature will flush your liquid waste away." A few months later Umbra wrestled with: Which is more earth friendly— traveling by car or plane? Well, it all depends . . .

710 2nd Avenue, Suite 860, Seattle, WA 98104, (206) 876-2020, www.grist.org

Herbivore. Another eat-your-vegetables periodical, *Herbivore* emerged in spring 2003, inspired, it says, by the idea that "there was exciting, vital culture coming out of the vegetarian community" and that *Herbivore* would cover it with "humor, sensitivity and passion." So it's no surprise that one issue had vegan congressman Dennis Kucinich as its cover boy, a fact sneered at by Fox News, inspiring this unpacific response from *Herbivore:* "We hate Fox news so thanks for nothing you knuckleheaded warmongers." *Herbivore* is run by creative young editors who write haikus to describe articles in the table of contents. It's published in Portland, which may explain the laid-back style and preference for the personal voice in its articles. In 2007 *Herbivore* joined the move to the Internet off-ramp. In 2008 it returned to quarterly print publication.

5519 NE 30th Avenue, Portland, OR 97211, www.herbivoremagazine.com

Orion. The *Boston Globe* once called *Orion* "America's finest environmental magazine." Suffice it to say, it is a well-written magazine that recruits talented contributors and gives them space to explore their themes in full. *Orion*'s bimonthly articles usually raise thoughtful solutions or even measured, long-run hopes for nature's own healing. The journal is published by the Orion Society, which has identified a grassroots network of more than 1,000 state and local groups working to salvage the environment and bolster community (these are listed on the Orion Society website). In 1996 the society moved from New York to Great Barrington. It has gone on to publish six books, and the magazine has expanded into commentary on cultural matters as well as nature.

187 Main Street, Great Barrington, MA 01230, (413) 528-4422, www.orionmagazine.org; www.orionsociety.org

Satya. This unslick, dedicated monthly, combining advocacy for vegetarianism, animal rights, environmentalism and social justice, unfortunately went extinct in 2007. It offered a commendably humane, holistic view of the ecosystem; its voice will be missed. Back issues are available on the website.

www.satyamag.com

WOMANTALK

Bitch. *Bitch* ("a feminist response to pop culture") is *Ms.*'s rebellious kid sister. It starts with that once opprobrious title that the editors construe as a badge of pride celebrating the outspoken women who don't take sexism like ladies. As *Nation* columnist Katha Pollit put it, *Bitch* dishes out "cheerfully attitudinous updated feminism." They may not do the solid investigative reporting of *Ms.* but they're full of reports and ideas. A composite table of contents from past issues gives a taste of *Bitch*, whose editors never met a pun that made them wince:

"Egos without borders: Mapping the new celebrity philanthropy";

"Green and Not Heard—Al, Rachel, and the feminizing of eco-activism";

"Troop Therapy—How the Girl Scouts made themselves over";

"Big Trouble—Are eating disorders the Lavender Menace of the fat acceptance movement?";

"The Shame Show—Revisiting your teenage angst for fun and profit";

"Multiply and Conquer—How to have 17 children and still believe in Jesus"

Bitch represents third-wave feminism, not postfeminism. The magazine was founded in San Francisco in 1996 by two young feminists, Andi Zeisler and Lisa Jervis, whose previous magazine experience consisted of working as interns at *Sassy*, and a colleague, Benjamin Shaykin. They've been poking a thumb in the world's eye ever since with stunts like a mock back cover ad showing a woman flaunting a purple vibrator, headed "Babes in Toyland." The magazine puts pop above politics, crusading against the stereotypes of women purveyed by advertising, fashion and the media. *Bitch*'s game plan is to reach younger women by leveraging pop culture to raise feminist issues and politics. Set up as a nonprofit, *Bitch* comes out four times a year. Like a lot of independent small magazines it's been hit by competition from the Internet and was bruised when its distributor folded. It now claims about 50,000 readers and its gadabout editors, seeking a lower cost of living, moved from San Francisco to left coastal Oakland and, in 2007, to Portland. Zeisler said she feels friendlier vibes.

4930 NE 29th Avenue, Portland, OR 97211, (503) 282-5699, www.bitchmagazine.org

Ms. The magazine rolled in with the 1970s feminist tide. It debuted in December 1971 as a supplement to *New York*. Contributors discussed sexism, marriage contracts; it included a comic strip (*Wonder Woman*), "which asks the question, Can the feminist movement laugh at itself?" The issue drew sufficient interest to attract start-up funding and pay the original editors—Pat Carbine, Nina Finkelstein, Joanne Edgar, Mary Peacock, Gloria Steinem, Letty Cottin Pogrebin—a living wage. The first stand-alone issue hit the stands in July 1972. After that, it was a bumpy ride but *Ms.* survived. Along the way it became the first American magazine to demand the repeal of laws criminalizing abortion, the first to push for the Equal Rights Amendment, to crusade against domestic violence and sexual harassment and to publicize the campaign against pornography. *Ms.* still fights the good feminist fight, but it has expanded its horizons beyond the original agenda, to cover issues of interest to the civic-minded of all genders. For example, it surveys global warming from the perspective of women who are leading the fight against it. Early in life, it gave up competing with the women's glossies and became an ad-free nonprofit owned by the Ms. Foundation. This freed the magazine from the need not to offend advertisers and enabled it to dare more investigative pieces. But virtue is only its own reward and financial problems ensued. In 2001, and four owners later, the magazine was subsumed into Eleanor Smeal's Feminist Majority Foundation (see page 227) and seems on a more stable footing as a quarterly.

433 S. Beverly Drive, Beverly Hills, CA 90212, (310) 556-2500, www.msmagazine.com

Off Our Backs. *Off Our Backs* was also a cheeky title when it was founded in 1970; it meant standing up to a patriarchal society in an era when radical feminist meant not shaving one's extremities and not wearing lipstick. Today, after twenty-something years of Reagan–Bush I–Bush II counterrevolution, it's interesting to read the brave words of *OOB*'s first issue in February 1970:

> Fifty years after we have won the right to vote we still do not have equal wages for equal work. We remain enslaved in myths of female inferiority, our lives limited to the home and children, often in poverty and isolation. We are considered only temporary workers and channeled into secondary and low-paying jobs. We do not have control over our own bodies, our own reproduction. Through the sexual "revolution" we have been cast in the role of sexual object, pleasure machines to be victimized by unsafe and unresearched birth control.

Now a quarterly, *OOB* is still talking up "reproductive justice" for women of color; discussing income inequality between single and married women and of course men and women; the injuries of class (as observed by a former academic turned truck driver); why working-class guys are less sexist than upper-class males; discrimination and rape problems of women in the military. *Off Our Backs* is run as a collective, printed on sensible stock and concentrates on unslick bread-and-butter issues with an international reach. Along with features and some reportage, it supplies a compendium of global news on women's issues, as well as a calendar of events and useful listings of relevant organizations and services.

2337B 18th Street NW, Washington, DC 20009, (202) 234-8072, www.offourbacks.org

FAKE NEWS BEAT

Adbusters. This Canadian magazine is based in Vancouver, but two thirds of its readers live in the United States. Its founders, Kalle Lasn, a filmmaker, and Bill Schmalz, a wilderness cinematographer, were fed up with consumerism, advertising, mass media. They were also disillusioned with the political Left (this was in the early 1990s). They envisioned an alternate Left movement of "culture jamming," which they defined as taking power back from the corporate forces. They set out to create "a new kind of left rag" that would avoid the boredom of the usual "heavy texttexttexttext." The result was *Adbusters,* a political-art magazine that draws its mojo not from the words but from the graphics. They would parody ads but not sell advertising; they would create a world of "design anarchy," a phrase that caught the eye of the design world. Prominent artists like Jeff Koons, Jerome Victore, Andres Serrano and others contributed their work for free. The Seattle anti-WTO riots boosted interest in the magazine. Circulation soared to 120,000, and Lasn thought, "My god, we've finally done it—we've finally got ourselves a slick subversive rag." Appropriating the lingua franca of our times, advertising, *Adbusters* does bimonthly battle with the mammoth global consumerist culture.

The Adbusters Media Foundation offers an intelligently strategized program for bolstering media democracy. They try to do this through publishing *Adbusters* and conducting various "social marketing" campaigns, including Buy Nothing Day, in which people in the sixty countries where the magazine is read join in a twenty-four-hour "consumer fast"; TV Turnoff Week, which encourages people to go seven days without TV to learn how addicted they have become; Blackspot shoes, "the world's first global anti-brand," a low-end sneaker made from organic, recycled materials in a union shop as a way of directly attacking the Great Sneaker Hype; and the Media Carta campaign, with a Culture Jammers network of some 75,000 members who strive to advance *Adbusters* campaigns in their own communities.

1243 W. 7th Avenue, Vancouver, BC, V6H 1B7, Canada, (604) 736-9401, www.adbusters.org

The Onion. One day in 1988 students at the University of Wisconsin-Madison found in their dorms an odd little tabloid bearing the sensational if untrue headline "Mendota Monster Mauls Madison." Though it's hard to conceive it, this paper with a current circulation of 3 million copies, appearing on stands in big cities across the land, started out as a parody of cofounding editor Tim Keck's hometown paper, the *Oshkosh North-western*. Keck and coconspirator Christopher Johnson produced it in their dorm room, and the title was, they claim, inspired by the numerous onion sandwiches they consumed during the summer that they gestated it, according to an article in the WU student newspaper. Gradually the satirical sheet caught on and expanded to other Wisconsin cities, then snuck across the border into Illinois, adding color pictures after it was settled. In 2001 the staff moved to New York, and, aided by slick business tactics, *The Onion* grew exponentially. Now a weekly, it has offices in ten cities, has published six collections and has a regular radio slot, Onion Radio News. The basic formula is mostly hilarious fake news items. This approach is now a staple of Jon Stewart's *Daily Show*, whose original executive producer was Ben Karlin, a former *Onion* editor. Like the *Daily Show*, it informs young people who otherwise glaze over stories about political goings-on and current events.

536 Broadway, 10th floor, New York, NY 10012, (212) 267-1972, www.theonion.com

World War 3 Illustrated. Founded in 1980 by Seth Tobocman and Peter Kuper, *WW3* publishes only political comics. Its biannual issues are the products of a collective of volunteer artists who cooperate in thinking up and assigning stories. Over them is a rotating, mutable editorial board. All profits finance the next issue. *World War 3 Illustrated* sums up its philosophy as follows: "*WW3* isn't about a war that may happen, it is about the ongoing wars our so-called leaders have been waging all our lives around the world and on our very own doorsteps. *WW3* also illuminates the war we wage on each other and sometimes the one taking place in our own brains." The editors say they place content above style; the contributors range from first timers to seasoned artists and activists. Since 1980 they've covered themes and topics ignored in commercial commix, not to mention the mainstream press. Nothing's out of bounds—race, religion, sex. A recent issue (2007) included "War Is Hell," a four-page picture layout with video stills created by a U.S. Army sergeant in Iraq.

P.O. Box 20777, Tompkins Square Station, New York, NY 10009, www.worldwar3illustrated.org

NEWSLETTER LAND

CounterPunch. The founding editor is the prolific radical journalist Alexander Cockburn, whom the *London Times Literary Supplement* called "the most gifted polemicist writing in English." His long-time collaborator Jeffrey St. Clair gets coeditor billing and contributes to the publication, working the enviro beat. The two partner on books as well, most recently *End Times: The Death of the Fourth Estate*, an autopsy of America's corporate press. (It and other CounterPunch books are available on the website.)

A caustic, witty writer and trenchant contrarian, the British-born Cockburn (rhymes with "slow burn") has had a long, productive career in left journalism, apprenticing with British socialist publications and moving on to New York and *The Village Voice.* Since 1982 he has written a regular column at *The Nation* called "Beat the Devil," the title of a novel by his father, Claud Cockburn, who published an antifascist newsletter in the early 1930s and covered the Spanish Civil War for the *British Worker.* Alex's brothers, Andrew and Patrick, are also journalists; his cousin Laura Flanders is a writer and radio personality (see Radio Nation, page 167). Cockburn often bemoans the timidity on the Left. He'll attack sacred cows such as "anthropogenic global warming" and soppy liberals. *CounterPunch,* in its twenty-two annual issues, fulfills its promise of extensive coverage of stories the mainstream media shy away from, and its website is prolific.

PO Box 228, Petrolia, CA 95558, (800) 840-3683, www.counterpunch.org

Hightower Lowdown. This monthly newsletter, which claims a circulation of 125,000, is a podium for Jim Hightower, who some years ago served two terms as Texas agriculture commissioner. His political beliefs have a Western populist tinge and his voice a folksy twang, but he's a shrewd and sophisticated analyst of the political scene. Planting himself firmly to the left of the national Democrats, he fires both guns at them and at Republicans and all politicians who place power and self above people. Of "centrist" Democrats, he famously cracked, "There's nothing in the middle of the road but yellow stripes and dead armadillos." He exhorts, "Let's make politics fun again," and once promoted county-fair-style political rallies with booths and music. In addition to his newsletter, he tapes *Common Sense Commentaries,* which air daily on several radio networks. He's a popular name on the speaker circuit and a prolific author, recycling column and newsletter fodder into books that include *If the Gods Had Meant Us to Vote, They'd Have Given Us Candidates; Let's Stop Beating Around the Bush* and *Swim Against the Current: Even a Dead Fish Can Go With the Flow.*

www.hightowerlowdown.org

RADICAL REVIEWS

Radical History Review. *RHR* is a scholarly voice of left-inclined historians. It was founded in the early 1970s (there is uncertainty about the precise year) and was, as Van Gosse, one of the editors, explained in 2001, "one part of a systematic effort among young untenured or often simply unemployed scholars across the humanities and social sciences to dig and give the New Left some long-term 'counterinstitutional' footing." Thirty years later it's snugly entrenched in left academe with ties to Duke University Press and New York University and directed by an editorial collective comprising twenty-five to thirty scholars, plus a steering committee. Published three times a year, its editorial office is appropriately situated in New York University's Tamiment Library, a major repository of documents related to U.S. labor and New York radical history. Each issue is a slim book, running nearly 200 large pages and containing articles, book reviews, essays or "Reflections," interviews with historians, a forum, pieces on "Teaching Radical History" and a regular column called "The Abusable Past," consisting of five or six linked short essays by R. J. Lambrose on various contemporary travesties of history (for example, how current Republicans misleadingly call themselves the "party of Lincoln"). Editorial guidelines laid out by one editor in 2001 suggested: "articles published in *Radical History Review* must have a political stance (not any particular politics—Marxist, socialist-feminist, radical democratic, anarcho-communist, or whatever—just some politics)." *RHR* is a formidable read but consistently offers solidly researched, if highly specialized, history of interest to left scholars, professional or amateur.

Tamiment Library, New York University, 70 Washington Square South, New York, NY 10012, (212) 998-2632, http://chmn.gmu.edu/rhr/rhr.htm

And Don't Forget . . .

International Socialist Review. Tough Marxist-infused commentary mingling topical reports with historical analysis. Published bimonthly by the Center for Economic Research and Social Change (see Haymarket Books, page 37).

PO Box 258082, Chicago, IL 60625, (773) 583-7884, www.isreview.com

Politics & Society. "Committed to developing Marxist, post-Marxist and other radical perspectives and to examining what Robert Lynd once called 'some outrageous hypotheses.' " Published quarterly.

Sage Publications, 2455 Teller Road, Thousand Oaks, CA 91320, http://pas.sagepub.com

Radical Society. "A review of culture and politics." A quarterly mixing graphics, photographs, poetry, reviews and fresh political analysis. *Nation* worker Timothy Don is editor.

67 Park Terrace East, C24, New York, NY 10034, www.radicalsociety.com

THE FAITH BASE

Catholic Worker. No one identified with the Religious Left embodied saintly idealism more than the late Dorothy Day, founder of the Catholic Worker movement. The eponymous monthly publication she cofounded in 1933 with Peter Maurin discussed Catholic social teachings, as articulated in Papal encyclicals, which she believed were more relevant to the problems of the Depression than Marxism. The penny paper was aimed primarily at the "poor, the dispossessed, the exploited" and it had no trouble finding an audience in the 1930s, appealing to radical Catholic intellectuals as well. By 1936 circulation had risen to 150,000. This growth continued until the eve of World War II, when the editors' pacifistic opposition to U.S. involvement caused readers to abandon the paper in droves. But the *Worker* carried on. A number of distinguished Catholic writers, such as Thomas Merton, Daniel Berrigan, Michael Harrington and Jacques Maritan, have contributed to its pages over the years. The price remains a penny a copy, but it is now issued seven times a year. A year's subscription is available for 25 cents. No online edition.

36 E. 1st Street, New York, NY 10003, (212) 777-9617, www.catholicworker.org

Jewish Currents. Once a Communist publication that faithfully trod the party line (see box), *Jewish Currents* has moved with the times. The magazine's current editor, Lawrence Bush, once a red diaper baby, has pronounced himself skeptical of all ideologies, though the magazine sticks to a left perspective. It is pro-Israel but critical of its policies, a stance that has earned it disfavor from parts of the Jewish establishment. Accused of Jewish self-hatred, it ventilated the issue in its pages, interviewing several prominent Jewish leftists, including Noam Chomsky, Dave Marash (Washington anchorman for International Al-Jazeera, the Arabic CNN) and Stanley Aronowitz, well-known CUNY professor of sociology. And in another issue, Melanie Kaye/Kantrowitz dealt with anti-Semitism from a progressive Jewish perspective, with

---

JEWISH CURRENTS: THE DIVIDED STREAM

When *Jewish Currents* (then called *Jewish Life*) was founded in 1946 by Communist Party members, the editors danced to the party's tune. But revelations of Stalin's crimes against Soviet Jewry infuriated many subscribers, who held *Jewish Life* to be in silent complicity, and three quarters of them canceled. The democratic socialists in Workmen's Circle (see page 373), a Jewish-Socialist welfare and cultural organization, had been feuding with *Jewish Life* since the 1920s and did not trust its editors. But after many veterans of the sectarian wars had passed on, the two merged. Workmen's Circle brought as dowry its considerable assets and dwindling membership; *Jewish Currents* contributed its journalistic voice and loyal subscription base. There was an actual marriage ceremony at Workmen's Circle headquarters in Manhattan, complete with a chuppah made of old photographs and magazine covers, around which the guests danced in accordance with Jewish tradition, followed by entertainment, singing and champagne. Thus did the divided stream of Jewish radicalism become one again.

observations on its manifestations in the antiwar left. In addition to tackling issues of the moment, every other month *Jewish Currents* dishes up a variety of articles on Jewish life and heritage, politics and literature. As Paul Buhle writes in an article celebrating the revival of the Students for Democratic Society, "I see youngsters in my classes, and in SDS, identifying as Jewish not only by virtue of either religion or Israel but also, in large numbers, based on their visions of social justice, of a better world in which Jews can live as Jews—as equals, not superiors—with a new sense of global possibility."

45 E. 33rd Street, 4th floor, New York, NY 10016, (212) 889-2523, www.jewishcurrents.org

Tikkun. The title is the Hebrew word meaning "to heal or repair the world." Founder Rabbi Michael Lerner earned his radical spurs in SDS and the free speech movement at UC Berkeley in the 1960s and founded the Seattle Liberation Front in 1970 as a nonviolent alternative to the Weather Underground. In the 1980s he started *Tikkun* as a voice of a spiritual liberal-left politics grounded in Judaism's teachings on the unity of creation, on the temptation of false idols and on the duty to feed the poor and do social justice. *Tikkun* vigorously opposed the Iraq invasion; it has long sided with Israeli peace groups, supported the two-state solution to the Israel-Palestine conflict and condemned the expansion of Jewish settlements on the West Bank and expulsion of Palestinians from their land. Lerner vociferously protests anti-Semitism at peace demonstrations. His Big Idea is a "Spiritual Left." He says progressives must stand for spiritual as well as material values and judge social worth by a "New Bottom Line," of maximizing "love and caring, kindness and generosity, compassion and creativity." Howard Zinn spoke for the secular Left when he said in an interview published in the May/June 2006 *Tikkun:* "My differences with Lerner . . . reside in the proportion of attention he pays to spiritual values. These are important, but they're not the critical issue. The issue is how are people living and dying. People are dying in Iraq and our wealth is being squandered on war and the military budget."

2342 Shattuck Avenue, #1200, Berkeley, CA 94704, (510) 644-1200, www.tikkun.org

INFIDELS

Free Inquiry. Paul Kurtz, a professor emeritus of philosophy at the State University of New York at Buffalo and founder of the Council for Secular Humanism (see page 219), is editor of this bimonthly, published by that organization. It's a philosophical but readable journal that features short articles by famous atheists like Christopher Hitchens, columns, reviews, features and departments. Kurtz described the council's credo in a recent editorial: "We are skeptical of traditional faith in God and salvation and are nonreligious. But we cannot be defined simply by our unbelief. . . . Clearly we believe in 'Life, Liberty and the pursuit of Happiness.' In ethical terms, this means the right of individuals to realize their own interests and aspirations on their own terms, so long as they do not harm others or prevent those people from pursuing their interests and aspirations." In 2006 Borders banned the April/May issue of *Free Inquiry*, which reprinted the caricatures of Muhammad that had appeared in the Danish newspaper *Jyllands-Posten.* The bookseller said it feared retributive violence by jihadists.

PO Box 664, Amherst, NY 14226, (716) 636-7571, www.secularhumanism.org

The Humanist. A bimonthly publication of the American Humanist Society (see page 218) covering issues at the abraded points between religion and democracy, such as proselytizing evangelical Christian beliefs in the U.S. Air Force, the perils of religious practices (for example, meditation and fasting), how Christian nationalism fuels intolerance and the (nonreligious) ethical case against genetically manipulating embryos. *The Humanist* could be said to offer a news-oriented approach, in contrast to *Free Inquiry*'s more philosophical bent.

1777 T Street NW, Washington, DC 20009, (202) 238-9088, www.thehumanist.org

FRIENDS OF LABOR

Labor Notes. *Labor Notes* the monthly magazine is sponsored by the foundation of the same name, which started up in 1979, as a voice for union activists "who want to put the *movement* back in the labor movement." Although labor got the short end of the stick from the global economy and the Bush administration, too many unions and their leaders also dropped the ball. Today, labor finds itself virtually invisible in the mainstream press. That's where *Labor Notes* tries to fill the gaps. It's an unfancy sheet that looks like your union paper but exhibits a lot of moxie in digging up stories that flay management and unions too when they're in the wrong. The stories tend to be short, to the point, ballasted with facts. *Labor Notes* covers grassroots union democracy movements seeking to prod their leaders to stand up for the membership. It writes about innovative organizing campaigns and smarter contract negotiations. It tells about activists who are allied with unions in Mexico and Canada to fight the depredations of NAFTA. It's blown the whistle on the downside of such half-bright management ideas as "quality circles," "team concept" and "reengineering," telling how these participation programs have co-opted union leaders into supporting the bosses' antilabor agenda. The magazine holds a national conference every two years at which a Montana railroad worker can compare notes with a Teamster trucker on wages and dues, or a California nurse can meet up with a Georgia electrical worker threatened by workplace "reengineering."

7435 Michigan Avenue, Detroit, MI 48210, (313) 842-6262, www.labornotes.org

New Labor Forum. The *New Labor Forum* began appearing two or three times a year in 1997, two years after John Sweeney's "New Voices" slate kicked out of the AFL-CIO the George Meany/Lane Kirkland old guard. In October 1996, a "teach-in with the labor movement" at Columbia University was held with the objective of rebuilding the alliance between labor and left intellectuals. It attracted prominent progressives like Betty Freidan, Eric Foner, Katha Pollitt, Richard Rorty, John Sweeney, Cornel West, Orlando Patterson, Patricia Williams and Steve Fraser, who started the *New Labor Forum* as an outgrowth of that event. It sets out to be a meeting place for a wide range of people who identify themselves with the labor movement and working-class politics; it draws contributions from trade unionists, academics, community activists and public intellectuals. (It has around 2,000 subscribers.) With its mix of contributors, *New Labor Forum* has succeeded in merging an academic and scholarly approach to labor politics with a rank-and-file perspective, focusing on the domestic labor movement, immigration, trade policy, low-wage work, the labor movement split, labor law reform and new approaches to organizing. The magazine also publishes reviews of books and films with a labor background.

Joseph S. Murphy Institute for Labor, Community, and Policy Studies, 25 W. 43rd Street, 19th floor, New York, NY 10036, (212) 827-0200, www.newlaborforum.org

ASSOCIATIONS

Center for Investigative Reporting. Since 1977 CIR has been supporting projects that the mainstream press has become increasingly reluctant to finance because they require a long-term investment, don't always pay off in circulation-building scoops, cost money and reporters and often tread on the toes of the rich and powerful. CIR is out to remedy the growing lack of risk-taking reporting. It puts up the money at the crucial time, that is, at the early stage of a project when the writer has maybe only a strong, informed hunch of some chicanery on high or injustice affecting the lowly. It has also developed the media chops to disseminate and promote a story once it has found a home in a paper, magazine or TV show. The center has a small West Coast staff that coordinates the production of independent reporters and producers from all over the country. One of the center's earliest projects originated in a *Mother Jones* article that became a book, *Circle of Poison: Pesticides and People in a Hungry World,* by David Weir, now a *Nation* editorial board member, and Mark Schapiro, a longtime *Nation* contributor who is editorial director of CIR.

2927 Newbury Street, Suite A, Berkeley, CA 94703, (510) 809-3160, www.centerforinvestigativereporting.org

Independent Media Center. These centers first cropped up in Seattle in 1999, amid the tumult of the anti-WTO protests. Activists made the unsettling discovery that the media on the scene were not telling the truth about what the street people were protesting, treating them as violent anarchists, though 99 percent of them were representatives of labor unions, churches, colleges and public interest groups. In Seattle several hundred media activists merged to create the Independent Media Center to provide coverage of the WTO meeting. They put out a publication called *The Blind Spot* and set up a website, which received some 1.5 million hits during the demonstrations. At subsequent protests—in particular the Biodevastation Convergence in Boston and the A 16 action against the World Bank and International Monetary Fund in Washington—similar media centers were created. These triggered a flurry of interest, and people began contacting the working centers asking how to set up centers in their own areas. There are now more than one hundred local IMCs all over the world, each independent and autonomous, controlling its own finances, membership and agenda. The central slogan is "become the media," and the aim is to empower people to become reporters and writers and tell their own stories on the IMC websites. The IMC sponsors the open publishing newswire, which provides a globally accessible space for self-published articles, stories, commentary, reviews, digital photos and audio. Each local IMC appoints volunteers to monitor the postings on its newswire. Inflammatory posts are not erased; they are hidden and can be accessed.

www.indymedia.org

The Independent Press Association–New York. This is a surviving local branch of the San Francisco–based national Independent Press Association, which went belly-up in 2006. After the fall, the New York chapter carried on, living off the goodwill it had accumulated from fruitful relationships with independent NYC-based papers and magazines. IPA–NY runs an advertising co-op, provides technical assistance for dozens of local ethnic and community papers, publishes *Voices That Must Be Heard,* a weekly online newsletter that features the best work of its member papers, sponsors the Ippies (community journalism awards) and runs the Campus Journalism Project and the George Washington Williams Fellowship, which funds journalists of color interested in the magazine field. IPA has ninety-four members, representing the eclectic mix of cultures and languages in New York, including *The KIP Business Report, Nowy Dziennik, Arab Voice, News India-Times, Russian Forward* and *Haïti Progres.* It also works with national IPA members located in the city, like *City Limits, Harper's* and *Lilith.*

115 W. 29th Street, #606, New York, NY 10001, (212) 279-1442, www.indypressny.org

Media Monitors

Ten or twenty years ago the idea that media issues could stir political passions would have seemed far-fetched. You might complain about your hometown paper, but issues relating to the media were left to J-school seminars and trade publications. Nowadays, mainstream media issues have become political issues. Media takeovers, once confined to the business pages of the paper, generate letters to editors and members of Congress. An FCC ruling that allowed an entertainment conglomerate to own newspapers and TV stations in the same city generated demos and 3 million letters of protest from people demanding local control. Changes in the national communications law provoked debate outside the Beltway. All this showed how intensely people want community-owned voices, responsible to the community. It's not the same when your hometown paper's home office is in New York or Chicago. In response to the public demand, media policy groups have proliferated.

WATCHDOGS

Center for Media and Democracy. CMD trains a spotlight on the shadowy nexus between news and public relations. It circulates on the web a smart, lively e-mail bulletin called "The Weekly Spin," featuring ten or so items exposing PR machinations but spilling over into wider media issues. CMD crusades against phony video news releases that PR firms distribute to copy-hungry stations too cheap to find their own news. It also issues a quarterly investigative newsletter, *PR Watch,* which exposes such techniques as "astroturfing" (creating a phony grassroots group to support a corporate cause; for example, Hands Off the Internet, which was designed to mislead bloggers into abandoning the fight for Internet neutrality). It awards Falsies annually to the most outrageous examples of corporate spin. Another valuable CMD service is SourceWatch, which covers PR campaigns and profiles oft-cited think tanks, industry-funded groups and industry-friendly experts. Then there's Congresspedia, a "citizen's encyclopedia," updated Wikipedia fashion, which gives you basic dope on members of the House and Senate.

520 University Avenue, Suite 227, Madison, WI 53703, (608) 260-9713, www.prwatch.org

Fairness and Accuracy in Reporting (FAIR). Founded in 1986, FAIR was one of the first groups to undertake the task of regular, objective media criticism. On its website it provides a good rundown of the day's crop of erroneous, misleading or misreported news stories. During the run-up to the Iraq War it exposed administration lies about WMDs that were carried uncritically by the mainstream media. It adds to diligent research seasoned analysis that comes from more than twenty years in the media-monitoring business. FAIR has an up-to-date list of some 50,000 supporters who receive "Action Alerts" on stories of urgent concern. Since 1987 FAIR has published a bimonthly magazine, *Extra!,* edited by former *Nation* intern Jim Naureckas. FAIR maintains a growing archive of past stories on its website, where selected articles from the current issue are available. *Extra!* is subscriber subsidized; it carries no ads and accepts no corporate underwriters.

112 W. 27th Street, New York, NY 10001, (212) 633-6700, www.fair.org

Free Press. The idea for a media action organization surfaced in a special big-media issue of *The Nation* in 1996. It was another seven years until the launching of Free Press by Bob McChesney, a journalism professor at the University of Illinois at Urbana-Champaign; John Nichols, *The Nation's* Washington correspondent; and Josh Silver, a campaign finance reformer. The organization took off. By 2007 Free Press's membership had climbed above 350,000, and it had become the coordinator of a sizable coalition of public interest groups; unions; churches; consumer, feminist and similar organizations. It maintains an outstanding website that presents updated posts on policy issues and "core concerns" related to the press, radio, TV and the Internet at the national and state levels. In pursuing its objectives of media diversity, openness and access, Free Press functions as a research and educational organization. It has a lobbying arm, the Free Press Action Fund, which works with Congress members in drafting reform bills and bird dogs the FCC's latest rulings. Free Press coordinates scores of organizations in the StopBigMedia.com Coalition; promotes citizen letter-writing and phone campaigns to key legislators and rallies opposition to corporate-friendly revisions of the Telecommunications Act. It sponsors an annual media reform conference. (A parallel organization, SavetheInternet.com, coordinates a campaign for net neutrality.) Free Press's January 2007 conference in Memphis drew an overflow crowd of 3,500 people to hear a roster of speakers that included Bill Moyers, the Rev. Jesse Jackson, Van Jones, Representative Ed Markey (chair of the House Telecommunications Committee), Senator Bernie Sanders and two commissioners from the FCC. Issues discussed, according to one attendee, included "assembly of radio stations (high and low power), creating viral media for online distribution, fighting to save the Internet and public access television, expanding the range of opinion on dominant corporate media (including public television and radio), increasing diversity in media representation and ownership and critiquing and challenging the major media and the policies that help shape them."

40 Main Street, Suite 301, Florence, MA 01062, (877) 888-1533, www.freepress.net

McCHESNEY ON FREE PRESS

I didn't expect such strong growth and wide interest when we started out. Like most people I thought "the media" was abstract or academic. I was surprised by how interested people are in media reform. Journalists are our strongest allies. They understand the need for changing the system. At our Memphis Conference, among the 3,500 people who attended, I'd guess one hundred of them were journalists.

When the politicians realize people do care about media issues, which are not exclusively left or right, they'll be more responsive to the voters. We need to build up pressure from the grass roots. We have two overarching objectives: 1. Making an open Internet the right of every citizen; that means keeping it from being colonized by the big companies like ATT or Verizon. 2. Promoting diversity of media. We need policies that encourage competition. You can't rely on the market to produce what's desirable. It's not getting the job done. It's going to take conscious policy measures and legislation.

Institute for Public Accuracy. The IPA specializes in finding and making available experts and organizations, mainly identified with the independent Left, for interviews or comments on issues of the day. Most of IPA's experts are people who aren't found on the Rolodexes of mainstream reporters. Subscribers daily receive one, two, even three e-mail reports on fast-breaking issues, supplying brief, to-the-point quotes from sources knowledgeable about the particular issue. The sources' contact information is provided, as well as links to their organizations and relevant articles. IPA was founded in 1997 by Norman Solomon, who serves as its current executive director and is author of books on political and media issues.

National Office, 65 9th Street, Suite 3, San Francisco, CA 94103, (415) 552-5378, www.accuracy.org

Media Access Project. MAP is a public interest telecommunications law firm that "promotes the public's First Amendment right to hear and be heard on the electronic media." It represents plaintiffs denied a voice before the Federal Communications Commission and other policy-making bodies and in the courts. The organization was started in the early 1960s after the United Church of Christ sued the FCC, claiming it had a First Amendment right to argue before the commission. It was siding with blacks in a Mississippi town who complained that a local TV station offered no minority programming. Since then, MAP has brought suits for antiwar and civil rights groups demanding to be heard on network TV, opposed the Time Warner merger, advocated hiring more minorities and women and promoted diversity of ownership of all electronic media. It has claimed legal victories in a suit establishing that the "must carry" provisions of the 1992 Cable Act require public access to cable channels and one challenging a law setting "decency" standards for the Internet.

1625 K Street NW, Washington, DC 20006, (202) 232-4300, www.mediaaccess.org

Media Matters for America. MMA is a web-based monitor that crusades against right-wing misinformation. It was started in 2004 by David Brock, who contributed some of those distortions as a right-wing journalist, concocting fables like the "Troopergate" scandal in *The American Spectator* and trashing Anita Hill as "a little bit nutty and a little bit slutty." But Brock became disillusioned and defected to the Left. He wrote a confessional book, *Blinded by the Right,* and came out as a gay man. Under his leadership, the MMA website has nurtured an instant-response team capable of exposing conservative misinformation in real time. It regularly blows the whistle on right-wing opinion misleaders like Ann Coulter and Rush Limbaugh but also hits on omissions and commissions by the mainstream press. Media Matters was the first website to feature a clip of shock jock Don Imus dissing the Rutgers University women's basketball team. As the scandal picked up media steam, MMA adroitly stayed on top of the twenty-four-hour cable cycle.

1625 Massachusetts Avenue NW, Washington, DC 20036, (202) 756-4100, www.mediamatters.org

SIGNIFICANT OTHER MEDIA WATCHDOGS

Center for Creative Voices in Media. This nonprofit ensures that "original, independent, and diverse creative voices" are heard on the media by opposing media concentration, FCC "decency" censorship rules, limitations on Internet access and so on.

1220 L Street NW, Suite 100-494, Washington, DC 20005, (202) 903-4081, www.creativevoices.us

Center for International Media Action. CIMA opposes discrimination in media access on the basis of race, ethnicity, religion, gender, age, physical and mental ability, sexual orientation, class status or socioeconomic situation. It provides advice on organizing and mounting campaigns.

1276 Bergen Street, #2, Brooklyn, NY 11213, www.mediaactioncenter.org

Media and Democracy Coalition. A network of twenty-five groups collaborating to halt media mergers, promote local media ownership and guarantee universal Internet and broadband access.

1133 19th Street NW, 9th floor, Washington, DC 20036, (202) 736-5757, www.media-democracy.com

Media Empowerment Project. MEP is sponsored by the United Church of Christ's Office of Communication. Launched in 1959, it has defended various groups' right to be represented on the media; it promotes causes like low power radio, children's television, equal employment opportunity in media and holding broadcasters to their statutory public interest obligations. It receives funding from the Ford Foundation and Fordham University.

Office of Communications, 100 Maryland Avenue NE, Room 330, Washington, DC 20002, (202) 543-1517, www.urc.org

What's Online

The Internet is an expanding universe, fluid, amorphous, a gaseous entity of information, commerce and endless chat. Political blogs proliferate by the day. Those leaning Left are great in number and diverse in character. This listing takes a broad view of what is available, interesting, relevant and valuable for an engaged left readership in search of news, analysis, commentary and other information online. And so rather than include all of the best-known members of the liberal blogosphere (most of whom seem to do more or less the same thing), we have tried to compile a diverse, useful list that covers a lot of bases. It numbers around seventy-five, but in no way do they constitute a top seventy-five blogs, let alone a definitive list.

For easier reference, this list has been organized rather arbitrarily into four categories: News, Commentary, Themes and Resources. News *includes broadly focused progressive websites that both aggregate stories from a range of sources and/or produce their own original content.* Commentary *refers to content that is more analytical than reportorial.* Themes *includes news sites and blogs that are organized around a particular theme or unifying conceit, for example, workplace health and safety issues, Third Worldism or drug policy.* Resources *comprises a hodgepodge of sites that make available information, statistics and other data that might complement or elucidate a progressive interpretation of news and politics. The websites listed within each category are in no particular order and may be appropriate in more than one category. Each has a succinct and, we hope, educational description.*

NEWS

Truthdig. (www.truthdig.com) Former *Los Angeles Times* columnist and veteran progressive journalist Robert Scheer is editor in chief of this award-winning online magazine that mostly produces its own content. It numbers many well-known lefties among its regular contributors.

Guerrilla News Network. (www.guerrillanews.com) This independent news organization produces original content as well as material from other publications. Its founders, former MTV execs Stephen Marshall and Josh Shore, have given it a multimedia character, with video productions—docs and feature films, shorts, even music videos—as well as blogs.

WatchingAmerica. (http://watchingamerica.com) This site collects and translates news articles and opinion about the United States and American political developments from the global media.

Women's eNews. (www.womensenews.org) This news service commissions women journalists to write articles, on a wide range of topics, distributed daily to subscribers and posted on the website, which also features blogs, cartoons and columns. Its content is also available in Arabic, to reach women in the Arab world.

Indian Country Today. (www.indiancountry.com) This website calls itself "the nations' leading American Indian news source." It's owned by the Oneida Nation, and covers issues and political developments relating to the Native American community.

Truthout. (www.truthout.org) This site aggregates news and opinion pieces and other content from online media; there is some original content as well.

BuzzFlash. (www.buzzflash.com) There's some original stuff, but the site mainly links to a huge number of articles and opinion pieces in the online media; guest contributors include Cindy Sheehan. The original stuff is especially noteworthy for elaborate, salty and pugnacious headlines and minieditorials.

Grist. (www.grist.org) (see also **Themes, Left Periodicals**) Formerly print (see page 132) now online magazine that covers environmental issues and the green movement. The magazine-like site adopts a deliberately hip and fun attitude in its coverage; home of Gristmill blog.

AlterNet. (www.alternet.org) Site is a news aggregate, progressive newswire; there's some original content; PEEK group blog, video, discussion boards. Columnists include well-known lefties.

TomPaine. (www.tompaine.com) Since 2004 site has been a project of the Institute for America's Future (see page 193). Content-heavy, it aggregates and commissions opinion pieces—"progressive perspectives on the pressing issues."

Common Dreams. (www.commondreams.org) The site compiles news and opinion pieces from online media with some original content. There's a progressive newswire section.

LabourStart. (www.labourstart.org) This UK-based daily aggregate of international labor news also has action alerts.

The Narco News Bulletin. (www.narconews.com) This online magazine/newsletter covers the drug war and inter-American politics from the perspective of Latin America. It generates much of its own content but also collects stories from online media.

Antiwar. (www.antiwar.com) This site reports on the Iraq War and U.S. foreign policy and also combines original content with news and opinion pieces drawn from online media. It's a libertarian site, a project of the Randolph Bourne Institute, and it brings together right-wing isolationists like Pat Buchanan and Ron Paul with leftist peace activists like Uri Avnery and Juan Cole. Justin Raimondo is the well-known editorial director.

Inter Press Service. (http://ipsnews.net) This independent, international nonprofit news organization was started as a journalists' cooperative in the 1960s and specializes in in-depth reporting and analysis on global issues, generally from the perspective of the global south and other marginalized peoples. Its site is updated regularly with original news stories by IPS reporters and is also home to the blog of well-known journalist Jim Lobe, who is IPS Washington bureau chief.

Black Agenda Report. (www.blackagendareport.com) This weekly online magazine is published every Wednesday, with all original content on black politics. BAR monitors the Congressional Black Caucus. It was started by *Black Commentator* (see page 126) cofounder Glen Ford and a few others after they left that webzine in 2006.

The Electronic Urban Report. (www.eurweb.com) Find news on black entertainment, black news, urban news, black expression, black television, black art and hip-hop news on this site.

Black America. (www.blackamericaweb.com) Site has news and commentary from an African-American perspective—heavy on entertainment.

MWC News. (http://mwcnews.net) This independent news site Media with Consequences relies heavily on grassroots sources to provide news coverage. The stories put heavy emphasis on action and progressive social change. The editorial staff includes Norman Solomon, Marjorie Cohn and Juan Cole.

The War in Context. (www.warincontext.org) This site collects news stories and opinion pieces from a range of national and international sources on Iraq, the war on terrorism, foreign policy and the Middle East; it's updated daily.

COMMENTARY

The Huffington Post. (www.huffingtonpost.com) A well-known group blog that features a range of links and contributions by prominent liberals, from Andy Stern to David Sirota, Bill Maher and Alec Baldwin. Its politics are generally Democratic/progressive.

Daily Kos. (www.dailykos.com) The grandfather of them all was started in 2002 by Markos Moulitsas Zúniga, who is now a media celebrity and a leading voice of the liberal blogosphere. His annual convention in Washington has become a must for bloggers; in 2007 it drew most of the Democratic candidates, who submitted to sharp questions from a strongly antiwar audience, the cream of the netroots.

TomDispatch. (www.tomdispatch.com) Tom Engelhardt's blog, sponsored by the Nation Institute, has long, high-quality posts on a wide range of subjects by prominent lefties.

TPM: Talking Points Memo. (www.talkingpointsmemo.com) The flagship blog of Internet elder Joshua Micah Marshall: its empire now includes TPMMuckraker, which does investigative reports on political scandals and ethical issues, and TPMCafé, a well-regarded group blog and online discussion forum. Their finest hour: TPM's crew was credited with playing a lead role in exposing Attorneygate, the politically motivated firing of eight U.S. attorneys under Bush.

Hullabaloo. (http://digbysblog.blogspot.com) This well-regarded political blog is written by the pseudonymous Digby, who received the Paul Wellstone Citizen Leadership Award at the 2007 Take Back America Conference in Washington.

Balkinization. (http://balkin.blogspot.com) This is the blog of Yale Law professor Jack Balkin. He drills a laser focus on constitutional and civil liberties issues and is fiercely critical of the Bush administration.

MyDD. (http://mydd.com) MyDD (direct democracy) is a group blog that emphasizes political analysis with an eye toward increasing the power of the progressive movement; it showcases well-known left bloggers and netroots figures like Matt Stoller (see *Open Left*) and founder Jerome Armstrong, who wrote *Crashing the Gate* with Markos Moulitsas Zúniga of Daily Kos.

Open Left. (www.openleft.com) A news analysis and action website founded by Chris Bowers, Mike Lux and Matt Stoller. Stoller writes: "If there is a core philosophy to what I call the 'Open Left,' it's a respect for pluralism, openness and participation. We like to hash things out. And hashing things out tends to create a sense of community and natural discipline, since you kind of figure out where the obvious areas of agreement are and move in that direction."

David Sirota. (www.davidsirota.com) An online publication/blog maintained by journalist, author and *Nation* contributor David Sirota; it carries progressive political analysis, with an emphasis on domestic issues, the economy, labor, trade and corporate power.

Altercation. (http://mediamatters.org/altercation/) This is home base for *Nation* columnist Eric Alterman. His blog has been subsumed into Media Matters. As in *The Nation*, his writing is loosely focused on media commentary.

Christopher Hayes. (www.chrishayes.org) This site publishes a blog by *The Nation*'s Washington editor and former *In These Times* editor who comments on political developments and issues.

Marc Cooper. (www.marccooper.com) The *Nation* contributing editor and frequent writer on the West wings it.

Washington DeCoded. (www.washingtondecoded.com) This nonpartisan online newsletter is edited by *Nation* contributing editor Max Holland. One new article is published on the eleventh day of every month on a range of contemporary issues pertaining to political economy, foreign policy, government and so on, usually from a historical-analytic perspective.

Nation Blogs (And Another Thing, Capital Games, The Online Beat, ActNow!, Editor's Cut, Campaign '08; The Notion). (www.thenation.com) The various blogs are displayed on the *Nation* website by your favorite *Nation* regulars with political commentary and analysis: Katha Pollitt, John Nichols, David Corn, Katrina vanden Heuvel and Peter Rothberg.

Burnt Orange Report. (www.burntorangereport.com) This political blog is run mostly by University of Texas at Austin students (hence "burnt orange"). It covers national as well as Texas and local politics from a progressive-Democratic perspective.

TAPPED. (www.prospect.org/csnc/blogs/tapped/) *The American Prospect*'s group blog with articles by contributors.

MoJoBlog. (www.motherjones.com) *Mother Jones*'s blog has daily updates, news and original commentary on Washington, the environment, health and other topics by staffers.

Salon. (www.salon.com) Full-blown limited-access webzine. **Broadsheet** is a good women's issues blog (www.salon.com/mwt.broadsheet).

White House Watch. (www.washingtonpost.com) The weekday column by veteran D.C. journalist Dan Froomkin provides good coverage of White House goings-on as well as analysis and commentary on administration-related news from online and print media.

The Dreyfuss Report. (http://robertdreyfuss.com/blog/) Here the veteran journalist Robert Dreyfuss holds forth with intelligent, probing analysis and coverage of issues pertaining to national security, war, foreign policy.

Rootless Cosmopolitan. (http://tonykaron.com) Time.com editor Tony Karon stars on his own blog. His analysis and commentary used to be more focused on the war on terror; now it includes stuff on food and soccer. The name is a positive co-optation of "Stalin's euphemistic pejorative for 'Jew' "; meant to suggest a worldly, culturally diverse liberalism.

Crooks and Liars. (www.crooksandliars.com) John Amato's political blog with a liberal-progressive bent mostly collects audio and visual content of political events, related media programming, talk shows. It does some original audio interview content also.

DMIBlog. (http://dmiblog.com) This group blog on the Drum Major Institute's (see page 198) website focuses pretty much in line with DMI's agenda, with fresh commentary on politics and policy, economic and social justice and middle-class issues.

THEMES

Just World News. (http://justworldnews.org) This blog is by frequent *Nation* contributor Helena Cobban, who keeps a close eye on Iraq, Palestine, the Middle East and American foreign policy in the region. Cobban is a Quaker, a longtime journalist and a member of the International Institute of Strategic Studies.

Afro-Netizen. (www.afro-netizen.com) Chris Rabb, a prominent black netroots activist, covers race politics and digital culture and media. Rabb is active in addressing the de facto segregation that pervades much of the online media and blogosphere, and he self-identifies as a part of a new "digital ethnorati."

Upside Down World. (http://upsidedownworld.org) This online magazine focuses on politics, activism and social movements in Latin America, with independent, grassroots reporting on the region; articles, news briefs, blogs.

Informed Comment. (www.juancole.com) Middle East historian Juan Cole writes this indispensable blog on Iraq and the Middle East. Cole won the 2005 James Aronson Award for Social Justice Journalism from Hunter College and web awards. He is on the history faculty of the University of Michigan. Because of his blog's outspoken criticism of U.S. foreign policy and, more significantly, Israel, Cole may have been denied a position at Yale; Cole says he never officially applied for the job.

Lapham's Online. (http://laphamsquarterly.org/online_b.php) The blog progeny of *Lapham's Quarterly*, edited by former *Harper's* editor Lewis Lapham. The blog reads current events onto historical antecedents on the premise that history affords an analytic lens for understanding the world around us.

History News Network. (http://hnn.us) This nonpartisan online publication and discussion forum is managed by historians and associated with George Mason University, and is meant to contextualize current events and political happenings via a historical lens.

Foreign Policy in Focus. (www.fpif.org) This think tank without walls is a project of the Institute for Policy Studies. Drawing on a stable of 600 experts, it analyzes U.S. foreign policy and international affairs; it produces briefs, reports and policy papers that are available on the website.

This Modern World. (http://thismodernworld.com) Prolific political cartoonist Tom Tomorrow (real name Dan Perkins) maintains his own web gallery, named after his syndicated weekly comic strip. It mainly showcases the drawings and jottings of Tom and a few others. TM's weekly comic is available online on Monday mornings at Salon.com and Tuesdays at the **Working for Change** blog at www.workingassets.com.

The Electronic Intifada. (http://electronicintifada.net) This site provides online coverage of Palestine and the Israeli occupation. It combines news, analysis, high-quality reporting, commentary and various other resources and media forms and serves as a counterbalance to mainstream media's neglect of the Palestinians' side of the conflict. Veteran journalist and activist Ali Abunimah is executive director and a cofounder.

Feministing. (www.feministing.com) This group blog is overseen by executive editor Jessica Valenti. It is one of the most respected blogs on feminism, gender, reproductive rights and women's issues. Valenti and her coeditors are all young, and her blog self-consciously reflects their youthful perspective and opinion.

Scienceblogs.com. (www.scienceblogs.com) This is a project overseen by Seed Media Group, which puts out *Seed* magazine ("Science is culture"). Its network of more than sixty blogs deals with science-related issues, much of which is naturally left-leaning: public health issues, evolution and climate change. It is dedicated to increasing science literacy among lay folk. One of the blogs, **Effect Measure** (http://scienceblogs.com/effectmeasure), is maintained by senior public health scientists and practitioners who use the pen name Revere.

Edge of Sports. (www.edgeofsports.com) Home base for sports journalist and *Nation* sportswriter Dave Zirin who posts a weekly column here, usually on the intersection of sports and politics, race and class issues.

AFL-CIO Now. (http://blog.aflcio.org) This group blog of the AFL-CIO is a useful place to go when you want the latest news from the federation with updates on legislative developments pertaining to labor issues, action alerts and campaign news, as well as reaction from the labor movement to political developments.

Ag Observatory. (www.agobservatory.org) This website, a project of the Institute for Agriculture and Trade Policy, monitors agribusiness, farm and trade legislation; it collects relevant news stories; makes briefs, reports and other publications of the IATP available to the public.

Media Channel. (www.mediachannel.org) This website monitors mainstream media; aggregates news and analysis on the media industry, consolidation, coverage, bias and so on; produces original content, including blogs by cofounders Danny Schechter (see page 80) and Rory O'Conner.

Workday Minnesota. (www.workdayminnesota.org) Another good source for local and national labor news, where you'll find clips from the labor press and mainstream media, newswires to some extent. The site also produces its own content, particularly Minnesota news and notes. It's a joint project of the Labor Education Service at the University of Minnesota and state labor organizations.

RESOURCES

Human Rights Watch. (www.hrw.org) The website of the oldest and best of the human rights organizations is where you'll find a wealth of useful publications, statistics, data and so on about global human rights issues, along with individual country profiles.

International Freedom of Expression Exchange. (www.ifex.org) The material here is produced by a global coalition of civil liberties groups, focusing on freedom of expression; the website includes updates, news and action alerts on speech and press issues from around the world; as well as a weekly e-mail publication called *IFEX Communiqué*.

Weekly Toll. (http://weeklytoll.blogspot.com) This site was formerly housed at the well-regarded, now defunct Confined Space website. It has spun off as its own blog and provides an unscientific but extremely comprehensive biweekly listing of workplace deaths, to draw attention to the scandalously underreported toll of casualties from unsafe working conditions.

LobbyWatch (www.publicintegrity.org/lobby), Project Vote Smart (www.vote-smart.org), OpenSecrets (www.opensecrets.org), Right Web (http://rightweb.irc-online.org), Political Money Line (http://moneyline.cq.com/pm/home.doc) All these websites are designed as user-friendly public resources for accessing information about the political process—funding and lobbying records, congressional voting records, connections between various right-leaning organizations and individuals and so on. Depending on the resource, some are more data heavy, others rely on written profiles; all are designed to further the objective of transparency in politics.

National Security Archive. (www.gwu.edu/~nsarchiv/) This valuable nongovernmental research institute and library, based at George Washington University, collects and publishes declassified government documents pertaining to issues of foreign policy, national security, intelligence gathering, economic policy and the like. It vigorously uses FOIA to gain access to new documentation, particularly regarding Cuba, Iran-Contra, Latin America and so on.

Real Clear Politics. (www.realclearpolitics.com) This daily aggregate of political news and commentary is entirely nonpartisan and very useful, particularly because it also collects polling data, video content, transcripts.

COMFOOD. (www.foodsecurity.org/list.html) This e-mail listserv of the Community Food Security Coalition, a group of organizations that work to create "sustainable, just, democratic and prosperous local and regional food systems"; listserv is a good resource for information sharing, networking and debate among subscribers who are interested in those issues.

Portside. (www.portside.org) Another e-mail listserv, it sends out about five articles daily, culled from online media, on issues of interest to the progressive audiences. It also posts reader responses, action alerts, short campaign updates—a very good collection of news and commentary, sent to your inbox every morning.

National Priorities Project. (www.nationalpriorities.org) This research organization makes accessible to the public information and data on how tax dollars are spent by the government. It analyzes budgetary allocations, prepares easily digestible briefs, reports, databases and the like.

Wal-Mart Watch (http://walmartwatch.com), Wake Up Wal-Mart (www.wakeupwalmart.com) Both sites are good resources for information on Wal-Mart, the engine—or at least the defining corporate model—of twenty-first-century global capitalism. The sites contain blogs, news, stats, publications and so on. The first site is a joint project of the Center for Community and Corporate Ethics and Five Stores, and the second is from the United Food and Commercial Workers International Union. They've squabbled with each other over the years.

Project Gutenberg (www.gutenberg.org), Internet Archive (www.archive.org), Folkstreams (www.folkstreams.net) Each of these digital archives is devoted to preserving archival recorded material as well as ensuring that it remains in the public domain. **Gutenberg** is a library of free e-books; **Internet Archive** preserves an assortment of digital media, including movies, live music performances, old websites and so on; **Folkstreams** preserves documentary films and makes them available on the Internet.

Radio Making Waves

For progressives in red places, where talk radio means all Rush all morning to drive time, and Clear Channel bland rock sucks up the remaining air, even a single local progressive show is a ray of light. In New York or Madison or Minneapolis or Portland it's a different story, of course. What follows is a list of stations nationwide that offer some progressive programming ranging from all Pacifica all the time to Democracy Now! *to some Air America or perhaps a liberal talk jock or two.*

STATIONS

Alaska

Anchorage, KUDO, 1080 AM. (www.kudo1080.com)

Arizona

Phoenix, KPHX, 1480 AM. (http://1480kphx.com)

Tucson, KJLL, 1330 AM. (www.tucsonsjolt.com)

California

Berkeley, KPFA, 94.1 FM. (www.kpfa.org)

Eureka, KGOE, 1480 AM. (www.kgoe.com)

Los Angeles, KTLK, 1150 AM. (www.ktlk.com). *Comment:* This is a satellite of the Clear Channel network that owns more than 1,200 stations and has a reputation for dominating markets, cost-cutting, killing off local radio voices, enforcing musical mediocrity and censoring liberal opinion. But even Clear Channel must bow to public tastes and lets in a breath of Air America, RadioNation and other syndies.

Los Angeles, KPFK, 90.7 FM. (www.kpfk.org). *Comment:* KPFK was the second Pacifica station in the country and is the most powerful public radio station in the western United States.

Monterey, KRXA, 540 AM. (www.krxa540.com). *Comment:* Hal Ginsberg, the station's manager and owner, also hosts a local progressive program live each weekday.

Palm Springs, KPTR, 1340 AM.

Sacramento, KSAC, 1240 AM. (www.1240talkcity.com)

San Francisco, KKGN Green 960 AM. *Comment:* An hour of progressive news, covering Bay Area politics. *Shake!*, otherwise known as "queer channel radio," handles all things LGBT.

Santa Cruz, FRSC, 101.1 FM. (www.freakradio.org). *Comment:* Free radio Santa Cruz is an anticorporate pirate radio station operating without an FCC license. It broadcasts Pacifica content and other nationally syndicated progressive shows as well as locally produced shows.

Colorado

Denver, KKZN, 760 AM. (www.am760.net)

Salida, KHEN, 106.9 FM. (www.khen.org). *Comment:* This station also broadcasts locally produced programs like Dave Bowers's *Local Motion*, a show that explores the local/sustainable movement and how it affects Salida's economy, food supply, energy and environmental concerns.

District of Columbia

WPFW, 89.3 FM. (www.wpfw.org). *Comment:* Real community radio in the D.C. area with Pacifica, jazz, Third World music, news and public affairs including traditionally underrepresented minority and ethnic groups.

Florida

Daytona Beach, WPUL, 1590 AM. (www.wpul1590.com). *Comment:* Progressive local station includes shows like *Free Your Mind* with C. Cherry and *On the Agenda* with city commissioner Dwayne Taylor.

Miami, WINZ, 940 AM. (www.supertalk940.com)

Miami, WQAM, 560 AM. (www.wqam.com). *Comment:* When sports talk is turned off from 10 A.M. to 2 P.M., semi–shock jock Neil Rogers entertains, making fun of Republicans, religion, pretensions and his own gay identity.

Tampa, WMNF, 88.5 FM. (www.wmnf.org). *Comment:* Station features news programming like *CounterSpin*, *RadioNation* and *Democracy Now!* followed by in-depth local coverage in the evening.

Georgia

Atlanta, WRFG, 89.3 FM. (www.wrfg.org). *Comment:* Here's 100,000 pulsing watts of community-service radio. A day's programming might include the *Progressive News Hour, Hard Knock Radio* (a hip-hop talk show), *Free Speech News, Soul Rhapsody* and *Labor Forum.*

Idaho

Moscow, KRFP, 92.5 FM. (www.radiofreemoscow.com). *Comment:* This listener-supported station broadcasts comments by the likes of Howard Zinn, Michael Moore, Greg Palast and Noam Chomsky; shows on bioengineering, corporate watchdog programs and a weekly labor report.

Illinois

Chicago, WCPT, 820 AM. (www.wcpt820.com)

Chicago, WVON, 1690 AM. (www.wvon.com). *Comment:* The town's only black talk radio station is dedicated to informing the community.

Louisiana

Eunice/Lafayette, KEUN, 1490 AM. (www.keunworldwide.com)

Maine

Bangor, WERU, 89.9 FM. (www.weru.org). *Comment:* Music (folk, blues, activist songs) is mixed with *Democracy Now!, Free Speech Radio News* and *RadioActive* during the evening stretch.

Massachusetts

Northampton, WHMP, 1400 AM. (www.whmp.com). *Comment:* Progressive talk hosted by long-time residents Tom Vannah and Chris Collins.

Michigan

Ann Arbor, WLBY, 1290 AM. (www.1290wlby.com)

Detroit, WDTW, 1310 AM. (www.1310wdtw.com)

Minnesota

Minneapolis/St. Paul, KTNF, 950 AM. (www.950airamerica.com). *Comment:* Air America stronghold with Mark Heaney hosting *Minnesota Matters*, a progressive take on local politics.

Missouri

Kansas City, KKFI, 90.1 FM. (www.kkfi.org). *Comment:* This station broadcasts *Radio-Nation*, music programming and locally produced political shows such as Vicki Walker's *KC Media Watch Dogs*.

Nevada

Black Rock City, RFBM, 99.5 FM. (www.rfbm.org). *Comment:* Call it YouTube radio. Anyone from Black Rock City and environs can go on the air by simply walking in and talking with whomever happens to be at the mike.

Reno, KJFK, 1230 AM. (www.1230kjfk.com). "AM with IQ."

New Mexico

Albuquerque, KABQ, 1350 AM. (www.abqtalk.com)

New York

Buffalo, WWKB, 1520 AM. (www.kb1520.com)

Ithaca, WNYY, 1470 AM. (www.1470wnyy.com)

New York City, WBAI, 99.5 FM. (www.wbai.org). *Comment:* Unconventional, rudely independent, free-form, uninhibited, radical radio Pacifica-style.

New York City, WWRL, 1600 AM. (www.wwrl1600.com). *Comment:* Air America's home base in Gotham. Rennie Bishop, the station's program director, hosts a local show, *All Things New York.*

Rochester, WROC, 950 AM. (http://wroc-am.firstmediaworks.com)

North Carolina

Asheville, WPEK, 880 AM. (www.880therevolution.com)

Asheville, WPVM, 103.5 FM. (www.wpvm.org). *Comment:* Their slogan is "The progressive voice of the mountains."

Chapel Hill, WCHL, 1360 AM. (www.wchl1360.com)

Oregon

Coos Bay, KBBR, 1340 AM. (www.1340kbbr.com)

Medford, KEZX, 730 AM. (www.talkradio730.com). *Comment:* Station features liberal faves mushed with right-wing ranters.

Portland, KPOJ, 620 AM. (www.620kpoj.com)

South Carolina

Columbia, WOIC, 1230 AM. (www.woic.com)

Tennessee

Nashville, WRFN, 98.9 FM. (www.radiofreenashville.org). *Comment:* This Pacifica affiliate features local programming like the *Tennessee Progress Report* hosted by activist-organizer Nell Levin.

Texas

Austin, KOKE, 1600 AM.

Dallas, KNON, 89.3 FM. (www.knon.org). *Comment:* Community-supported radio features music and talk and working-folk programming, for example, *ACORN Hour, Workers' Beat* (SEIU Local 100) and *Empowerment Radio.*

Houston, KPFT, 90.1 FM. (www.kpft.org). *Comment:* The station's slogan is "Radio for peace." It's part of the Pacifica network.

Utah

Salt Lake City, KRCL, 90.9 FM. (www.krcl.org). *Comment:* Station broadcasts locally produced shows such as *RadioActive* (progressive politics) and *Now Queer This.*

Virginia

Charlottesville, WVAX, 1450 AM. (www.wvax.com)

Vermont

Brattleboro, WKVT, 1490 AM. (www.1490wkvt.com)

Washington

Seattle, KPTK, 1090 AM. (www.am1090seattle.com). *Comment:* Progressive regulars, plus green pages on the website and local gardening on the weekends, are broadcasted along with *Community Matters Weekend Edition,* which features interviews with Seattle politicos.

Spokane, KPTQ, 1280 AM. (www.1280kptq.com)

West Virginia

Wheeling, WVJW, 94.1 FM. (http://wvjw.info)

Wisconsin

Madison, WXXM, 92.1 FM, "The Mic." (www.themic921.com). *Comment:* In 2006 Clear Channel wanted to trade in left programming for all-sports radio. Madison progs rallied for the Mic and won.

TALK, TALK, TALK

Doug Basham. (www.dougbasham.com). Basham's a progressive radio voice in the Nevada desert, broadcasting on KLAV, 1230 AM.

Between the Lines. Broadcast from noncommercial, listener-supported WPKN (see page 162) in Bridgeport, Connecticut (89.5 FM), since 1991, *Between the Lines* "provides a platform for individuals and spokespersons from progressive organizations generally ignored or marginalized by the mainstream media." Each weekly show begins with the underreported news stories gleaned from the alternative press. Interview segments include phone numbers and Internet addresses so listeners can get in touch with activist groups. The show's website (www.btlonline.org) offers an archive and web stream.

Lynn Cullen. (www.1360wptt.com). Named one of Pittsburgh's fifty most influential cultural brokers by the *Pittsburgh Post-Gazette,* she's on WPTT, 1360 AM every morning, and she's a real liberal.

Deconstructing Dinner. (http://kootenaycoopradio.com/deconstructingdinner). Produced in Canada, *Deconstructing Dinner* tackles current food issues and seeks to create smarter consumers. Topics range from fair-trade foods to genetically modified crops to discussions of peak oil and workers' rights. The show is currently syndicated in the United States at KRBS in Oroville, California; KEIF in Enid, Oklahoma; KOWA in Olympia, Washington; KRFP in Moscow, Idaho; WZBC in Boston, Massachusetts; KQRP in Salida, California; WRFA in Jamestown, New York; WMRW in Warren, Vermont.

Jim Hightower. (www.jimhightower.com). Proprietor of *Hightower Lowdown* newsletter (see page 138). His *Common Sense Commentary* is aired daily on many radio networks.

RadioNation. (www.lauraflanders.com/pages/radionation.html). This syndicated weekly program hosted by Laura Flanders, showcases *Nation* writers, editors and authors talking about political, social and cultural questions of the day, as reported in a recent issue.

Mario Solis-Marich. (http//gotomario.com). His show features progressive talk—with a Latino host—broadcasting on KTLK, 1150 AM out of Los Angeles and streaming over the Internet.

Bree Walker. (www.breewalker.com). A former TV anchorwoman, Walker hosts a Saturday show on KTLK, 1150 AM to promote awareness of and support for new programs for the disabled. In June 2007 she made headlines when she purchased Camp Casey from Cindy Sheehan for a reported $87,000. Walker plans to build a memorial on the five-acre site and will also keep it open to protesters.

Jon Wiener. (www.jonwiener.com). *The Nation* contributing editor hosts a weekly show on KPFK, 90.7 FM in LA and 89.3 FM in Santa Barbara, while also streaming live on the web. Guests have included *Vanity Fair* columnist Christopher Hitchens, *Fast Food Nation* author Eric Schlosser and British journalist Andrew Cockburn. Wiener teaches history at the University of California, Irvine, writes and interviews like a journalist.

Peter Werbe. (www.peterwerbe.com). He has hosted a weekly show on WRIF, 101.1 FM for nearly forty years. He discusses Michigan politics as well as national.

Your Call. (www.yourcallradio.org). Rose Aguilar and Sandip Roy preside over a daily show on San Francisco's KALW, 91.7 FM.

Labor Radio

The menu of programs by and about working people on U.S. Radio is sparse but here are a few outlets.

America's Work Force. (www.awfradio.com). "The live labor radio voice for northern Ohio and America's working people." Ed Ferenc, the son of a steelworker, hosts it every morning on WKTX, 830 AM (Cortland) and WELW, 1330 AM (Willoughby).

Building Bridges. (www.buildingbridges.org). New York City's community labor report airs on Pacifica's WBAI, 99.5 FM on Mondays.

Heartland Labor Forum. (www.umkc.edu/labor-ed/radio.htm). Kansas City's only show about labor and the workplace is broadcast weekly on Thursdays and Fridays on KKFI, 90.1 FM. Live streaming available.

Labor Express. (www.laborexpress.org). Chicago's labor and current affairs radio program covers labor locally, nationally and internationally every Sunday night on WLUW, 88.7 FM.

Labor Radio. (http://wort-fm.org). This show airs every Friday evening on Madison's WORT, 89.9 FM. The station says its mission includes "strengthening local unions, increasing the breadth and depth of media coverage on labor issues, and providing for the information needs of the community."

Voices at Work. (www.voicesatwork.net). A weekly radio show for and by workers airs on KPFT, 90.1 FM in Houston, Texas. Podcasts and downloads are available on its website.

Workers Independent News. (www.laborradio.org). Founded in 2000 as a labor-oriented news service, WIN sustains a staff of producers and reporters who gather and package news items and feed them to radio stations and print publications. You can listen to them on the website.

The World of Work. (www.wdvrfm.org). Hosted by labor lawyer Shep Cohen, the show airs on Friday evenings on southern New Jersey's WVDR, 89.7 and 91.9 FM.

NETWORKS AND PRODUCTION SHOPS

Air America Radio. Launched in 2004, America's first progressive talk network was platformed as an antidote to right-wing bloviators. The network ran through some rough patches but built an audience, proving there were hundreds of thousands of

---

LATINO JOCKS STEAL A MARCH

It is widely acknowledged that an unlikely band of ribald, prankster disc jockeys played a crucial role in generating the massive turnout [of Latinos for immigration reform in Los Angeles on March 25, 2006]. In what may go down as a historic meeting of the mouths, four rival morning DJs—KSCA's El Piolín (Eduardo Sotelo), KLAX's El Cucuy (Renán Almendárez Coello), KBUE's El Mandril (Ricardo Sánchez) and KHJ's Humberto Luna—held a joint news conference announcing their support for the March 25 rally. Sotelo, whose show on Univision-owned KSCA is the highest-rated radio program in LA, called the meeting and became the most recognized for his passionate support of the rally. "It was fascinating, to say the least," said LA march organizer Javier Rodríguez. "Here were [El Piolín and El Cucuy] the two top [morning show] DJs, competitors, coming forth and saying, We're going to march with you, we're going to get everybody together." Rodríguez laid much of the groundwork for the DJ détente by organizing a breakfast March 14 that not only resulted in massive local news coverage but also prompted an invitation from El Mandril to appear on his show. Two days later, El Mandril called his rival El Piolín on the air, and the DJ movement was on. "Radio, unlike TV, focuses on how to effectively speak to the common man and woman and thus has been able to generate a great deal of enthusiasm," said Angelica Salas, executive director of the Coalition for Humane Immigrant Rights of Los Angeles, one of the march organizers. "Many of the disc jockeys are themselves immigrants and can relate to the struggle that their listeners face and motivate them to be active."

—ED MORALES, *The Nation*, May 15, 2006

Americans who were starved for alternative points of view. By 2006, however, the network was struggling, having developed business problems. It filed for Chapter 21 bankruptcy protection. Then, in March 2007, the Green brothers—Mark, the former New York City public advocate, senatorial and mayoral candidate, and Stephen, the real estate magnate—purchased the franchise, took over operations and started rebuilding. They lost their morning star, comedian Al Franken, who left to run for the Senate in his native Minnesota, but a new lineup slowly emerged, and AAR was offering twenty hours of progressive programming, including daily talk shows hosted by Randi Rhodes, the Young Turks, Thom Hartmann, the Air Americans, Rachel Maddow and Jon Elliott. On weekends a lineup of familiar personalities holds forth, including *Ring of Fire* (Robert F. Kennedy, Jr., Mike Papantonio and John Morgan) and *RadioNation.* The shows are syndicated around the country on smaller community stations. At last count, Air America claimed around seventy affiliates and a weekly audience of 1.7 million.

www.airamerica.com

National Radio Project. In 1994 a group of community activists, journalists and visionaries sat down in an Oakland café to discuss how to counter the pullulating blab of right-wing "hate radio." They set up the National Radio Project in self-defense. First, they created a series of thirteen weekly programs called *Making Contact,* which they continue to produce and distribute via the Internet and which are picked up by many stations throughout the country. They offer interviews, discussions, call-ins from overseas hot spots like Damascus and Baghdad. NRP has five desks covering neglected issues—women, globalization, prisons, environment and labor. Go to its website and click on "Where to Listen." New York, New York? Answer: WBAI, 99.5 FM (occasionally). Enid, Oklahoma? Answer: KEIF, 104.7 FM.

1714 Franklin Street, #100-251, Oakland, CA 94612, (510) 251-1332, www.radioproject.org

Pacifica Foundation. KPFA in Berkeley—the first station in the Pacifica chain of publicly owned, independent stations—was founded in 1946 by a couple of pacifists. Now the oldest public network in the United States, Pacifica comprises five sister stations: KPFA (Berkeley); KPFK (Los Angeles and Santa Barbara); KPFT (Houston); WBAI (New York City) and WPFW (Washington, D.C.), plus 120 community affiliates. During the 1990s, temblors of dissent, originating along the San Francisco–Berkeley fault, rippled through the network. A significant faction of listeners were convinced that the Pacifica Board under Mary Frances Berry intended to nullify each station's independent control over programming and to standardize content, replace listener-supported radio with corporate underwriters and/or sell off the New York and Washington stations for hundreds of millions. Listeners and local staff raised hell. Strikes, sit-ins and lawsuits were met by firings, lockouts and countersuits. Eventually, the constitution was changed to give local listeners the power to elect board members at their stations, and these people in turn chose the Pacifica National Board. The network seemed back on track, and the national production facility started making new programs like *From the Vault*, drawing material from Pacifica's historic archives, and *Informativo Pacifica*, a daily Spanish-language program. Staple shows also survived the storm. *Democracy Now!*, the jewel in the Pacifica crown—a popular news, interview and investigative show hosted by the indomitable Amy Goodman—spun off to become an independent operation; it's now syndicated on 450 stations. Shows like *Uprising Radio* (produced by KPFK in Los Angeles and syndicated nationally) and *Free Speech Radio News* are heard from Fairbanks, Alaska, to Tampa, Florida. And the network's programming is enriched by the fare served up by independent local stations, dealing with national and international issues but also local ones, underscoring the "community" in community radio.

1925 Martin Luther King Jr. Way, Berkeley, CA 94704, (510) 849-2590, www.pacificafoundation.org

Public Radio Exchange. PRX is an online marketplace for distribution, review and licensing of public radio programming—kind of an online bulletin board where radio producers post content and radio stations eyeball and acquire it. Part of PRX's service is taking care of rights and collecting royalties. The website previews offbeat shows as well as many documentaries. Sample entries: *Only in America: 350 Years of the American Jewish Experience*, *Living with Lou Gehrig's Disease*, *The Tale of the Allergist's Wife* by the LA Theater Works. All these could be acquired by your local station.

2 Arrow Street, 4th floor, Cambridge, MA 02138, (617) 576-5455, www.prx.org

Transom.org. This website describes itself as a "showcase & workshop for new public radio." It's a subsidiary of Atlantic Public Media. Transom.org founder and director Jay Allison recognized the need to find alternatives to that smoothly professional "NPR voice." So Transom.org solicits programs by unknowns and trots out the pick of the litter on its website. ("Over the transom" is the journalistic term for unsolicited manuscripts.) Call it a farm club. It encourages aspiring producers with advice, discussions of technique and descriptions of new technology. Transom.org accepts radio show submissions from almost anyone with a voice and equipment to record them, so long as they meet the formatting guidelines laid out on the website. Some submissions are heard on the website or broadcast on local stations or even picked up by one of the NPR shows. If you fancy you have a *This American Life* episode in you, or an *All Things Considered* segment, this website could be your point of entry.

PO Box 445, 3 Water Street, Woods Hole, MA 02543, (508) 548-5527, www.transom.org

ADVOCACY GROUPS

Grassroots Radio Coalition. This outfit is a loose assemblage of community media activists who in the mid-1990s coalesced around a common dissatisfaction with the increasing commercialization of National Public Radio and other community stations and a concomitant slump in support for the volunteer-run stations. Out of their discontent flowered the first annual Grassroots Radio Conference in Boulder, Colorado, in the summer of 1996. It was sponsored by two community radio stations—KGNU in Boulder and WERU in Blue Hill, Maine. The GRC has a listserv and holds a conference every year. These get-togethers give radio communitarians a chance to chat about areas of common interest, from advocacy to outreach to the mundane chores of running a radio station.

www.grradio.org

Liberal Talk Radio. Styling itself your "alternative media radio resource," this blog devotes itself to reporting on the comings and goings in liberal talk radioland. It's a good place to go if you want to know which affiliates are adding syndicated hosts or shows to their lineups. LTR is also a good resource for tracking down liberal radio stations across the country when you find yourself a stranger in a strange land.

www.ltradio.blogspot.com

National Federation of Community Broadcasters. This association of local, noncorporate stations is not overtly left (or right), but its fight to keep community radio alive in big cities as well as rural areas is of necessity anticorporate and is surely pro–Joe and Jane Listener. Its core values are localism, collaboration, quality public service, cultural preservation and building community. It's proud to have member stations that broadcast in English, Spanish, Navajo, Apache, Lakota, Russian, Creole and Hmong in a wide array of radio formats. NFCB projects include National Youth in Radio Training Project, Low Power FM, Rural Programming Initiative, Native Public Media, Radio for People, Basic Radio Station Website Strategies.

1970 Broadway, Suite 1000, Oakland, CA 94612, (510) 451-8200, www.nfcb.org

Prometheus Radio Project. In 1998 a band of radio activists who wanted to preserve diverse community radio founded Prometheus. They sought "easy access to media outlets and a broad, exciting selection of culture and informative media resources." The main path to that goal, they figured, was the support of low-power FM (LPFM) radio stations. Two or three times a year Prometheus Radio Project members turn out to help a community group that has successfully applied for and received a radio construction permit to operate a low-power FM station. Their website conjures up a vision of

Prometheus volunteers rushing by train, plane and automobile to the site of the new station, where "Low Power FM radio applicants, journalists, radio engineers, students, lawyers, musicians, activists and folks from across the country" commingle "to raise the antenna mast, build the studio, and flip on the station switch . . . all over a long weekend!" At last count, with the Malcolm X Grassroots Center's WXMP, they had helped eleven stations get up and broadcasting.

PO Box 42158, Philadelphia, PA 19101, (215) 727-9620, www.prometheusradio.org

TV: Oases in the Wasteland

CABLE AND SATELLITE NETWORKS

Deep Dish TV. Calling itself "the first national grassroots satellite network," Deep Dish TV was created in 1986 as the distribution arm of the five-year-old Paper Tiger Television video collective (see page 177). DDTV is a content distributor that brings together independent video makers and activists with local public access producers and programmers. Deep Dish TV helps local independent producers edit and package programming and then beams it via satellite to more than "200 cable systems around the country, as well as selected public television stations, and received by thousands of satellite dish viewers nationwide." Programming has featured *Shocking & Awful* (2004–2005), a thirteen-part series that represented the work of more than one hundred artists, video makers, producers and editors bent on challenging the purpose, legitimacy and conduct of the U.S. war on Iraq, and *Iraqi Women Speak Out,* made with the feminist antiwar organization Code-Pink. Deep Dish TV is not a separate channel. You can view its programming on other cable systems and public-access stations. Check your cable or DISH Network listings.

339 Lafayette Street, New York, NY 10012, (212) 473-8933, www.deepdishtv.org

Free Speech TV. Founded in 1995, Free Speech TV uses "the power of television to expand social consciousness . . . by exposing the public to perspectives excluded from the corporate-owned media." The unit traces its roots to *The '90s*, a progressive television program that was syndicated by PBS, and the 90s Channel, a full-time progressive cable network that carried programming like the *Gulf War Crisis TV Project*. Both were created in 1989 by media activist John Schwartz. After they were forced off the air in 1995 when cable giant TCI imposed a massive rate increase, Schwartz bounced back with Free Speech TV, distributing the programs to a network of fifty community cable channels. In 2000, after the FCC began enforcing a clause of the 1992 Cable Act that satellite companies must reserve at least 4 percent of their broadcast spectrum for noncommercial educational use, Free Speech acquired a twenty-four-hour satellite channel on the DISH Network. With this platform and its distribution network of more than 150 community-access cable stations, it reaches more than 25 million homes. Free Speech TV disseminates a daily schedule of independently produced documentaries, commissioned works, serial programming and live broadcasts. Programming covers the waterfront of social, cultural, political and environmental issues. Free Speech made the Iraq War a major focus of its programming.

PO Box 44099, Denver, CO 80201, (888) 378-8855), www.freespeech.org

Link TV. Link TV is a nationwide, noncommercial television network devoted to presenting diverse and alternative perspectives on national and international issues. Since 1999 it has reached more than 29 million homes. Link combines news and documentaries with music and other cultural programming from around the world, along with "innovative participatory programs promoting citizen action" and outreach to underserved communities. The Peabody Award–winning Link TV program *Mosaic* compiles daily news reports from more than thirty TV broadcasts throughout the Middle East and airs them unedited with English translation. Producer Jamal Dajani has said, "Our mission is to bring a window to what people in the Middle East watch on a daily basis" and to give American viewers an inside perspective on regional issues. Another program, called *Latin Pulse*, was launched in April 2007 to present a similar perspective on current events in Latin America. A large percentage of the documentary programming on Link TV consists of foreign-made productions being shown in the United States for the first time. The Iraq War has been a persistent focus.

Link Media, PO Box 2008, San Francisco, CA 94126, www.linktv.org

INDEPENDENT PRODUCERS, FUNDERS AND SUPPORTERS

Denver Open Media. After Denver Community Television went out of business in September 2005, a local nonprofit called Deproduction created Denver Open Media as the city's public-access channel. First aired in December 2006, Denver Open Media is an extension of the broader mission of Deproduction, which aims to "put the power of the media into the hands of the community." Denver Open Media has featured viewer-run programming in the spirit of eBay, Wikipedia, Facebook and YouTube on the Internet. Viewers vote online for the programming they want to see and when. Denver Open Media also makes available to the public video equipment, media training, studio production and editing technology. According to Tony Shawcross, executive director of Deproduction, the Denver Open Media production model seeks to achieve "the ultimate promise of media: the strongest force in the world for engaging communities and bringing society together. . . . The future is decentralization. . . . Centralization will fall, and the people will take the driver's seat."

700 Kalamath Street, Denver, CO 80204, (720) 222-0160, www.denveropenmedia.org

Downtown Community Television Center. Founded by documentary filmmaker and journalist Jon Alpert and his wife, Keiko Tsuno, in 1972, DCTV is a New York community center devoted to supporting and facilitating independent media production by a diverse public. It offers free or low-cost courses on electronic media production and makes available high-quality production equipment and studio space. DCTV has won a trunk full of awards. It targets low-income, minority and at-risk youths, gives them training in television and documentary filmmaking and hooks them up with mentors. In 1999, DCTV birthed ConnecTV, a program that equips and trains people with disabilities. Some of the work that has come out of DCTV's training programs has been professionally distributed and shown on networks like PBS, HBO and the BBC and on cable access or satellite channels. Since the early 1980s, DCTV has been located in a nineteenth-century firehouse in Chinatown. The building was recently renovated and equipped with wireless technology. (See *Democracy Now!* page 179.)

87 Lafayette Street, New York, NY 10013, (212) 966-4510, www.dctvny.org

EnviroVideo. A group project of the nonprofit Envision Environmental Media Center, Enviro generates half-hour documentary programs on subjects like the weaponization of space, alternative energy sources and the legacy of the Three Mile Island meltdown; hour-long EnviroVideo specials are on subjects like voter fraud and the effects of economic globalization. A regular half-hour interview series, *Enviro Close-Up,* is hosted by Karl Grossman, a veteran investigative journalist and SUNY Old Westbury professor. He interviews experts on issues such as global warming, environmental pollution, public health and biodiversity. *Enviro Close-Up,* along with other EnviroVideo programs, can be seen on Free Speech TV and public-access cable stations; all EnviroVideo programming is available for order on the center's website.

Envision Environmental Media Center, PO Box 311, Fort Tilden, NY 11695, (800) 320-8846, www.envirovideo.com

Independent Television Service. ITVS has its origins in legislation passed by Congress in 1988, which required the Corporation for Public Broadcasting to support a coalition of independent producer groups. ITVS functions as "a bridge between producers and public television," supporting video makers with funds, training and editorial feedback, as well as "a comprehensive public television launch which includes marketing, publicity, website, station relations and outreach support." With an annual budget of more than $7 million, almost all of which is reserved for production, ITVS is one of the largest financiers of independently produced public television in the country.

651 Brannan Street, Suite 410, San Francisco, CA 94107, www.itvs.org

Paper Tiger Television. This collective of video makers was inspired by a course cofounder Dee Dee Halleck took in 1981 with the media savant Herbert Schiller, for many years an analyst for *The Nation*. This open, nonprofit volunteer collective has made well over 400 programs, which address and critique issues pertaining to media, culture and politics with the objective of "increasing public awareness of the negative influence of mass media and involving people in the process of making media." In 1986, Halleck and Paper Tiger created Deep Dish TV (see page 174) to distribute the collective's shows to public-access and satellite channels.

339 Lafayette Street, 3rd floor, New York, NY 10012, (212) 420-9045, www.papertiger.org

Saveaccess. This website is devoted to monitoring legislative developments pertaining to community media issues. It makes available detailed analyses of the important issues in the struggle to preserve community television and does general movement-building work.

www.saveaccess.org

LEFT TV: AN ALL-STAR LINEUP

Alternate Focus. A Muslim, a Jew and a Christian walk into a broadcasting studio and start covering the Middle East. No, it's not the setup for a joke, it's how this group really started in 2002. Its three founding directors were Al Maaz (the Muslim), Ed Sweed (the Jew) and George Nasser (the Christian). They figured that their multiethnic mix would produce alternative views to the mainstream coverage of the region, particularly the Israel-Palestine Sixty Years War. They produce shows broadcast on various channels. Productions have included *Wall of Shame*, a half-hour report on the separation wall under construction by the Israeli government; *Refuseniks*, a fifty-two-minute program on two Israeli Army reserve soldiers who joined 500 others in signing a letter

refusing to participate in the occupation; *Curfew,* an account of restrictions imposed on people in the Palestinian city of Jenin; and *The Empire Strikes Out,* a dark view of the war in Iraq. More than twenty producers contribute shows to Alternate Focus, which also works with a number of independent video producers who make their documentaries available for broadcast. Volunteers, predominantly young activists, perform other tasks. Shows are broadcast on public access channels in cities around the country and on Free Speech TV. (See website for schedule.)

3830 Valley Centre Drive, Suite 705-PMB741, San Diego, CA 92130, (858) 551-0191, www.alternatefocus.org

America's Defense Monitor. This highly regarded, multiple award–winning television program was broadcast weekly on scores of PBS affiliates and cable stations around the country from 1987 to 2000. It was produced by the Center for Defense Information, a Washington think tank advocating reduced and more-transparent defense budgets and greater reliance on international diplomacy. Though the show has been off the air for nearly a decade, the episodes are still available on the website and can be used as informational and instructional videos to facilitate discussions in classrooms, peace groups, political parties, MoveOn house parties—wherever serious citizens gather.

Center for Defense Information, 1779 Massachusetts Avenue NW, Washington, DC 20036, www.cdi.org/adm/

Bill Moyers Journal. Bill Moyers retired and turned over his program, *Now,* to the able David Brancaccio, who does more field reporting. But Moyers is back, telling listeners: "I retired from *NOW with Bill Moyers* two years ago because it was time. Now it's time to come back. Old journalists, like old soldiers, never die; we just tell new stories." The show features Moyers sitting down one-on-one with political figures, activists, authors, poets, artists, preachers. He proves himself yet again to be one of the most intelligent and empathetic interviewers on the medium. He intersperses insightful commentaries and filmed reports.

www.pbs.org/moyers/journal/index-flash.html

The Daily Show with Jon Stewart and The Colbert Report. Satirical reality TV: put-ons and parodies of punditry.

www.thedailyshow.com, www.comedycentral.com/shows/the_colbert_report/index.jhtml

Democracy Now! Amy Goodman and Juan Gonzalez's highly successful, truth-digging daily radio news program is, according to its website, "the only public media program in the country that airs on radio, satellite and cable television, shortwave radio, and the internet." *Democracy Now!* is produced out of the DCTV Firehouse in Chinatown. See website for local schedules and stations.

87 Lafayette Street, New York, NY 10013, (212) 966-4510, www.democracynow.org

International News Net World Report. Daily news and political affairs with a focus on international politics, the Iraq War and the Middle East, globalization and counter-intelligence operations. Though the show's politics appear to range broadly enough to interview as guest experts and contributors well-known lefties—like Dennis Kucinich, Daniel Ellsberg, Cynthia McKinney, Robert Dreyfuss and Laura Flanders—as well as some libertarians and a smattering of 9/11 conspiracists. The show is broadcast regularly on Free Speech TV and also on cable channels.

56 Walker Street, New York, NY 10013, (888) 905-2835, www.innworldreport.net

Labor Beat. This cable TV news program is produced by the Chicago-based Committee for Labor Access, which also produces a radio show called *Labor Express* (see page 169). Shows are broadcast regularly on Chicago public access, and rebroadcast in St. Louis; Rockford, Illinois and New York City. *Labor Beat* covers local doings (organizing campaigns, strikes, pickets, union elections, May Day celebration in Haymarket Square); national stories (*Sicko*, Labor against the War, Employee Free Choice Act) and international developments (solidarity with Iraqi trade unionists, humanitarian crisis in Gaza). It's affiliated with Local 1220 of the International Brotherhood of Electrical Workers; most funding comes from workers' organizations and individual donations.

37 S. Ashland Boulevard, #1W, Chicago, IL 60607, (312) 226-3330, www.laborbeat.org

Liberty News TV. A kind of progressive, public-access alternative to cable news, this totally independent, unsponsored half-hour monthly special wrestles with corruption, loss of individual freedoms, corporatism and religious intolerance. Although it's put together "in a Portland basement studio the size of a broom closet," the technical quality is remarkably high. The show is written by professional journalists and produced by professional technicians, who turn out smooth shows with titles like *Impeachment Time?*, *Spinning Rove* and *Nuclear Roulette*. The first show aired in 2005. Liberty News TV shows are broadcast on DISH Network and Free Speech TV, and on public-access channels around the country. It produced a "futurementary" called *Pax America 2031* that covers the 2008 election from the perspective of thirty years in the future.

PO Box 10847, Portland, ME 04104, www.libertynewstv.com

P.O.V. Television's longest-running showcase for independent nonfiction films premiers fourteen to sixteen films a year in keeping with PBS's long, if diminished, tradition of providing an outlet for documentary filmmakers.

www.pbs.org/pov

Left Heritage Trail

ALABAMA

Sixteenth Street Baptist Church. At this, the first black church in Birmingham, on September 18, 1963, Youth Day, a bomb blasted four little girls—Addie Mae Collins, Denise McNair, Carole Robertson and Cynthia Wesley—to heaven. Years later Klansman Robert Edward "Dynamite Bob" Chambliss was convicted of the murder of Denise McNair and sentenced to life in prison. This atrocity, plus police beatings of Selma marchers and the unleashing of dogs against peaceful demonstrators in Birmingham, swung public opinion behind the civil rights cause.

6th Avenue and 16th Street, Birmingham, AL

MY FAVORITE AMERICAN PLACE

Selma, Alabama, is my favorite place. I remember it for an inspiring moment in November of 1963 when the black citizens of Dallas County jammed into a church the night before they were to defy police and state troopers in an attempt to register to vote, and we all listened to the Selma Freedom Chorus raise the spirit of the crowd to the heavens.

—HOWARD ZINN

MISSISSIPPI

Ronald Reagan Speech. We suggest the following Historical Marker for the town of Philadelphia, Mississippi: "On this spot in early August 1980, presidential candidate Ronald Reagan declared, 'I believe in states' rights,' and promised to 'restore to the states and local communities those functions that properly belong there.' He deliberately made no mention of an atrocious crime that occurred in Philadelphia in 1964: the murder of three civil rights workers, Michael Schwerner, Andrew Goodman and James Chaney. In 2005—forty-one years after the murders—Edgar Ray 'Preacher' Killen was convicted of manslaughter for instigating the murders and sentenced to sixty years in prison. He was then eighty years old. Seven other surviving Klansmen who participated in the murders never did time."

Ronald Reagan Speech Marker, to be erected, Philadelphia, MS

Robert Johnson's Crossroads. The intersection of Highway 69 and Highway 41 has been pinpointed by scholars, seers and conjure persons as the spot where early bluesman Robert Johnson made a pact with the devil, selling his soul for musical success. Perhaps the durability of the myth derives from Johnson's immortal impact on the history of blues, folk and rock music. Clarksdale is also home to the Delta Blues Museum, established in 1979, which exhibits old instruments, pictures and recordings of great Delta bluesmen and women.

LOUISIANA

Kate Chopin House. In 1878 Kate Chopin arrived in Cloutierville, which she described as "two long rows of very old frame houses, facing each other closely across a dusty roadway." After her husband's death in 1882, Chopin was left at age thirty-one with their two children and his debts. The rumor in Cloutierville was that she had an affair with a married man; scandal seemed to seek her out. She spent only a few years in the town, leaving to join her mother in St. Louis, where she started writing seriously. Many of her stories are set in a fictionalized Cloutierville. *The Awakening,* her finest novel, scandalized contemporaries with its frank portrayal of a woman's sexuality. She died in 1904, disgraced and forgotten; she is now a feminist heroine.

243 State Route 495, Cloutierville, LA 71416, (318) 379-2233

Congo Square. Here is the birthplace of jazz in New Orleans, if any single place can be so pinpointed. In the late eighteenth and early nineteenth centuries, slaves as well as free blacks and American Indians gathered every Sunday at the "square," a marketplace of goods and entertainment where displaced Africans could play their traditional music—drumming, songs and dances. This music, infused with the savory, pleasure-loving, interracial ambience of New Orleans, ended up in the pot simmering America's native musical gumbo—jazz. A square in the southern part of the park honors Louis Armstrong.

Louis Armstrong Memorial Park, bounded by Saint Philip Street, North Rampart Street and Orleans Avenue in the Treme neighborhood, New Orleans, LA

THE BAMBOULA.

OHIO

Auto-Lite Workers Strike. In 1934, workers at the Electric Auto-Lite Company went out on strike, and the company promptly hired strikebreakers. Hundreds of men showed up to close the factory by blocking the gates; each day thousands more joined them. Special police charged in and beat up the strikers, injuring 200. The crowd fought back. It took hundreds of National Guardsmen and Auto-Lite's promise to close its plant temporarily to disperse the crowd. Ultimately, Auto-Lite recognized the union and rehired the strikers. A memorial in Union Memorial Park features a male and a female worker with signs reading "Solidarity Forever" and "Dignity in the Workplace."

Union Memorial Park, Elm and Champlain streets, Toledo, OH

INDIANA

Madam C. J. Walker Factory. She made black woman more beautiful. Born Sarah Breedlove in Louisiana in 1867, the daughter of former slaves, she built a beauty products empire with its headquarters in Indianapolis. The formula of her first product, Wonderful Hair Grower, came to her in a dream. Moving to Denver, she

beloved hometown. He was the respectable leader of the locomotive firemen's craft union and well-paid editor of the union paper. His wife had inherited money, and the Debses were esteemed by Terre Haute's bourgeoisie. But his work as a labor leader plunged him into the maelstrom of late-nineteenth-century industrial unrest. During the great Pullman Strike (see page 109) when he was president of the striking American Railway Union, he was thrown in jail. Kate visited him wearing her best diamonds. His campaigns for the presidency frequently took him away from home. The marriage was unhappy, and he found companionship outside it. He was buried separately from the Debs family plot because he feared his controversial reputation might attract vandals who would desecrate his wife's grave. Now his grave is beside hers.

451 N. 8th Street, Terre Haute, IN 47807

married C. J. Walker, an advertising salesman who helped her market a growing line of beauty products. In 1910, she moved her operation to Indianapolis. Madam Walker became one of America's richest women, and built herself a $350,000 mansion in Irvington-on-Hudson, New York. She made Horatio Alger an equal-opportunity inspirer, telling the National Negro Business League in 1913: "I want to say to every Negro woman present, don't sit down and wait for the opportunities to come. . . . Get up and make them!" She ordered her lawyer to sue a movie theater that charged her more for a ticket than it did whites, protested segregation in the U.S. military and denounced lynching and federal segregation in Washington, D.C. She died in 1919, aged fifty-one, eulogized by her friend W. E. B. Du Bois for her financial support of the NAACP.

Madam C. J. Walker Theatre, 617 Indiana Avenue, Indianapolis, IN 46202, http://walkertheatre.com, www.madamcjwalker.com

Eugene V. Debs Home. Debs and his wife, Kate, built this Queen Anne–style house in 1890 in Terre Haute, his

KENTUCKY

Federal Correctional Institution, Ashland. In June 1950, John Howard Lawson, screenwriter and first president of the Screenwriters Guild, and Dalton Trumbo, novelist and screenwriter, began serving one-year terms at this low-security federal prison. Lawson and Trumbo were jailed for refusing to testify at the 1947 HUAC hearings whether they belonged to the Communist Party. Rather than cooperate with the HUAC inquisitors, Lawson railed against "self-appointed dictators, ambitious politicians, thought-control gestapos, or any other form of censorship this Un-American Committee may attempt to devise," before being dragged from the witness stand. The Hollywood blacklist of the politically heterodox lasted for decades. Lawson's career never recovered. Trumbo, however, sold scripts under pseudonyms. In 1953 he won an Oscar for *The Brave One* under the pseudonym Robert Rich.

State Route 716, Ashland, KY 41105, (600) 928-6414

Chicago is, of course, my favorite city. Nelson Algren said of it: "Like loving a woman with a broken nose, you may well find lovelier lovelies. But never a lovely so real." It is the home of labor battles royal. Here it was the eight-hour day became part of the world's vocabulary. Four men were hanged in an obscene, farcical trial. Yet—we finally achieved. The Republic Steel Massacre on Memorial Day, 1937. It was during a picnic that Chicago cops shot ten picnickers in the back. Yet, steel was organized. The Newspaper Guild's most important victory was cinched at the Hearst *Herald-Examiner*. What is lacking today is the old Chicago spirit. With older workers out of a job, due to automation used against the have-nots and have-somewhats, Chicago's god is Janus, the two-headed one. Jane Addams, Al Capone, Samuel Insull; Mayor Harold Washington versus the hacks who sabotaged his every effort on behalf of the working folks. There is an increasing number of the young who form organizations for Peace, Civil Rights and whatever sanity our society has left.

Riccardo's was the great restaurant—here it was writers, actors, activists of old stripe gathered. It was Riccardo who broke the Loop color line. The role Humphrey Bogart played in *Casablanca* was really our Riccardo; that he was called Rick was a happy accident. And, of course, the lobby of the Wells-Grand Hotel where the arguments were definite and idiomatically eloquent. Finally, there was Bughouse Square, with its soapbox orators, who caused us to laugh and to heckle but, mostly, to think.

—**STUDS TERKEL** is author of the Pulitzer Prize–winning *The Good War, Division Street: America, Hard Times, Working* and other oral histories.

ILLINOIS

Haymarket Riot. On May 4, 1886, Chicago anarchists and workers held one of the many labor rallies for an eight-hour day that were sizzling around the country. (See Bay View Massacre, page 187.) The mood of the crowd was anticop because police violence had killed four strikers at the McCormick Reaper plant the previous day. As the speaker ended his peroration, the police started rousting the crowd. A person unknown hurled a bomb into a contingent of police, killing an officer and injuring one hundred demonstrators. The police started firing wildly, killing and wounding more people, including several officers. In the aftermath, a firestorm of anger scapegoating the anarchists swept Chicago. Police rounded up eight well-known radicals, who were convicted on no evidence other than their political beliefs. Four were hanged, one committed suicide in jail and the remaining three were pardoned by Governor John Peter Altgeld. The new Haymarket Square Monument, a tablet describing the riot and its aftermath, is

located at the corner of Randolph and Des Plaines streets. The square is the scene of the Illinois Labor Historical Society's yearly May Day celebration.

Randolph and Des Plaines streets, Chicago, IL

Hull House. The first settlement house was founded in Chicago in 1889 by Jane Addams to educate, train and organize immigrants, poor and working people. Two of the original buildings survive. They are open to the public, displaying objects and information related to the buildings and to the settlement house movement, which spread to other cities in the early twentieth century. Addams was the first American woman to win the Nobel Peace Prize.

800 S. Halsted Street, Chicago, IL 60607, (312) 413-5353, www.uic.edu/jaddams/hull/

Wobbly Sites. The Industrial Workers of the World was founded at Brand's Hall on Clark Street. On June 27, 1905, 186 hobos, bindle stiffs and dreamers gathered to create "One Big Union." They heard Western Federation of Miners organizer William D. "Big Bill" Haywood shout: "Fellow workers . . . this is the Continental Congress of the working class. We are here to confederate the workers of this country into a working class movement that shall have for its purpose the emancipation of the working class from the slave bondage of capitalism." The latter-day IWW has its national headquarters in Cincinnati and a branch in Chicago. The Solidarity Bookshop, the last of the Wobbly bookstores, is no more. The annual Lilac Festival in suburban Lombard was largely the brainstorm of IWW organizer and poet Ralph Chaplin, author of the labor anthem "Solidarity Forever!"

Chicago GMB Office, The New World Resource Center, 1300 N. Western, Chicago, IL 60622 (312) 638-9155, www.iww.org

Pullman Historical District. George Pullman built his eponymous town in 1880 for employees of his sleeping-car company. All the workers' expenses for rent, water, food, library, and so on were deducted from their paychecks. Some original houses survive. (See Great Pullman Strike, page 109.)

Historic Pullman Foundation, 112th Street and Cottage Grove Avenue, Chicago, IL 60628, (773) 785-8901, www.pullman.org; A. Philip Randolph Pullman Porters Museum, 10406 S. Maryland Avenue, Chicago, IL 60628, (773) 928-3935, www.aphiliprandolphmuseum.com

Forest Home Cemetery. So many famous radicals are interred at this graveyard in Forest Park that it is called "the Forest Lawn of the Left." Here stands the Haymarket Martyrs' Monument, one of the most famous statues of the American labor movement, marking the graves of five of the eight anarchists wrongly condemned to hang for the deaths of seven policemen during a demonstration for the eight-hour day in Haymarket Square (see page 184) on May 4, 1886. The sixteen-foot-high shaft, erected in 1893, features the figure of Justice laying a wreath on the brow of a dying man and drawing her sword with her other hand. Emma Goldman, who was inspired by the Haymarket tragedy to become an anarchist, is buried nearby. The monument has been a favored site of labor rallies commemorating the Haymarket riot, part of the original May 1 rallies for the eight-hour day, which inspired Europe's May Day workers' holiday. (See Union Square, page 13.) Other heroes of labor in residence are IWW chief William D. "Big Bill" Haywood, leader of the 1913 Patterson textile strike; Elizabeth "Rebel Girl" Gurley Flynn; hobo doctor and anarchist Ben Reitman and U.S. Communist Party chief William Z. Foster.

900 South Des Plaines Avenue, south of the Eisenhower Expressway, Forest Park, IL 60130

Municipal Swimming Pool. The municipal pool in suburban Maywood was racially segregated until well into the 1960s. Now it is called the Fred Hampton Family

Aquatic Center, after the Chicago Black Panther leader harassed by the FBI COINTEL program and murdered in 1969 by Chicago lawmen.

Fred Hampton Family Aquatic Center, 300 Oak Street (Fred Hampton Way), Maywood, IL 60513

Union Miners Cemetery. This labor shrine began as an alternative resting place for four miners killed by guards in the Virden strike after other cemeteries refused to admit them. In the fall of 1898 the Chicago-Virden Coal Company, maneuvering to weasel out of an industry-wide eight-hour-day agreement with the UMWA, imported African-American strikebreakers. In the resulting melee between miners and detectives, seven union members and five detectives were killed. When Mary "Mother" Jones heard about the miners' cemetery she reserved a plot for herself, stating: "When the last call comes for me to take my final rest, will the miners see that I get a resting place in the same clay that shelters the miners who gave up their lives on the hills of Virden, Illinois, on the morning of October 12, 1897, for their heroic sacrifice on behalf of their fellow men. They are responsible for Illinois being the best organized labor state in America. I hope it will be my consolation when I pass away to feel I sleep under the clay with those brave boys." When she died in 1930, aged 100, her wish was granted. Her picture is engraved on a granite obelisk flanked by two bronze statues of coal miners guarding her with raised sledgehammers.

Off I-55, Mt. Olive, IL

MICHIGAN

Sit-Down Strike Memorial. In the 1930s labor's fortunes began to turn around with the momentous General Motors–United Automobile Workers sit-down strike in Flint. The tactic (workers occupying their factories) was first used briefly by the Akron, Ohio, Firestone Tire workers and inspired the GM workers. Their strike

---

GRAVES OF THE LEFT AND FAMOUS

SUSAN B. ANTHONY, nineteenth-century feminist, suffragist leader, buried in Mount Hope Cemetery, 791 Mount Hope Avenue, Rochester, NY 14620.

EUGENE V. DEBS, labor leader, presidential candidate, buried in Highland Lawn Cemetery, 4420 E. Wabash Avenue, Terre Haute, IN 47803.

FREDERICK DOUGLASS, former slave, abolitionist leader, buried in Mount Hope Cemetery, 791 Mount Hope Avenue, Rochester, NY 14620.

EMMETT TILL, lynching victim, civil rights martyr. He and his mother, Mamie Till—who became a national civil rights figure—are buried in Burr Oak Cemetery, 440 W. 127th Street, Alsip, IL 60803.

PAUL ROBESON, singer, actor, activist (epitaph: "The artist must elect to fight for freedom or for slavery. I have made my choice") is buried in Ferncliff Cemetery and Mausoleum, 280–284 Secor Road, PO Box 217, Hartsdale, NY 10530.

MALCOLM X, civil rights leader, black Muslim teacher, also is buried in Ferncliff Cemetery and Mausoleum, 280–284 Secor Road, PO Box 217, Hartsdale, NY 10530.

See also: Forest Home Cemetery (page 185), Frank Little's Grave (see page 251), Union Miners Cemetery (see page 186), Jack London State Historical Park (see page 325).

---

lasted much longer, into 1937, but on their side they had the Wagner Act, an administration in Washington sympathetic to labor (FDR intervened personally with GM management), planning, organization and solidarity. In the end, the company agreed to bargain with the UAW. There was some violence but management did not use it as a tactic, unlike Henry Ford, whose security chief Harry Bennett employed spies and gun thugs to harass union organizers and finger prounion workers, who were fired and/or beaten bloody. UAW leader Walter Reuther himself was worked over in the 1937 "Battle of the Overpass" at the River Rouge plant. Old Henry capitulated in 1941, after his soft-spoken wife, Clara, threatened to divorce him if he didn't stop the violence by talking with the UAW.

Sit-Down Strike Historical Marker, Flint, MI

WISCONSIN

The Bay View Massacre. In the aftermath of Milwaukee's May Day parade for the eight-hour day in 1886, scuffling broke out when Knights of Labor demonstrators at the North Chicago Rolling Mill sought to persuade workers inside to join their ranks. They were blocked by National Guard troops. The governor (urged on by businessmen and galvanized by the Haymarket Riot) had ordered the guardsmen to shoot to kill if the unionists made menacing moves. At nine the next morning, unaware of the order to use lethal force, the workers approached the mill; guardsmen shot seven of them. A subsequent investigation praised the guardsmen for their "restraint" (they were rewarded by bonuses from local businesses). Twenty Polish demonstrators were found guilty of unlawful assembly and "riot and conspiracy" and sentenced to a minimum of three months of hard labor. This injustice triggered a backlash, and in the next municipal election voters swept in the People's or Labor Party ticket.

Bay View Martyrs Historical Marker, Russell Avenue at South Superior Street, Milwaukee, WI

Part III.

Policy, Advocacy and Action Organizations

THE THINKING PERSON'S GUIDE TO THINK TANKS

Think tanks (centers staffed by experts devoted to researching economic and social problems and devising solutions) are the spawn of the Progressive era, when public-minded citizens advocated applying the scientific method to political questions in the faith that facts should guide policy. Since the 1980s, with the rise of conservative foundations and think tanks, these centers of nonacademic research have become more political, even ideological. Whatever one thinks of this development, research and policy, outreach and activism are now part of many think tanks' missions. We present here a roster of the most prominent left-progressive think tanks, followed by a gallery of some of the more interesting policy and advocacy groups on the Left.

Americans for Democratic Action. The ADA is one of the oldest liberal lobbying organizations in the country. It was founded in 1947 by prominent anticommunist liberals, among them Walter Reuther, Joseph L. Rauh, Reinhold Niebuhr, Eleanor Roosevelt, Hubert H. Humphrey, John Kenneth Galbraith and Arthur M. Schlesinger, Jr., whose 1949 book *The Vital Center* was the galvanizing text of Cold War liberalism. ADA jumped into the presidential fray in 1948, rallying liberals behind Harry Truman's beleaguered bid for the presidency. This campaign underscored the deepening fissure between

THE TEN MOST-CITED THINK TANKS

One imperfect measure of think tanks' political muscle is how often their findings are cited in press stories or how many articles and op-eds their fellows publish in the mainstream media. It's a nonacademic variant of the old publish or perish syndrome. More crucially, according to media watchdog *Extra!*, it's a measure of the media's rightward shift. In surveys from 1996 to the present, *Extra!* has consistently found that conservative and centrist think tanks received more citations by far than progressive ones. In 2007 the number of citations overall was down 17 percent. Citations of conservative policy groups dropped by 3 percent from the previous year, though they still made up 37 percent of the total; centrists like the venerable Brookings Institution and the establishmentarian Council on Foreign Relations led with 47 percent. The center-left or progressive sector garnered only 16 percent, holding steady with the previous year.

1. Brookings Institution (centrist)
2. Council on Foreign Relations (centrist)
3. American Enterprise Institute (conservative)
4. Heritage Foundation (conservative)
5. Center for Strategic and International Studies (conservative)
6. RAND Corporation (center-right)
7. Kaiser Family Foundation (centrist)
8. Center for American Progress (center-left)
9. Cato Institute (conservative-libertarian)
10. Urban Institute (center-left)

The following left-leaning groups made the top 25:

14. Economic Policy Institute (progressive)
16. Carter Center (center-left)
22. Center on Budget and Policy Priorities (progressive)
25. Center for Economic and Policy Research (progressive)

Source: Extra! March/April 2008. Citations are defined as "appearances in major newspapers and TV and radio transcripts that appear in the Nexis database."

Popular Front liberals, and Cold War liberals. Many of the former supported Henry A. Wallace's challenge to Truman under the Progressive Party standard. The ADA stayed firmly in the Democratic fold, contributing to Truman's come-from-behind victory. In the aftermath the ADA continued to oppose communism at home and abroad and lent a heavy hand to the campaign to purge CP members and sympathizers from liberal groups like the ACLU and the NAACP. The upshot was, as one historian put it, "a victory of the liberals over the Left." The ADA continued to honor the ideals of the New Deal and the best of Truman's Fair Deal and LBJ's Great Society. In 1968, led by Allard Lowenstein,

ADA members worked politically against Johnson's war in Vietnam and promoted Eugene McCarthy's peace candidacy. Today, with strongly liberal chapters in California, New York and other places, and some 65,000 members by latest count, the ADA continues to back progressive candidates and lobby for liberal legislation. Perhaps its best-known activity is rating members of Congress on the basis of their backing for a list of liberal measures, a score of 100 meaning they bought all the items in the ADA's shopping cart.

1625 K Street NW, Suite 210, Washington, DC 20006, (202) 785-5980, www.adaction.org, www.eliberal.org

Campaign for America's Future. CAF is an example of the trend toward diversifying the think tank's mission and going beyond the traditional policy-pondering function. While it does issue political prescriptions in bright-colored booklets with graphs and pie charts, CAF also does "issue advocacy, communications, and coalition building to forge a new American majority for progressive reform." CAF's major public splash is the annual Take Back America conference, which brings the best and brightest of Left America into conference rooms to talk, network, listen and learn. CAF coexists with the Institute for America's Future, which performs research, analyzes issues and publishes reports, specializing in environmental, energy and health care issues; Social Security, education and congressional accountability. (CAF draws on IAF research in creating activist agendas that offer solutions to problems of the day and ways of implementing them.) IAF also sponsors TomPaine.com (see page 152). CAF also publishes an annual called *Straight Talk* (http://straighttalk.ourfuture.org), a source of data in support of the goals of economic security, putting people first and national defense.

1825 K Street NW, Suite 400, Washington, DC 20006, (202) 955-5665, www.ourfuture.org

Center for American Progress. Another of the younger generation of progressive think tanks, CAP, founded in 2003, is led by John Podesta, former White House chief of staff

under Bill Clinton and professor at Georgetown University Law Center. *US News &
World Report* called CAP "one of the best funded of the leftist think tanks." CAP's
2005 budget totaled $2.2 million, a minor amount compared to $20 million for Cato
(conservative) and $56 million for Brookings (centrist). It was the most frequently
cited progressive think tank in 2006. The core of its advocacy is its 15 New Ideas project, which includes improving teacher quality, increasing college opportunity, reform-
ing banks' lending practices, strengthening pensions with a universal 401(k), adopting
universal health coverage and comprehensive worker adjustment assistance, curbing
abuses of congressional power and so on. CAP also sponsors various programs, such
as the Americas Project, which studies U.S. relations with Latin America; Campus
Progress, which "works to strengthen progressive voices on college and university campuses nationwide, counter the growing influence of right-wing groups on campus, and
empower new generations of progressive leaders."

1333 H Street NW, 10th floor, Washington, DC 20005, (202) 682-1611, www.americanprogress.org

Center on Budget and Policy Priorities. Robert Greenstein, a former government economist and MacArthur Fellow, founded the center in 1981 and is its executive director.
It received a big kiss from George Soros's Open Society Institute in the form of a
$2,250,000 grant. It analyzes federal budget priorities and tax policies, particularly
their impact on low-income Americans. Projects include assessing whether federal and
state governments are fiscally responsible and taking in enough tax revenue to address
important social problems, especially those affecting the poor and working families.
The CBPP delves into tax policies; when the GOP wealth lobby in Congress was zero-
ing in on the elimination of the estate tax, the center weighed in with a report pointing
out that "the estate tax can be reformed in a way that would exempt large numbers of
estates from the tax while preserving much-needed revenue that would be lost if the tax
were permanently repealed." Executive Director Greenstein called President Bush's
attacks on the proposed expansion of the State Children's Health Insurance Program
full of "distortions, misuse of data, and false claims." During the 1990s, when Congress
increasingly fobbed off its spending responsibilities on the states via unfunded man-
dates, the center devoted more of its time to its State Fiscal Project and working with
state governments and nonprofits concerned with state policies. The Center has provided research and program advice on Medicaid, unemployment insurance (for example, analyzing whether existing benefits pay enough to help jobless workers); food
stamps, Temporary Assistance for Needy Families and programs like Supplemental
Security Income; Women, Infants and Children; and the Earned Income Tax Credit
(EITC). On the theory that programs are of little value if poor people don't know
about them, the center funds outreach efforts in two areas: EITC and children's health
insurance. Much of its work is posted on its website, which *National Journal* rated top

drawer on budget, tax and social security issues. The *New York Times*'s resident economist Paul Krugman regularly pulls into its website for a statistical fill-up, writing on his website in 2003: "The Center's statistical work is absolutely impeccable; there is nothing at all like it on the Right or anywhere else."

820 1st Street NE, Suite 510, Washington, DC 20002, (202) 408-1080, www.cbpp.org

Center for Economic and Policy Research. Economists Dean Baker and Mark Weisbrut, both *Nation* contributors, launched CEPR in 1999. They still head it, overseen by an Advisory Board that numbers Nobel laureates Robert Solow and Joseph Stiglitz; Richard B. Freeman, professor of economics at Harvard University; and Eileen Appelbaum, professor and director of the Center for Women and Work at Rutgers University. CEPR has issued some innovative and accessible studies that tend to win media attention. In a study of the number of media citations received for every $10,000 think tanks spent that year, CEPR found it had made the best showing with 3.53 citations per $10,000 spent. The Center for American Progress, another low-budget leftish tank, was number two, it said, followed by the well-respected Economic Policy Institute and the Center for Public Integrity—both progressives. CEPR pointed out that although conservatives blast liberals for being big spenders, when it comes to throwing around their patrons' money, the right-wing think tanks live high on the hog.

1611 Connecticut Avenue NW, Suite 400, Washington, DC 20009, (202) 293-5380, www.cepr.net

Center for the Study of Responsive Law. In 1968, investing the royalties from his bestseller *Unsafe at Any Speed,* Ralph Nader opened his first Washington base of operations and launched his consumer-rights crusade against the unresponsive Washington regulatory agencies that had become somnolent, toothless watchdogs. He recruited a small band of smart, idealistic law students for summer jobs at paltry pay and turned them loose on the Federal Trade Commission, at the time a bureaucratic swamp devoted mainly to helping its business clients avoid being regulated. The Nader group's FTC report made a big splash, and news stories spread the word about his crusade, attracting more young, idealistic law students. In 1969 some 3,000 of them applied for 2,000 slots, and it was said that one third of the Harvard Law School graduating class applied. These investigators took on the corruption-riddled Interstate Commerce Commission, air pollution and lax oversight of the food industry. The first four Nader reports, published as books, sold more than 450,000 copies. In 1969, his ideas bearing lush fruit, Nader set up the Center for the Study of Responsive Law as a permanent Washington office. Every summer a new class of Raiders scoped out other lax agencies and hot consumer issues. More books ensued, some of them best sellers. In a skeptical time, the public liked the new muckraking, absent in the press. But Nader believed in going beyond muckraking to citizen action. An inner-directed visionary, Nader believed in the power of the individual. Flash forward thirty years to a 2007 conference on Taming the Giant Corporation. Nader observed in a speech: "There have never been as many exposés of corporate scandal in the progressive and mainstream media as there are today, and there has never been less impact to these disclosures." That hasn't kept the CSRL from turning out the reports. The total number now approaches one hundred. Nowadays, many of them are published by the center itself.

PO Box 19367, Washington, DC 20036, (202) 387-8030, www.csrl.org

Citizens for Tax Justice. CTJ can trace its ancestry back to 1979. Its mission involves analyzing tax policies at the federal, state and local levels from the perspective of their impact on the nation's fiscal health. CTJ talks back to the megacorporations that for over a decade have been shifting the tax burden off their shoulders and onto those of Joe Taxpayer. Its main weapon is raising the temperature of public indignation with a media bombardment of facts, statistics and interpretations. Its analyses of corporate tax avoidance were packed into three books: *130 Reasons Why We Need Tax Reform* (1986), *Corporate Taxpayers & Corporate Freeloaders* (1985) and *Money for Nothing: The Failure of Corporate Tax Incentives, 1981–1984* (1986). These tomes played a key role in ginning up support for the passage of the Tax Reform Act of 1986, which carpet bombed tax shelters for corporations and the rich and cut the rates for poor and middle-income families. CTJ's reports were said by the *Washington Post* to have been a "key turning point" in the tax reform debate. During Bill Clinton's stint in the White House, CTJ's house economists brought out *Inequality and the Federal Budget Deficit* (1991), an exposé of the correlation between tax cuts for the wealthy and the mounting federal deficit, and helped stiffen Democratic support for passage of the 1993 budget act, which required legislators actually to repeal some cuts for fat cats adopted during the Reagan era. CTJ research has also produced change or at least better-informed opinion at the state and local levels. It showed how Wal-Mart had evaded some $2.3 billion in state taxes by using real estate investment trusts as tax shelters.

1616 P Street NW, Suite 200, Washington, DC 20036, (202) 299-1066, www.ctj.org

Citizens Trade Campaign. CTC emerged amid the fight against NAFTA back in 1992. Working with allies, it has brought into the sunshine Congress members' votes on trade issues, asking, Were they for the people or for the corporations? The group has highlighted the major downsides of free trade policies and advocated for international trade rules and fair-trade coalitions. In 2006 CTC formed Citizens Trade PAC, which circulated questionnaires to congressional candidates and ended up endorsing fifteen who demonstrated the best comprehension of the issues. The PAC hired organizers for seven campaigns and made financial contributions to the rest. All this boosted the Democratic tide, as twelve out of fifteen CTC PAC–supported candidates won. An analysis in the publication *Democratic Strategist* concluded that "a majority of victorious Democratic candidates prevailed on a fair trade platform against anti–fair-trade incumbents."

PO Box 77077, Washington, DC 20013, (202) 778-3320, www.citizenstrade.org

Democracy Alliance. This organization was created as a response to the chronic problem of inadequate funding of progressive policy groups. The initial spark was ignited by former Clinton Commerce Department official Rob Stein, who made presentations to a conclave of wealthy liberals in Phoenix sounding the alarm about the Right's superior financial firepower. He calculated it pours out $170 million a year to its think tanks compared to the Left's $85 million. Stein attracted a group of eighty wealthy progressives, who each pledged to donate $1 million to support left think tanks and policy advocacy groups. By October 2006, an article in *The Nation* reported that the alliance had distributed $50 million to center-left groups. The article criticized the group's inability to agree on a central purpose, its "early stumbles" and being "poorly run." It operates like an investment partnership, recommending to its "partners" a "portfolio" of progressive groups. Partners commit to making a minimum level of financial contributions. Many of the alliance's donors remain anonymous, but they include George Soros, Norman Lear, Drummond Pike, Anne Bartley, Fred Baron and Gara LaMarche. Beneficiaries have included ACORN, Air America Radio, Emily's List, Media Matters for America, Sierra Club, USAction, Center for Progressive Leadership and Women's Voices. Democracy Alliance has brought about more than $100 million in grants to liberal groups.

PO Box 18607, Washington, DC 20036, www.democracyalliance.org

Demos. Demos proclaims it is seeking to meld "the commitment to ideas of a think tank with the organizing strategies of an advocacy group." Initially, its main focus was on expanding democracy and bridging the income gap. Out of that concern grew the Democracy Program, which comes up with ideas and strategies to eliminate obstacles blocking new voters and making the tallies fair and honest. Demos has given a special push to voter registration. The Economic Opportunity Program, started in 2002, has zeroed in on credit card debt and predatory lending and on programs to build the middle class by promoting college education and home ownership for low-income Americans. In 2007 Demos and the Project on Inequality and the Common Good (based at the Institute for Policy Studies) launched a new website, inequality.org, which reports on the "growing economic divide." A third program is Public Works, which has generated ideas for improving government efficiency and educating Americans disillusioned with government to support its resuming the appropriate and productive role it once had in this country. The Demos Forum sponsors discussions on public policy in New York. David Smith, chief economist with the House Financial Services Committee, who had been a fellow at Demos, told us: "Demos regards itself as doing both policy and advocacy and is getting better at both."

220 5th Avenue, 5th floor, New York, NY 10001, (212) 633-1405, www.demos.org

Drum Major Institute for Public Policy. Drum Major Institute for Public Policy has an action-oriented perspective similar to Demos. Its name comes from Martin Luther King's drive to be "a drum major for justice." Under its present director, Andrea Batista Schlesinger, DMI pays special attention to people of color, immigrants and the middle class. It has barged into such local issues as congestion pricing (Mayor Bloomberg's plan to discourage cars from entering midtown Manhattan), predatory lending in poor areas of New York City and local crackdowns on illegal immigrants on Long Island. Credit DMI with living up to its credo of challenging the "tired orthodoxies of both the right and the left" and having the guts to butt into the policy fights of its times and in its neighborhood. Even its policy papers are all about making a difference. As Schlesinger admonishes: "If a report isn't read, it wasn't written."

40 Exchange Place, Suite 2001, New York, NY 10005, www.drummajorinstitute.org

Economic Policy Institute. From the start in 1986, EPI's founders intended it to be a think tank devoted to achieving "a prosperous and fair economy" with special emphasis on improving the lot of low- and middle-income workers. EPI operates on a budget of $5 to $6 million a year. The *Nation*'s national affairs correspondent, William Greider, wrote that through Reaganomics and Clinton globalization EPI was "the premier left-liberal think tank standing up to the dominant conservative orthodoxy. EPI seldom prevailed in major policy debates, but it won high regard, even among conservative rivals, for its meticulous research and powerful analysis of the economic realities." Since the congressional Democratic victory of 2006, it has generated a Shared Prosperity agenda that offers practical measures to address the growing inequality under the Bush administration. It outlines plans for setting up a new national pension system parallel to Social Security, improving employer-based national health care, restarting the commitment to full employment and using public investment to stimulate high-wage growth (see www.sharedprosperity.org). The initiative was thrashed out in discussions among more than fifty outside economists, policy experts and political activists.

1333 H Street NW, Suite 300, East Tower, Washington, DC 20005, (202) 775-8810, www.epinet.org

Essential Information. This Nader-founded group publishes *Multinational Monitor* (see page 128), books and reports; sponsors investigative journalism conferences; makes grants to writers to probe problems and performs research on Internet access. It operates its Multinational Resource Center, which addresses the needs of countries in the global south that find themselves victims of antisocial practices by multinational corporations. The resource center answers requests from activists and citizens in the south who want to know the name and history and legal status of the corporations that are exploiting them, and technical information about laws and, say, alternative waste management methods. An action arm called Essential Action sponsors an Access to Medicine project that strives to free essential medicines from big pharma's patent stranglehold and make them widely available to the poor. One of its biggest accomplishments was persuading an Indian drug manufacturer to produce generic AIDS medicines that would cost ailing Africans only pennies.

PO Box 19405, Washington, DC 20036, (202) 387-8030, www.essential.org

Global Exchange. GE was cofounded in 1988 by Kirsten Moller, Kevin Danaher and Medea Benjamin. Using a multifarious array of techniques, it provokes and promotes international action in the areas of human rights and social, economic and environmental justice. Global Exchange tries to educate the public about problems of globalization, defend the Universal Declaration of Human Rights, change U.S. policy to support sustainable development and connect people here and abroad who share similar political goals. It reports on human rights violations in war zones; fights the corporate-friendly policies of the WTO, World Bank and International Monetary Fund; opposes all free trade agreements; promotes regionalism and sponsors fair-trade stores in San Francisco, where artisans and craftsmen in other countries can sell their wares at a good price; conducts Reality Tours that take people to various countries to study social conditions and runs a public education program that produces books, videos, articles and editorials.

2017 Mission Street, 2nd floor, San Francisco, CA 94110, (415) 255-7296, www.globalexchange.org

Institute for Policy Studies. IPS, born in 1963, was the first liberal think tank. It was cofounded by Marcus Raskin and Richard Barnet, both of whom worked in the Kennedy administration, with financial backing from Sears heir Philip Stern, a journalist and author, and international banking heir James Warburg. Some of its ideas, such as Model Cities and the Teacher Corps, were given a legislative tryout by the Kennedy-Johnson administrations. IPS supplied a different sort of model to those of conservatives. Marcus Raskin recalled, "Heritage Foundation published a study paper on IPS, one of its first, which said that they would pattern themselves after IPS with the difference that they would have more funding." That was the birth of the right-wing think tank counterrevolution. Despite internal schisms and financial shortfalls, IPS entered its forty-fifth year as timely and relevant as ever under the leadership of brilliant international economist John Cavanaugh. IPS fellow Phyllis Bennis, director of the New Internationalism Project, was a reliable source of facts and research for the few editorial voices on the Left raised against the Iraq invasion. IPS sparked a Cities for Peace initiative under which more than 200 cities and towns passed resolutions against the Iraq war. (This is now called Cities for Progress, a network of progressive mayors and other local government officials with an urban agenda.) The institute collaborated with United for a Fair Economy (see page 205) on an investigative report *Executive Excess 2006*, exposing bloated CEO salaries. The groups reported that the top thirty-four defense CEOs made a combined total of $984 million, enough to pay a year's wages to 1 million Iraqis.

1112 16th Street NW, Suite 600, Washington, DC 20036, (202) 234-9382, www.ips-dc.org

Institute for Southern Studies. Founded in 1970 by veterans of the civil rights movements, the institute has helped generate the Brown Lung Association, Southerners for Economic Justice, the Georgia Power Project and the Gulf Tenants Leadership Development Project. It also studies the southern contribution to culture and social change, from gospel music and the blues to the civil rights movement and community organizing. It publishes the magazine *Southern Exposure* (edited by former *Nation* intern Chris Kromm), which has won a National Magazine Award and a George Polk Award for reporting. Julian Bond calls it "the single best resource about the changing South." Celebrated for gritty investigative reporting, it has published special issues on the military culture in the South and the Ku Klux Klan. It has covered the poultry industry, civil rights movement, folk life, Native Americans, prisons, economic development, the nuclear industry and regional theater.

PO Box 531, Durham, NC 27702, (919) 419-8311, www.southernstudies.org

New America Foundation. This relatively recent addition to the policy ranks, founded in 1999, is more centrist than left. It has described itself as "a home for the ideologically homeless." Founder Ted Halstead, who founded a public policy institute (Redefining Progress) at the age of twenty-five, would presumably position himself in the "radical center," the title of a book he wrote with Michael Lind. It is a brief for a cross-breeding of proposals. Some of these ideas are evident in the NAF's Next Social Contract Initiative. For example, the NAF says that because there's so much turnover in American workplaces, health insurance should be individually funded rather than employer based. They'd provide assets to every child and ditch Social Security for a universal 401(k), because they encourage saving. They call for a new centrist politics and an opening up of the system to new parties and candidates and local action. In ten years the staff at NAF grew from ten to ninety people, with an annual budget of $10 million. It has attracted policy thinkers like Middle East expert and *Nation* contributor Anatol Lieven, global economist Joel Kotkin, Paraq Khanna (author of *The Second World*) and others. Arms-trade experts William Hartung and Frida Berrigan, formerly of the World Policy Institute, now hang their hats at NAF. Its board includes mainstream-liberal journalists like James Fallows, Fareed Zakaria, Walter Russell Mead and Francis Fukuyama. In September 2007, Steve Coll, *New Yorker* writer and two-time Pulitzer Prize winner at the *Washington Post,* became president and CEO.

1630 Connecticut Avenue NW, 7th floor, Washington, DC 20009, (202) 986-2700, www.newamerica.net

New Politics Institute. Born in 2006, NPA is in the business of helping progressives use the new media more effectively to reach the millennium gen and the growing Hispanic demographic, both fertile fields for Democratic Party recruitment. SourceWatch reports NPI had a start-up budget of $1.5 to $2 million, with funding from Bay Area philanthropists Andy and Deborah Rappaport. The Service Employees International Union was also reported to be a major partner in the start-up phase. Among the early plans: studies of the Hispanic electorate, the future of progressive media and Internet television technology. NPI presents the question: Can the Left be saved by a technological fix alone? First off, NPI has vowed to devote its time and money to politics, not policies, to finding practical strategies that work in today's political environment. Their basic ideas are contained in "The New Politics Begins," which they presented at various meetings and conferences. They also exhort progressives to focus on cable ads, blogs and search engine ads. Oh yes: learn Spanish! They're also experimenting with doing politics via mobile media and user-generated video and reaching young people through networking sites like YouTube, Facebook and video and computer games and creating dynamite viral videos and MySpace extravaganzas. Beyond these are mobile phone text messages and sophisticated social networking. They advise focusing on the nineteen to twenty-niners, who became hyperactive in 2008. Internet-active Barack Obama was definitely their kind of candidate.

660 York Street, Suites 213 and 211, San Francisco, CA 94110, (415) 593-1973; 729 15th Street, 2nd floor, Washington, DC 20005, (202) 544-9200, www.newpolitics.net

OMB Watch. *Quid custodiet ipsos custodes?* Who will watch the watchers? OMB Watch was founded in 1983 with that question in mind. Its purpose was to penetrate the veil of secrecy surrounding the White House's Office of Management and Budget, which is supposed to be the executive branch's monitor of the other branches—the regulatory agencies; the congressional budget committees; the torrent of reports, facts and statistics and legislative proposals. OMB Watch takes its mission as throwing light on OMB's arcane doings and informing and guiding nonprofit groups of the status of this or that program or legislation. OMB Watch has set up Citizens for Sensible Safeguards, uniting almost 300 groups that try to correct and strengthen regulatory protections and enforcement; and OpenTheGovernment.org, a variegated constituency of journalists and issue groups pressuring government agencies to make their dealings more transparent. OMB Watch reports on government actions on many other fronts in projects such as Fair Estate Tax, Community Toxics Watch and the Regulatory Resource Center, which helps citizens understand the agency process and participate in it by, say, submitting comment on a new rule or searching the *Federal Register* for the last rule made by an obscure but influential agency (this was a necessity under the secretive Bush administration). OMB Watch issues action alerts to members, publishes a biweekly e-newsletter, *The Watcher*, and disseminates information on government and the regulatory process.

1742 Connecticut Avenue NW, Washington, DC 20009, (202) 234-8494, www.ombwatch.org

Open Society Institute. The multibillionaire financier, currency speculator and political do-gooder George Soros, who had previously set up foundations to promote democracy in former Soviet satellite nations, established OSI in 1993. His institute has global reach, with autonomous branches in twenty-nine countries, as well as Southern Africa and West Africa. In the United States, the OSI directs funding from the Soros Foundation to a number of left organizations such as the ACLU, Alliance for Justice, Drug Policy Alliance, Families USA, Proteus Fund, Justice at Stake, Center for Policy Alternatives, People for the American Way, NARAL, Center on Budget and Policy Priorities, Campaign for America's Future and many others. Its grants totaled $82 million in 2005. OSI's Washington and New York offices plan and fund substantive programs for drug policy reform, equal access to the legal system, inner-city education, reproductive choice, campaign finance reform, care of the dying, women's rights and other initiatives. Its Open Society Policy Center in Washington functions as a separate 501(c)(4) policy advocacy group on behalf of OSI causes. Overall, Soros's various foundations are dedicated to transforming closed societies into open ones, hence his initial funding of clandestine prodemocracy groups in Eastern Europe before the collapse of the Soviet Union. Soros's well-funded opposition to Bush's reelection in 2004 made him a favorite villain of ultraright conspiracy theorists, drawing on age-old nativist stereotypes of "international bankers." The money for his political activities, of course, comes out of his personal pocket, unlike the millions for OSI projects from his foundation.

400 W. 59th Street, New York, NY 10019, (212) 548-0600, www.soros.org; Open Society Policy Center, 1120 19th Street NW, 8th floor, Washington, DC 20036, (202) 721-5600, www.opensocietypolicycenter.org

Political Research Associates. PRA is a comparatively small think tank with a special focus on the U.S. Right in its various political, religious, racist and violent incarnations. Born in Chicago in 1981, it was founded by political scientist and feminist activist Jean Hardisty. Among the original staff of three was Chip Berlet, a veteran writer-researcher on right-wing affairs. PRA grew, moved to Boston, changed its name and celebrated its twenty-fifth birthday in Somerville, Massachusetts, where it now resides. With a sinewy staff of seven and a budget in the high six figures, it continues to publish well-researched reports that penetrate the rhetorical smoke screen to reveal the real motives of many organizations on the Right.

1310 Broadway, Suite 201, Somerville, MA 02144, (617) 666-5300, www.publiceye.org

Progressive States Network. Established in 2005, this strategy center helps progressive state legislators achieve their policies and seeks to elect more of their kind. It also nourishes with the latest information and expertise the progressive nonprofits and grassroots organizations working within a given state to affect legislation. As Executive Director Joel Barkin said, "State legislators are on the front line of the most important issues affecting the country." Nathan Newman, PSN's policy director, points to a concerted conservatives' effort to steer corporate-friendly legislation through state legislatures; for example, laws helping ExxonMobil block global warming legislation and assisting pharmaceutical companies to stop the import of cheaper drugs from Canada. The PSN enunciates a set of progressive policies for the states, including minimum wage increases, making union membership easier, protecting working families through family leave legislation and affordable health care and supporting clean energy policies that reduce emissions while creating green jobs. PSN's active website serves as a clearinghouse for information on legislation, state policy news and rising stars in the legislative ranks; it also provides access to special resources for journalists and bloggers. When President Bush ordered his "surge" in Iraq in 2007, PSN worked with state legislators to oppose it, with the result that twenty-nine states issued resolutions of condemnation. Barkin and cochair David Sirota (a *Nation* contributor) both earned their spurs working for Senator Bernie Sanders, the Vermont independent.

101 Avenue of the Americas, 3rd floor, New York, NY 10013, (212) 680-3116, www.progressivestates.org

Project on Government Oversight. POGO started in 1981 as the Project on Military Procurement, amid a rising public outcry against Pentagon scandals, such as $7,600 coffeemakers and $436 hammers. Founder Dina Rasor was a protégée of Ernie Fitzgerald, the famous Pentagon whistle-blower who tooted loud and long about gold-plated weaponry and cozy contracting. She acknowledges her debt to other Pentagon whistle-blowers, including contractors of conscience who blew the whistle on fraud and waste. Rasor now serves on the board of POGO, with Danielle Brian as its executive director. POGO has broadened its mandate to encompass systemic waste, fraud and abuses in all the federal agencies.

666 11th Street NW, Suite 900, Washington, DC 20001, (202) 347-1122, www.pogo.org

Public Citizen. In 1971 Ralph Nader expanded his agenda to develop what would be his greatest contribution: consumer action. He imagined an ideal type, a "public citizen," empowered by knowledge of the threats to his well-being and motivated to act politically to rectify these conditions. Public Citizen was at the center of a loose federation of specialized advocacy groups, including the Health Research Group, Congress Watch and the Litigation Group. It acted as an administrative and fund-raising body, freeing up the action groups to focus on engendering change in their particular areas. Today, under Joan Claybrook, Public Citizen's six divisions reflect Nader's original priorities:

Auto Safety: highway safety, driver protections, higher fuel economy standards

Regulatory Policy Group: monitoring regulation of business

Congress Watch: public interest legislation, campaign finance and lobbying reform, freedom of information

Energy Program: nuclear safety and waste disposal, alternative energy sources

Litigation Group: bringing lawsuits for consumers

Global Trade Watch: globalization issues

Health Research Group: unsafe drugs and medical conditions, information on doctors' disciplinary rates, patient access to medical records, affordable health care and prescription medicines

During its years of public interest lobbying, Public Citizen was deeply involved in the first energy conservation legislation and in auto fuel economy standards; in halting construction of hazardous nuclear reactors; pushing through the Superfund law mandating cleanup of polluted areas by the companies responsible; removing the carcinogen formaldehyde from home insulation; defeating the Reagan administration's attempts to gut the Clean Air Act and trash the Consumer Product Safety Commission; overturning in court Reagan's veto of auto safety standards; exposing over-the-counter pills that don't work; defending a tobacco industry whistle-blower; opposing fast-track trade authority and more. On the Internet, PC sponsors WhiteHouseForSale.org and a blog called Watchdog, which issues up-to-date reports on the legislative dance in Congress.

1600 20th Street NW, Washington, DC 20009, (202) 588-1000, www.citizen.org

United for a Fair Economy. This think tank is dedicated to sounding the tocsin about the growing concentration of wealth and power in America, which threatens to "undermine the economy, corrupt democracy, deepen the racial divide, and tear communities apart." Regarding itself as a "movement support group," it goes beyond the cogitating to engage the public on these subjects by running workshops for churches, neighborhood groups, businesses and like groups. UFE also runs a Racial Wealth Divide project that sponsors forums on race issues. In furtherance of its opposition to great wealth as antidemocratic, UFE organizes grassroots support for progressive income taxes and opposition to the repeal of the estate tax.

29 Winter Street, Boston, MA 02108, (617) 423-2148, www.faireconomy.org

GRASSROOTS, ADVOCACY AND PUBLIC INTEREST LOBBIES

Americans United for Change. This advocacy group was organized in 2005 around a single issue: Bush's scheme to privatize Social Security. It received labor union funding, and one of its main tools was issue ads. In the run-up to the 2005 election it sponsored a television spot mocking Bush's "Stay the Course" rhetoric and one that highlighted the Jack Abramoff scandal with glimpses of that photogenic political villain in his trademark black overcoat. It ran anti–Iraq War ads with the slogan "It's the will of one nation against the stubbornness of one man," and demanded Bush sign a bill bringing American GIs home. In another antiwar tactic, AUC targeted Senate Republicans up for reelection. In 2008, it sponsored an $8.5 million advertising campaign to expose Bush's dismal record. The effort included the Bush Legacy bus, a "museum on wheels." To support its various campaigns AUC has staff members posted in twenty-three states, finances national advertising, engages in press outreach and sponsors high-profile events and grassroots organizing.

1825 K Street NW, Suite 210, Washington, DC 20006, (202) 263-4577, www.americansunitedforchange.org

Common Cause. Common Cause was part of the public interest lobby explosion touched off by Ralph Nader. In 1970, John Gardner, a Republican who had served as secretary of health, education and welfare in the Johnson administration, announced the formation of Common Cause as a "citizen's lobby." After a few months the new organization had attracted more than 100,000 members, most of them interested in opposing the Vietnam War. Defunding the war was one of the group's early successes. Flash forward to still another war: Now it has some 300,000 members and thirty-six state organizations, funded mainly by contributions from members. Its primary issues these days are holding the Bush administration accountable for costs and consequences of its illegal invasion of Iraq, promoting media diversity in voices and ownership, achieving campaign reform, making government more ethical and accountable and increasing voter participation by flattening partisan barriers.

1133 19th Street NW, 9th floor, Washington, DC 20036, (202) 833-1200, www.commoncause.org

MoveOn. MoveOn has brought the netroots to the grass roots, spreading the word that all it takes is a click of the mouse to petition the powers that be. Two Silicon Valley entrepreneurs, Wes Boyd and Joan Blades, founded MoveOn.org in 1998, to campaign for "moving on" beyond the Clinton impeachment mud wrestle. Then a twenty-three-year-old Bard grad and Internet genius named Eli Pariser came aboard to promote antiwar activities and moved up to become executive director of MoveOn.org Political Action. MoveOn stirs up phone-ins, petition drives, letters-to-the-editor campaigns and local media events. It promotes bake sales and virtual town halls and living room showings of documentaries. In 2005, some 125,000 people contributed $9 million to various MoveOn campaigns. Structurally, MoveOn.org Civic Action takes care of education and advocacy on important national issues; and

MoveOn.org Political Action, a federal PAC, mobilizes people across the country to take part in congressional debates and help elect candidates who reflect progressive values. MoveOn has become one of the most effective netroots groups and the largest, boasting links to some 3.2 million minutemen and -women standing by their computers, ready to click. It tries to be independent yet supportive of the Democratic Party but has caused it the wrong kind of grief, as with an ad rhyming "General Petraeus" with "Betray us." The comment gratuitously incensed the right-wing attack dogs. MoveOn's critics say it's too cozy with the Democratic Party and doesn't do demos. But its members like it cool.

www.moveon.org

People for the American Way. PFAW is another familiar station on the Left Internet, broadcasting almost daily bulletins to its ready-alert membership. Usually they are cogently argued broadsides that pique, inform, motivate. PFAW was founded by Hollywood producer Norman Lear, the original Hollywood liberal, who decided to put his mouth where his money was. After its founding in 1981, PFAW gained fame as one of the few institutions that dared talk back to the religious Right. If PFAW sometimes sounded like Lear's creation Maude, the quintessential glib-lib, it made scads of enemies in the "Right" places. PFAW engages in a variety of activities from rallying its 1 million members to write their representatives to lobbying on Capitol Hill. Its PFAW Foundation publishes reports on issues like discrimination against African Americans at the polls and civil rights and civil liberties. It mounts legal challenges to groups undermining the constitutional wall between church and state and to censorship of art and acts of discrimination against gays. Its foundation runs a lawyers network of 300 pro bono counselors nationwide. PFAW sponsors a Democracy Campaign for electoral reform and voter rights. Among its resources is a Progressive Network on the website, which will help you find progressive organizations in your area.

2000 M Street NW, Suite 400, Washington, DC 20036, (202) 467-4999, www.pfaw.org

Progressive Democrats of America. Since Democratic Party Chair Howard Dean and Representative Dennis Kucinich inaugurated it in July 2004, PDA has worked to engineer a progressive takeover of the Democratic Party, expunging what they perceive as the alliance of Wall Streeters, free traders and Democrat Leadership Council types that have dominated the party. It's committed to ousting the Clintonite coterie by an "inside-outside" strategy. As the organization sums up: "We will reach our goal by working *inside* the Democratic Party to return it to its roots as the party that represents the workers and the less fortunate, and by building coalitions *outside* the Democratic Party on shared issues." The PDA folk burrow into the party to put progressive ideas on its agenda, while rallying party members into pressuring their elected reps to carry through on those ideas. Lacking a lot of money or a large membership, they haven't succeeded, of course, but their members take satisfaction out of a close working relationship with the Congressional Progressive Caucus. They claim success in their core effort to "translate grassroots issues into Progressive Caucus goals." So far, they've mostly preached to the choir, but that choir is growing.

PO Box 150064, Grand Rapids, MI 49515, (877) 239-2093, www.pdamerica.org

Progressive Majority. Progressive Majority was set up after the 2000 election by labor, Congress members and progressive donors to "serve as a multi-issue political action committee (PAC) and to enhance the political effectiveness of the progressive movement." By 2007 it claimed 50,000 members, who concentrate on grooming winning candidates in their home states. The heart of it is the Candidate Recruitment & Development program, which is building a farm team of dedicated progressives to run for municipal, state and national office and giving them the kind of logistical and financial support they need to win. A subset is the Racial Justice Campaign, recruiting progressive people of color who are also the best candidates for a particular campaign. Executive director is Gloria Totten, a veteran political organizer, who previously served as political director of NARAL and before that masterminded several political campaigns.

1825 K Street NW, Suite 450, Washington, DC 20006, (202) 408-8603, www.progressivemajority.org

U.S. PIRG. When we caught up with Anna Aurilio, federal legislative director of U.S. PIRG, she was fresh off a "great victory" in Congress: the House had just passed a PIRG-backed bill that included a requirement that 15 percent of U.S. electricity be generated by renewable energy. Aurilio had just been talking to an assistant about the next step—writing the renewable-energy requirement into the bill that emerges from the House-Senate conference. The National Federation of State Public Interest Research Groups is another Ralph Nader spin-off. Headquartered in Boston, it has an active Washington office that carries on public interest lobbying, working closely with the state PIRGs. The independent citizen-funded PIRGs uncover local threats to public health and safety and act to alleviate them through exposure, lobbying and activism at the statehouse level. They tackle issues from air and water pollution to campaign finance reform. U.S. PIRG was formed in 1985 when the state PIRGs decided they wanted Washington to extend their state victories to the federal level. The national federation of PIRGs "tightly controls" U.S. PIRG's legislative priorities, according to Aurilio. The state PIRGs oversee College PIRGs on more than one hundred campuses nationwide. College PIRGs were started in the early seventies and serve as farm clubs for state and national PIRGs.

44 Winter Street, 4th floor, Boston, MA 02108, (617) 747-4370; Federal Advocacy Office,
218 D Street SE, Washington, DC 20003, (202) 546-9707, www.uspirg.org

PEACE, DISARMAMENT, ANTINUKE AND ANTIWAR ORGANIZATIONS

Arms and Security Initiative. The project was established as the Arms Trade Resource Center in 1993 by William D. Hartung under the wing of the World Policy Institute at the New School for Social Research in New York City. The center monitored and reported on the international arms trade and published and disseminated reports, magazine articles and op-ed pieces on the U.S. weapons trade and U.S. arms sales policy. In 2007 Hartung moved to the New America Foundation in Washington (see page 201) and adopted the present name.

(see page 201)

New America Foundation, 38 Greene Street, 4th floor, New York, NY 10013, (212) 431-5808, www.newamerica.net

CODEPINK Women for Peace. The name originated as a play on the Bush administration's code alerts—yellow, orange, red. "Pink" signaled that the antiwar women were coming. The "women-initiated grassroots peace and social justice movement" mounted some of the most vigorous, daring and noisy protests against the Iraq War in 2007–08. Their reasoning, according to one member, was that the Bush administration was set in stone. So they decided: " 'Let's move who we can move, let's change the Congress,' and so we went out and worked like hell to get Democrats elected. Now we are putting pressure on the Democrats who control Congress." CODEPINK has spawned 250 active local groups around the country and the world. The national headquarters coordinates these local groups, which are invited to set up their own contact link on CODEPINK's website. It has dispatched all-women peace delegations to Iraq—the first in February 2003—and sent groups to countries neighboring Iraq to deliver humanitarian aid to refugees and make connections with fellow peaceniks. It thinks up demos and direct actions to provoke pro- or insufficiently antiwar political figures, starting with Congress.

Regional Offices: 2010 Linden Avenue, Venice, CA 90291, (310) 827-4320, www.codepinkla.org; 2017 Mission Street, #200, San Francisco, CA 94110, (415) 575-5555, www.bayareacodepink.org; 712 5th Street NE, Washington, DC 20002, (202) 290-1301, www.codepinkdc.org; 630 9th Avenue, Suite 216, New York, NY 10036, (646) 723-1781, www.codepinknyc.org

Declaration of Peace. This grassroots group, set up in response to the Iraq War, organized in September 2006, a "week of action," in which people from hundreds of organizations and groups participated in 375 Declaration of Peace events all over the country. They reprised this chorus in 2007.

2501 Harrison Street, Oakland, CA 94612, (773) 777-7858, www.declarationofpeace.org

Democracy Rising. This national effort based in Washington, D.C., was kicked off in February 2005 by Ralph Nader and Kevin Zeese. Nader called not only for an end to the war but also for a congressional investigation into the "institutionalization of corruption and secrecy that is taking hold in Washington, D.C., particularly in the military budget and its corporate contractors, as a result of the Iraq War." He pointed to the insider deals that are profiting Bush family members and called them "the biggest war profiteering First Family in history." Democracy Rising draws on capital public policy wonks and works with other groups inside the coalition of United for Peace and Justice (see page 212). The organization maintains an active website. A running feature is Iraq War Facts, which provides key information on the ongoing war, updated daily.

PO Box 18485, Washington, DC 20036, http://democracyrising.us

Friends Committee on National Legislation. Representing effectively the ideals of the Religious Society of Friends, an antiwar church throughout its long history, the FCNL calls itself "the largest peace lobby in Washington, D.C." It was founded in 1943, in the middle of a "good war," of which the Friends think there are none. The FCNL aims to "promote global security through peace-building, active diplomacy, nuclear nonproliferation, arms control and disarmament, and the peaceful prevention and resolution of deadly conflict." They opposed military intervention in Iraq and supported resorting to the UN and multilateral diplomacy to contain Saddam. The Friends demand that the United States dismantle all its military and paramilitary forces and bases in Iraq, return to the people full control over their nation's assets and natural resources and provide funds to rebuild Iraq through "accountable intergovernmental, non-governmental and Iraqi agencies." Typically, FCNL joined a dialogue with the Iranian president on his 2007 visit to the United States while politicians and academics shunned him.

245 Second Street NE, Washington, DC 20002, (202) 547-6000, www.fcnl.org

Peace Action. This historic group is the result of the merger of the Committee for a SANE Nuclear Policy and the Nuclear Weapons Freeze Campaign. SANE, founded in 1957 by Coretta Scott King, Dr. Benjamin Spock and other notable liberals, was the first organized citizens movement against the nuclear arms race in the United States. During John F. Kennedy's administration, SANE, led by Dr. Spock, aroused public sentiment against nuclear testing, moving Kennedy to propose and Congress to adopt the 1963 Partial Test Ban Treaty. In 1987 SANE merged with the Nuclear Freeze Movement to form SANE/FREEZE, which in 1993 became Peace Action. With more than 100,000 members, 28 state affiliates and 100 chapters at the local level, it continues to speak out on such nuclear issues, opposing modernization of the U.S.

nuclear arsenal and calling for compliance with the nuclear nonproliferation treaty. Eight years of Bush nuclear policies has only strengthened the need for groups like Peace Action. The administration dumped arms control agreements; withdrew from the antiballistic missile treaty; deployed a smaller, still unworkable version of Reagan's Star Wars; blocked treaties on biological and chemical weapons; opposed the Comprehensive Test Ban Treaty and the treaty to ban land mines; halted nuclear disarmament talks and developed a new generation of nuclear weapons. Although he surely did not intend it, George W. Bush established conclusively the need for groups like Peace Action.

1100 Wayne Avenue, Suite 1020, Silver Spring, MD 20910, (301) 565-4050, www.peace-action.org

Ploughshares Fund. The buck starts here for many peace organizations. Ploughshares was founded in 1982 by the heiress activist Sally Lilienthal, who wanted a peace fund that would help groups whose objective was "preventing the spread and use of nuclear, biological and chemical weapons and other weapons of war, and preventing conflicts that could lead to the use of weapons of mass destruction." In little more than a quarter of a century the Ploughshares Fund has distributed $450 million in gifts and subsidies, usually in the form of start-up funding, that is, relatively modest donations that enable projects to get up and running and go for more substantial support. Among its beneficiaries: the International Campaign to Ban Landmines, which helped win adoption of a global treaty to abolish antipersonnel land mines by most nations of the world. In 2007 Ploughshares Fund sponsored a "Peace Primary," in which citizens could "vote" for one or more organizations from a list of twelve (American Friends Service Committee, Center for Arms Control and Non-proliferation, Citizens for Global Solutions, Faithful Security, Genocide Intervention Network, Global Green USA, National Religious Campaign Against Torture, Peace Action Education Fund, Refugees International, TrueMajority, Union of Concerned Scientists, Women's Action for New Directions) that best articulated the issues important to them (a vote being a $1 contribution). The organization receiving the most dollars would win a $100,000 donation from Ploughshares.

Fort Mason Center Building B, Suite 330, San Francisco, CA 94123, (415) 775-2244, www.ploughshares.org

SOA Watch. This small but energetic organization is in the business of antimilitarism in South America. The initials refer to School of the Americas, a training post at Fort Benning, Georgia, for military officers from South and Central American nations. Its graduates have long been prominent among the dictators and death squads of the countries where the military runs things. In 1996 the Pentagon released training manuals used at the school that advocated torture, extortion and execution. SOA Watch advocated closing the school (now known as the Western Hemisphere Institute for Security Cooperation) and it faithfully holds annual demonstrations at Fort Benning that attract hundreds of demonstrators, dozens of whom are arrested, convicted and sentenced to prison for trespassing on federal property and related offenses. SOA Watch has sent delegates to meet with governments throughout Latin America and ask them not to send their military to Fort Benning. Venezuela, Argentina and Uruguay have stopped the practice. Bolivia is phasing out its participation, and Chile is reconsidering its plans to send troops.

PO Box 4566, Washington, DC 20017, (202) 234-3440, www.soaw.org

United for Peace and Justice. This group was the wheelhorse of the antiwar movement from late 2002 through 2007. UFPJ was founded in October 2002 by Leslie Cagan, a veteran antiwar and political activist, with leaders of a number of progressive groups alarmed by increasingly ominous signs that the Bush administration was brazenly taking the country into a preemptive war with Iraq. An organizational conclave in Washington on October 25, 2002, was attended by representatives of more than seventy labor, peace, socialist, antiglobalization and other progressive organizations. They agreed to form an antiwar coalition under the umbrella of United for Peace and Justice. The coalition grew rapidly and was able to stage its first big march on the eve of the war. On February 15, 2003, it joined other organizations here and abroad in calling for a day of global protest, "The World Says No to War." Huge demonstrations were held in major cities across the globe. In August 2004, UFPJ and the ANSWER Coalition, which was formed by the radical Workers World Party (distrusted by some on the Left), turned out 500,000 people during the Republican National Convention in New York. The UFPJ coalition also engaged in other political actions, such as sounding alarms about Bush's intentions toward Iran, condemning Israel's invasion of Lebanon and opposing the use of torture. It has supported immigrant rights and demonstrated for Katrina victims and social welfare. In December 2005 UFPJ split with ANSWER because, Cagan said, too much energy was being wasted in disputes. The two groups accused each other of bad faith and broken promises. Being a coalition with an ideologically diverse membership, it has avoided being too specific in its proposals for ending the war—or endorsing candidates for that matter. This way it can avoid the sectarianism and divisive debates that have plagued the Left. Cagan told *Nation* editors in 2008 that UFPJ was reaching out to more potential coalition partners, such as labor unions, liberal churches and feminist organizations. She insisted the coalition's 1,400 member groups were still alive and kicking about the war nationally and in hundreds of cities and towns. Against the backdrop of economic downturn its proposed 2008 election slogan was "It's the war economy, stupid."

PO Box 607, Times Square Station, New York, NY 10108, (212) 868-5545, www.unitedforpeace.org

War Resisters League. This venerable but feisty group has a long career of antiwar action. It was organized in 1923 by pacifists, many of whom had been jailed for refusing military service in World War I. During World War II its members continued their opposition to all wars, and did alternative service as conscientious objectors, or more commonly went to prison. The ex-cons radicalized the league when they got out. When the civil rights movement emerged in the 1950s, WRL members were in the ranks of its marchers. They opposed nuclear testing and were the first peace group to call for withdrawal from Vietnam, organizing draft card burnings, antiwar rallies and legal help for draft resisters. They organized peace vigils and coffin displays against the Iraq War. WRL publishes an internationally oriented quarterly magazine called *WIN*.

339 Lafayette Street, New York, NY 10012, (212) 228-0450, www.warresisters.org

War Times/Tiempo de Guerras. The Center for Third World Organizing is a "racial justice organization dedicated to building a social justice movement led by people of color." The organization opposes the U.S. government's racist, imperialist "permanent war against terrorism at home and abroad, which has endangered the lives and liberties of millions." The organization used to put out a paper called *War Times/Tiempo de Guerras* but now produces bilingual outreach materials with the same purpose. Using the Internet and e-mail, it distributes leaflets and flyers that can be downloaded, reproduced and distributed.

PO Box 99096, Emeryville, CA 94662, www.war-times.org

Win Without War. This organization sprang out of dissatisfaction among some antiwar people with the prominent role played in the antiwar movement by organizations they considered extremist or violent. Win Without War comprises some forty moderate-to-far-left groups such as Greenpeace, MoveOn, National Council of Churches, National Gay and Lesbian Task Force, NOW, Peace Action, Physicians for Social Responsibility, Shalom Center, United Church of Christ and Veterans for Peace. It called for achieving peace and security through "international cooperation and enforceable international law" and working through multilateral agencies rather than military action and inveighed against the "militarization" of U.S. foreign policy. It is for "prompt" withdrawal of U.S. troops from Iraq and a declaration that the United States desires no permanent bases. The coalition has organized demonstrations against the Iraq War and monitored and criticized legislation on the war. It helped organize StandUpCongress.org, which works at the grassroots level and tells people how to put pressure on their Congress members to stop the war.

1320 18th Street NW, 5th floor, Washington, DC 20036, (202) 822-2075, www.winwithoutwarus.org

VETS

Iraq and Afghanistan Veterans of America. IAVA calls itself "the nation's first and largest group dedicated to the Troops and Veterans of the wars in Iraq and

Afghanistan, and the civilian supporters of those Troops and Veterans."

770 Broadway, 2nd floor, New York, NY 10003, (212) 982-9699, www.iava.org

Iraq Veterans Against the War. IVAW emerged at the convention of Veterans for Peace in July 2004 with the mission of giving a voice to antiwar service people on active duty. IVAW has members in forty-three states and at numerous bases, including some in Iraq, who speak in debates to clubs and in classrooms and counsel gung ho youngbloods about the realities of war. IVAW pushes for more Veterans Administration funding and full health care for vets. It calls for immediate withdrawal from Iraq and reparations to the Iraqi people. According to Garett Reppenhagen, "Through our military experience we have learned that the continued presence of U.S. troops in the Middle East is instigating further hatred toward American Armed Forces and undermining our nation's security. As a result, our military in Iraq is viewed by the majority of the world as occupiers and not peacekeepers. The Iraq Veterans Against the War stands by the belief that funding the war is killing the troops."

PO Box 8296, Philadelphia, PA 19101, (215) 241-7123, www.ivaw.org

Military Families Speak Out. This group started with two families in 2002 and has grown to some 3,700 who are against the war and have relatives or loved ones who are serving or have served in Iraq. In 2007 they added a new chapter, Gold Star Families Speak Out, made up of those who have lost loved ones in the war.

PO Box 300549, Jamaica Plain, MA 02130, (617) 983-0710, www.mfso.org

Veterans for Peace. Although it was only started in 1985, VFP numbers among its members veterans of the Spanish Civil War, World War II, the Korean and Vietnam wars and Gulf Wars I and II; it is dedicated to stopping current and future wars. Its headquarters is in St. Louis and it has chapters around the country.

216 S. Meramec Avenue, St. Louis, MO 63105, (314) 725-6005, www.veteransforpeace.org

VoteVets. This was cofounded by Jon Soltz, who worked for John Kerry's presidential campaign in 2004, organizing the veterans' vote in Pennsylvania. Soltz became chairman of the organization, whose board is dominated by Democratic pols, including former senator Bob Kerrey. VoteVets has 20,000 members, of whom 1,000 served in Iraq and Afghanistan. The organization has a PAC, which encourages vets to run for public office and backed eight candidates for Congress in 2008.

303 Park Avenue South, #1293, New York, NY 10010, (646) 415-8429, www.votevets.org

PEOPLE OF FAITH

Faith in Public Life. This umbrella organization was assembled by an interdenominational task force of liberal divines, who met in Washington following the 2004 election. They were unanimously disturbed by the religious right's choke hold on the political discourse, transforming it into a one-note rant against abortion and homosexuality. The leaders felt this kind of tunnel vision ignored the rich tapestry of religious values and creeds and their applicability to a wide range of social problems and issues of social justice. Their website contains news items, links and commentary on faith and politics, and publishes case studies of faith at work (for example, reports on an African-American ministers conference's evaluation of the federal response to hurricane Katrina; the efforts of a group of church leaders to persuade Congress to treat the federal budget as a moral document and evangelicals' espousal of a proenvironment program of "creation care"). The website also displays a Mapping Faith database that lists by state some 3,000 progressive religious organizations representing all denominations.

1333 H Street NW, 10th floor, Washington, DC 20005, (202) 481-8165, www.faithinpubliclife.org

Muslim WakeUp! This organization "champions an interpretation of Islam that celebrates the Oneness of God and the Unity of God's creation through the encouragement of the human creative spirit and the free exchange of ideas, in an atmosphere that is filled with compassion and free of intimidation, authoritarianism, and dogmatism. In all its activities, Muslim WakeUp! attempts to reflect a deep belief in justice and against all forms of oppression, bigotry, sexism, and racism."

PO Box 196, Pleasantville, NY 10570, (646) 485-1163, www.muslimwakeup.com

Progressive Muslim Union of North America. PMU is a grassroots group that provides a home for U.S. Muslims who support a progressive political agenda. They "affirm the importance of . . . culture and the pursuit of joy" and oppose bans on some forms of instrumental music and art depicting human figures; revere Islamic ritual but oppose imposing a specific form of it by coercive means; support equality for women and oppose gender segregation; approve of equal rights for LGBT people and "affirm that justice and compassion should be the guiding principles for all aspects of human conduct." PMU favors universal health care, public education, the protection of our environment and the eradication of poverty around the world. "We reject the authoritarian, racist, sexist and homophobic interpretations of our faith as antithetical to the principles of justice and compassion."

www.pmuna.org

Shalom Center. Rabbi Arthur Waskow founded this Jewish center in 1983 as a division of the Reconstructionist Rabbinical College, where he taught and where his cofounder, Ira Silverman, was president. Waskow has had a long career in left politics, thought and activism, going back to the early days of the Institute for Policy Studies (see page 199). Shalom Center's foundational project was halting the out-of-control nuclear arms race. In the Jewish scriptural tradition, the nuclear threat should be seen as presaging a Flood of Fire, an ecological disaster of biblical proportions. It is this reinterpretation of political questions in light of Jewish scriptural tradition that has infused Shalom Center's progressive politics. The center has addressed the Israel-Palestine conflict, and Waskow has called for an independent Palestinian state long before it was kosher to do so. He is a frequent sponsor of and/or participant in interfaith causes, engaging in various initiatives in opposition to the Iraq War. He formed the Green Menorah Covenant coalition to work for progreen change in government policies and in personal behavior.

6711 Lincoln Drive, Philadelphia, PA 19119, (215) 844-8494, www.shalomctr.org

Sojourners. The organization is headed by the Rev. Jim Wallis, a charismatic, progressive evangelical preacher and author of the religious best seller *God's Politics: Why the Right Gets It Wrong and the Left Doesn't Get It.* He also edits and writes for *Sojourners* magazine, a subscription-based monthly that serves as the voice of the organization. The magazine and an active website address issues of politics from a biblical perspective in a deliberate response to the better-organized and better-funded media machine of the Christian Right. The website beams almost daily messages to viewers, reporting the doings and sayings of Wallis and featuring a God's Politics blog.

3333 14th Street NW, Suite 200, Washington, DC 20010, (202) 328-8842, www.sojo.net

PROGRESSIVE PROTESTANTS

For lists of progressive churches by city and state consult Sojourners Faith & Justice churches database (www.sojo.net/index.cfm?action=network.search_fjc_directory). Also, Faith in Public Life's Mapping Faith database lists by state some 3,000 progressive religious organizations of all faiths (www.faithinpubliclife.org/map/index .html).

PROGRESSIVE RABBIS

Adam Berman	David J. Cooper	Fred Scherlinder Dobb	Michael Feinberg	Joshua Levine Grater
Isabella Freedman Jewish Retreat Center	Kehilla Community Synagogue	Adat Shalom Reconstructionist Congregation	Greater New York Labor-Religion Coalition	Pasadena Jewish Temple and Center
116 Johnson Road	1300 Grand Avenue	7727 Persimmon Tree Lane	40 Fulton Street, 22nd floor	1434 N. Altadena Drive
Falls Village, CT 06031	Piedmont, CA 94610	Bethesda, MD 20817	New York, NY 10038	Pasadena, CA 91107
(860) 824-5991	(510) 547-2424, ext. 103	(301) 767-3333, ext. 106	(212) 406-2156, ext. 4637	(626) 798-1161
http://isabellafreedman.org	www.kehillasynagogue.org	www.adatshalom.net	www.labor-religion.org/ local_greater.ny_bar.htm	www.pjtc.net

Linda Holtzman
Mishkan Shalom
4161 Freeland Avenue
Philadelphia, PA 19128
(215) 508-0226

Steven B. Jacobs
Congregation Kol Tikvah
20400 Ventura Boulevard
Woodland Hills, CA 91364
(818) 348-0670
http://koltikvah.org

Mordechai Liebling
Jewish Funds for Justice
8459 Ridge Avenue
Philadelphia, PA 19128
(215) 483-4004
www.jewishjustice.org

Ellen Lippmann
Kolot Chayeinu
1012 Eighth Avenue
Brooklyn, NY 11215
(718) 390-7493
www.kolotchayeinu.org

David Shneyer
Am Kolel Sanctuary and
    Renewal Center
19520 Darnestown Road
Beallsville, MD 20839
(301) 349-2799
www.am-kolel.org

Toba Spitzer
Congregation Dorshei Tzedek
60 Highland Street
West Newton, MA 02465
(617) 965-0330
www.dorsheitzedek.org

Susan Talve
Randy Fleisher
Central Reform Congregation
5020 Waterman Avenue
St. Louis, MO 63108
(314) 361-3919
www.centralreform.org

Brian Walt
Rabbis for Human Rights
PO Box 810
West Tisbury, MA 02575
(508) 696-1880

PROGRESSIVE MUSLIMS

Imam Al-Hajj Talib 'Abdur-Rashid
Mosque of Islamic
    Brotherhood, Inc.
130 W. 113th Street
New York, NY 10026
(212) 662-4100
www.mosqueofislamicbrother
hoodinc.org

Parvez Ahmed
Awad Nihad
Council on American-Islamic
    Relations (CAIR)
453 New Jersey Avenue SE
Washington, DC 20003
(202) 488-8787
www.cair.com

Ahmed Bedier
CAIR, Florida
8056 N. 56th Street
Tampa, FL 33617
(813) 514-1414
www.cair.com

Imam Yahya Hendi
Georgetown University
    Campus Ministry
37th & O Streets NW
    Healy 112
Washington, DC 20057
(202) 687-4272

Iftekhar Hussain
CAIR, Philadelphia
1218 Chestnut Street, Suite
    510
Philadelphia, PA 19107
(215) 592-0509
www.cair.com

Imam Ibrahim Kazerooni
Abrahamic Initiative
St. John's Cathedral
1350 Washington Street
Denver, CO 80203
(303) 831-7115
www.sjcathedral.org

Ibrahim Ramey
Imam Mahdi Bray
Muslim American Society
    Freedom Foundation
1050 17th Street NW, Suite
    600
Washington, DC 20036
(202) 496-1288
www.masnet.org

Imam Feisal Abdul Rauf
Daisy Khan
American Sufi Muslim
    Association
475 Riverside Drive, Suite
    248
New York, NY 10115
(212) 870-2552
www.asmasociety.org

Dr. Sayyid Muhammad Syeed
Islamic Society of North
    America
PO Box 38
Plainfield, IN 46168
(317) 839-8157
www.isna.net

UNBELIEVERS

American Humanist Association. The AHA maintains a vigorous defense against the encroachments on the First Amendment by the religious Right. It functions to explain the doctrines of humanism but also to afford nonbelievers the support they need in a predominantly sectarian culture. It "actively defends the civil liberties and constitutional freedoms of Humanists—indeed of all peoples—and leads both local and national Humanist organizations toward progressive societal change." With more than one hundred grassroots organizations, the association campaigns in the national media as the leading American voice of humanism. It has drawn support from prominent unbelievers like Kurt Vonnegut (who was honorary president until his death in 2007), John Kenneth Galbraith, Edward O. Wilson, Carl Sagan, Isaac Asimov, Erich Fromm, Margaret Sanger, John Dewey, Bertrand Russell and Albert Einstein. The association has branches in thirty-six states and publishes *The Humanist* magazine (see page 142).

1777 T Street NW, Washington, DC 20009, (202) 238-9088, www.americanhumanist.org

Americans United for Separation of Church and State. This freedom-from-religion group dates back to 1947. Its emphasis, of course, is on the separation of church and state as the sine qua non of religious liberty in America—a pragmatic, working truce between believers and nonbelievers and among people of different faiths; the idea is that all peacefully coexist and avoid the lethal hubris of one sect claiming a superior truth and forcing it on unbelievers with an AK-47. Claiming a membership of around 75,000, AU is nonsectarian and nonpartisan, open to people of all faiths and value systems, from Buddhists to nudists, who share its view on church-state separation. It backs lawsuits against religious observances in public schools and government facilities. Yet it's not against student exercises relating to religion so long as they are "truly voluntary." The magazine *Church & State* provides sharp analyses of recent church-state issues, and the website reports daily on the latest controversies. Ignoring the divine curses and imprecations hurled at it, AU continues to patrol the heavily contested border between church and state. The job brings it up against groups like the Christian Reconstructionists who, according to a January 7, 2008, article in *Church & State*, seek to institute the death penalty for homosexuality, adultery, fornication, witchcraft, cursing parents and propagating false doctrines.

518 C Street NE, Washington, DC 20002, (202) 466-3234, www.au.org

Council for Secular Humanism. This freethinking group was founded in 1980 as the Council for Democratic and Secular Humanism. The council publishes *Free Inquiry* (see page 141). It opened a research center in 2007, adjacent to the State University of New York at Buffalo, Amherst Campus, which contains the Center for Inquiry libraries and archives, including the books and papers of philosophers Paul Edwards and Richard Taylor; Martin Gardner's collection on the paranormal and extensive correspondence; commentary and news clippings compiled by Steve Allen, along with 65,000 books.

PO Box 664, Amherst, NY 14226, (716) 636-7571, www.secularhumanism.org

CONSUMER NATION

Center for Science in the Public Interest. In 1971 the center was founded by its executive director, Michael Jacobson, who holds a Ph.D. in microbiology, and two scientists, all products of Ralph Nader's Center for the Study of Responsive Law. Its declared mission was to give consumers the latest science on questions of food safety, nutrition and related issues. CSPI educates the public and advocates new laws and policies on the basis of the best scientific information. It remains a determined scold on issues of "nutrition and health, food safety, alcohol policy, and sound science." CSPI led the charge for such advances in consumer awareness as inclusion of nutrition information on packaged foods. The center has vied with agribusiness over how to define "organic" and with the liquor interests over slapping warning labels on alcoholic beverages. It calls for levying heavy taxes on unhealthy food, particularly alcoholic beverages, a bête noire of Jacobson's. He is also a fanatical foe of soft drinks and coined the terms "junk food" and "empty calories" for these products and their ilk. CSPI has analyzed the nutritional values and dangers in fast-food meals and movie house popcorn and campaigned against soda and junk foods in schools. When New York City passed the first ordinance in the nation banning trans fat in restaurants and requiring calorie information on menus, CSPI was there, providing the backup science. CSPI boasts a membership of 900,000 as it brings about the consumer-welfare state prophesied by Nader.

1875 Connecticut Avenue NW, Washington, DC 20009, (202) 322-9110, cspinet.org

CLEAN GOVERNMENT

Center for Public Integrity. Despite his dream job doing investigative stories for *60 Minutes,* Charles "Chuck" Lewis was finding TV journalism more and more unsatisfying. Good stories were sometimes spiked because they were offensive to an advertiser or to network executives or simply too controversial. In November 1988, Lewis resigned with a vision of doing uncompromising, proactive investigative reporting that uncovered systemic corruption. The result was the nonprofit, foundation-supported Center for Public Integrity. Its first story exposed the revolving door of White House trade officials who left to take lucrative jobs lobbying for foreign governments. The CPI's exhaustive investigation into the provenance of campaign donations to the presidential candidates, *The Buying of the President* (1996), got people talking; sequels in 2000 and 2004 became best sellers. Within a decade the center had quintupled in size and was spewing out books, articles, reports and TV shows. It became journalists' go-to source on campaign finance, telling which industry was bundling how much to which candidate. Its Collateral Damage document warehouse collects hidden information on U.S. aid to dictatorships and human-rights-challenged regimes. By the new century the center was recognized as an authoritative data bank on international corruption following its 750,000-page online report *Global Integrity.* This led to the formation of an independent organization with the same name, which publishes the *Global Integrity Report* using "integrity indicators" to monitor international corruption.

910 17th Street NW, 7th floor, Washington, DC 20006, (202) 466-1300, www.publicintegrity.org

Center for Responsive Politics. The CRP is a nonpartisan, nonprofit research group that "tracks money in politics, tracing its effect on elections and public policy." The CRP "conducts computer-based research on campaign finance issues for the news media, academics, activists, and the public at large." This information is disseminated on www.opensecrets.org, the indispensable website that tells you what pol gets big bucks from what special interest. Support for the center comes from a combination of foundation grants (Carnegie: $500,100; Ford: $300,000) and individual contributions. It refuses money from businesses and labor unions.

1101 14th Street NW, Suite 1030, Washington, DC 20005, (202) 857-0044, www.opensecrets.org

CHILDREN, LABOR AND IMMIGRATION

ACORN. That acronym stands for Association of Community Organizations for Reform Now. It is the largest national community organization protecting the interests of low- and moderate-income families. Its origins trace back to the 1960s and the National Welfare Rights Organization, which became one of the first national organizations championing the rights of poor people. By 1966 NWRO had 170 groups in 60 cities. Under the dynamic organizer Wade Rathke, NWRO's Arkansas branch grew into a political powerhouse called Arkansas Community Organizations for Reform Now. Rathke's idea was to concentrate on issues close to poor people. In 1978 ACORN held its first national convention in Memphis and drew up a "People's Platform" that it presented to the Democratic national convention about to nominate Jimmy Carter (the platform was ignored). Subsequently, ACORN continued to grow, and its local units worked to unite welfare recipients with needy working people around issues of free school lunches, unemployed workers' concerns, Vietnam veterans' rights and hospital emergency room care, environmental justice (no situating of polluting centers in poor neighborhoods and cleanup of toxic dumps), housing foreclosure, more paid sick days and increased voter registration and participation. ACORN still works through community organizations, which employ demonstrations, picketing, negotiation, legislation and voter activism. It campaigns for many other causes. It has more than 850 neighborhood chapters in more than 100 cities across the United States. There are also chapters in Argentina, Canada, the Dominican Republic, Mexico and Peru. Funding comes from member dues and fund-raisers. ACORN umbrellas various organizations, including two radio stations, a voter registration network, a housing corporation and various publications.

739 8th Street SE, Washington, DC 20003, (202) 547-9292, www.acorn.org

Center for Human Rights & Constitutional Law. The center is a nonprofit, public interest legal foundation dedicated to furthering and protecting the civil, constitutional and human rights of immigrants, refugees, children and the poor. It is supported by the California Legal Services Trust Fund, private donations and attorneys' fees in major cases. It has used some of this money for the Immigrant Litigation Fund, which helps nonprofits and pro bono attorneys with the costs of representing immigrant and refugee appeals. It distributed more than $200,000 in 2006 to about fifty organizations around the country that represent immigrants needing legal help, such as victims of violent crime, domestic violence, drug trafficking, child abuse. The ILF finances such actions with no-interest loans, paid back only if attorney fees are reimbursed.

256 S. Occidental Boulevard, Los Angeles, CA 90057, (213) 388-8693,
www.centerforhumanrights.org

Children's Defense Fund. The Children's Defense Fund spotlights the needs of poor and minority children and those with disabilities. It was founded in 1973 by Marian Wright Edelman, a lawyer from Mississippi who had been counsel for the Rev. Martin

Luther King's Poor People's Campaign. Salient concerns include affordable child care, prevention of violence, welfare reform, teenage pregnancy, health insurance coverage for children. It works with coalitions of local organizations on child welfare problems and runs Freedom Schools, staffed by college students, that offer six- to eight-week sessions for boys and girls ages five to eighteen to help them improve reading, learn conflict resolution and social skills.

25 E Street NW, Washington, DC 20001, (800) 233-1200, www.childrensdefense.org

Mexican American Legal Defense and Educational Fund. MALDEF is the largest legal advocacy group representing the interests of millions of Latinos residing in the United States. It works for fairer immigration laws and protects the rights of Latin Americans. It has branch offices in Atlanta, Chicago, Houston, Sacramento, San Antonio and Washington, D.C., with a total staff of around seventy-five, twenty-two of them attorneys. MALDEF was founded in 1968 in San Antonio by Pete Tijerina, a San Antonio lawyer with a background in antidiscrimination law, who started out fighting for Mexican-American representation on trial juries as a crack in the door to equal rights. Under his leadership MALDEF expanded its mission beyond civil rights cases to working for accurate census counts and fair districting and running workshops to train new business and community leaders and instill parenting skills. Amid the recent anti-immigrant backlash, the Texas branch of MALDEF worked with the ACLU Foundation of Texas to challenge local ordinances penalizing landlords who rented to illegals. It strives for equal educational opportunities for Mexican-American children. MALDEF maintains a newsy website updated daily and publishes a weekly newsletter, *The MALDEFian.*

634 S. Spring Street, 11th floor, Los Angeles, CA 90014, (213) 629-2512, www.maldef.org

National Housing Institute. For more than three decades the National Housing Institute has studied the growing housing crisis for the working poor in an era of increasing income inequality, stagnant wages, rising housing costs and predatory lenders. Founded in 1975 as an independent nonprofit organization, NIH's scope is broad, embracing issues interwoven with housing—jobs, safety, education, poverty and racism, disinvestment and unemployment and breakdown of the social fabric. It does scholarly research and publishes books and papers as well as a lively bimonthly called *Shelterforce* that covers such topics as saving subsidized housing, homelessness prevention, predatory lending and creating jobs as a component of affordable housing construction.

460 Bloomfield Avenue, Suite 211, Montclair, NJ 07042, (973) 509-2888, www.nhi.org

National Immigrant Solidarity Network. This coalition of groups—including labor, human rights, religious and student activist organizations—supports immigrant rights.

It organizes letter-writing campaigns, sends out speakers and devises campaigns on various issues.

Action LA/The Peace Center, 8124 W. 3rd Street, Suite 104, Los Angeles, CA 90048, (213) 403-0131, www.immigrantsolidarity.org

National May 1st Movement for Worker & Immigrant Rights. This coalition of more than one hundred organizations supportive of immigrant rights organized the May 1 Great American Boycott and March by immigrants. In 2007 more than 500,000 people participated nationwide, a lower figure than the previous year. The march in LA was marred by a police riot in MacArthur Park, during which tactical patrol cops attacked marchers gathered for a postmarch celebration. These groups were galvanized by Congress's failure to pass a reasonable immigration reform bill and have sounded off against punitive anti-immigration bills, such as the Immigration Enforcement and Border Security Act of 2007, which emphasizes sanctioning immigrant families, adding border agents and detention space, worksite roundups and border fences.

5274 W. Pico Boulevard, #203, Los Angeles, CA 90019, (213) 995-0694, www.maydaymovement.blogspot.com

OTHER ACTIVIST GROUPS THAT HAVE BEEN DOING GOOD WORK:
Coalition for Humane Immigrant Rights of Los Angeles, 2533 W. 3rd Street, Suite 101, Los Angeles, CA 90057, (213) 353-1333, www.chirla.org
National Day Laborers Organizing Network, 675 S. Park View Street, Suite B, Los Angeles, CA 90057, (213) 380-2784, www.ndlon.org
Dolores Huerta Foundation. PO Box 9189, Bakersfield, CA 93309, (661) 322-3033, www.doloreshuerta.org

Worker Centers. There are numerous immigrant support groups at the city or state level, formed to deal with immediate workplace and community issues. The rise of these immigrant self-help organizations has been one of the big labor stories in the past two decades. Worker centers are located all over the country and take many forms, but basically they are set up to deal with problems facing a group of immigrant workers in a given area. These employees are below the radar, toiling in industries that labor laws don't reach and unions can't or won't. The centers are the products of immigration laws that have created an underclass of people who toil long hours for little money and no benefits and, most of all, have no rights. Often worker centers have been formed as an ad hoc response to some specific employer injustice such as illegal firings or withholding of wages. According to Janice Fine, a labor economist from Rutgers, who wrote the definitive study on worker centers for the Economic Policy Institute, there

When I was growing up in Perth Amboy, New Jersey, it was largely a second-generation immigrant enclave, with a sizable Eastern European population, clannish Jewish neighborhoods, and a rising, first-generation Puerto Rican bloc in the poorer areas. Economically, Perth Amboy was on the way down in the late 1960s, the 1970s and early 1980s. A former industrial and manufacturing town, it was in the process of being left behind by the new economy. But now, when I make my annual pilgrimage, instead of boarded-over stores and depressing graffiti, I find a booming place—not yuppified or gentrified so much as Dominicanized. The later generations of Puerto Ricans have assimilated, and Smith Street, the main boulevard of downtown, is now a booming *avenida* that could be dropped intact into Santo Domingo.

Along with lower Manhattan, Perth Amboy was my family's gateway into America. We came here fleeing poverty, as did so many others. And it's still a real American town with real American contrasts: there are pawnshops and 99-cent stores on Smith Street, as well as chains and successful local businesses; and city politics is dominated by third- and fourth-generation immigrants. But there is also real Latino street life and, down by the bay—half a mile from the house where William Franklin, Ben's son, governed New Jersey for King George III—a newly refurbished marina park established by longtime residents, with a band shell where an orchestra plays Sousa's "Stars and Stripes Forever" every Fourth of July to an audience, many of whom were born in the Caribbean.

—AMY WILENTZ is a former assistant literary editor at *The Nation,* is the author of *The Rainy Season: Haiti Since Duvalier*; *Martyrs' Crossing* (a novel) and *I Feel Earthquakes More Often Than They Happen.*

were more than 140 by 2006, up from forty in a decade.* Workers centers serve a gateway function, helping recently arrived, undocumented people from Central and Latin America, China and other parts of the globe. The worker centers are diverse in nature; they tend to have small staffs of less than five with budgets of less than $250,000 a year. They deal with basic workplace problems, ranging from employers who cheat their people to bosses who work them long hours in dangerous workplaces. Here are some prominent ones:

Carolina Alliance for Fair Employment, 1 Chick Springs Road, Suite 114, Greenville, SC 29609, (864) 235-2926, www.cafesc.org

Chinese Staff and Workers Association, PO Box 130401, New York, NY 10013, www.cswa.org

Interfaith Worker Justice, 1020 W. Bryn Mawr Avenue, 4th floor, Chicago, IL 60660, (773) 728-8400, www.iwj.org

Korean Immigrant Workers Advocates, 3465 W. 8th Street, 2nd floor, Los Angeles, CA 90005, (213) 738-9050, www.kiwa.org

*Janice Fine, *Worker Centers: Organizing Communities at the Edge of the Dream* (Ithaca, NY: ILR Press/Cornell University Press, 2006).

New York Taxi Workers Alliance, 37 E. 28th Street, #302, New York, NY 10016, (212) 627-5248, www.nytwa.org

Restaurant Opportunities Center of New York, 275 7th Avenue, 17th floor, New York, NY 10001, (212) 343-1771, www.rocny.org

Tenants' and Workers' United, PO Box 2327, Alexandria, VA 22305, (703) 684-5697, www.tenantworkers.org

Workplace Project on Long Island, 91 N. Franklin Street, Suite 207, Hempstead, NY 11550, (516) 565-5377, www.workplaceprojectny.org

TAMING THE WILD CORPORATION

Center for Corporate Policy. This comparatively new outfit was set up to look into corporate shenanigans. It has rounded up an impressive board, which includes Sarah Anderson, a fellow with the Institute for Policy Studies' Global Economy Program,  and John Cavanagh, director of IPS, both experts on the global economy. The center's director, Charlie Cray, is a policy analyst and former director of the campaign for corporate reform at Citizen Works, and former associate editor of *Multinational Monitor* magazine. CCP deals with issues like bloated executive pay, corporate crime waves, monopolies and concentration.

PO Box 19405, Washington, DC 20036, (202) 387-8030, www.corporatepolicy.org

CorpWatch. Founded in 1996 as Transnational Resource & Action Center, this research center has been on the transnational corporations' case since even before Seattle. It has campaigned against Nike sweatshops, private military contractors, war and disaster profiteering, the World Trade Organization and the UN Global Compact. In 1997 CorpWatch's founder, Joshua Karliner, published an influential book *The Corporate Planet: Ecology and Politics in the Age of Globalization.* In that year CorpWatch exposed inhuman working conditions in Nike's sweatshops in Vietnam, sparking a wave of demos against the company. Fearing for its image among its predominantly young customer base, Nike agreed to inspections and took steps to improve the working conditions in its contractors' factories. As early as 1998, CorpWatch was looking into the bizarre accounting practices of a firm named Enron. Its report *Greenhouse Gangsters vs. Climate Justice,* which looked at climate change from the standpoint of environmental justice and human rights, mobilized communities already adversely impacted by the fossil fuel industry. By 2002 CorpWatch was cocking an eye on companies like Bechtel, DynCorp and Halliburton that were making out like thieves during the war on terrorism. A CorpWatch team filmed corporate boondoggling in Iraq, and some of this footage enlivened Michael Moore's film *Fahrenheit 9-11*. All this poking around led to its War Profiteers website (www.warprofiteers.com) and in November 2004, *Iraq, Inc., A Profitable Occupation*. Amy Goodman of *Democracy Now!* called it "the ultimate primer on how modern U.S. invasion and occupation for profit is being waged." CorpWatch has prepared subsequent books on bungled reconstruction in Afghanistan and the New Orleans mess post-Katrina.

1611 Telegraph Avenue, #720, Oakland, CA 94612, (510) 271-8080, www.corpwatch.org

ON AND OFF DEATH ROW

National Coalition to Abolish the Death Penalty. Since 1976, NCADP has opposed the death penalty and claims to be the only fully staffed national organization doing so. It serves as a resource for opponents of the national capital punishment lottery by providing information, advocacy for public policy and other support. NCADP publishes a death penalty blog that features personal stories of inmates on death row, of the victims of their crimes and of activists working to stop the death lottery. It amasses information on the effect of race on death sentences (African Americans account for 43 percent of all death row inmates). It maintains a list of inmates approaching execution dates and tells you how to send a message to the state governor. It publishes reports such as "Judging Innocence" by University of Virginia law professor Brandon Garrett. Garrett studied 200 cases of wrongful convictions and found that in each one there was conclusive (DNA) evidence that the condemned man was innocent. Another publication, called *Innocent and Executed*, tells the stories of four men later proven to have been wrongly executed.

1705 DeSales Street NW, 5th floor, Washington, DC 20036, (202) 331-4090, www.ncadp.org

FEMINIST

Feminist Majority Foundation. FMF was set up in 1987 by Eleanor Smeal, former president of NOW, as a research and education organization, and since 2001 it has underwritten *Ms.* magazine (see page 135). It is dedicated to "women's equality, reproductive health, and non-violence," and its program includes plotting long-term strategies for achieving solutions to problems that women face, sponsoring a variety of health information and access programs such as National Clinic Access Project, the Campaign for Afghan Women and Girls and Rock for Choice, a series of concerts by rock stars held since 1991. More recently, it helped defeat a ballot measure in Michigan that eliminated affirmative action and a South Dakota measure that banned abortions.

1600 Wilson Boulevard, Suite 801, Arlington, VA 22209, (703) 522-2214, www.feminist.org

NARAL Pro-Choice America. For more than thirty years, NARAL Pro-Choice America has supported full reproductive rights for women. NARAL maintains a choice action center that disseminates current information on issues relating to reproductive rights. The group has collected stories of women's actual experiences in exercising their rights locally that provide a picture of the state of reproductive rights in the United States:

Women in some states must pay for their prescription birth control pills because their insurance plan refuses to cover them.

Young people face an unintended pregnancy or contracting a sexually transmitted disease as a result of misinformation taught in abstinence-only programs in their schools.

Sexual assault survivors are routinely denied a chance to prevent pregnancy because the hospital emergency rooms they visit refuse to provide them emergency contraception (the "morning-after" pill).

1156 15th Street NW, Suite 700, Washington, DC 20005, (202) 973-3000, www.prochoiceamerica.org

National Organization for Women. NOW was established on June 30, 1966, in Washington, D.C., at the Third National Conference of Commissions on the Status of Women. Its first president was Betty Friedan, author of *The Feminine Mystique*, who had earlier scribbled "NOW" on a napkin during lunch. NOW's original Statement of Purpose has a familiar urgency:

We believe that the power of American law, and the protection guaranteed by the U.S. Constitution to the civil rights of all individuals, must be effectively applied and enforced to isolate and remove patterns of sex discrimination, to ensure equality of opportunity in employment and education, and equality of civil and political rights and responsibilities on behalf of women, as well as for Negroes and other deprived groups.

These concerns would classify NOW as centrist. Yet the rightward drift of the political culture made it seem almost radical in 2008. NOW has surely succeeded beyond the dreams of its founders, with 500,000 members all over the United States and 550 chapters in fifty states and D.C. The organization under its current president, Kim Gandy, remains combative and ready to take to the streets for women's rights. It promises to resort to direct and indirect actions like rallies, picketing, civil disobedience, grassroots political organizing and class-action lawsuits. It has a political action committee, NOW-PAC, which endorses candidates in federal elections and accepts contributions from NOW members only. The NOW Equality PAC endorses candidates at state, county and city levels; and state and local chapters may have their own PACs that endorse candidates in their area. NOW's program of action includes protesting the denial of emergency contraceptives to U.S. servicewomen; demanding health care for all; supporting the Healthy Families Act; working for repeal of the military's antigay "don't ask, don't tell" policy; calling for prosecution of all hate crimes and telling Congress members to support the Freedom of Choice Act.

1100 H Street NW, 3rd floor, Washington, DC 20005, (202) 628-8669, www.now.org

Third Wave Foundation. This feminist, activist foundation's constituency comprises young women and transgender youth from fifteen to thirty. The inspiration for the Third Wave Foundation came in a 1992 article in *Ms.* magazine by Rebecca Walker, "Becoming the Third Wave." So favorable was the reaction to the piece that Walker and Shannon Liss founded the Third Wave Direct Action Corporation, which took on the job of motivating young women to become more politically active. It sponsored Freedom Summer '92, a voter registration drive, which also drew more young women to the cause. As the organization grew, its principals discovered that only 4 percent of philanthropic grants were going to programs for young women and girls. They held discussions that led to the reconstitution of the group as the Third Wave Fund, then as the Third Wave Foundation, with a new set of priorities: "emergency funding for abortions, scholarships, building young-women-led reproductive rights organizations, and providing general operating support for young-women-led groups and projects." Grants have supported groups engaged in environmental justice, prison reform, living-wage campaigns and reproductive rights.

25 E. 21st Street, 4th floor, New York, NY 10010, (212) 228-8311, www.thirdwavefoundation.org

Radical Women. A socialist-feminist group affiliated with the Freedom Socialist Party. The women held their Forty-first Anniversary Conference in San Francisco in 2008 with speakers from Central America, China and the U.S. They maintain Freedom Hall in New York's Harlem and Roses Center in Portland. Meetings and panels are held at these and other venues in other cities.

5018 Rainier Avenue, Seattle, WA 96118, (206) 722-6057, www.radicalwomen.org

LESBIAN, GAY, BISEXUAL AND TRANSGENDER

THINK LOCAL: LGBT CENTERS

The gay rights movement might be said to have decentralized. Since the 1980s LGBT centers (often called simply that) have sprung up in numerous cities, providing all manner of services to the local LGBT community. A model would be the New York City LGBT center (www.gaycenter.org). With 6,000 drop-ins a week and 300 organizations holding meetings there, it claims to be the second largest LGBT center in the world. It is a testament to community service and political organizing—running everything from group therapy sessions and after-school programs to political forums, reading groups, social events, family centers, libraries, courses and addiction recovery—kind of like a megachurch only it's secular, left and gay. Wingspan in Tucson is also great (www.wingspan.org), as are the Los Angeles Gay and Lesbian Center (www.laglc.org) and San Francisco LGBT Center (www.sfcenter.org). The Audre Lorde Project in the very progressive Lafayette Avenue Presbyterian Church in Brooklyn is a great drop-in center for queers of color (www.alp.org). Salt Lake City, of all places, has a good LGBT center, Utah Pride Center (www.glbtccu.org). And you'll find others in most states. Search for "LGBT centers" on the Internet.

Our Earth, Our Rights

MONKEY WRENCHERS, ARCHDRUIDS AND SEA SHEPHERDS

These should be boom times for the numerous environmental organizations in America, what with annual contributions reaching an all-time high of $1.7 billion, the global warming threat much in the news and polls showing people of all political stripes placing the environment and global warming as major concerns. But, as Mark Hertsgaard reported in a Nation *article, a lot of Americans who love their environment don't like environmentalists. Critics say they've become too establishment, too timid, too Capitol Hill–oriented and too neglectful of the local groups working at the state level. Nevertheless, the Bush years of obstructionism and sabotage were marked by a countervailing rise in proenvironmental legislation by state governments prodded by local groups. And young people are flocking to the banner of ending global warming with the commitment of civil rights workers in the sixties. The 1Sky initiative has united many groups around a few basic principles (see Step It Up, page 239). Energy Action Committee, a student group, has also been active in organizing students on 200 campuses and mobilizing them in national actions. The environmental community is learning from past mistakes, becoming less conservative, less establishment and industry centered and more activist, more politically oriented, more grassroots conscious. But global warming was steaming toward Earth in Distress like a locomotive in the* Perils of Pauline *serial and the survival of the planet itself hung in the balance. What follows is a quickie rundown on the principal environmental groups, large and small.*

ENVIROS

Apollo Alliance. Apollo started out as a project of the Center on Wisconsin Strategy, which joined with the Institute for America's Future (see page 193); it's now flying free. The basic idea was to link environmentalism with job creation. For too long corporate America and unions had regarded environmental measures, such as fuel economy standards, as profit and job killers. The Apollo Alliance said, "Okay, why not create green jobs?" and it won the support of the AFL-CIO and twenty-one international labor unions, the major national environmental organizations, businesses and organizations in the nation's states and cities. The alliance's program calls for investment in a sustainable and clean energy economy that will create 3 million new jobs and reduce oil imports. In 2007 Jerome Ringo, who is also head of the National Wildlife Federation, took over as president. Ringo once worked in the petrochemical refineries in Louisiana's Cancer Alley as a labor and community organizer and knows firsthand how polluting industries and toxic waste dumps always cluster in low-income neighborhoods. One would expect a simple long-term solution— *disinvestment* in pollution manufacturing industries and *investment* in green-collar jobs for the people who are forced to live by them. AA joined with the Ella Baker Center (see page 365), Center for American Progress (see page 193) and others in lobbying Congress to pass the Energy Independence and Security Act, which will spend $125 million annually on training for "green collar" jobs.

330 Townsend Street, Suite 205, San Francisco, CA 94107, (415) 371-1700; 1825 K Street, Suite 400, Washington, DC 20009, (202) 587-1616, www.apolloalliance.org

Earth First! This aggressive cadre has acquired a reputation for extreme activism. Moderates chastised it for acts of civil disobedience such as erecting log tripods to block vehicles from entering ancient growth forests or members chaining themselves to stately trees or perching on their highest boughs to prevent arborcide. The FBI and other agencies have been on Earth First!'s case, accusing it of plotting violence, though nothing was ever proved. It does admit to admiring the end-of-saving-the-planet-justifies-the-means philosophy of Edward Abbey's characters in his 1975 novel *The Monkey Wrench Gang*. Its priorities listed on its website are:

1. Stopping the dangerous spread of genetically modified organisms (GMOs)
2. Halting the Biscuit logging project [direct-action protests against the U.S. Forest Service's introduction of logging into the rain forests of the Siskiyou Mountains of southwest Oregon]
3. Stopping the Camisea project in Peru [saving a rain forest there]
4. Promoting fair trade for farmers
5. Saving the Arctic National Wildlife Refuge from oil drilling
6. Protecting the Tongass National Forest from logging
7. Stopping the seal slaughter in Canada
8. Jackson Forest [restoring the state forest of 50,000 acres of redwoods]
9. Stopping mountaintop mining [strip mining in Appalachia]

www.earthfirst.org

Friends of the Earth. FOE traces its lineage back to 1969, when it was founded in San Francisco by the great environmentalist David Brower (writer John McPhee's "arch-druid"), who also organized the Sierra Club and the League of Conservation Voters. It continues to be an influential, international network of grassroots groups with offices in seventy countries. In 1995 it merged with the Bluewater Network (www.bluewaternetwork.org), a bunch of West Coasters working to stop air and water pollution and damage to public lands by jet skis, snowmobiles and other rec-road vehicles. FOE claims to have blown the whistle when genetically engineered corn infiltrated the supermarkets. It has persuaded a number of companies to pledge not to use carcinogenic chemicals in their products and mounted an ad campaign calling on the Ford Motor Company to make more hybrid cars. For years it fought wrongly sited dams, international whaling, strip mining and taxpayer giveaways to corporate polluters.

1717 Massachusetts Avenue NW, Suite 600, Washington, DC 20036, (877) 843-8687, www.foe.org

Greenpeace. Greenpeace is one of the most courageous and in-your-face environmental groups, its members challenging eco-invaders at the risk of their lives and liberties. Some of its feats have become the stuff of legend, such as sailing into the French nuclear test zone in the South Pacific, though in recent years it has adopted nonviolent modes of protest (for example, in confronting Japanese whalers with its ship *Esperanza*). Its operations have always been global in reach and it has branches in more than thirty countries and 200,000 members. Greenpeace is currently dedicated to:

   Alerting the world to the need to save ancient forests that are threatened by economic development, as are the native peoples who depend on them

   Waking the world to the threat to the oceans from overfishing and global warming

   Using one-person submarines to take a census of underwater life in previously unexplored ocean canyon habitats

   Lobbying the U.S. government to take the lead in reversing global warming

   Cleaning up toxic chemicals in the water, air and land

   Shutting down all nuclear power plants

   Putting a halt to genetic engineering

702 H Street NW, Washington, DC 20001, (202) 462-1177; 75 Arkansas Street, San Francisco, CA 94107, (415) 255-9221; www.greenpeace.org

National Resources Defense Council. The NRDC calls itself a national, nonprofit organization of scientists, lawyers and environmental specialists dedicated to protecting public health and the environment. It's been fighting polluters since 1970 and its membership now numbers 1.2 million with offices in New York, Chicago, Los Angeles, San Francisco, Washington and Beijing (it's advising Chinese greens, once an endangered species). Much of its Washington lobbying effort has been conservation of existing environmental laws under attack by the administration. As Frances Beinecke, NRDC president, told Mark Hertsgaard: "It was critical to be in Washington the last few years to resist the [Bush] rollback, which we've done." Now, however, they recognize that pressure points exist outside Washington. When the administration's tools in Congress sneaked a proviso into a law allowing untreated sludge to drain into coastal waters, the NRDC decided to mobilize state firepower. It's been working at the local level, allying with other nature and environmental groups to expose the Bush administration's environmental depredations. For example, the Bushies were not cracking down on ocean polluters, so NRDC joined with some other concerned groups from the fishing industry to the Surfrider Foundation to prepare a report on the major problems threatening Florida's ocean waters and coastlines and the actions needed to solve them. NRDC also drafted and helped California pass the Global Warming Solutions Act, one of the most advanced anti-global-warming laws to be passed in the United States. The NRDC gets its word out through *OnEarth* magazine and a newsletter, *This Green Life*, and it runs the breezy reports of *Grist* (see page 132) on its website.

40 W. 20th Street, New York, NY 10011, (212) 727-2700, www.nrdc.org

Sierra Club. With 1.3 million members, the Sierra Club claims to be the oldest environmental action group. Founded in 1892, its first president was John Muir, and the club's first battles involved saving scenic lands that would become Yosemite, Grand Canyon, Mount Rainier and Glacier National parks. In 1952 David Brower took over as the club's first executive director and stayed on until 1969, when he was edged out by more conservative board members who resented his command-and-control management style. He went on to found Friends of the Earth (see page 233). In recent times, members complained that the club was paying more attention to national politics than to grassroots environmental activists. That has changed and Sierra focuses on local chapters, though it retains its Washington lobbying office. It promotes expeditions to exotic places and ecotourism and disseminates a number of publications, including the handsome *Sierra* magazine, Sierra Club Books and *The Hotline* (a twice monthly global warming e-newsletter). President Carl Pope's blog "Taking the Initiative" features trenchant political commentary. The club's website links you to important environmental news stories and provides a legislative tracker on bills before Congress of interest to greens, and issues frequent reports on efforts such as building new green homes in New Orleans. Expanding beyond nature, the Sierra Club has been a strong opponent of the Iraq War.

National headquarters, 85 2nd Street, 2nd floor, San Francisco, CA 94105, (415) 977-5500; legislative office, 408 C Street NE, Washington, DC 20002, (202) 547-1141; www.sierraclub.org

SMALLER BUT BEAUTIFUL

Bioneers. Somebody must think, as well as act. Here are some thinkers. Bioneers holds annual conferences devoted to finding solutions to environmental problems with a spiritual-environmental nexus. Bioneers was founded in 1990 by Kenny Ausubel and Nina Simons. The first conference set the pattern for future conclaves, drawing together "scientific and social innovators." Bioneers tries to go beyond sustainability to restoration and recovery.

Old Lamy School House, 6 Cerro Circle, Lamy, NM 87540, (505) 986-0366, www.bioneers.org

Bronx River Alliance. Ask a New Yorker about the Bronx River and he's likely to think you're talking about the Bronx River Parkway. Well, there really is an actual Bronx River running beside the highway. This body of water rises in Westchester County and flows to the East River and the sea through desperately poor neighborhoods in the South Bronx. The alliance is a coalition of community groups that has spent more than three decades working to bring back the river, seeking to link, both ecologically and socially, its northern and southern parts. As a result of these efforts, Tracy Tullis reported in *The Nation* ("A Bronx Tale," August 13, 2007), "Oysters . . . are spatting on manmade clamshell reefs. Hundreds of herring were released in the past two springs; when their fry return to spawn, volunteers will scoop them over the dams that have blocked their migration since the 1600s. And last winter, a beaver built his dam on the bank. . . ."—the first in, oh, about 200 years.

1 Bronx River Parkway, Bronx, NY 10462, (718) 430-4665, www.bronxriver.org

Center for Biological Diversity. The folks here seriously believe that galloping extinction of flora and fauna threatens humanity's tenure on this planet. Some action alerts in recent years: "Help Protect Idaho's Backcountry Forests!" "Protect Panama's Biosphere Reserve from Dam!" "U.S. Military Base in Okinawa Threatens Rare Dugongs."

PO Box 710, Tucson, AZ 85702, (520) 623-5252, www.biologicaldiversity.org

Colorado Environmental Coalition. Here's an example of an effective local coalition, which reaches out to other groups that share interests rather than ideology. In 2004, even as John Kerry was losing Colorado, a state of crimson hue, the coalition passed three progressive ballot initiatives and helped Dems take back the state legislature and win a U.S. Senate seat. Said Executive Director Elise Jones: "Seeing how the conservatives who orchestrated the Gingrich revolution [in 1994] went back to the grass roots made me realize that we needed to do the same thing."

1536 Wynkoop Street, 5C, Denver, CO 80202, (303) 534-7066, www.ourcolorado.org

E. F. Schumacher Society. This group follows the precepts of E. F. Schumacher, author of the seminal work *Small Is Beautiful: Economics as If People Mattered*. It was founded by Robert Swann, an early admirer and disciple of Schumacher. The society sponsors an annual lecture series, and the lectures are then published as pamphlets. Participants have included Gar Alperovitz, Ivan Illich, Winona LaDuke, Kirkpatrick Sale and numerous others. The society promotes local currencies and has worked with the chamber of commerce and local citizens to issue a script called Berkshares, which circulates in Great Barrington and environs.

140 Jug End Road, Great Barrington, MA 01230, (413) 528-1737, www.schumachersociety.org

Garrison Institute. A combined retreat and conference center near the Hudson River in New York that is devoted to encouraging a spiritual approach to environmentalism—applying the great religious and meditative traditions to civil and environmental issues. It contends that "[a]uthentic contemplative practice generates deep insight into the essential interdependence of all forms of life . . . and awakens unselfish compassion for others, and the combination of contemplative insight and compassion represents the purest and surest force for positive social change."

PO Box 532, Garrison, NY 10524, (845) 424-4800, www.garrisoninstitute.org

Planet Drum Foundation. Founded in 1973, Planet Drum was the first enviro to develop the concept of a bioregion, "a distinct area with coherent and interconnected plant and animal communities, and natural systems, often defined by a watershed." Planet Drum devises projects on bioregional issues, publications and supplies speakers to help other bioregional groups start up and live within the limits of their own bioregion. They sponsor bioregional workshops in various places in the West.

PO Box 31251, San Francisco, CA 94131, (415) 285-6556, www.planetdrum.org

Rainforest Action Network. With forty-three staff members, plus thousands of volunteer scientists, teachers, parents, students and other engaged citizens around the world, and an annual budget of just over $3 million, RAN is considered one of the more sophisticated and creative proenvironment agitators around. It uses marketing campaigns to pressure multinational corporations to adopt more environment-friendly policies. "We believe that logging ancient forests for copy paper or destroying an endangered ecosystem for a week's worth of oil is not just destructive, but outdated and unnecessary." RAN was created in 1985 to spread the word about the destruction of the rain forests. Its first campaign was a successful boycott of Burger King, which was buying cheap Central American beef, thus encouraging cutting down the rain forests for pasturage. RAN has employed other tactics. As part of its Dirty Money campaign, which seeks to stop banks from investing in coal-burning utilities, it sponsored a Billionaires for Coal demo at Merrill Lynch. More straightforwardly it opposed a loan by the ANZ Bank to Gunns Ltd., an Australian lumber company notorious for destroying virgin forests to build a pulp mill in Tasmania. Says an admirer: "It's a cool group. More in your face than most but in an effective way."

221 Pine Street, 5th floor, San Francisco, CA 94104, (415) 398-4404, www.ran.org

Rocky Mountain Institute. This green technology nonprofit was founded in 1982 by Amory B. Lovins, a pioneering thinker in "soft" energy and conservation fields, and his wife, L. Hunter Lovins. It turns out practical moneymaking (or saving) fuel-conserving solutions for environmental problems. It calls itself a "think and do tank" that advises individuals and organizations of every imaginable kind on how to use energy and resources efficiently while being ever better stewards of the environment. Supported by foundations, corporations and individuals, RMI also earns money by consulting for corporations and governments. It now has a staff of eighty and a budget of nearly $12 million. It is actively working for hydrogen fuel-cell technology and is opposed to nuclear energy; it designs technology that achieves greater energy efficiency.

1739 Snowmass Creek Road, Snowmass, CO 81654, (970) 927-3851; 1215 Spruce Street, Suite 301, Boulder, CO 80302, (303) 245-1003; www.rmi.org

Ruckus Society. Another occasionally confrontational group, Ruckus was cofounded by Mike Roselle, formerly of Greenpeace and Earth First!, his companion Howard "Twilly" Cannon and others. The name and purpose came from a disaffected enviro's remark that "we don't need a wilderness society any more, we need a ruckus society." As former director John Sellers described its earliest days in *A Movement of Movements*, edited by Tom Mertes, "Basically they took the Greenpeace direct-action model, threw away the little rubber boats, and imposed it on the forests." Nowadays they go beyond environmental activism to dissuading young people from joining the military, hanging a huge antiwar banner from the Plaza Hotel in New York during the GOP National Convention, placing Wal-Mart stores under mock quarantine and pushing for single-payer health care.

369 15th Street, Oakland, CA 94612, (510) 763-7078, www.ruckus.org

Sea Shepherd Conservation Society. Paul W. Watson was founder of Greenpeace but in 1977, impatient with that organization's increasingly pacific ways, he resigned and started a new mission with one ship, an old fishing trawler he purchased with a grant from the Fund for Animals. He christened her *Sea Shepherd* and took her out and rammed a whaler that was operating illegally. Rather than be captured by other whalers in the area, Captain Watson scuttled *Sea Shepherd.* Since then he and his supporters have acquired several used but seaworthy craft, stoutly constructed to operate in extreme climates and conditions. His miniature "navy" criss-crosses the seas on the hunt for poachers, whalers, long-liners and illegal dumpers. They board malefactors and confiscate illegal fishing devices. They've intervened to protect whales, turtles and other endangered creatures and can be quite rude about it, throwing stink bombs and acid at whalers, even boarding vessels and opening stopcocks in an attempt to sink them. Often, however, just the threat of a confrontation is sufficient to shame a wrong-doer into desisting (for example, Icelander fishermen hunting fin whales in 2007). That tactic's known as the "art of fighting without fighting." If you have a boat you want to donate to Watson's fleet, give him a jingle.

PO Box 2616, Friday Harbor, WA 98250, (360) 370-5650, www.seashepherd.org

Step It Up 2007. Here's Bill McKibben's group. As author of the seminal environmental text *The End of Nature,* he knows well the dangers to the environment and preaches them to an awakening America. After teaching he moved on to leading students in protest marches, and now he's trying to stir up "a really passionate commitment" to the environment, one that is as strong as the civil rights movement's was to its goals. His group has been organizing demos nationwide to pressure Congress to take action against global warming by adopting the 1Sky initiative, which calls for three simple science-based actions:

Cut carbon dioxide by 80 percent by 2050 (cut it by 10 percent in three years—
    hit the ground running)
Build no new coal-fired power plants
Establish a Green Jobs Corps

Here is the account in *Grist* of one Step It Up demo: "On April 14, 2007, gaggles of enthusiastic Americans gathered at more than 1,400 spots around the United States to demand action against climate change, part of a coordinated Step It Up campaign. . . . At all the rallies, marches, parties, and other hullabaloos, the message was the same: Step it up, Congress! Enact immediate cuts in greenhouse-gas emissions, and pledge an 80 percent reduction by 2050." Or as McKibben likes to say: "Screw in the new lightbulb but then screw in the new federal policy." Proclaiming 2007's actions had "helped jump start the national climate movement," McKibben said that Step It Up would be pulled into 1Sky (see www.1sky.org), a kindred group.

931 Elm Street, Manchester, NH 03101, (877) 839-8957, www.Stepitup2007.org

Sustainable South Bronx. Sparked by a dynamo named Majora Carter, who says, "Economic degradation begets environmental degradation," a South Bronx Greenway Project has been laid out that will bring parks and bicycle and pedestrian paths to the people of the area, giving them clean air, physical exertion and healthy recreation. The neighborhood around Hunts Point, where the Bronx River flows into the East River, is Pollution City, a transit point for trucks bound for a huge produce and fish market. It is also home to numerous scrap metal yards, garbage transfer stations, power plants, a sewage treatment plant and a factory that makes fertilizer from baked sewage sludge. Ms. Carter says she wants to bring about the economic rebirth of the South Bronx and perhaps inspire solutions for other poor communities. "You gotta meet people where they are," she says, meaning you don't talk ecology or environmentalism here. You talk jobs, asthma rates, obesity and crime.

890 Garrison Avenue, 4th floor, Bronx, NY 10474, (718) 617-4668, www.ssbx.org

Time's Up! This all-volunteer group has been working since 1987 to improve environmental conditions in New York City. They partner with groups like Critical Mass, a cyclist collective, as well as with city transportation people on projects to make cycling easier and safer, and speak out in the media. They have engaged in self-styled "playful" demo tactics, such as using clown cars to protest cars parking in bike lanes, and have held a march to save community gardens on the Lower East Side, complete with puppets, seed balls and the Rude Mechanical Orchestra's lively music.

PO Box 2030, New York, NY 10009, www.times-up.org

We Act for Environmental Justice. WE ACT started in 1988 with $1.1 million won in a successful lawsuit against the city for operating a sewage treatment plant in Harlem. It continues the fight against other kinds of environmental racism, for example, provoking New York City Council hearings on pollution emitted by MTA buses, a factor in Harlem's high asthma rate among children. It has called for an environmental study of Columbia University's plans to preempt an eight-square-block area in West Harlem for a new campus, which will displace some residents.

271 W. 125th Street, Suite 308, New York, NY 10027, (212) 961-1000, www.weact.org

POLL WATCHERS

The name of the game for voting rights groups in the Bush years was defending poor and minority voters against "voter fraud" challenges by Republican Party operatives seeking to cut the Democratic vote, defeating voter ID laws, ensuring a fair vote count and working to register more voters. Nonprofit activist groups also had to expose attempts to mislead potential voters or practices designed to create voter backlash, such as "robo-calling" (automated calls ostensibly for a candidate but actually sponsored by his or her opponent and put through very late at night or early in the morning). Many groups, including Internet activists like Black Box Voting, tested electronic voting machines for hacking or rigging. Finally, the nonprofits engaged in expanding the electorate by registering new voters. ACORN, for example, registered 540,000 voters during the 2006 election—the biggest such effort in the nation's history.

Public Campaign. Public Campaign promotes "clean money laws" in the states, meaning public campaign financing for candidates to eliminate their grubbing for dollars from special interests. Here's how it works. A state candidate may choose whether to take public funding or not. Candidates who opt for public money must collect a minimum number of signatures and/or a minimum number of small contributions in the $5 range. Once they meet these standards they are eligible to receive a set amount of public funding to pay for their campaigns (and to point with pride to the fact that they are untainted by special interest money). Those who decline public funding may cadge money from individual and corporate donors—as long as they comply with state and federal campaign finance laws. "Clean" candidates get additional money if their opponent outspends them. Voters like public campaigns because they get candidates unbeholden to special interest groups. Candidates like the idea because it frees them from the endless dollar chase and gives them more face time with the voters. Campaign finance reformers like it because it's a simple way of pushing special interest money out of politics. You can find out who in your state is backing clean money by checking out the Public Campaign website. Veteran activist Nick Nyhart is cofounder, CEO and public face of the group.

1320 19th Street NW, Suite M-1, Washington, DC 20036, (202) 293-0222, www.publiccampaign.org

CIVIL RIGHTS, JUSTICE AND LEGAL AID

Alliance for Justice. This research organization is perhaps best known for its Judicial Selection Project, which publishes thoroughly researched analyses of the records of federal judiciary appointees. AFJ researchers sniff down the appointees' paper trails to discover their real views on abortion and other issues and publicize their findings in plain language, empowering activists to deliver informed testimony at confirmation hearings or vent their opposition in letters to Judiciary Committee members. Alliance for Justice sponsors other initiatives: for example, getting students involved with legal issues; its Nonprofit Advocacy Project and Foundation Advocacy Initiative provide information on the relevant laws governing the policy process in an effort to strengthen the voice of the nonprofit and philanthropic sectors in important public policy debates.

11 Dupont Circle NW, 2nd floor, Washington, DC 20036, (202) 822-6070, www.afj.org

American Civil Liberties Union. The ACLU is an old and flawed and great and honorable and indispensable organization, whose history is intertwined with the great courtroom battles over constitutional liberties in this country. What other organization has placed so much legal talent and membership resources so effectively in the service of civil liberties in America? The ACLU was born in 1920, amid the acrid smell of repression that descended on the nation in the aftermath of World War I. It braved the Red Scare and intervened in the trial of the decade, the Scopes Monkey Trial on teaching high school students about evolution. Most of the cases that followed embodied sharp legal controversies. In our own time, against the backdrop of 9/11, the ACLU launched legal challenges to warrantless surveillance of citizens' electronic communications by the National Security Agency. It has defended gun owners, opposed Megan's Law publicizing sex criminals, defended Iran-Contra plotter Lt. Col. Oliver North and former CIA agent Frank Snepp, challenged the Patriot Act and opposed anti-spam legislation in 2003. Amid all the tumult and pressures of changing times, the ACLU has taken principled stands, derived from its reading of the Constitution and Bill of Rights, for free speech, religious freedom, separation of church and state, freedom of the press, affirmative action, decriminalization of drugs, prisoners' rights and on and on. To those who believe it is only "common sense" that police should be able to use racial profiling, the ACLU is a bunch of bleeding hearts. But to those who understand that when the authorities are allowed to violate the rights of the despised Other today, they will be free to violate our own rights tomorrow, the ACLU is precious. It is our constitutional fire department, even when it is fighting the wrong fire. The ACLU has more than 500,000 members and autonomous chapters in every state that bring important suits of their own. It is run by an elected board of directors, a president and an executive director. It provides free legal assistance to worthy plaintiffs and defendants through its state branches and has effectively defended undocumented immigrants.

125 Broad Street, 18th floor, New York, NY 10004, www.aclu.org

Brennan Center for Justice. The Brennan Center (named in honor of the liberal Supreme Court Justice William Brennan), located at New York University School of Law, tries to combine in a single agenda scholarship, public education and legal action in the service of equal economic opportunity, especially for those who can't compete in the job marketplace. A key program sought to improve the lives of restaurant workers in New York City, selected because—as with other low-wage service sectors, particularly those employing a lot of immigrants—employers routinely violate labor laws relating to minimum pay, overtime, safety, racial discrimination and other subjects. The plight of the restaurant workers became part of a larger study, *Unregulated Work in the Global City,* which looked at fourteen industries where laws regulating working conditions and pay were laxly enforced, including supermarkets, retail establishments, child and health care, construction, light manufacturing and taxis. The Brennan Center has been in the vanguard of the living-wage movement. The center helped home care workers win raises in four states and is seeking national legislation to overrule the U.S. Supreme Court's decision upholding the exclusion of home care workers from federal wage laws. Now that Congress passed a raise in the minimum wage in 2007, the Brennan Center and other groups are planning a campaign to set the federal minimum wage at 50 percent of average wages and to index it to inflation. The center has helped craft public funding legislation in statehouses and in Congress (the Fair Elections Now Act); publicized special interest contributions in state judicial elections and studied abuses of presidential power post–9/11, resulting in the book *Unchecked and Unbalanced: Presidential Power in a Time of Terror,* by Frederick A. O. Schwarz, Jr., and Aziz Z. Huq. Another book, *Liberty Under Attack: Reclaiming Our Freedoms in an Age of Terror,* edited by Richard C. Leone and Greg Anrig, Jr., deals with the rights of Muslim communities. The Prosecutorial Discretion in Sentencing Project studies disparate outcomes in prisoners' sentences as a result of prosecutors' arbitrary decisions. The Brennan Center is noted for its timely, thoughtful, comprehensive analyses of frontline legal and social problems.

161 Avenue of the Americas, 12th floor, New York, NY 10013, (212) 998-6730,

www.brennancenter.org

Center for Constitutional Rights. CCR started in 1966 defending civil rights activists in the South. Founders included Morton Stavis, Arthur Kinoy, Ben Smith and William Kunstler, whose experiences representing workers in Mississippi had convinced them of the need for a privately funded legal center that would work out new courtroom strategies for defending social justice movements. CCR lived up to that challenge, becoming a creative, determined legal strategist, defending the cases of unpopular people against prosecutions that might ultimately threaten the rights of ordinary citizens. It lawyered the case of *Abramowicz v. Lefkowitz,* a landmark challenge to New York State's law banning abortion (1972). That same year Kunstler and Leonard Weinglass defended the antiwar activists known as the Chicago 7. In 1980, in the case of *Filártiga v. Peña-Irala,* CCR ingeniously revived a forgotten statute called the Alien Tort Claims Act as a tool for suing against human rights violations committed in foreign lands. Under Michael Ratner, who has worked for CCR most of his legal career and now is its president, the center took up the cause of Guantánamo detainees and uncovered testimony of brutal treatment. It has challenged their detention without legal and constitutional rights and fought as well for aliens caught up in post-9/11 dragnets and successfully litigated the closing of a U.S.–installed Haitian HIV refugee camp. Ratner and CCR have challenged the constitutionality of the Bush administration's war in Iraq and its serial assaults on civil liberties. In *CCR v Bush*, CCR, in collaboration with the National Lawyers Guild, challenged the NSA's warrantless wiretapping program and the expanded powers granted to the agency in a law bulldozed through Congress in the summer of 2007. In *Arar v. Ashcroft* CCR represented a Canadian who had been a victim of the CIA's extraordinary rendition policy.

666 Broadway, 7th floor, New York, NY 10012, (212) 614-6464, www.ccrjustice.org

Center for Guerrilla Law. Founded by Paul Harris, the center consists of associates who work in the fields of litigation, mediation and legal education. Harris—who pioneered the "black rage defense" (experience of racism as a mitigating factor) and who is the author of *Black Rage Confronts the Law*—is a radical lawyer who helped win acquittals for Black Panther chairman Huey P. Newton, feminist health worker Stephanie Kline and lawyer-activist Stephen Bingham. A former president of the National Lawyers Guild, he teaches guerrilla law at New College of California's School of Law in San Francisco. What is guerrilla law? "Guerrilla law is guided by four principles: 1. to demystify the law; 2. to help build the power of community groups; 3. to protect radical political activists; 4. to dignify the client in and out of the courtroom." It draws on three primary writings: J. R. R. Tolkien's *Lord of the Rings*, in which justice and injustice are at war and the small and seemingly insignificant play a role in the transformation of this continual struggle; the works of Che Guevara, in which men and women are urged to live today according to the values that they hope to make a reality tomorrow; and *A Book of Five Rings* by Miyamoto Musashi, in which the warrior strives to be one with his or her vocation and prepares with great discipline to achieve the Way of Being. Harris was a cofounder of the San Francisco Community Law Collective in 1970, an interracial firm in which lawyers and secretaries alike received the same pay.

20 Quickstop Lane, #1, San Francisco, CA 94115, (415) 567-3494, www.guerrillalaw.com

National Lawyers Guild. NLG lawyers have regarded the law as an instrument for social and economic change, not the foundation of the status quo. This view automatically placed them far to the left of the legal establishment. Strong adherence to left principles has embroiled it in conflicts with more conservative legal groups and generated internal conflicts that ripped it apart but ultimately strengthened the guild's commitment to dissident advocacy. Its main distinction has been mobilizing the courage, idealism and skill of its lawyers—the ones on staff and the volunteers—all willing to fight

ATTORNEYS FOR THE DAMNED

A poll showed that approximately 90 percent of Americans distrust lawyers. Another poll showed that 90 percent of Americans would call a lawyer if they got in trouble with the law. The following list is a pantheon of people's lawyers who have taken on the hard cases in behalf of the underdog, the powerless and the unjustly accused. Our thanks to Marjorie Cohn, president of the National Lawyers Guild, for her help. We welcome readers' nominations to this Hall of Fame.

Stephen Bingham.

Representing Black Panther and prison author George Jackson in San Quentin prison, he was falsely accused of smuggling a gun to him. He was acquitted of this charge in 1986. He was staff attorney at San Francisco Neighborhood Legal Assistance Foundation (now a regional office of Bay Area Legal Aid) and founding director of its Legal Barriers to Employment Project.

Leonard Boudin (1912–1989).

Boudin argued more civil liberties cases before the U.S. Supreme Court than any other constitutional lawyer. He won the landmark passport case, *Kent v. Dulles* (1958), establishing the right of all U.S. citizens to have a passport. His clients have included Daniel Ellsberg (the Pentagon Papers case), Julian Bond (denied a seat in the Georgia legislature), Dr. Benjamin Spock (charged with conspiracy during the Vietnam War) and Jimmy Hoffa (banned from union activities). He represented Cuba's interests in the United States from the beginning of the Cuban revolution. Founded (1952) and was general counsel (1952–1989) for the National Emergency Civil Liberties Commission, which merged with the Center for Constitutional Rights.

Ken Cockrel (1938–1989).

A Detroit radical lawyer in 1960s and 1970s who helped found the League of Revolutionary Black Workers and the Labor Defense Coalition and defended working and poor people in numerous cases. He was a friend and colleague of Chuck Ravitz.

David Cole.

A professor at Georgetown Law School and the *Nation*'s legal affairs editor, Cole emerged even before 9/11 as a champion of immigrants' rights, taking unpopular cases like the Los Angeles 7. He has spoken out in timely and eloquent fashion against the depredations of the Patriot Act and the Bush administration's immigrant roundups.

George Crockett (1909–1997).

Cofounder of the first racially integrated law firm in 1946, and vice president of the National Lawyers Guild, he defended Communist Party Smith Act defendants and served four months for contempt of court. He established the NLG's office in Mississippi and managed its Mississippi Project defending Freedom Summer workers. He personally searched, unsuccessfully, for missing civil rights workers Schwerner, Chaney and Goodman, while police and the FBI turned their backs. He was Michigan representative in Congress from 1980 to 1991.

Earl Dickerson (1891–1986).

The first black graduate of the University of Chicago Law School, he helped organize the NAACP Legal Defense and Education Fund in 1939. He was a member of FDR's first Fair Employment Practices Committee and led the movement that broke the color barrier to membership in the Illinois Bar Association. He handled *Hansberry v. Lee,* which ended restrictive real estate covenants in Hyde Park.

Charles Garry.

He's defended tough, unpopular cases like Huey P. Newton in the 1967 killing of Oakland police officer John Frey. He won freedom for Black Panther chairman Bobby Seale, who was accused of murdering a police informant. Garry defended the Oakland 7 (anti–Vietnam War activists involved in the planning of Stop the Draft Week) and the San Quentin 6.

Ann Fagan Ginger.

She challenged the Ohio Un-American Activities Commission in the Supreme Court and won (1959). She founded Meiklejohn

Civil Liberties Institute in Berkeley (1965), a think tank on human rights and peace law. She lectures on using the International Covenant on Civil & Political Rights and Conventions Against Torture, and on Elimination of Racial Discrimination to protect rights of U.S. citizens. Ginger convinced the city of Berkeley to make reports required under these treaties, and made presentations to UN committees and conferences.

Ernest Goodman (1907–1997).

He has argued numerous labor and civil liberties cases before the Supreme Court. He represented GIs during the Vietnam War and successfully defended the Detroit 15, Black Panthers charged with conspiracy and a convict accused of murder in the Attica Prison riot. As president of the NLG (1964–1967), he made civil rights activist work the guild's top priority, a turning point which led to its involvement with the student antiwar movement.

Bill Goodman.

Son of Ernest Goodman, he represented defendants in the 1967 Detroit riots and inmates involved in the Attica Prison rebellion.

Susan B. Jordan.

She was first to use the battered spouse defense in the murder trial of Inez Garcia, who killed the man who raped her. She's famous for defending radical women, for example, Emily Harris, who kidnapped Patty Hearst, and Sara Jane Olson, Symbionese Liberation Army member; Marilyn Buck, alleged Black Liberation Army associate; Earth First! leader Judy Bari; New York lawyer Lynne Stewart.

C. B. King (1923–1988).

Practicing in Georgia in the 1950s, he was the only black lawyer who would take criminal cases. He demanded equal treatment by judges in court. In the sixties he led defenses of the Albany Movement; freedom riders; the Americus Four (incarcerated civil rights protestors); and represented clients like Ralph Abernathy,

Andrew Young, Martin Luther King, Jr., and William G. Anderson, leader of the Albany Movement. He challenged voter literacy tests and worked to integrate public employment, juries and schools.

Arthur Kinoy (1920–2003).

A radical lawyer who represented victims of HUAC, he was attorney for the Rosenbergs. He represented the leftist United Electrical Workers, Students for a Democratic Society, the Emergency Civil Liberties Committee. He successfully argued before the U.S. Supreme Court that wiretaps were a violation of constitutional protections against unreasonable searches. During the 1950s and 1960s he worked on behalf of the civil rights movement. He was a cofounder of the Center for Constitutional Rights (see page 243) and a partner of William Kuntsler, another great radical lawyer.

Bill Quigley.

In New Orleans he has represented thousands of displaced public housing residents, stopping evictions and bulldozing of homes. He's also taken the cases of hundreds of people charged with civil disobedience: protesters at the School of the Americas in Georgia (see SOA Watch, page 211), Plowshares antinuclear activists in North Dakota and Arizona, Catholic Workers protesting the start of the Iraq War by pouring their blood on the walls of a military recruiting station. He went to Iraq before the war with the blockade-breaking Voices in the Wilderness and represented the group in federal court; he has represented several people on death row and been active in cases from living wage to tax resistance to public education. A Loyola University law professor, Quigley has written extensively on social justice and the need for revolutionary lawyering.

Victor Rabinowitz (1911–2007).

A legendary figure, his clients have included the government of Cuba, many trade unions, Alger Hiss, Jimmy Hoffa and Benjamin Spock. He established that the McCarthy Committee had no authority to investigate "subversive activities" (*Yellin v.*

United States) and that Cuba had a right under international law to nationalize U.S. property (*Banco Nacional de Cuba v. Sabbatino*). A founding member of the National Lawyers Guild, he was its president from 1967 to 1970.

Justin (Chuck) Ravitz (1940–2007).

This Detroit lawyer represented the local countercultural hero John Sinclair in a marijuana bust set up by the police. Ravitz raised one of the earliest challenges to the constitutionality of the state's marijuana laws.

Catherine Roraback.

A pioneering attorney who defended victims of McCarthyism and was of counsel in the landmark reproductive rights case *Griswold v. Connecticut*, she was lead attorney in *Women v. Connecticut,* which established right to an abortion in Connecticut.

Mark Soler.

He did groundbreaking work on keeping juveniles out of adult prisons and antiracist juvenile work.

Fay Stender (1932–1980).

She started out as a feminist lawyer working in the law office of Charles Garry (see page 245) and founded the Prison Law Project, which represented many hard case cons, notably George Jackson, one of the Soledad brothers. In 1979 she was shot and seriously wounded by a delusional man who accused her of betraying Jackson. She survived but committed suicide a year later, worn down by the physical deterioration resulting from her wounds.

Michael E. Tigar.

This lawyer, law teacher and author has represented Angela Davis, H. Rap Brown, Kiko Martinez, Fernando Chavez, Rosalio Muñoz, the Chicago 7, the Seattle 8, Allen Ginsberg, Leonard Peltier and Lynne Stewart. He was involved in efforts to bring to justice members of the Chilean junta, including Augusto Pinochet. In 1999, he came in third in the California Attorneys for Criminal Justice ballot for "Lawyer of the Century" (behind Clarence Darrow and Thurgood Marshall).

Doris Walker.

UC–Berkeley law school grad who became a union organizer then joined the defense team in *Yates v. United States,* which ended Smith Act prosecutions of Communist Party members; involved in sedition case during the Korean War and defended Angela Davis; subpoenaed by HUAC for membership in NLG; first woman president of NLG.

Leonard Weinglass.

His clients include Abbie Hoffman, Tom Hayden and Rennie Davis of the Chicago 7; Daniel Ellsberg in the Pentagon Papers trial; Jane Fonda in a suit against Richard Nixon; Barry Commoner in a battle to enter a presidential primary; Angela Davis, a discharged Communist professor; Bill and Emily Harris, charged with kidnapping Patty Hearst; Amy Carter, daughter of former president Jimmy Carter, charged in a demo; Mumia Abu-Jamal, African-American journalist and death row inmate; Kathy Boudin, former Weatherman; five Cubans charged with conspiracy to commit espionage in Miami.

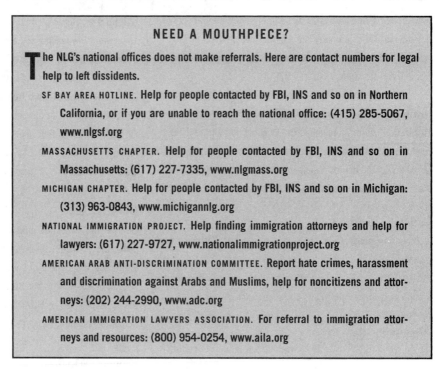

NEED A MOUTHPIECE?

The NLG's national offices does not make referrals. Here are contact numbers for legal help to left dissidents.

SF BAY AREA HOTLINE. Help for people contacted by FBI, INS and so on in Northern California, or if you are unable to reach the national office: (415) 285-5067, www.nlgsf.org

MASSACHUSETTS CHAPTER. Help for people contacted by FBI, INS and so on in Massachusetts: (617) 227-7335, www.nlgmass.org

MICHIGAN CHAPTER. Help for people contacted by FBI, INS and so on in Michigan: (313) 963-0843, www.michigannlg.org

NATIONAL IMMIGRATION PROJECT. Help finding immigration attorneys and help for lawyers: (617) 227-9727, www.nationalimmigrationproject.org

AMERICAN ARAB ANTI-DISCRIMINATION COMMITTEE. Report hate crimes, harassment and discrimination against Arabs and Muslims, help for noncitizens and attorneys: (202) 244-2990, www.adc.org

AMERICAN IMMIGRATION LAWYERS ASSOCIATION. For referral to immigration attorneys and resources: (800) 954-0254, www.aila.org

injustice in the streets, on the picket lines, in the jails. They have championed the causes of the outsiders, the workers, the poor, the dissenters. From the industrial organizing drives of the thirties through the McCarthyite repression of the fifties, the civil rights movement in the sixties, the draft resistance movement of the seventies, the nonviolent antinuclear protests of the eighties to the anti–Iraq War marches and immigrant roundups in the 2000s, NLG lawyers have been out on the front lines, defending arrested demonstrators, collecting examples of violations of the right to protest, helping people on the wrong side of the law—but on the right side of the Constitution.

132 Nassau Street, Suite 922, New York, NY 10038, (212) 679-5100, www.nlg.org

IF AT FIRST YOU DON'T SECEDE . . .

The Middlebury Institute. For those who find themselves alienated from the powers that be, there's a less-drastic course than moving to Canada or Tierra del Fuego: secession. All it takes is convincing fellow citizens in your town, city or state to officially and collectively resign from the United States. Actually, this is no alienated fantasy. All over the country there are determined folk working for secession in their region: it's an idea that gathered steam under Bush. One group wants to found the Republic of New

Hampshire as a libertarian haven where the federal government would be forever off your back. The Second Vermont Republic has a similar goal. In the epicenter of this movement is the Middlebury Institute, which serves as a clearinghouse and coordinator of secessionist and separatist groups in the United States and Canada. The director is Kirkpatrick Sale, a well-known author, deep ecologist and Luddite who used to shatter computers with a sledgehammer but now uses one to communicate with far-flung secessionists. Sale and colleagues promoted the First North American Secessionist Convention, held in November 2006 in Burlington, Vermont, and two more since then. The conclaves drew representatives of separatist groups from Hawaii, Alaska, Oregon, Washington, British Columbia, Texas, Louisiana, South Carolina, Tennessee, Virginia, New Hampshire and Maine. They represented a variety of shadings from libertarian to anarchist, but as one delegate affirmed: "We are decentralists, all of us, and we're up against a monster"—the bloated, imperialist U.S. government.

127 E. Mountain Road, Cold Spring, NY 10516, www.middleburyinstitute.org

Left Heritage Trail

MINNESOTA

Bob Dylan Home. The two-story stucco residence at 2435 7th Avenue East in Hibbing where Bobby Zimmerman was raised is not open to the public. But the owners tolerate fans taking pictures of the house and the garage door with the cover of *Blood on the Tracks* painted on it. Other Dylan sites around town include Zimmy's Bar and Restaurant, which displays Dylaniana and sponsors Dylan Days in conjunction with the annual Dylan Arts Celebration on May 24, Bob's birthday. Programs include singers, readings, tributes and the like. Hibbing High School, where young Zimmerman matriculated, still stands, a popular pilgrimage for extreme fans. (Duluth, Minnesota, Dylan's birthplace, has Bob Dylan Way running through town.)

Zimmy's, 531 E. Howard Street, Hibbing, MN 55746, www.zimmys.com; Hibbing High School, 800 E. 21st Street, Hibbing, MN 55746

KANSAS

***Brown v. Board of Education* National Historic Site.** A Topeka student named Linda Brown wanted to transfer from her all-black, distant Monroe Elementary School (now a National Historic Landmark) to the more convenient all-white Sumner Elementary School (National Historic Landmark). Linda Brown's little case grew into a mighty constitutional oak, the Supreme Court's 1954 decision declaring "separate but equal" unconstitutional and calling for desegregation of public schools "with all deliberate speed." The *Brown* decision expanded the Fourteenth Amendment's guarantee of equal protection under the law.

Monroe Elementary School, 1515 Monroe Street, Topeka, KS 66612, (785) 354-4273, www.nps.gov/brvb/

OKLAHOMA

Woody Guthrie's Home. Woody said: "Okemah was one of the singingest, square dancingest, drinkingest, yellingest, preachingest, walkingest, talkingest, laughingest, cryingest, shootingest, fist fightingest, bleedingest, gamblingest, gun, club, and razor carryingest of our ranch towns and farm towns, because it blossomed into one of our first Oil Boom Towns." The town is at its Woodiest every July when the Woody Guthrie Folk Festival happens. The Okfuskee County Historical Society Museum in downtown Okemah has memorabilia; there's also a statue to Woody and a landmark sculpted cedar tree, carved by a local chain saw artist out of a tree that stood beneath the front balcony of Woody's boyhood home.

Woody Guthrie Folk Festival, every July, London House (boyhood home), 301 S. 1st Street, Okemah, OK, www.woodyguthrie.com;

Woody's cemetery marker, Highland Cemetery on N. Woody Guthrie Street, Highway 27; Woody Guthrie Statue and Mural, 510 W. Broadway, Highway 56, Okemah, OK; Okfuskee County Historical Society Museum, 407 W. Broadway, Okemah, OK

COLD WAR TOURISM: UNITED STATES OF AMNESIA*

The bus tour of the Nevada Test Site, where the United States tested nuclear weapons from 1951 to 1991, leaves from the Department of Energy building, behind the Circus Circus casino in Las Vegas. Once a month, forty people get a free, all-day trip to the most bombed place on earth, a place where a thousand nuclear weapons were exploded, a hundred in the open air, many of which exposed Americans to radiation comparable to that from Chernobyl. . . .

Every historic site needs some explanation, but our guide Drew was strangely inarticulate about the significance of what went on here. "The tests here were all coordinated with Civil Defense Activities," Drew explained. "Those who are a little older will remember we just knew we were gonna be attacked by Russia. Well, they discovered out here that the biggest casualties from bombs dropped on downtown L.A. or New York or Washington would be from glass—glass would be the most crippling projectile. Their work here led to the conclusion that people should open their windows when the warning sirens went off to equalize the air pressure."

That's it? The significance of the Nevada Test Site is that it showed that people should open their windows before the Soviet bombs fell? . . .

—JON WIENER, "Cold War Tourism, Western Style," *The Nation*, October 6, 1997

*In Gore Vidal's phrase.

MONTANA

Frank Little's Grave. Wherever there was a strike or a free speech demonstration or an organization drive, Frank Little, the "hobo agitator," was there stirring up trouble for the IWW. Thus it was that he limped into the tough copper mining town of Butte on a broken leg (courtesy of the previous town's cops) to organize the miners and preach against America's entry into the capitalistic European war.

On the night of July 31, 1917, three days after the union presented the copper bosses its demands for better working conditions, vigilantes snatched Little, beat him and hanged him from a railroad trestle. Butte authorities did nothing, but hundreds of miners turned out for Frank Little's funeral, making it the biggest in Butte's history. Slain by capitalist interests for organizing and inspiring his fellow men.

Mountain View Cemetery, Butte, MT

UTAH

JOE HILL'S ASHES

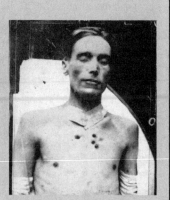

Tradition holds that after Joe Hill was executed by firing squad for the robbery-murder of a Utah storekeeper in 1915, his ashes were released to the winds on May 1, 1916, by fellow Wobblies as stipulated in his "Last Will" composed on death row: "Let the merry breezes blow / My dust to where some fading flowers grow. / Perhaps some fading flowers then / Would come to life and bloom again." Actually, the Wobblies placed some of the ashes in envelopes and mailed them to every IWW branch. U.S. postal inspectors intercepted one envelope and impounded it as subversive remains. It was detained in FBI files for many years. Yet at the funeral of six miners killed in a 1927 riot by state police in Columbine, Colorado, some of Joe's ashes were reportedly sprinkled on the gravesites. It is also claimed that Joe had visited the Haymarket Martyrs' graves in Forest Home Cemetery (see page 185) and asked that his ashes be strewn there. And it is told that one of the original IWW envelopes of ashes was sent to a Swedish labor union, which interred it in the wall of its headquarters. The building is now a public library, but Joe Hill's ashes abide. Flash forward to 1988: The living branch of the IWW in Chicago obtained the ashes from the FBI (sans original envelope warning of its subversive contents). The socialist monthly *In These Times* asked readers to suggest how best to dispose of Joe Hill's remaining dust. The winning suggestion came from radical provocateur Abbie Hoffman, who proposed that sympathetic radicals eat it. Folksinger Billy Bragg confirmed that while he was in Chicago he was offered a pinch, which he swallowed, chased by a glass of beer. All these reports seem somehow appropriate to the restless spirit of Joe Hill.

Part IV.

Goods

CLOTHING: FAIR TRADE FASHIONS

Conscious Clothing. Fashion note: For the green bride—wear a hemp dress at your wedding. It's a cool thing to do. Check out Conscious Clothing, which sells wedding gowns, bridesmaids' dresses and flower girl frocks, all made of hemp and hemp-blend fabrics (hemp and silk, hemp/silk/satin and hemp/Tencel). And they also have a line of elegant evening gowns, "cut and sewn to order, with exquisite attention to detail." Choose among the Goddess Gown, the Mermaid Gown and many other styles.

Santa Fe, NM (505) 982-7506, www.getconscious.com

Cynthia King Dance Studio. Cynthia King, who is an ex-dancer turned teacher with her own studio in Brooklyn, wondered, "Why can't someone make an animal-friendly ballet shoe?" She got her answer from the "renowned dance shoe maker Jim Brown of Brooklyn." Jim came up with a shoe that was *en point*: fit for the pickiest dancer, in children's and adults' sizes, with synthetic suede soles (instead of leather). You can buy it at Madame King's studio or order online.

1256 Prospect Avenue, Brooklyn, NY 11218, (718) 437-0101,

www.cynthiakingdance.com/slippers.htm

Global Exchange. This antiglobalization policy center (see page 199) sponsors three stores where developing-world artisans can sell their products at decent prices.

4018 24th Street, San Francisco, CA 94114, (415) 648-8068; 2840 College Avenue, Berkeley, CA 94705, (510) 548-0370; 3508 SE Hawthorne Boulevard, Portland OR 97214, (503) 234-4049; www.globalexchange.org

MooShoes. A Lower East Side (NYC) boutique, founded by vegan sisters Erica and Sara Kubersky in 2001, that sells only "cruelty-free" [no animals killed] footwear, bags, T-shirts, wallets, books and other accessories. It offers women's and men's shoes fashioned from such materials as faux leather or natural cloth. An example of their leather-free craftsmanship is the men's tweed shoe, which has canvas uppers and rubber soles. Or slip your arm through a handcrafted Charleston Brown hobo handbag or try the Calculator Belt, crafted from synthetic microfiber. MooShoes won *VegNews* magazine's 2006 Veggie Award for Favorite Vegan Storefront.

152 Allen Street, New York, NY 10002, (212) 254-6512, www.mooshoes.com

No Sweat Apparel. This well-known and (relatively) successful online retailer sells only exploitation-free, union-made gear. It offsets higher costs (from paying decent wages) by eschewing advertising and relying on a community of ethically inclined consumers to spread the word about the website. No Sweat engages in open-source production, which means it makes public the sources of its clothing. No Sweat hurls this challenge at its competitors: "Let them, too, reveal their sources. Let them suffer the shame and loss of revenue for favoring sweatshops. Let them reap the rewards of choosing union shops and respecting workers' rights." Looking for the union label is one way to ensure your article of clothing was made by fairly paid workers.

Newton, MA, www.nosweatapparel.com

The Peace & Justice Store. As the name implies, this place sells stuff symbolizing ideas that are integral to left political culture. Appropriately, it is a subsidiary of (and helps support) the Peace & Justice Center, a Vermont-based progressive activist organization founded in 1979. The store's job is to purvey "meaningful products and educational materials that foster cooperation, equality, and a sustainable society." The inventory includes No Sweat sneakers, T-shirts, books, bumper stickers, posters and magazines, including *The Nation*. The center hosts weekly *Nation* discussion groups. (Walt Vanderbush recommended this place all the way from Franklin, Indiana.)

21 Church Street, Burlington, VT 05401, (802) 863-2345, www.pcjvt.org/store.htm

Peacecraft. *Sharon Cantrell, a Peacecraft volunteer and work study coordinator, sent us this description of the store:*

"Behind a bright-red awning and tucked in between other Albuquerque independent businesses is Peacecraft, a nonprofit and New Mexico's only fair-trade store. As of June 2007, Peacecraft had served the New Mexico community for eighteen years, providing beautiful handmade crafts from the developing world. Peacecraft purchases these crafts either directly from cooperatives or from alternative trade organizations. Sixty percent of the register price is returned to the cooperatives, giving the cooperative members and their families a sustainable income. A fair price, not the lowest price, is offered to the cooperatives in exchange for their crafts. Community members help support the store by either working a four- to five-hour shift in the store, working at off-site sales or providing entertainment at an in-store event."

3215 Central Avenue NE, Albuquerque, NM 87106, (505) 255-5220, www.peacecraft.org

RECYCLEDS AND RESALES

Boomerangs. If you seek a fairly classy resale store for a classy cause in the greater Boston area, go to Boomerangs. It comes recommended by our Secondhand Rose, aka Maureen O'Connor, and sells men's and women's clothes, furniture and secondhand goods of all descriptions. The beauty part (aside from the clothes) is that the proceeds go to support the AIDS Action Committee of Massachusetts. Boomerangs sells online, but the staff recommends you visit the store, because the stock is in constant turnover with new items walking in and out daily. Most of the merchandise is retailers' overstock or stuff with small imperfections, but the store also takes donated duds from the general public.

716 Centre Street, Jamaica Plain, MA 02130, (617) 524-5120,
www.aac.org/site/PageServer?pagename=boom_home

Freecycle. When Tucson environmentalist Deron Beal started up this not-for-profit online operation in 2003, his purpose was to reduce waste, save resources and curtail landfill growth by creating an online gifting network that allows people to recycle used and/or unwanted items instead of throwing them out. Members list items they want to donate and/or post requests for stuff they want to receive. Everything listed must be absolutely free. The Freecycle Network claims more than 4,100 constituent groups with more than 3.8 million members in some 75 countries and a membership surpassing 3 million. The basic Indy Freecycle Network rules boil down to: Keep it free, legal and appropriate for all ages.

www.freecycle.org

Freegan.info. Another anticonsumerist online community, this one facilitates "freegans," or "people who employ alternative strategies for living based on limited participation in the conventional economy and minimal consumption of resources." Essentially, this is Dumpster diving as a political movement: freegans boycott corporate-dictated consumerism. They live off the grid, as much as possible. Instead of exercising their fundamental American right to "consumer choice," which may mean patronizing one ecologically distressing company rather than another, freegans just say no to buying. They collect free stuff from recycling networks like Freecycle, avoid car travel when possible, scavenge food and other necessities from trash containers or grow their own and support "rent-free housing." Living totally off the grid means reducing or eliminating the need to hold down a regular job. The Freegan website includes a Dumpster directory, a guide to Dumpsters in various cities—where to find them, what times they're accessible, what you can expect to find in them and the provenance and freshness of the food.

P.O. Box 344, New York, NY 10108, http://freegan.info

Food

COUNTRY TO CITY: FARMERS' MARKETS

Farmers' markets are older than the republic. New Orleans's French Market started in 1779 and continued until Katrina's floods shut it down. (Two Crescent City markets have since reopened.) Harrisburg's market dates back to the Civil War. A new chapter in the city-rural story started in the 1980s, and farmers' markets have grown in number from 1,755 in 1994 to 4,385 in the last five or so years. Go to the Department of Agriculture's website (www.ams.usda.gov/farmers markets) to find one near you, whether a full-blown market or a modest farm stand.

Most farm markets are producer's markets, where the farmer sells only what he grows. A growing number, though, mix several kinds of food artisans (butchers, bakers, fishmongers, candle makers) with the produce. It's impossible to describe the quality range of farmers' markets in this country. Some are as well stocked as the country markets in France. Some (a few) are more like the one in Nevada described by a Nation *reader as "nothing more than an alcoholic street fair. Two local produce booths (neither of which is organic), three guys who haul fruit in from warehouses in California and two blocks of deep-fried food . . . and a lot of schlock for sale." We present a few of the best ones nominated by* Nation *readers and staff.*

Alaska

Arctic Organics. A farmers' market in Palmer, Alaska? That's what Connie Ozer tells us, referring to Arctic Organics, the name of a twenty-acre spread owned by River and Sarah Bean at the foot of the Chugach Mountains. The Beans grow more than fifty varieties of vegetables plus flowers. It's all organic and "tastiest in the area," writes Ozer. "They bring their veggies, etc. to a market in Anchorage every Saturday; they offer a subscription service throughout the summer and once a week they deliver the freshest produce of the week to subscribers in Anchorage and the surrounding areas." Ozer adds this footnote regarding local fish: "Most restaurants serve fresh wild salmon and fresh wild halibut all summer long. In Alaska it's considered 'bad taste' to eat farmed salmon—at any time of the year."

Palmer, AK 99645, (907) 746-1087, www.beansalaska.com

California

Alemany Farmers' Market. San Francisco's Ferry Building Market on Fisherman's Wharf is the most famous Frisco market, specializing in upscale gourmet foods in great variety and abundance. But we'll focus on Alemany, which is older and considered "the people's farmers' market" because the produce is cheaper and more diverse. It opened in 1943 to sell the surplus of the Victory Garden program. After the war, San Franciscans voted to keep Alemany going under the direction of the county agriculture commissioner. The city purchased the present site for the market's exclusive use, and it has been a boon to California's small farmers under the California Department of Agriculture. Alemany is a self-supporting operation financed by vendor fees. It is open on Saturdays dawn to dusk year-round. The granddaddy of California's markets, it sells fish, live chickens and exotic produce, grown by Vietnamese, African, Filipino, Hispanic and other ethnic vendors.

100 Alemany Boulevard, near the junction of Highways 101 and 280, San Francisco, CA; open rain or shine

The Vineyard Farmers' Market. Fresno is in the heart of farm country, and several markets are located here. Our man Robert Merrill goes to his neighborhood spot, which is called the Vineyard because it's set in the shade of a grape arbor. It's a small, more casual operation than some, with about twenty vendors, and it's been around for more than fifteen years. Richard Erganian launched the operation in the parking lot of the O.K. Market, which his family owned. Starting a farmers' market in the heart of an area that called itself "the agricultural capital of the world" was no easy task. Central Valley farm operators supplied the big wholesalers or brokers or were too high on the food chains to concern themselves with selling a couple of tomatoes to neighborhood people. Anyhow, the people started coming and buying, which encouraged the vendors. Soon some of them were making $100 a day and eliminating the middleman. Back then, there was no arbor and hence no shade. Customers and vendors shopped and worked in 105-degree heat. Enter the arbor, which shades stalls for twenty-four growers, though the actual number varies. The place is open year-round, produce changing with the seasons.

Northwest corner of Shaw and Blackstone, Fresno, CA; Wednesdays, 3 to 6 P.M.; Saturdays, 7 to noon; www.vineyardfarmersmarket.com

Connecticut

CitySeed. In Connecticut twenty years ago there were twenty-two farm markets; by 2007 there were ninety. A woman named Jennifer McTiernan and colleagues started New Haven's CitySeed network in Wooster Square in 2004. She'd left her job in the Yale admissions office with an idea that just about everybody told her wouldn't work. But she rounded up some farmers, and they sold out the first day and the New Haven market was off and running. It has since multiplied fourfold, and McTiernan successfully agitated the city to set up a food policy commission and state legislators to create greater community access to fresh food. The Wooster Square location now operates into December, thus assuaging somewhat the hunger pangs of fanatical locavores. The winter market people offer a cornucopia of produce: oysters and clams, grass-fed veal and lamb, milk, cheese, breads and greenhouse grown salad fixings. As McTiernan told Melissa Waldron-Lehner in *Edible Nutmeg* magazine: "The important thing about this winter market is that . . . you can go out and still buy local foods in February."

P.O. Box 2056, New Haven, CT 60521, www.cityseed.org

Georgia

Coastal Health District Farmers' Markets. This operation is primarily a State of Georgia initiative, run jointly by the Coastal Health District and the Farmers' Market Nutrition Program. The fresh fruits and vegetables are trucked in to each of the county health department locations within the Coastal Health District, which comprises eight counties in southeast Georgia. Its favored customers are mothers in the local

Women, Infants and Children (WIC) program, who come to their health department on the appointed days, receive vouchers and, if they want, pick up produce right outside the office. The WIC vouchers are also usable at other GFMNP stands anywhere in the state, and WIC clients are given seed packets and instructions on planting small gardens of their own. The vegetables are also on sale to the general public, and that's where our agent, Nancy Shea, comes into the picture. She writes that she goes to the Health Department market in Savannah, where she picks up, depending on availability, "fresh okra; fresh tomatoes; Silver Queen corn on the cob; sweet potatoes; new potatoes; green beans; summer squash; 'northern turnips' [rutabagas]; onions; green peppers; cabbage [we're still with you]; peaches; eggplant and sometimes fresh, washed, cut collard greens. The people are nice, cooperative and always throw in a few extras." There's another market in Savannah and of course those at Health Departments in other counties.

Health Department, Eisenhower and Sally Vood Drive, Savannah, GA; Tuesdays and Thursdays, 9 to noon.

Illinois

Green City Market. Chicago is no slouch when it comes to supporting farmers' markets. But reader Nora Fox Handler chooses the Green City Market, located at the south end of Lincoln Park, as her personal best. "It is committed to promoting local sustainable food," she writes. "The selection is fabulous and I shop until I can't carry any more or my money runs out, whichever comes first." Not only does Green City Market promote healthy eating and sustainable agriculture but it also has more than forty sustainable or certified organic farmers bringing their products to market every Wednesday and Saturday 7–1. In addition, Green City features the Edible Garden at the zoo, where staff teaches kids about gardening and cooking, and a breakfast club, where mature citizens receive tips on nutrition and health. Oh, yes, don't overlook the Green City Market chefs' summer barbecue starring fifty top Windy City chefs. Alice Waters (see Chez Panisse, page 277) calls Green City "the best sustainable market in the country."

1750 N. Clark Street, Chicago, IL 60614, (773) 435-0280, www.chicagogreencitymarket.org

Iowa

Cedar Falls Farmers' Market. This is a bit of small-town Americana in Iowa. Says a reader: "It is a pleasant Saturday morning experience to stroll through the market buying the best and freshest and often one-of-a-kind items. If you get tired, you can stop to rest in the park." Or stroll into the town center and kick back with a latte or have lunch or take in an art show. The vendors are mostly regulars, who return year after year and are treated like friends—funny, you don't even know the name of the lettuce and tomato lady. Most Saturdays local artist Gary Kelley is on hand selling posters that evoke the spirit of the market. Much of the produce is organic and nothing fancy—just the sweetest corn, meatiest tomatoes and tartest rhubarb; and don't forget the creamiest homemade ice cream. Imagine the background sounds of live fiddle music performed by a family of kids who bring their violins to market. Ah, yes, Cedar Falls Saturday: "Sometimes the main thoroughfare of our market is so crowded with people stopping to chat, hug, cuddle babies and admire each other's market 'finds' that it becomes difficult to shop. Those are the moments when I feel like I am in exactly the right place on earth." That's signed "Stephanie Clohesy (transplanted from my beloved NYC to Iowa in 1993)."

Overman Park, 3rd Street, Cedar Falls, IA 50613

Missouri

Webb City Farmers' Market. Carol Smith reports: "All vendors come from within seventy miles of the market, basically a radius taking in bits of southeast Kansas, northeast Oklahoma and southwest Missouri." There are around fifty vendors. "All small, family-owned farms and businesses. Products available include vegetables, fruits, grass-fed beef and pork, chicken and eggs, honey, plants and baked goods." The meats are guaranteed free of hormones and antibiotics. Open Tuesdays and Fridays, 11 A.M. to 3 P.M.; on Tuesdays local charitable groups can prepare and sell lunches to raise money. Musical groups are usually playing as well. Market master Eileen Nichols stands on a chair and rings a bell to open the market (a custom going back to the one in Philadelphia).

Main Street entrance to King Jack Park; Tuesdays and Fridays, 11 A.M. to 3 P.M.; second Saturday of the month, 10 A.M. to 1 P.M.

Montana

Missoula Farmers' Market. This space opened in July 1972, on a blustery Saturday, temperature peaking at 47 degrees, a handful of brave vendors shivering at their stalls. So recalls Greg Patent, whose memory is so precise because he and his family had moved to Missoula the previous month. Now, thirty-five years later, there are dozens of sellers offering only local produce, some of it organic; a separate area for crafts and knick-knacks; bakeries, coffeehouses, flower sellers. "The specialness of this market," Greg writes, "is the incredible sense of community it has created. Every Saturday is a happening; we run into old friends; families come with their children and the feeling of joy is palpable." Also open Tuesday evenings, 5:45 to 7:15 P.M. in July and August.

Circle Square, North Higgins Street, Missoula, MT

New Hampshire

Pete's Stand. Pete has passed on. The stand is run by his son Mike and *his* son John. The provender is fresh, local and unfancy—no heirloom tomatoes, Japanese eggplants or purple potatoes. Pete's mainly caters to a local clientele who like their vegetables fresh and familiar. The stand supplies special orders like bushels of overripe cukes for picklers and cabbages for the neighborhood Polish ladies. As one regular summed up, Pete's supplies "vegetables for the community they are grown in, a relationship between three generations and one stretch of fertile ground and the memory of Pete bellowing, 'No stripping the corn!' in English, Polish and, when appropriate, Ukrainian."

Route 12, North Walpole, NH 06308, off Route 91 near Westminster

New York

Bedford-Stuyvesant Greenmarket. In the Bedford-Stuyvesant and Bushwick sections of Brooklyn, as in many poor neighborhoods of the city, residents make do (if they do at all) with the scraggly produce found in bodegas and delis. Now, thanks to the drive of community activist Gail Harris, a green market has grown in this part of Brooklyn. Harris became interested in racial disparities in health and conceived the idea of giving the community greater access to nutritious vegetables. Her group, the Community Action Council, recruited a Jamaican farmer with a spread in upstate New York and a Vermont farmer, both black; and now every Saturday area residents can buy organic produce, including peaches, plums and apples and even callaloo, a vegetable popular among Caribbean immigrants. The challenge now is to spread this nutritional message into other poorly served neighborhoods, connecting city dwellers with green-thumbed farmers.

Hecksher Playground, Lewis Avenue at McDonough Street, Brooklyn, NY, (718) 636-2220, ext. 2227; Saturdays 8 A.M. to 3 P.M., July through mid-November

Ithaca Farmers' Market. Benjamin Nichols, who was mayor of Ithaca from 1990 through 1996, called this a "community gathering place on Saturdays and Sundays." Located in DeWitt Park on an inlet of Cayuga Lake, it is a project often cited as one of Ithaca's prime assets, a cooperative that features some 165 vendors of fruits, vegetables, meats, eggs, baked goods, jellies, honey and homemade sauces, natural clothing, pottery, local wine, pastries. The cuisine includes Cambodian, Vietnamese and Mexican. Also on sale is locally produced art and furniture, and the ASPCA offers pets for adoption. The site is surrounded by green lawns, trees and flowering plants, and you can access it by boat at Steamboat Landing. Composting and recycling are strongly encouraged and demonstrated, and even the small cafés use recyclable tableware.

P.O. Box 0575, Ithaca, NY 14851, (607) 273-7109, www.ithacamarket.com

Union Square Market. Walking through the Union Square Market in New York City, some old urbanites reflexively smile. You plunge into a street fair of the senses, a mélange of sights, colors and smells: fresh-cut flowers; grilling turkey sausages, silvery striped bass, pink squid and fat floun-

ders on ice; bulbous heirloom tomatoes in shades of bright yellow to blood red, musky-smelling corn, fat red radishes and white Japanese eggplants, punnets of blueberries and raspberries; loaves of whole grain bread, crisp scones and homemade jelly to spread on them and on and on. The green market was the idea of Barry Benepe, an MIT-trained urban planner who had grown up on a farm in Maryland. According to Roberta Gratz in *Cities Back from the Edge*, while working in upstate New York he worried about the rapid encroachment on small farms by urban sprawl and, with the help of a rep from the New York State Department of Agriculture, conceived the idea of a farmers' market in the city, which he called Greenmarket. In 1976, he established the first and moved it to the northern end of Union Square (see page 13). Today there are some twenty-seven markets in New York under the Greenmarket brand that are managed by New York's Council on the Environment. Greenmarket not only brought fresh produce, it revitalized Union Square Park, which had been overrun by pushers and addicts, a dangerous place at night. Greenmarket brought in people and stimulated commerce in the neighborhood. Restaurants like Danny Meyer's four-star Union Square Café and many others moved in, drawn by the accessibility of fresh produce.

They in turn drew people and other businesses. The market continues to thrive, as do the farmers who set up their stands year after year and become familiar faces—friends—to the city dwellers who trade with them. It's open year-round but blooms in spring-summer-fall, Monday, Wednesday, Friday, Saturday, 8 A.M.–6 P.M.

Union Square between 14th and 17th streets, Broadway and Union Square West, New York, NY 10003

West Farmers' Market. Phipps Houses Group, a nonprofit builder of low-cost housing in New York City, started this operation in the Bronx. It's supplied by two Phipps-owned community gardens, where local children can spend summers growing vegetables, raising butterflies and studying native plants. There's a summer youth employment program that gives the neighborhood kids a chance to farm. It's a tough neighborhood—they've had more than $1,000 worth of equipment stolen—but the kids learn how things grow and develop a taste for a healthier diet and sharing the gifts of the soil. Wednesday's the day.

Drew Gardens, East Tremont Avenue, near Boston Post Road, Bronx, NY; Wednesdays, 9 A.M. to 4 P.M., July through mid-November

North Carolina

Matthews Community Farmers' Market. Matthews is southeast of historic Charlotte. All the food on sale is organic, reports our agent Laura Paynter, who also likes the coffee shop and the tasting events (for example, heirloom tomato, local honey). And they have an ask-a-chef tent in which a local chef cooks a meal designed around that day's fresh produce. Born in 1991, Matthews is run by a nonprofit corporation made up of member farmers. They collect fees, sell T-shirts and fair trade coffee and hold fundraisers, including the peach festival at the height of the season and the September barbecue serving up Grateful Growers organic pork. Market offices are in the community house, a building more than one hundred years old that was once a rest stop for farmers waiting for their cotton to go through the machine on the grassy lot (site of the present market's parking lot) next to Cotton Gin Alley. There are about forty vendors who all live within a fifty-mile range of Matthews. See website for hours.

105 North Trade Street, Matthews, NC 28015, (704) 821-6430, www.matthewsfarmersmarket.com

Ohio

North Market. This large spread features outdoor farm stands in summer with indoor stands in winter. There's Bluescreek Farms for meats; North Market Poultry and Game for chickens, ducks and the like and the Fish Guys, who service the seafood side of your diet. North Market, established in 1876, is the last remaining public market in central Ohio. After World War II customers ran off to the suburbs, and in 1980, fearing the city was eyeing the grounds for a parking lot, a group of shoppers and merchants formed the North Market Development Authority to keep it running. The NMDA continues to manage the market, on a long-term lease that appears to preclude parking lot conversion anytime soon. A popular fixture is the autumn Columbus Microbrew Festival, with the products of six Columbus-based microbrewers, along with a ringer from Zanesville. And with 1 million people visiting the place annually, it looks like they may be able to count on a sufficient customer base. Hours are varied: see website.

59 Spruce Street, Columbus, OH 43215, (814) 463-9664, www.northmarket.com

Oregon

Portland Farmers' Market. In an ecofriendly city like Portland you'd expect a strong green market presence, and you'd be right. There are four of them, but the one at Albers Mill is the biggest and oldest. It started in 1992 with thirteen vendors; now it has hundreds, a paid staff and a governing board made up of volunteers. It is supplied by harvests in the Willamette Valley, a huge area for organic produce, and in the Hood River Valley, where the famed pears and other fruits are grown. All that makes this one of the top markets in the country, and on Saturdays the venue is a magnet for Portlanders, who come to shop, read, listen, relax. The Taste the Place Market booth is open, offering samples of what's available. The market has lots of festivals, with perhaps the Tomato Festival in September being the best known. This is one of the EatingWell website's picks as "the Best of the Bunch" (www.eatingwell.com). See website for locations and hours of Portland's markets.

South Park Blocks, between SW Harrison and Montgomery, www.portlandfarmersmarket.org

Pennsylvania

Broad Street Market. Harrisburg's central market was founded in 1860 and fed Yankee soldiers who passed through nearby Camp Curtin. Once there were six markets in Harrisburg with more than 750 vendors, but only Broad Street remains. Now run by the city's Broad Street Market Corporation, it was once an outlet for Amish and Mennonite farmers. Nowadays it's an ethnic salad of Germans, Austrians, Italians, Russian Jews, Hungarians and native-born Americans. It's located in a poor neighborhood only three blocks from the state capital. We interrupt this item for a green real estate tip (pre-housing-prices collapse) from reader Chris Wonders, who suggests: "If you're willing to invest in great historic urban neighborhood living, you can buy a restored townhome nearby at a great price (for example, below $200,000) and walk to the market so you're using your feet and not your car."

1233 N. Third Street, Harrisburg, PA 17102, (717) 236-7923, www.broadstreetmarket.org

Millheim Farmers' Market. This cornucopia is picturesquely set in Penns Valley about twenty miles from State College, home of Pennsylvania State University. The market started in 1880; the produce and meats are all organic and locally raised. There's a friendly, welcoming spirit permeating the place, reports Frank Fentry, and you can enjoy a cup of fair trade coffee with your homemade scone or cookie and stroll about visiting the vendors. Open 9–2 P.M. mid-May to October, it's sheltered under a pavilion. Offerings include vegetables, fruits, flowers, herbs, baked goods, maple syrup, cider, heritage turkeys, candles, raw milk, butter, yogurt, wool yarn and more.

State Route 45, West Millheim, PA

Wisconsin

Dane County Farmers' Market. Located near Capitol Square in Madison since 1972, this produce haven greatly pleases Nelly Mitchell, which is a recommendation because she's a tough sell. "As a French citizen," she writes, "I grew up with weekly or biweekly trips to the farmers' market." Madison's facility is open on Wednesdays and Saturdays, from April through November. "We have *wonderful* organic farmers, lots of CSAs and it is such a privilege to be able to eat healthy food. I barely go to food stores for six months of the year." There are vendors that have been coming for years—like the people of Golden Dreams Ostrich, who raise the ungainly creatures right there in Wisconsin; the Carpenters, who've been selling organic vegetables for more than a quarter of a century; and Harmony Valley Farm, which sells sorrel, black radishes, heartchokes and other exotic flora. The many Scandinavian-heritage dairy farmers bring a wide assortment of cheeses to market. The only rule governing vendors is that their produce must be grown in Wisconsin. The local restaurants key their menus to what's in the market that day; there are community gardens, where children can learn to grow and sell their crops; and branch markets in different neighborhoods. There are street musicians and arts and crafts vendors. Citizen Mitchell gives the Dane County Market her highest ranking: "I call the market my 'church' even; one can live without religion but not without food—so I choose the market." Check the website for hours of operation.

Capitol Square, Saturdays, 6:30 A.M. to 2 P.M.; Wednesdays, 9 A.M. to 2 P.M.; Martin Luther King Jr. Boulevard, early May to early November; www.madfarmmkt.org

FARM CLUBS (CSAs)

CSA stands for community-supported agriculture. CSA members buy "shares" in their local farm; these shares usually cost between $350 and $550 per season. Each week in summer (or year-round), the farm puts together a basket of vegetables, fruit, and/or flowers for each member household. CSA programs mean the difference between life and death to many small family-owned farms. By participating in a CSA program, members support sustainable agriculture, contribute to the local economy and are able to enjoy fresh produce that hasn't traveled thousands of miles in a freezer to reach them. There are more than a 1,000 CSA programs throughout the United States. What follows are a few of the more interesting ones. Some, you'll note, include a worthy social agenda, such as helping troubled youths. You can find your closest CSA program by heading to www.localharvest.org.

Community CROPS. CROPS stands for "combining resources, opportunities and people for sustainability." The people here provide food security for the immigrants, refugees and low-income residents of Nebraska. In 2003 this spot was a small community garden divided into plots that were worked by immigrants and refugees in the area. Soon enough, the gardeners—many of whom had been farmers in their own countries—began to ask for more land so that they could actually farm (instead of garden). Now there are eleven plots (acquired through a private donation of land); each is divided into quarter-acre lots that are loaned to Lincoln's immigrants and refugees, who use them to grow vegetables to feed their families or sell at the Community CROPS stand at the Old Cheney Road farmers' market. The crops are also sold through Community CROPS's twenty-four-member CSA. One of these gardens, the Women's Community Garden, is worked by residents of Fresh Start, a Lincoln women's shelter. The people working the other gardens come from places like Sudan, Bosnia, Mexico and surprisingly, Iraq—Lincoln has a small population of Iraqi refugees. Community CROPS also offers English-language classes.

1551 S. 2nd Street, Lincoln, NE 68502, (402) 474-9802, www.communitycrops.org

Fairview Gardens. In 1954, Goleta, a few miles north of Santa Barbara, was covered by a patchwork of farms. Today, it is a densely settled suburb, complete with shopping malls, tract houses and extremely high land values. Fairview Gardens, a twelve-acre green island in a sea of concrete cul-de-sacs, was founded in 1895, and the owners claim it's one of the oldest organic farms in Southern California. Michael Ableman was the last farmer standing; he continued selling produce to regular customers until the new suburban neighbors complained about the roosters crowing in the morning and the smell of compost in the air. In the early 1990s, the owners of the land decided to sell. Ableman and his customers pooled their resources and formed the Center for

Urban Agriculture, an educational nonprofit, which came up with enough money to buy the property. Now the farm organizes educational programs, apprenticeships, gardening classes and a summer camp. They also operate a farm stand.

598 N. Fairview Avenue, Goleta, CA 93117, (805) 967-7369, www.fairviewgardens.org

GRuB. That stands for "garden-raised bounty." It operates two main programs out of Thurston County, Washington. The first one, Cultivating Youth, invites low-income teens and young folk with learning problems to come learn how to grow their own gardens to provide food for their families and for local food banks. The other is the

Kitchen Garden Project, in which GRuB travels to the homes of low- or no-income families and digs three raised-bed gardens in their backyards, where they can grow healthy produce. According to GRuB's website, 80 percent of the recipients of these gardens now consume fresh fruits and vegetables five to seven times a week, and 88 percent usually produce extra food that they donate to the community. People interested in buying the produce harvested by the participants in Cultivating Youth can drop by the GRuB market stand or join the vegetable CSA; people simply interested in donating to the cause can "donate a garden"—give enough money for GRuB to build a garden for a low-income family in the area—or they can buy their own garden, which will be transported to their homes and assembled. In the latter arrangement GRuB will match the donation by building a garden for a needy family.

711 State Avenue NE, Olympia, WA 98506, (360) 753-5522, www.goodgrub.org

Indian Line Farm. Created in 1985, Indian Line Farm was one of the earliest Community Supported Agriculture operations in the United States. It was initiated by Robyn Van En and a small circle of friends, who were influenced by the programs that had been around for decades in Switzerland and Japan and by the biodynamic farming principles espoused by Austrian philosopher Rudolf Steiner in the 1920s. Steiner taught that the farmer should treat the whole farm as a single, self-sustaining living ecosystem. In 1992 Van En founded CSA North America, a nonprofit group that propagates the CSA message. Today, there are nearly 2,000 CSA programs in the United States, thanks in large part to Van En's missionary work. After her untimely death, her son wanted to sell the place, but the farmers who worked the land couldn't afford to buy it. Indian Line was saved from the developers when an agreement was reached between the farmers, the Community Land Trust in the Southern Berkshires, Inc. and the Nature Conservancy, by which the farmers received a ninety-nine-year lease on the property so that the farm would be affordable for future generations. Produce from the farm can be found on summer Saturdays at the Great Barrington farmers' market.

57 Jug End Road, South Egremont, MA 01230, (413) 528-8301, www.indianlinefarm.com

Long Hungry Creek Farm. A 300-acre farm north of Nashville, Tennessee, the spread is run by the "barefoot farmer" Jeff Poppen, a long-haired, bearded eternal hippie who has owned the farm for more than twenty-five years. The crops are produced through methods that are both organic and biodynamic, following the techniques of Rudolf Steiner. Poppen is an active member of the community, writing a weekly newspaper column and producing a public-access television show about organic gardening methods. The farm has sponsored an annual summer solstice festival, held on June 21, marking the end of the chaotic planting season and the beginning of lazier summer days. Most of the twenty-five tons of food produced annually on the farm is distributed through the CSA program, which Poppen says "offers hope for rural America," allowing city folk to connect with the land and small organic farms to prosper. Poppen encourages his CSA members to take full advantage of the farm by picnicking, swimming, hiking and frolicking on the grounds.

PO Box 163, Red Boiling Springs, TN 37150, (615) 699-2493, www.barefootfarmer.com

Moon in the Pond Organic Farm. This spread, which sits in the Housatonic River Valley of the southern Berkshires, is run by Dominic Palumbo. He found an outlet for his fresh vegetables and beef from Scotch Highland cattle at the nearby Route 7 Grill. Palumbo's farm provides its CSA members with fresh, organic heritage duck, pork, chicken and beef. He now sells organic vegetables at the Union Square Greenmarket in Manhattan (see page 265).

816 Barnum Street, Sheffield, MA 01257, (413) 229-3092, www.mooninthepond.com

PEAS Farm. In the early twentieth century Missoula was known as the Garden City and grew food for the entire region; today over 90 percent of the fruits and vegetables consumed in Montana are shipped in from out of state. The Program in Ecological Agriculture and Society (PEAS), founded in 1997 with a grant from the USDA Community Food Project, aims to change that. PEAS is an urban organic farm (also called Rattlesnake Farm) that is one of several organizations run by Garden City Harvest. It produces tens of thousands of pounds of produce each season that is given out to low-income folk by the Missoula Food Bank. In 2004 the organization started the Youth Harvest Program at PEAS Farm as "an employment program for 'at-risk' teens." That spring, five area kids (four of them fresh from Youth Drug Court) were chosen to work on the farm, harvesting vegetables and delivering them to the Missoula Food Bank. It's a therapeutic approach to nonviolent youthful offenders.

Garden City Harvest Project, 103 Hickory Street, PO Box 205, Missoula, MT 59806, (406) 523-3663, www.gardencityharvest.org

Red Wiggler Community Farm. The CSA at Red Wiggler is the backbone of this farm. It started in 1996 with twelve members—it now has eighty. Though not certified organic, the farm, which covers twelve acres of Ovid Hazen Wells Park, uses no chemically based fertilizers, pesticides or herbicides, nor does it use GMO seeds. What makes Red Wiggler unique, though, is that its main mission is to "provide gainful employment for adults with developmental disabilities through a unique horticulture program." The vegetables at Red Wiggler are grown and sold by people afflicted with disabilities like autism or Down's syndrome, with each worker delegated a task that suits his or her strengths and limitations. In addition to growing the vegetables, the workers also sell them to local families through the CSA, which provides them "valuable social and business interaction." The farm also provides an agrarian education for children (many of them disabled), who work alongside the growers and learn about sustainable agriculture and farming methods.

23400 Ridge Road, Germantown, MD 20876, (301) 916-2216, www.redwiggler.org

Temple-Wilton Community Farm. Temple-Wilton Community Farm competes with Indian Line Farm for the title of oldest CSA program in the United States. Like Indian Line, Temple-Wilton was opened in the mid-eighties, but Trauger Groh, one of the founders, said, "As with all great ideas, the idea of CSA had arrived. It just needed to emerge." Groh had recently migrated to New Hampshire from Germany, where he had studied Rudolf Steiner's methods. With two other farming families he created Temple-Wilton as a biodynamic, organic farm cooperative. Unlike many CSA programs, the members of Temple-Wilton are actively involved in the farms, meeting annually to draw up a budget based on the projected expenditure needs of each farmer. At the start of each season, members make a pledge (either of money or of labor) based on how much they can afford and how much they think they will be consuming, part of an attempt to "sever the direct link between food and money." They have finally managed to secure a ninety-nine-year lease on the current property, where they provide food for more than a hundred households annually through the cooperative.

195 Isaac Frye Highway, Wilton, NH 03086, (603) 654-5751, www.templewiltoncommunityfarm.com

Voluntown Peace Trust. In 1962, when the Herbert family of Voluntown, Connecticut, sold their farm to Mary Meigs for $12,500, they had no idea that Meigs was going to turn around and give the property to her friends Robert and Marjorie Swann, a politically active couple closely tied to the New England Committee for Nonviolent Action. They had met Meigs through her then partner, Barbara Deming, a pacifist journalist who was at the time writing for *The Nation*. VPT evolved into both a retreat and a center for political activism, regularly hosting forums with titles like "Pillars of War/Sectors of Struggle: Strategic Nonviolence in the Anti-war Movement and Beyond." Occupying fifty-seven acres, VPT houses facilities where grassroots organizers and activists meet to develop strategies for social change. VPT is also embroiled in environmental issues and food sustainability. In summer 2007 it created a small CSA that works with local farmers to provide fresh, organic produce during summer months.

539 Beach Pond Road, Voluntown, CT 06384, (860) 376-9970, http://voluntownpeacetrust.org

CITY FARMS

Farms planted in gritty urban soil are, well, cropping up all over—gardens in urban spaces cleared of rusty cans, broken glass and rocks, where people from the neighborhood coax forth

vegetables, raise chickens and honeybees and fruits of the soil. Jason Mark in E Magazine *describes the growing trend toward small urban farms: a backyard garden in Oakland, California, called City Slicker Farms; a spread called Food from the 'Hood (see below) in Los Angeles; Jones Valley Urban Farm on a vacant lot in Birmingham, Alabama; Mill Creek Farm in Philadelphia. In Chicago, heirloom tomatoes climb on land that was once a parking lot. And in Brooklyn, New York, young people from the neighborhood learn about growing food or building a greenhouse.*

Added Value. Added Value is a nonprofit, youth-oriented community service program located in Red Hook, Brooklyn, a neighborhood cut off from the rest of the borough by the Brooklyn-Queens Expressway, inaccessible by subway and, until recently (when a Fairway store opened), lacking grocery stores where residents could buy healthy, fresh food. As a result, a disproportionate number of residents came down with nutrition-related health problems. The purpose of Added Value is to provide young people in the neighborhood with meaningful work, to stimulate economic growth in the community and to provide residents with nutritious food. The organization laid out a 2.75-acre urban farm on what used to be a run-down playground. The farm is run by staff members, volunteers and neighborhood teens who participate in the youth empowerment program, where they learn about gardening, food sustainability and nutrition. The food grown on the farm is sold at the Red Hook Farmers' Market (itself a creation of Added Value), which is run by youth participants, who thus also learn about business. Added Value also sells food through their CSA program, and additional food is donated to people in need.

305 Van Brunt Street, Brooklyn, NY 11231, (718) 855-5531, www.added-value.org

Food from the 'Hood. In 1992, high school students in Crenshaw, Los Angeles, an area that had been hit hard by the riots earlier that year, decided to plant a garden in a weed-choked plot of land behind the football field. The first harvest was donated to local shelters and food banks. When the next harvest came in, the students decided to try to sell their produce at a local farmers' market. Within thirty minutes of setting up shop, they had sold $150 worth of produce. They partnered with Sweet Adelaide, a salad dressing manufacturer, and by 1994 they were selling "Straight Out of the Garden Creamy Italian Dressing" as the first product from Food from the 'Hood. Through the project students learn the basics of running a business and of operating an urban organic garden. Half the profits go into a scholarship fund for the student-managers. The salad dressing can be purchased at all major grocery stores in Southern California, as well as online at amazon.com.

6109 S. Western, #102, Los Angeles, CA 90047, (323) 759-7000, www.foodfromthehood.com

The Food Project. Founded in 1991, the Food Project is located on a thirty-one-acre farm in a suburb of Boston; it also operates three urban farm lots within the city itself. Combined, these farms produce more than a quarter million pounds of pesticide- and chemical-free food every year. The crops are harvested by a diverse group of teenagers—some from the inner city and some from the suburbs—who participate in summer and/or academic year programs that "bridge communities through farming." Forty percent of the food grown on the land is donated to local homeless shelters and soup kitchens, providing about 250,000 meals a year; the rest is sold through the organization's CSA and at local farmers' markets. The Food Project also offers an urban education and outreach program that provides tours and workshops on the benefits of organic farming, working with a "backyard gardener," and teaching the community about the dangers of gardening in contaminated soil. The Food Project runs two summer CSAs, one at its large farm in Lincoln and the other at locations within the city; there is also a winter CSA.

10 Lewis Street, Lincoln, MA 01773, (781) 259-8621; 555 Dudley Street, Dorchester, MA 02125, (617) 442-1322; www.thefoodproject.org

The Homeless Garden Project. A training program created in 1990 by the Citizens Committee for the Homeless in which the homeless citizens of Santa Cruz gain farmwork experience on a 2.5-acre organic farm. They are provided with hot meals for their services. Advanced trainees are allowed to work in the project's edible plants nursery, where they gain horticultural skills. The project offers a Women's Organic Flower Enterprise, which teaches flower arrangements and selling flowers to restaurants and other businesses. Produce from the farm is sold through their store at 101 West Cliff Drive and through the CSA, and is donated to local shelters and other organizations. The farm is also open to visitors (Shaffer Road at Delaware Avenue in Santa Cruz).

PO Box 617, Santa Cruz, CA 95061, (831) 426-3609, www.homelessgardenproject.org

New Roots Urban Farm. Inspired by the Catholic Worker Community, New Roots is a nonprofit urban "micro-version of a small organic farm" that occupies six city lots in St. Louis Place, a low-income, predominantly African-American neighborhood just north of downtown St. Louis. It was established in 2005 by four young organic farmworkers. They saw New Roots's mission is growing healthy produce for the lower-income residents of St. Louis, connecting them with the source of their food and integrating biodiversity and social diversity. Many neighborhood children volunteer to work on the farm on weekends. In summer, New Roots invites fifteen kids from the neighborhood to come and harvest the vegetables and help cook them. New Roots also takes part in City Seeds, a project that aims to provide training in farmwork to St. Louis residents who are homeless or afflicted with drug addiction or mental illness. The farmers at New Roots act as mentors, teaching them how to run the farm and harvest vegetables. Each week during the growing season, New Roots produces 300 pounds of food for their small CSA and 75 pounds of food for the local food bank. Everything left over is donated to local women's and children's shelters.

1830 Hogan Street, St. Louis, MO 63106, (314) 588-7116, http://newrootsurbanfarm.org

WHOLESOME FOOD: LOCAVORE, SLOW FOOD AND ORGANIC RESTAURANTS

The reason that eating well in this country costs more than eating poorly is that we have a set of agricultural policies that subsidize fast food and make fresh, wholesome foods, which receive no government support, more expensive. Organic foods seem elitist only because industrial food is artificially cheap, with its real costs being charged to the public purse, the public health environment.

—ALICE WATERS, *The Nation*, Sept. 11, 2006

We list below some prominent restaurants emphasizing slow food and serving local produce in accord with the motto: "Think globally, eat locally," including Alice Waters's Chez Panisse. (See also www.slowfoodusa.org.)

Blue Hill at Stone Barns. Though it's less than an hour's drive north of New York City, diners arriving at Blue Hill at Stone Barns might think they've been magically transported to rural Vermont. Tucked in the hills of the Hudson Valley, Stone Barns is an eighty-acre operational farm, situated on land purchased by John D. Rockefeller in the 1890s. In the mid-1990s, his grandson David created the Stone Barns Center for Food and Agriculture, in honor of his late wife, Peggy, a farmer herself who had started a cattle ranch on the property and was the founder of American Farmland Trust, an organization dedicated to protecting American farmland. Blue Hill at Stone Barns was born in 2000, when Dan, David and Laureen Barber, the owners of Blue Hill restaurant in New York City, were invited to open a restaurant on the property in the old dairy barn, which is surrounded by organic vegetable gardens and pastures for the farm's cows, pigs and chickens. A 22,000-square-foot greenhouse provides vegetables during the off-season. Visitors may tour the facilities, but we advise you not to fraternize with the livestock since that cute little lamb whose ear you scratched could end up on your plate. Most of the menu, a sort of create-your-own prix fixe, changes daily and is made up of ingredients that come from the farm, like grass-fed lamb and Hudson Valley beef.

630 Bedford Road, Pocantico Hills, NY 10591, (914) 366-9600, www.bluehillstonebarns.com

Burgerville, USA. Burgerville is a Northwest fast-food chain with a conscience. Though the chain dates back to 1961, it wasn't until the 1990s that current CEO Tom W. Mears, faced with declining profits caused by competition from national franchises, decided that Burgerville was no longer "going to play the cheap-hamburger game." Now the focus at Burgerville is "fresh, local, sustainable" and most of its beef—which is all antibiotic and hormone free—comes from Oregon, as does the cheese on the burgers and the onions for the onion rings. The milk shake flavors change with the seasons (autumn's is pumpkin). The chain also purchases 100 percent wind power, uses transfat-free canola oil, which is then recycled into biodiesel, and pays 95 percent of the health insurance costs of its nearly 400 hourly employees.

The Holland Inc., 109 West 17th Street, Vancouver, WA 98660, (888) 827-4369, www.burgerville.com

Casa Nueva. In 1985 the owner of a Mexican restaurant in Athens, Ohio, skipped town. Eight workers at the restaurant stepped in and opened a cooperative. The enterprise has since expanded to include a bar (Casa Cantina) and deli (Casa Bodega); it is now owned and managed by roughly forty-five co-op members, all of whom have a vote. Though Casa Nueva began as a Mexican restaurant, over the years the menu has evolved to offer other choices. Eighty-five percent of Casa Nueva's supplies come from local producers, and each season the cooks devise a new menu that revolves around what the restaurant calls "the trinity"—three peak-season items that are incorporated in all their dishes. Wednesday is "Bounty Hunter" night, when one member of the staff runs around trying to find the freshest and tastiest produce available. Even the bar is locally minded, serving a rotating line of eight Ohio beers on tap. Aside from traditional recycling methods, Casa Nueva also donates bottles to a local artist who makes furniture with them, boxes to farmers who reuse them, and compost to people who fertilize their gardens with it. Used cooking oil is saved and recycled as biodiesel.

6 W. State Street, Athens, OH 45701, (740) 592-2016, www.casanueva.com

Chez Panisse. Fifteen years before Italian journalist Carlo Petrini officially founded the Slow Food Movement, Alice Waters was already seeking out local farmers, ranchers and fishermen to provide the food for her newly opened restaurant, Chez Panisse, which has served as a model for the hundreds of organic, local-food restaurants that have been opened in its wake. From the beginning, Chez Panisse has offered only one prix fixe dinner menu, of three to four courses. The menu changes daily, working off seasonal ingredients. In 1980, Waters opened the Café at Chez Panisse, upstairs from the restaurant, which offers a more moderately priced à la carte menu. In 1996, she organized the Chez Panisse Foundation, whose biggest success has been its work with the Berkeley school district, where the lunch program features student-grown fresh and organic ingredients and hardly any processed foods. The foundation also created the Edible Schoolyard project, a one-acre organic garden in what used to be an empty lot next to Martin Luther King, Jr., Middle School. Students work in the garden and are taught about the origins of the food they eat; they also help in Edible Schoolyard's kitchen, learning how to turn the vegetables they have grown into meals. The foundation aims to replicate these programs at schools throughout the United States, imparting to younger generations an awareness of how and what they eat affects themselves and the planet. (Waters was involved in planning and editing a special September 11, 2006, issue of *The Nation* on food.)

1517 Shattuck Avenue, Berkeley, CA 94709, (510) 548-5525, www.chezpanisse.com

The Corn Exchange Restaurant and Bistro. This relatively upscale restaurant emphasizes local, organic meat and produce. The chef and owner, M. J. Adams, spent over a decade learning her art in New York before returning to the Midwest in 1996 to open the Corn Exchange. "People in and around Rapid City have forgotten how food—real food—should look and taste," she said. Apparently, at first it was a hard sell: South Dakotans wanted sixteen-ounce rib eyes and French fries, not Swiss chard and pan-roasted quail. However, the following year, after a fire destroyed the restaurant, which was uninsured, the people of Rapid City threw a benefit for Adams. The town had realized that, in the words of one customer, "Rapid City had become home to the best restaurant between Minneapolis and Denver." Adams was able to build a new space, and the restaurant has been thriving ever since. Adams regularly visits the local farmers' market for produce, and she is active in Women Chefs and Restaurateurs, an organization that promotes education and support for women in the food industry.

727 Main Street, Rapid City, SD 57701, (605) 343-5070, www.cornexchange.com

Devotay. Devotay is a small Spanish-inspired restaurant in Iowa City whose motto is "Local food, worldly flair." It debuted as a farmers' market spice stand in 1994, evolving into a gourmet food shop and then into the restaurant it is today. Owners Kurt and Kim Friese buy as many ingredients as possible through Devotay Local Farm Partners, a group of more than thirty local producers, and the menu changes seasonally to utilize what's fresh and available. Nearly all the dinnerware used in Devotay was hand-thrown by Kim, a professional potter. Kurt Friese is the founder of Slow Food's Iowa City chapter and represents the Midwest region on the Slow Food USA national board of governors. He is also editor of the local food magazine *Edible Iowa River Valley,* "a seasonal magazine that celebrates the abundance of Eastern Iowa, from the bluffs of Decorah to the Des Moines metro area, and from our Mississippi river towns to our fertile farms and fields."

117 North Linn Street, Iowa City, IA 52245, (319) 354-1001, www.devotay.net

Habana Outpost. Habana Outpost, in the leafy Fort Greene neighborhood of Brooklyn, is an offshoot of the popular Café Habana in Manhattan. At Habana Outpost, though, the emphasis is on sustainability—the restaurant describes itself primarily as "ecologically oriented" and claims to be New York's first "eco-eatery." Most of the seating is outdoors, where diners pick up their orders of Latin and Cuban-inspired food (the most popular dish is the grilled corn) from a colorful food truck. The dining takes place on picnic benches or under the solar-panel awning that supplies much of the electricity for the restaurant, including "the world's first sunlit chandelier." Another source of power is the bike blender, a stationary bike that powers the smoothie blender (customers can pedal to blend their own smoothie or, for a dollar more, have one of the waitstaff pedal it for them). Diners who choose to sit inside can admire *Howard the Duck,* a reproduction of the famous mural by graffiti legend Lee Quinones, considered to be "the Jackson Pollock of New York graffiti." The entire restaurant is made of earth-friendly materials, right down to the biodegradable cornstarch utensils. Each weekend from May through October Habana Outpost hosts "Recycled Rejects," an outdoor flea market of vintage goods. Sunday afternoons feature the ASPCA "Adopt a Pet" events, and on Sunday nights there are movie screenings.

757 Fulton Street, Brooklyn, NY 11217, (718) 858-9500, www.habanaoutpost.com

Heartland. Since it opened in 2002, Heartland has received numerous accolades and has been featured in *Bon Appetit* and the *New York Times.* The restaurant buys all its food, most of which is organic, locally from small, independent producers who practice sustainable agriculture methods. Though chef Lenny Russo (who, along with his wife, Mega Hoehn, owns the restaurant) hails from Hoboken, New Jersey, he celebrates Midwestern cuisine. The menu changes daily.

1806 St. Clair Avenue, St. Paul, MN 55105, (651) 699-3536, www.heartlandrestaurant.com

Highlands Bar and Grill. Opened in 1982 by chef Frank Stitt, an Alabama native, Highlands offers an interesting fusion of French provincial cooking techniques and traditional Southern food. According to the website, Stitt "combines consummate French technique and the seasonal flavors of 'both souths,' " meaning the South, and the south of France. The menu incorporates local and regional foods, sustainably raised meats and organic produce. Before opening Highlands, Stitt honed his craft while apprenticing with Alice Waters at Chez Panisse. Stitt demonstrated his commitment to sustainable agriculture when he put up the money for a former Highlands waiter to open an organic farm in the area, which now provides Highlands's produce.

2011 11th Avenue, Birmingham, AL 35205, (205) 939-1400, www.highlandsbarandgrill.com

Hominy Grill. It would be hard to find a restaurant more beloved by locals and critics alike than Hominy Grill, a low-key restaurant that specializes in simple but beautifully done low-country cuisine (think shrimp creole with okra and sesame-crusted catfish). Owner-chef Robert Stehling is a North Carolina native who, while growing up, helped his parents tend their organic garden in rural Kernsville. After spending some time working in restaurants in New York, he returned to his roots and opened Hominy Grill in 1996 in a space that used to be a barbershop. Now he goes out of his way to support local producers, from whom he buys vegetables, meat, eggs and fish. Hominy Grill's grits are stone ground in an eighteenth-century water-powered grist mill in North Carolina, near where Stehling grew up (his father drives down every month with a supply of grits).

207 Rutledge Avenue, Charleston, SC 29403, (843) 937-0930, www.hominygrill.com

Kerbey Lane Café. Kerbey Lane Café was opened in 1980 by David Ayer and Patricia Atkinson, two students about to graduate from the University of Texas who realized that there was no place in Austin to get affordable, healthy food. Twenty-seven years later, Kerbey Lane is now a popular local minichain, with four locations throughout Austin, though it bears little resemblance to your average chain restaurant. Ayer and Atkinson's breakthrough came in the mid-eighties, when they asked their friends Cora and Bobby Lamar, local farmers, to provide the restaurant with fresh tomatoes for a season. Once customers had their first taste of fresh ripe tomatoes, there was no going back. Now, Lamar Farms provides Kerbey Lane with pesticide-free produce year-round from their sixty-acre farm. What the Lamars don't grow is purchased from other local farms or farmers' markets. Ayer and Atkinson got such a positive response from their customers that they decided to start buying their eggs, honey, chicken and tofu from local suppliers as well. Every summer (prime tomato time), the restaurant celebrates the season with a tomato festival. As an added benefit, all four Kerbey Lane restaurants are open twenty-four hours a day, a particular bonus to all the UT students who crowd into the Guadeloupe Street location after the bars close.

For addresses see website: www.kerbeylanecafe.com

The Kitchen. The Kitchen is an upscale, hip bistro in Boulder. Chef and co-owner Hugo Matheson grew up in England and says his mother's meals consisted of whatever she had picked from the garden or bought from their local butcher. In his restaurant, Matheson uses local and organic ingredients as much as possible. The menu changes daily, depending on what's available. The restaurant also makes a point to recycle or reuse nearly 100 percent of its discards. Uncooked food and opened bottles of wine are given to staff and food scraps are composted. Electricity for the restaurant comes from wind power. *Natural Home* magazine named it one of the top five eco-eateries in America, and *Organic Style* named it one of the top twenty restaurants in the United States.

1039 Pearl Street, Boulder, CO 80302, (303) 544-5973, www.thekitchencafe.com

Local Burger. When Hilary Brown opened the restaurant in 2005, her goal was "to do 'slow food' fast." That means her burgers—in addition to beef, there are also elk, buffalo and lamb—come from producers in the surrounding area, who adhere to organic or natural farming practices. At Local Burger, all the ingredients are listed on the menu, as is their place of origin. A burger made of grass-fed elk from Winchester (twenty-five miles away), along with a side of organic, trans-fat-free russet potato fries costs $7.50. In 2007, Brown—inspired by Morgan Spurlock's *Super Size Me,* in which the director consumed nothing but McDonald's for a month straight and practically died—decided to make a documentary of her own with the same premise, called *Localize Me.* It starred a twenty-nine-year-old Lawrence resident who was used to eating at traditional fast-food places. For thirty days he ate all three meals a day at Local Burger. By the end of the month, he had lost twenty pounds and cut his cholesterol in half.

714 Vermont Street, Lawrence, KS 66044, (785) 856-7827, www.localburger.com

Quiessence Restaurant and Wine Bar. Unlike many restaurants in Phoenix, Quiessence is housed in a historic structure on the Farm at South Mountain, which *Gourmet* called "a twelve-acre organic oasis," covered in gardens and pecan trees. The restaurant's motto is "local, seasonal, delicious," and diners can gaze out of floor-to-ceiling windows on the gardens that provided the produce on their plates. The four-course menu changes daily. The printed menu often describes the place of origin of the ingredients in the dishes.

Farm at South Mountain, 6106 S. 32nd Street, Phoenix, AZ 85042, (602) 276-0601,
www.quiessencerestaurant.com

Sublime Restaurant and Bar. A committed animal rights activist, Nanci Alexander is the founder and president of the Animal Rights Foundation of Florida, the state's largest animal rights organization. This ideology is reflected in her restaurant that is not only 100 percent vegetarian but also donates all its profits to organizations that promote animal welfare. Though the menu is strictly vegetarian, more than half of Sublime's customers are omnivores, a testimonial to the quality of the food. Sublime's dishes are also cholesterol free. When asked if she was worried about losing business to the new BBQ joint next door, Alexander replied, "People will have the option of eating 100 percent cholesterol-free food or food that's laden with cholesterol, which is the decaying bodies of dead animals. Which would you choose?" Well, if you put it that way . . .

1431 North Federal Highway, Fort Lauderdale, FL 33304, (954) 539-9000, www.sublimeveg.com

Don and I ate twice recently at the friendly, unassuming, spacious Town Restaurant, in the sleepy hill district of Kaimuki, Honolulu, which buys organic produce from a Waianae farm (the impoverished district that has Makua Valley), as well as from local small fishermen, green markets, etc. In the rural district of Waianae, where unemployment is three times the state average and the native Hawaiian residents suffer some of the state's highest rates of obesity and cardiovascular disease, one small organic farm and café have begun to make a very healthy difference. Most of the produce goes to the café, which also buys from the edible gardens program at Waianae High School. Ma'o Organic advises the school farm, employs twelve paid student interns, and has augmented the full-time staff. Soon they'll be adding another 2.5 acres to help meet the demands of the Town Restaurant for Ma'o's lettuces, kale, chard and orchard fruit. "We [also] focus on directly marketing to the consumers through farmers' markets, rather than adding on costs by using a distributor," says Gary Maunakea-Forth, founder of the Ma'o Organic Farm. . . . As sustainable farming takes root, thanks in large part to demand for such niche foods as poi and organic mesclun, it helps Hawaii to feed itself and preserves the environment that makes it such a fabulous place to visit and live.

—MINDY WALLACE, a native Hawaiian, is an editor at *Plenty* and greenpenny.org.

Aloha Aina Café, 808-697-8808; Town Restaurant, 808-735-5900; Ma'o Organic Fruits and Vegetables, PO Box 441, Waianae, HI 96792, (808) 696-5569; www.maoorganicfarms.org

Tipu's Restaurant. Finding a vegetarian restaurant in Montana cattle country ain't easy, folks; finding a restaurant that is vegetarian and run by a group of ordained Buddhists is almost unbelievable. When the owners of Tipu's (named after the eighteenth-century sultan who died defending his kingdom against a British invasion) opened their first restaurant, Tipu's Tiger, in 1997, it was the only Indian restaurant in Montana. Luckily, their vindaloo found a market in Missoula; two years later the owners opened Tipu's, which serves traditional East Indian vegetarian cuisine. Their chai is also sold at coffee shops around town. The restaurant is not 100 percent organic, but the owners use locally grown ingredients when available and recycle where possible. Their full-time salaried staff receives health benefits and is given paid leave to "attend retreats and renew themselves," all in keeping with the restaurant's "commitment to create a sustainable lifestyle that supports personal and spiritual growth."

115½ S. 4th West, Missoula, MT 59801, (406) 452-0622, www.tipustiger.com

FOOD COOPERATIVES

The Bozeman Food Co-op. "Be a yokel, buy local" is the proud slogan here. Says our friend Norm Doebel: "The Bozeman Food Co-op . . . sells organic produce, dairy and meats along with bulk items, convenience foods and vitamins. A very good deli with upstairs enclosed and open eating areas. The bad part is I have to go back to eating my own food." The co-op is politically active; for example, it organizes a Farm Bill letter-writing campaign.

908 W. Main Street, Bozeman, MT 59715, (406) 587-4039, www.bozo.coop

The Cleveland Food Co-op. Secundra Beasley says: "The co-op is staffed and run by college students, parents and farmers, just a cross section of Ohio in one of the richest sections of Cleveland (University Circle). The co-op is a place where ministers such as the Rev. Otis Moss, Sr., political activists and people who care about the world around them can commune to hang out to talk and shop for food. The co-op has a children's area, a message board (where people are not afraid to let their opinions about how the co-op is running be known) and is lately the new home for Cleveland's Food Not Bombs. It is a beacon of light in a place where Clevelanders are well known for quickly telling you what is wrong with their city."

11702 Euclid Avenue, Cleveland, OH 44106, (216) 791-3890

The Community Mercantile. *Nation*ista David Burress shared this great description of his favorite store: "As Lawrence, Kansas, grows to the west its 80,000 citizens are increasingly segregated—not by race and not primarily by income, but by politics and lifestyle. Eastsiders are Democrats more often than not and live in older houses, often restored. Westsiders tend to vote Republican and live in newer and often larger houses. Eastsiders are required by informal law to love downtown Lawrence, which we think is the best preserved and most vibrant downtown in Kansas. Some Westsiders never go there. The Community Mercantile, surprisingly, is physically and socially in the middle, the one place in town where the two sides are most likely to rub shoulders. (Full disclosure: I live almost a mile west of the Merc, but still in the transition zone.) The Merc is superficially a full-service grocery store, with almost every kind of food you might want. However, many of the labels and types of food and even places of origin are ones you never heard of, organic or grass fed or free range or fair traded more often than not, with a lot of locally grown produce and bulk commodities. It's organized as a consumer cooperative with spin-off institutions and a long history. Its customer loyalty has defeated efforts by chains like Wild Oats to colonize the city. As far as I know, no food store in either Greater Kansas City or Topeka has a comparably strong sense of place. The one downside is prices. Really poor people go elsewhere."

901 Iowa Street, Lawrence, KS 66044, (785) 843-8544, http://communitymercantile.com

La Montañita Food Co-op. This mainly organic and natural food co-op in New Mexico comes in four locations and boasts more than 13,000 members. Says our reader Paul Zolbrod: "Here in Albuquerque, I shop at La Montañita, the city's venerable co-op market. . . . The produce is consistently fresh, as are the meats and cheeses. Although the store is small and unpretentious, it is well stocked and well run, and has an air of familiarity scarce at the city's larger, more pretentious and pricier 'health foods' outlets. Checking out is an extra pleasure, especially for an older person such as myself, because of the way the younger clerks consistently exchange greetings and carry on easygoing banter. It may be a subtle point, but their reliable good cheer suggests that employees are well treated. Albuquerque keeps growing, but along with its well-run efficiency, La Montañita maintains the comfortable charm of a neighborhood store."

105 E. Coal Avenue, Gallup, NM 87301, (505) 863-5383; 913 W. Alameda, Santa Fe, NM 87501, (505) 984-2852; 3500 Central SE, Albuquerque, NM 87106, (505) 265-4631; 2400 Rio Grande NW, Albuquerque, NM 87104, (505) 242-8800; www.lamontanita.coop

Middlebury Natural Foods Co-op. Says *Nation* associate Louise Giovanella: "Regarding favorite co-ops, I would like to suggest the Middlebury Natural Foods Co-op in Middlebury, Vermont, which is a self-described democratic, member-owned cooperative committed to providing healthy, competitively priced foods, encouraging ecologically sound and healthful patterns of production and consumption and responding to members' needs accordingly. It is committed to forging partnerships with local growers and has been in the forefront of the growing locavore movement here." We can't add to that.

9 Washington Street, Middlebury, VT 05753, (802) 388-7276, www.middleburycoop.com

Nebraska Food Cooperative. A producer/consumer co-op (as opposed to just a consumer co-op), NFC, Deborah Hunsberger tells us, is intended to connect the residents of cities like Lincoln and Omaha to the sources of their food. You order online and then pick up your order later, and the website has detailed profiles of all its producers (all family farms), so you really know where your food is coming from.

PO Box 94691, Lincoln, NE 68509, (800) 993-2379, www.nebraskafood.org

Oklahoma Food Cooperative. The OFC is an online membership food co-op that connects its members with a network of local producers. Everything sold at the co-op is produced in Oklahoma, and much of the food is organic. The co-op was created in

2003 by Bob Waldrop, whose aim was to support local growers. OFC's website profiles the individual farms, so customers feel more of a connection with their food source.

1524 NW 21st, Oklahoma City, OK 73106, (405) 613-4688, www.oklahomafood.coop

The Park Slope Food Co-op. Founded in 1973, Park Slope is the largest member-owned and operated co-op in the United States, with 12,000 members. Unlike many co-ops, this one is members only. Each member is required to work at the co-op for two hours and forty-five minutes every four weeks. Another rule is that every adult family member must belong. Members pay a $25 annual fee and the $100 refundable "investment." The strict rules and the progressive politics of Park Slope have led the co-op's detractors to compare it with the collective farms of Stalinist Russia and call it "the People's Republic of Park Slope." But the members says it's well worth the hassle; the produce is fresher and cheaper than that in the neighborhood stores.

782 Union Street, Brooklyn, New York 11215, (718) 622-0560, http://foodcoop.com

People's Food Co-op. Incorporated in 1973, this member co-op allows all comers to shop in its premises. Our woman Cara LaLumia-Barnes reports: "Kalamazoo is a medium-sized college town (Western Michigan University, Kalamazoo College) that is both large enough to offer great arts and entertainment and small enough that you still see people you know at the store. This very thing happens almost every time I visit the People's Food Co-op (PFC). People's Food Co-op has been in the same downtown location . . . since 1978. The store is tiny; it is incredible how much product they can fit in it, all in an orderly manner. And you normally can find what you need at PFC; today's list was organic quick oats, butter, lemons. Check, check, check. And I got distracted by the CD section, which is crammed with CDs by local/Michigan artists. PFC is looking to expand in the next few years, and then will without question be able to offer the best food-buying experience in town."

436 S. Burdick Street, Kalamazoo, MI 49007, (269) 342-0194, www.peoplesfoodco-op.org

Tidal Creek Cooperative Market. Says *Nation*ista Bill DiNome: "Tidal Creek shares a similar history to countless other co-ops around the country, having been started on a shoestring by a small number of anachronists (most wearing sandals), survived the ups and downs of a precarious business run mostly by nonprofessionals and now grown into a thriving (if still comparatively small) brick-and-mortar market with its own kitchen, bakery, hot and cold fresh buffet, organic meats and poultry, local honey and much more. It's the kind of place where you meet plenty of friends and acquaintances who greet one another by their first names. Some stop in for lunch or a snack after working out at the yoga studio upstairs." The co-op started, as Bill says, in the 1970s when a buying club bought out a natural foods store. It struggled for a while but slowly gained members. As the official history states: "The co-op was 'open to the public' but its size, unconventional offerings, and funky atmosphere meant that it still mainly catered to shoppers already committed to the 'alternative' natural food lifestyle. Nevertheless, sales and memberships both grew slowly and the co-op gradually put aside the resources to expand into two increasingly larger storefronts, staying in its last home, an old house of around 2,400 total square feet (1,340 in retail), for eleven years."

5329 Oleander Drive, Wilmington, NC 28403, (910) 799-2667, www.tidalcreek.coop

The Upper Valley Food Co-op. An active participant in the locavore movement, UVFC also screens films about food politics. Says Lauran "Birdie" Emerson: "The Upper Valley Food Co-op . . . is the best food store and community gathering spot I know. It creates markets for local growers and producers; provides a refuge from the industrial shopping model; and offers a library, film series, kids' corner, workshops and lots of volunteer opportunities. As a customer said recently, 'It's like walking into another ecosystem.' I'm biased, and I work there, but it's the most positive work environment I've ever encountered."

193 N. Main Street, White River Junction, VT 05001, (802) 295-5804, www.uppervalleyfood.coop

Whole Foods Co-op. Not *that* Whole Foods. These guys recently helped promote the Paul Wotzka Whistleblower Fund-raiser, something you wouldn't catch the other Whole Foods doing. (Wotzka was a hydrologist for the Minnesota Pollution Control Agency who was fired after sixteen years on the job, allegedly because he was willing to testify to the state legislative committee about the levels of atrazine in the state's water.) Says Carol Orban: "I nominate Whole Foods Co-op. . . . It started, as many did, in the early seventies and has grown and matured a lot since then. They moved into a new store a year and a half ago—they remodeled a big old restaurant into a showcase! New digs include lots of space, green heating and cooling, an expanded deli; and I know they seek as many local foods as possible. They sponsor community-directed events around living and eating closer to the earth too. I live 120 miles away, up near Canada, so I don't get there nearly as often as I'd like."

610 E. 4th Street, Duluth, MN 55805, (218) 728-0884, www.wholefoods.coop

Willy Street Co-op. This member-owned, open-to-the-public food co-op has more than 10,000 members. Says Brenda Morris: "With its colorful shopping experience and emphasis on quality products, sourced locally when possible and as environmentally friendly as possible, it is a one-stop shopping experience in sustainability. While I don't always have time to research the most environmentally friendly option in wet wipes, for example, I can trust that the people at Willy Street have done so and that they carry the best option on their shelf." Willy Street has a boycott policy, to wit,

"WSGC will recognize boycotts called by reputable and informed organizations." They notify customers if a product is the target of a boycott and will remove the product if enough patrons demand it.

1221 Williamson Street, Madison, WI 53703, (608) 251-6776, www.willystreet.coop

GROCERY STORES

People's Grocery. In West Oakland (a low-income community), the People's Grocery, founded by Brahm Ahmadi, says its mission is to "change the way the food system works" by developing a self-reliant, sustainable local food distribution system. They preach "food justice," the human right to healthy food. To that end, PG operates several urban gardens and runs education programs about nutrition and sustainable agriculture; also gardening classes, nutrition workshops and cooking classes for young people. They also have operated a "Mobile Market"—a familiar purple-and-orange food truck that trolled Oakland neighborhoods like the Lower Bottom, which are mostly off the grid, selling residents healthy food at low prices. As one customer said, "I would have to go to Berkeley to get anything close to this—or a farmers' market. We don't have a lot of options."

3236 Market Street, #103, Oakland, CA 94608, (510) 652-7607, www.peoplesgrocery.org

The Root Cellar. The Root Cellar is an all-Missouri grocery: every product in the place was grown, bred or baked in the state. It has its own line of sauces, jams, frozen foods and pies made from Missouri produce. It says: "By building a healthy circle of supporting the farmers in our community who work hard every day to earn your food dollar, you too can be part of galvanizing your community against urban sprawl, water contamination, excessive fossil fuel consumption, monetary exploitation and help lay the groundwork for your state to be more food secure."

814 E. Broadway, Columbia, MO 65201, (573) 443-5055

MEAT

Lava Lake Lamb. The owners of this ranch that sells grass-fed, organic lamb boast, "Other than using cell phones and pick-up trucks, we are raising lamb pretty much the way it has been raised for centuries by cultures all over the world." They are very involved in land and wildlife conservation efforts—they even have a "predator-friendly" method of deterring wolves, bears and mountain lions from eating their sheep, because they understand the importance of all these animals to the Plains ecosystem. Lava Lake sells nearly all cuts.

PO Box 2249, Hailey, ID 83333, (208) 788-9778, www.lavalakelamb.com

Whippoorwill Farm. Anyone who's read Michael Pollan's *The Omnivore's Dilemma* on why American food is so high-calorie (among other issues) knows that mainstream, industrial cattle farms rapidly speed up the cow's growing process with injections of hormones. That's because the sooner they get the cow to the slaughterhouse, the more money they make. Allen and Robin Cockerline of Whippoorwill Farm let their cows mature naturally, grass fed and hormone free, taking two years to reach their full size. Says *Nation*ista Al Ginouves: "Not only do Allen and Linda Cockerline of Salisbury sell great beef, pork and eggs from their farm, they are active on local boards, committees and social service organizations." They specialize in beef that's dry aged thirty days and frozen. Drop by Saturdays in the summer between noon and two and they'll have samples sizzling on the grill.

189 Salmon Kill Road, Lakeville, CT 06039, (860) 435-2089, www.allenandrobin.com

Wild Idea Buffalo Company. Wild Idea sells grass-fed buffalo meat to customers by mail. Its guiding philosophy is raising buffalo where they were meant to be raised—on the prairie with lots of room to roam. It's kind of letting the animals revert to their natural habitat, the prairie, and letting the prairie revert to its natural plants and grasses. Wild Idea was conceived in 1997 by Dan O'Brien, a biologist, rancher, falconer and novelist. When Wild Idea started, he had a single herd of 50 buffalo; now he has more than 400 of the critters. Testimonials and recipes are available on the website.

PO Box 1209, Rapid City, SD 57709, (866) 658-6137, www.wildideabuffalo.com

COFFEE

Dean's Beans. This coffee roasting company sells 100 percent fair-trade (and 100 percent organic and 100 percent shade-grown) coffee. The 100 percent is key: most coffee companies that advertise themselves as fair trade actually buy only a very small percentage of their beans at fair-trade prices (for example, Starbucks buys only 1 percent of its beans at fair-trade prices). Dean Cycon, the Dean of Dean's Beans, blasts the way these bigger companies have "turned fair trade over to their marketing departments." He says there are only a dozen coffee companies in the United States that are 100% fair trade (see box). Cycon also works with the foreign communities from whom he buys his beans, sponsoring People-Centered Development projects, which include Miriam's Well, a revolving loan fund in Ethiopia that helps farmers build wells in their communities.

50 Moore Avenue, Orange, MA 01364, (800) 325-3008, www.deansbeans.com

WINE AND BEER

Coturri Winery. Coturri Winery grows organic, all-natural grapes in vineyards on Sonoma Mountain, a former active volcano whose ash and lava eruptions greatly affected the soil in the area, which in turn influences the taste of the wine (according to Coturri's website). The vineyards and company were started in 1967 by Harry "Red" Coturri, who learned how to make wine during Prohibition from his Italian immigrant father, and Coturri's two sons, Tony and Phil, bearded fellows who now run the place. Most wines, even those labeled "made with organically grown grapes," add a hefty amount of sulfites, which act as a sort of preservative during the postharvest winemaking process. The Coturris pride themselves on not adding anything—they just grow the grapes, crush the grapes, ferment the juice and bottle it. Whether or not added sulfites actually do any damage to health is questionable, though a small percentage of the population is allergic to them. But the Coturris believe that they cause greater health problems than anyone realizes. Coturri wines are probably the most acclaimed natural wines in the United States.

6725 Enterprise Road, PO Box 396, Glen Ellen, CA 95442, (707) 525-9126, www.coturriwinery.com

Free State Brewery Company. The Free State Brewing Company has the distinction of being the first legal brewery in Kansas in more than 100 years. To add to its pre-Prohibition quaintness, it's located in an old interurban trolley station. Free State is trying to revive the Kansas tradition of fine hand-crafted beers, produced close to home. Drink locally—as do the sociable members of Drinking Liberally, who meet regularly at the brewery's attached brauhaus and restaurant.

636 Massachusetts Street, Lawrence, KS 66044, (785) 843-4555, www.freestatebrewing.com

New Belgium Brewery. Say hello to the first wind-powered—maybe the first green—brewery in the United States. This operation was started by electrical engineer Jeff Lebesch after a bike trip across Europe. He returned to Colorado inspired by the Belgian breweries he had visited and set out to create an American version of their product. In the early days, he brewed in his basement, and persuaded a neighbor to paint watercolors to reproduce on the bottle labels. In 1995, Jeff and company moved into their current space and started using wind-generated electricity. For every barrel of beer sold, New Belgium donates one dollar to a cause within their distribution territory. A lot of beer has flowed and a lot of kegs have been tapped and the dollars have mounted up to

a total of more than $2 million. After a year working for New Belgium, employees are invited to become co-owners of the company, which keeps its books open to them at all times. New Belgium brews are distributed throughout the western United States, and

Lebesch encourages road trips to the brewing facility, which offers free tours and tastings. They have six kinds of beer plus a seasonal brew, but their main label is Fat Tire Amber Ale.

500 Linden Street, Fort Collins, CO 80524, (888) 622-4044, www.newbelgium.com

PRETZELS

Hempzel's. With beer you need pretzels. They make hemp pretzels at Hempzel's. They also make and sell horseradish hemp mustard, hemp baklava, hemp seed snack. The proprietors of Hempzel's are prohemp activists who believe that the government unfairly bans growing hemp. Says the owner: "The real confusion started in the early 1930s with the federal government referring to *Cannabis sativa* in racial, derogatory slang terms as marijuana. Prior to that the federal government and USDA had hemp listed in the farm yearbooks as any other needed crop. Cannabis was medicine or recreation and hemp was industrial and the hearty crop that produced fiber, seed and oil for a growing free nation." So eat a hemp pretzel and make a political statement! As far as we know hemp pretzels won't make you high, though hemp wedding dresses just might. (See Conscious Clothing, p. 255.)

PO Box 302, Lancaster, PA 17608, (717) 684-9808, www.hempzels.com

GREEN ARCHITECTS

Alchemy Architects. They make modular housing units that look like LEGO boxes of varying sizes, which you can combine into what Alchemy calls weeHouses. They're single or multiunits, dwellings or hideaways or summer cottages. Alchemy also designs larger "not-so-wee houses" and does other types of residential and commercial building utilizing recycled and reused materials. They specialize in building strategies that reduce waste.

856 Raymond Avenue, St. Paul, MN 55114, (651) 647-6650, www.weehouse.com

ArcheWorks. This alternative design school, instead of teaching a traditional curriculum, encourages its students to work with nonprofit partners to design for social needs. An example of their work is a current project in partnership with the Notebaert Nature Museum aimed at developing "a long-range plan to systematize a sustainable, natural food cycle at the Museum."

625 N. Kingsbury Street, Chicago, IL 60610, (312) 867-7254, www.archeworks.org

D.I.R.T. Studio. This Charlottesville studio professes a "love for the landscape, a concern for marginalized communities and an obsession with urban regeneration." They like to transform derelict ground—brown fields and Superfund sites—into "renewed land-scapes of ecological and cultural production." Julie Bargmann, founding principal, con-fesses to having a soft spot for abandoned land, because people once lived and worked there. *Design & Architecture* wrote of her: "Julie Bargmann, of D.I.R.T. Studio, knows how to turn trash into treasure. Literally. Her reclamation, decontamination, and development of urban landfill, manufacturing, and other industrial sites goes beyond superficial beautification to a transformation of these 'undesirable' spaces into produc-tive landscapes of economic, cultural, and environmental significance." Projects include reclamation of New York City's High Line and Ford's River Rouge Plant in Dearborn, Michigan. One project, rehabilitating a town park in Antioch, Illinois, located on a toxic site, involved tapping the methane gas it produced to heat the local high school. The goal is to revive the community by creating vital public space where once was trash and pollution.

700 Harris Street, #104, Charlottesville, VA 22903, (434) 295-1336, www.dirtstudio.com

Ecoshack. Ecoshack was started in 2004 as a green "design lab" in the Joshua Tree, Cal-ifornia, desert. It is now an LA-based design studio and manufacturer, with a focus on low-impact living. Ecoshack's first product, the Nomad, is an updated version of the Mongolian tent for today's "urban nomad." (www.thenomadyurt.com).

2404 Wilshire Boulevard, 11F, Los Angeles, CA 90057, (323) 463-5291, www.ecoshack.com

Marilyn Crenshaw: The Green Architect. Crenshaw and her consultants promise to help with any or all of the following stages of building a new green house or greening a house already built: design consultation, retrofit consultation, permit application, mas-ter planning, construction cost estimates, product/material selection, bidding adminis-tration, construction period observation, landscaping and interior design.

PO Box 3158, Taos, NM 87571; PO Box 4204, Santa Cruz, CA 95063, (831) 469-0489;
www.thegreenarchitect.com

Natural Building Network. NBN is a not-for-profit membership group founded in 2005. Here's a definition by a member: "Natural building is any building system which places the highest value on social and environmental sustainability. [It] is about using the resources we need and leaving the rest. You can create *beautiful* buildings that are safe, renewable and healthy, often for much less money than you might think—sometimes without debt or a mortgage." According to the group, natural building might use any of the following materials and procedures: "straw bale, cob, mud, straw-clay, cordwood, bamboo, timber frame, stone, roundwood, adobe, earth bags, rammed earth, salvaging and scrounging, recycling and repurposing, retrofitting and remodel-ing, environmentally preferable products, passive and active solar, rainwater, graywater, composting toilets, blacksmithing." The NBN publishes lists of its member builders throughout the country, accompanied by descriptions of themselves and of the kind of work they do. Typical is Seven Generations Natural Builders, which will teach you how to build a house out of straw bales and other natural materials. NBN is a good source for books and consulting services listings. It sponsors colloquiums, conferences and forums where members can cross-fertilize ideas.

PO Box 23631, Eugene, OR 97402, www.naturalbuildingnetwork.org

Project Locus. The reigning philosophy here is that "the architecture profession has an ethical responsibility to help improve living conditions for the poor and disadvantaged." They want "an architecture of decency." Their goal is to design, at zero cost, practical and beautiful architecture for underserved communities. They work on "small projects located in troubled communities in U.S. inner-cities and rural areas," and also work abroad to learn the techniques of indigenous architects. Their projects include several housing sites in New Orleans, small-scale installations in five Kansas "dead" towns, and the Seven Hills Homeless Center, Fayetteville, Arkansas.

4428 Harding Avenue, Los Angeles, CA 90066; 527 Delaronde Street, Unit B, New Orleans, LA 70117, (617) 477-6130; www.projectlocus.org

Public Architecture. Public Architecture started in 2002 is dedicated to encouraging pro bono work by architects. Its 1% program calls on architecture firms to devote a set percentage of their time to public interest work. Public Architecture achieved some celebrity with a project called ScrapHouse, which entailed designing and constructing a 1,200-square-foot house in front of San Francisco City Hall, completely from salvaged materials in conjunction with World Environment Day 2005. It was built in only six weeks and looked like a real suburban house, although one with a wall made of 500 old phonebooks, which "provide both insulation and texture." Floors were covered in tiles made from leftover leather scraps. Instead of landscaping, they surrounded the house with day-old flowers donated by local shops in vases made from garden hoses, "growing" out of the green grass lawns.

1211 Folsom Street, 4th floor, San Francisco, CA 94103, (415) 861-8200, www.publicarchitecture.org

The ReBuilding Center of Our United Villages. One of more than 500 building material reuse centers in the United States and Canada, this one, in Portland, was opened in 1998 and the next year moved to its present 24,000-square-foot warehouse. They stockpile over five tons of construction and demolition waste that otherwise would have been dumped in a landfill. The ReBuilding Center works like a thrift shop–cum–recycling center: you can either buy and use or bring in and donate (with a tax write-off) waste materials. They pick up big loads and accept waste from drive-in visitors—though the stuff must meet their criteria. To give you an idea of what they take and/or keep in stock: lumber trim and siding, doors, windows, kitchen and bathroom cabinets, sinks, tubs, toilets, carpets, appliances, furnaces, woodstoves, drywall, vinyl flooring, wood window blinds and curtain rods, hardware.

3625 N. Mississippi Avenue, Portland, OR 97227, (503) 331-1877, www.rebuildingcenter.org

The Straw Bale Cottage. Straw bale is becoming the material of choice among sustainable home buyers. It provides good insulation when used in walls. But it also requires plastering on both sides, adding to cost, so typically, it doesn't greatly save on the cost of the wood it replaces. The specialty of this construction company, run by Greg Walter and Terri Dunn, is the straw bale cottage, a hand-built structure primarily made of straw and recycled and local natural materials. They might, for example, construct a ceiling out of recycled newspaper, as well as locally grown and sustainably harvested wood for the detailing. They also run workshops out of their home, Creative Mountain, located at an elevation of 8,500 feet on 70 acres in "de-facto wilderness."

C.M.E.I., 410 H Street, Salida, CO 81201, (719) 221-8506, www.thestrawbalecottage.com

TerraLogos: Eco Architecture. TerraLogos is a women-owned business that has developed the Green Rowhouse Solution©, a design method that applies green design practices to Baltimore row house and town house renovations.

1101 E. 33rd Street, Suite B301, Baltimore, MD 21218, (443) 451-7130, www.terralogos.com

The Thread Collective. This design firm, formed by friends from UC-Berkeley, majors in sustainable architecture and landscapes. It renovates old factories and turns them into apartments. It designed a green apartment building in the Bushwick section of Brooklyn, the first green building of its size in New York. One of the group, Gita Nandan, who lives with her husband in the newly hot neighborhood of Red Hook, Brooklyn, exemplifies the Thread ethic. The pair was profiled by the *New York Times* in their once derelict apartment, which they restored themselves, avoiding toxic materials. The ground floor, for example, was made of salvaged oak and Russian pine. For effective insulation they filled the wall spaces with a fiber called Ultratouch made from shredded blue jeans.

117 Grattan Street, Studio 205, Brooklyn, NY 11237, (718) 366-3988, www.threadcollective.com

GREEN BUILDING SUPPLIES

Here is a quick rundown of stores offering environmentally friendly building materials and furnishings of unusual kinds.

American Wetwood. Professional diver Scott Mitchen was searching for shipwrecks when he found "a bunch of logs that never made it to their destinations back in the days of river shipping." Now he searches for this kind of underwater salvage full-time, checks it for rot and imperfections, then sells it to you.

310 Stuntz Avenue, Suite 201, Ashland, WI 58406, (715) 682-6338, www.americanwetwood.com

Eco Supply Center. A family-owned showroom and warehouse started in 2005 by woodworker Anthony Brozna that showcases an eco-friendly furniture line.

1310 Roseneath Road, Richmond, VA 23230, (805) 355-3547, www.ecosupplycenter.com

Eco Terric. The owners follow the principles of "Bau-Biologie," the study of the effect of the built environment on human health. The store aims to help clients make their home environments healthier and to become more environmentally conscious.

1812 Polk Street, San Francisco, CA 94109; 716 E. Mendenhall Street, Bozeman, MT 59715, (866) 582-7547, www.eco-terric.com

Ecohaus. The former Environmental Home Center "grew out of a little despair and a lot of hope back in 1991." Company founder Matthew Freeman-Gleason, who worked for many years in the building industry, had grown increasingly unhappy with it. In 1992 he and his wife, Alison, opened the first store in an 800-square-foot storefront on Bainbridge Island near Seattle. By 1995 the business had outgrown its space, and the couple moved the store to downtown Seattle. They cater to a wide range of customers, from parents looking for low-toxic paint for the nursery and carpenters looking for sustainable lumber to shipbuilders looking for durable flooring.

4121 1st Avenue S., Seattle, WA 98134, (800) 281-9785, www.environmentalhomecenter.com

Environmental Home Store. Originally located in Lansdale, Pennsylvania, they've recently opened a branch in Philadelphia—a Philly first, they claim. Examples of products they carry: clay earth plaster, safecoat paints, sustainable wood and organic mattresses, recycled concrete and glass countertops, recycled cotton insulation (produced locally in Philadelphia).

1684 Kreibel Road, Lansdale, PA 19446, (215) 368-2589; 550 Carpenter Lane, Philadelphia, PA 19119, (215) 844-4733; www.environmentalhomestore.com

Green Building Center. This store (and online business) promotes environmentally friendly building products. The center's four staff members are all from Utah or the Northwest.

1952 E. 2700 South, Salt Lake City, UT 84106, (801) 484-6278, www.greenbuildingcenter.net

Green Building Supply. This store sells natural and environmentally friendly home-building products.

508 N. 2nd Street, Fairfield, IA 52556, (800) 405-0222, www.greenbuildingsupply.com

Green Foundations Building Center. A building and home supply store (think tables made out of recycled corn husks) that was founded by Lisa Scales and Heidi Caye after Scales found out her son's chronic ear infections were caused by allergies to materials commonly used in building materials, furniture and carpeting. In the course of researching her son's condition, she realized that these materials weren't just bad for her son—they were bad for all of us.

5242 W. Chinden Boulevard, Boise, ID 83714, (208) 321-1400, www.greenfoundations.com

Green Living. This firm, which does business in the Dallas–Fort Worth area, was launched by Kate Macaulay and Michael Johnson in June 2003 after a stint abroad had opened their eyes to green living. They like to call Green Living a local community resource center because, beyond selling green products, it also provides information about local and global issues and about living green. Our designated shopper liked "their recycled flip-flop doormats and recycled newspaper place mats."

1904 Abrams Parkway, Dallas, TX 75214, (214) 821-8444, www.green-living.com

Green Things. Green Things focuses on supplying building products that are healthy and sustainable.

118 East Street, Rutland, VT 05701, (802) 388-4445, www.greenthings.com

The Organic Mattress Store. As the name says, these people specialize in bedding and sell some interesting products like organic buckwheat pet beds and Peruvian organic pima cotton sheets.

1075 Main Street, Hellertown, PA 18055, (866) 246-9866, www.theorganicmattressstore.com

Prairie Technologies. Designs and implements green roofing systems, such as its prairie green roofs (roofs covered with soil with growing plants), which mitigate urban "heat island" problems in the big cities. It is estimated that widespread use of green roofs could drop a city's ambient temperature by 12 degrees Fahrenheit in summer. Chicago has been promoting these roofs for years.

6900 Bleck Drive, Rockford, MN 55373, (800) 403-7747, www.prairie-tech.com

Straw Sticks & Bricks. They sell green building materials and sustainable lifestyle products online and in two stores. The couple that started it did so after a fruitless search for green materials in the Midwest during the construction of a straw bale home.

720 O Street, Lot B, Lincoln, NE 68508, (402) 435-5176; 15 W. 18th Street, Kansas City, MO 64108, (816) 421-7171; www.strawsticksandbricks.com

TerraMai. TerraMai reclaims and certifies wood from old buildings, bridges, railroads, orchards that are being replanted, abandoned logging operations and so on, then resells it as flooring, lumber, beams and timbers, decking, siding and paneling.

PO Box 696, 1104 Firenze, McCloud, CA 96057, (800) 220.9062, www.terramai.com

Your Home Your World. This independently owned and operated store sells things like organic mattresses and is run by interior designer Meredith Gonzales. Its motto is "eco design, eco living, eco elegance."

38 N. Main Street, Concord, NH 03301, (603) 223-9867, www.yourhomeyourworld.com

COHOUSING

The Cohousing Association of the United States defines cohousing on its website as "a type of collaborative housing in which residents actively participate in the design and operation of their own neighborhoods. Cohousing residents are consciously committed to living as a community. The physical design encourages both social contact and individual space. Private homes contain all the features of conventional homes, but residents also have access to common facilities such as open space, courtyards, a playground." It attracts people seeking a sense of community in reaction against the rootlessness and lack of community in suburbia. Cohousing communities might be made up of old friends or contemporaries or (as in one place) a group of lesbians. They are often demographically heterogeneous, that is, residents come in all ages, sexes and sizes. There are many cohousing communities in the United States; readers looking for one in a specific area should visit http://directory.cohousing.org/us_list/all_us.php. The Cohousing Association's website also lists some of them (www.cohousing.org).

East Lake Commons. This cohousing community is in Decatur, Georgia (six miles from downtown Atlanta), with a comparatively large membership who share several community meals per week. There is gardening on five acres of certified organic land.

900 Dancing Fox Road, Decatur, GA 30032, www.eastlakecommons.org

EcoVillage at Ithaca. Located in the Finger Lakes region of upstate New York, a mile and a half from Ithaca, EcoVillage has two different cohousing developments with plans for a third. It offers a common house with cooperative dining; a swimming pond; gardens; hiking trails; play spaces and sixty passive-solar, energy-efficient homes. It includes people of all ages, emphasizes environmental sensitivity and lives by the principles of sustainability. It's surrounded by woods, with a ten-acre organic farm and a five-acre berry farm. (See Liz Walker's *EcoVillage at Ithaca: Pioneering a Sustainable Culture.*) The following footnote on EcoVillage came from *Nation* associate Deborah Emin:

My partner and I stayed at a bed and breakfast hosted by one of the best hosts we have ever met, Gail Carson. Her Wild Goose Bed and Breakfast is at 111 Rachel Carson Way at EcoVillage in Ithaca, New York. A truly planned community, it is the largest ecovillage in the country but has a very small footprint on the 170-plus acres where over 100 families live in two separate sites. It is definitely a "conscious and conscientious" environment. I can't think of a more enjoyable way to spend some time away from home than in a setting as gorgeous as this one and as comfortable as well as with the knowledge that it is not using up the resources but maintaining them.

115 Rachel Carson Way, Ithaca, NY 14850,
www.ecovillage.ithaca.ny.us

Greater World Earthship Community. Earthships are weird-looking compact houses made entirely of the effluvium of modern society and designed to be extremely energy efficient. They can be purchased in both prepackaged and modular designs. Often, Earthship

dwellers form communities based on principles of conservation and ecologically harmonious living. In New Mexico, Taos's Greater World Earthship Community claims to be 95 percent independent of the cost and global effects of municipal utilities, which it barely uses, since most utility lines don't even go to the site. It's on 347 acres of land with several parks, a community center, playgrounds and other facilities. Water is caught and reused. Even if the community is full, don't fret: you can build and install your own Earthship just about anywhere (see Earthship.net for details).

PO Box 1041, Taos, NM 87571, (800) 841-9249, www.earthship.net

Heartwood Cohousing. This 250-acre, 24-home, green-designed community in southwest Colorado shares labor and ownership of community spaces (greenhouse, gardens, common house, athletic facilities) and emphasizes mutual, neighborly support and interaction. It has communal ownership, communal meals and communal decision making.

800 Heartwood Lane, Bayfield, CO 81122, (970) 884-4055, www.heartwoodcohousing.com

Los Angeles Eco-Village. This is a rarity—an ecovillage in a densely populated urban area. It was started after the LA uprising of 1992 as a project of the nonprofit Cooperative Resources & Services Project (CRSP) to encourage city dwellers to enter into more cooperative, ecologically sensitive living arrangements. Now there's a very ethnically diverse community that is constantly working out a common vision. Over the past decade, CRSP has purchased two apartment buildings (forty-eight units of housing, including two common units), which they are slowly eco-retrofitting and planning to make permanently affordable for low- to middle-income households. There are regular meetings of residents to decide on priorities and policies. There are organic gardens in the village and nearby, and the residents hold regular community dinners to which the entire neighborhood is invited. They provide tours and workshops.

117 Bimini Place, #221, Los Angeles, CA 90004, (213) 738-1254, www.laecovillage.org

Prairie Crossing. Here is a community designed around principles of responsible development, preservation of open land (677 acres of it) and easy rail commutes. Single-family homes and condominiums are available. Residents purchase food from their own organic farm, gather in a barn turned community center and send their children to the environment-focused charter elementary school on the premises. It's located forty miles northwest of Chicago.

977 Harris Road, #113, Grayslake, IL 60030, (847) 548-5400, www.prairiecrossing.com

Ten Stones. A very ecoconscious group has constructed a wetland for wastewater treatment and at least five straw bale and several other types of environmentally conscious homes. It is modeled after Findhorn, a famous "intentional community" in northern Scotland.

463 Ten Stones Circle, Charlotte, VT 05445, (802) 425-2931, http://tenstones.info

Wasatch Commons. Cohousing can take many forms. This consists of twenty-six town houses. The traditional cohousing emphases on the environment, diversity and community are augmented by an explicit commitment to affordability and the accommodation of federally assisted rent-to-own programs—also: weekly meals, community votes on decisions, organic garden plots.

1411 S. Utah Street, Salt Lake City, UT 84104, (801) 908-0388,

www.econ.utah.edu/~ehrbar/coho/index.htm

Winslow Cohousing. Winslow, on Bainbridge Island, is about one mile from the ferry and a thirty-five-minute ride to Seattle. It is home to a collection of like-minded people of all ages, from infants to grandparents, living in thirty energy-efficient houses. In the cohousing spirit they support, respect and regularly interact with their neighbors and make community decisions by consensus, contribute labor to community needs and gather sometimes for shared meals.

353 Wallace Way NE, Bainbridge Island, WA 98110, (206) 780-1323, www.winslowcohousing.com

Services

PUBLIC RELATIONS

Fenton Communications. Founded in 1982 to do PR work for progressive campaigns and now with offices in three major cities, Fenton Communications calls itself "the largest public interest communications firm in the country." Its employees pledge they "aren't guns for hire" and are selective about the clients they represent. Those clients have included over the last twenty-five years: the antiapartheid boycott, MoveOn.org, Greenpeace, National Center for Bicycling, Open Society Institute, Amnesty International, Save Darfur Coalition, Air America Radio, Robert Greenwald's film *Outfoxed*, the AFL-CIO and SEIU, the Hip Hop Action Summit, Common Cause and the NAACP Voter Fund. Its successful campaign for the human rights group Global Exchange (page 199) against Nike's use of sweatshop manufacturers promoted "a steady stream of high-profile news stories designed to incite public backlash and force Nike's hand," among them a nationwide tour by a migrant worker from Indonesia who was fired after asking for the minimum wage.

260 Fifth Avenue, 9th floor, New York, NY 10001, (212) 584-5000; 1320 18th Street NW, 5th floor, Washington, DC 20036, (202) 822-5200; 182 Second Street, 4th floor, San Francisco, CA 94105, (415) 901-0111; www.fenton.com

Riptide Communications. A PR firm that takes the side of the angels, for a change. Riptide, founded in 1989, limits its clientele to individuals and organizations striving for progressive social change. It has represented, among others, the Center for Constitutional Rights (most recently on CCR's Guantánamo lawsuit); the Workplace Project (a worker center that does advocacy and service work on behalf of Long Island day laborers); activist actor Danny Glover; the Pace University School of Law Social Justice Center (on racial profiling in the NYC taxi industry); Local 1199/SEIU (New York's health and hospital workers union); also, *The Nation* and the Nation Institute. Its forte is organizing media and public outreach campaigns, producing print and web-based press and advertising material, running workshops on press relations and producing special events. Actor-activist Tim Robbins has called David Lerner, president and cofounder of Riptide, "the best progressive publicist in the United States."

270 Lafayette Street, Suite 1300, New York, NY 10012, (212) 260-5000, www.riptideonline.com

SPAS AND RETREATS

Breitenbush Hot Springs. This is a worker-owned cooperative community that's been around since 1981. There's a permanent community of 50 to 70 adults and children, and some 20,000 guests annually. The place functions as a conference center, hot springs and retreat offering a hippie ambience with communal living, natural and spiritual regeneration, "organic vegetarian megameals," and so forth. They offer workshops, daily well-being programs, hiking over ancient mountain trails, a historic lodge—all in 154 acres of wildlife preserve.

PO Box 578, Detroit, OR 97342, (503) 854-3320, www.breitenbush.com

Windcall. For the past two decades, the Windcall Residency Program has developed a successful approach for supporting and sustaining social change leaders who were burned out or experiencing compassion fatigue. It was founded by Susan and Albert Wells on their Montana ranch, nestled amid scenic mountain ranges. The idea was that a few guests could spend a few weeks doing exactly nothing if they felt like it or reading or writing or thinking or hiking or swimming in the pond. Their choice. They're free from the burden of saving the world or their little patch of it. More than 430 low- to moderate-income social- and environmental-change agents have benefited from their stay, and a great majority of them continued in the social justice field. One Windcaller, Van Jones, head of the Ella Baker Center for Human Rights in Oakland (see page 365), says his time there so renewed him that he now divides his life into "before Windcall" and "after Windcall." He was able to break the destructive cycle of workaholism that threatened to derail his career. The founders of Windcall have retired, but a group of former residents stepped forward to create the Windcall Futures Project to find a new home for the program. It is now run by the Common Counsel Foundation, which administers the Mesa Refuge writers retreat (see page 45). (See Susan Wells's book *Changing Course*.)

c/o Common Counsel Foundation, 678 13th Street, Suite 100, Oakland, CA 94612, (510) 834-2995, www.commoncounsel.org

CLINICS AND ALTERNATE THERAPIES

Berkeley Free Clinic. Founded in 1969 in downtown Berkeley, the Free Clinic was a product of the street medicine movement and gradually became a fixture in the Berkeley community. It's operated as a worker's collective; no fees are charged—funds are generated through donations and government programs. Service is provided by specially trained lay health care workers, all volunteers, along with volunteer professionals, who provide referrals if necessary. Lay workers handle men's STDs, colds and sore throats, rashes and skin problems, some ear and lower respiratory problems, urinary tract infections and testing for STDs and pregnancy. There's a free dental clinic that will do extractions and fillings. There is also an HIV prevention service, "talking therapy" and hepatitis testing.

2339 Durant Avenue, Berkeley, CA 94704, (800) 6-CLINIC, (510) 548-2570, www.berkeleyfreeclinic.org

Emma Goldman Clinic. The Women's Health Project, a not-for-profit organization, owns this well-run, woman-friendly facility in Iowa City. It dates back to 1973, founded only eight months after *Roe v. Wade* was decided, and is the first women-owned and -operated health center in the Midwest. The clinic believes that: "Every woman has the right to become an informed participant in her own health care. We want women to be empowered by the information they gain, and through the choices they make." And so patients (who come for a full range of women's health issues) receive full information about their diagnoses and treatments, medications and access to medical records and each is assigned a personal advocate or support person. It offers first- and second-trimester abortions.

227 N. Dubuque Street, Iowa City, IA 52245, (319) 337-2111, www.emmagoldman.com

---

EMMA GOLDMAN ON ABORTION

When [Goldman] occasionally lamented the high US abortion rate . . . it was because of the "utmost danger" to the lives of the women involved and the fact that most of the unwanted pregnancies could have been prevented, not because she opposed abortion in theory. . . .

—"What the Founders of Feminism Really Thought about Abortion" (Part One), by **BARBARA FINLAY, CAROL WALTHER** and **AMY HINZE**, *The Touchstone*, vol. X, no. 3, Summer 2000.

Niroga Institute. This nonprofit yoga center has spread the application of yoga techniques to a variety of conditions and communities. It was started by Bidyut Bose, who was taught the art by his father while still a child. He's now a "teacher's teacher," training people known as the Yoga Corps™ to take the yoga message to children with special needs, at-risk youth, seniors and people with cancer. He is now researching "the science of flexibility, the mechanisms of aging, and the scientific application of the principles of Yoga Therapeutics for many common chronic conditions," including chronic back pain, asthma, arthritis, osteoporosis and repetitive strain injuries.

3101 Arizona Street, Oakland, CA 94602, (510) 336-7060, www.niroga.org

SOCIAL CAPITALISM

Amalgamated Bank. Founded by Sidney Hillman and the Amalgamated Clothing Workers of America in 1923, the Amalgamated is "the only fully union-owned U.S. bank still in operation." It provides a full line of commercial and individual banking services, plus trust, investment advisory, custodial and benefit remittance services for Taft-Hartley and public sector employee benefit plans since 1973. There are branches in New York City, California, Nevada and Washington, D.C.

275 7th Avenue, New York, NY 10001, (212) 255-6200, www.amalgamatedbank.com

Ceres (Coalition for Environmentally Responsible Economies). Ceres (pronounced "series"), founded in 1989, works with investors, environmental groups and other stakeholders to persuade companies to operate within social and environmental standards. Among its achievements are: launching the Global Reporting Initiative (GRI), which advocates corporate reporting on environmental, social and economic performance; taking certain actions against global companies, such as getting Nike to disclose "the names and locations of its 700-plus contract factories worldwide in 2005," or Dell Computer "to support national legislation to require electronic product recycling and 'take back' programs;" holding a successful conference at the UN on the financial risks posed by climate change.

99 Chauncy Street, 6th floor, Boston, MA 02111, (617) 247-0700, www.ceres.org

Citizens Funds. Citizens Funds works for both institutional and small investors, steering them to socially responsible companies that are considered better investments. For example, studies show businesses that practice diversity in hiring policies are more profitable. Citizens Funds also supports the Carbon Disclosure Project calling on companies to track carbon emissions.

PO Box 182456, Columbus, OH 43218, (800) 223-7010, www.citizensfunds.com

Domini Social Investments. This fairly large fund oversees a portfolio totaling $1.8 billion. It's open to individual and institutional investors who wish to integrate social and environmental standards into their portfolios. Domini's social conscience works with Wellington Management's financial expertise. For details on how they choose their holdings and try to instigate greater corporate responsibility and help people in need, go to the website or write for a prospectus.

PO Box 9785, Providence, RI 02940, (800) 762-6814, www.domini.com

Green Century Capital Management. GCCM is the administrator of Green Century Funds, a family of environmentally responsible mutual funds. Because of its nonprofit status, 100 percent of its net profits and management fees go to the nonprofit advocacy organizations that founded it: California Public Interest Research Group, Citizen Lobby of New Jersey, Colorado Public Interest Research Group, Com PIRG Citizen Lobby, Fund for Public Interest Research, Massachusetts Public Interest Research Group, MOPIRG Citizen Organization, PIRGIM Public Interest Lobby and Washington State Public Interest Research Group. Their environmental activities include campaigning for the protection of clean air, clean water and open space; filing lawsuits against companies that illegally pollute; advocating for reduced use of toxic chemicals and reduced emissions of global warming gases. GCCM engages companies in which it holds shares on environmental issues, lobbying with them to change harmful policies. It offers two "green" funds: a balanced fund and an equity fund.

14 State Street, Suite 200, Boston, MA 02109, (800) 934-7336, www.greencentury.com

Invested Interests. Invested Interests takes a laid-back view of investing, saying they are "offering something different, something people need and we're having a good time doing it." They say investing in the right stock, like buying a green product, can be an instrument of social change.

96 Miller Avenue, Mill Valley, CA 94941; 954 63rd Street, Emeryville, CA 94608; (800) 613-7875, www.investedinterests.com

Pax World Mutual Funds. "We refused to invest in a retail giant because they sold rugs made by children. We divested our position in a Silicon Valley company because of the increased volume of their Defense Department business. We intentionally invest in community development banks that work in low-income minority areas. What would you expect of us? We were founded during the Vietnam War by ministers who felt it was wrong to own a company that made napalm. From that day to this, our principal has followed our principles."

30 Penhallow Street, Suite 400, Portsmouth, NH 03801, (800) 767-1729, www.paxworld.com

Permaculture Credit Union. This unique credit union espouses a "permaculture ethic" of "care of the earth, care of people, and reinvestment of surplus funds for the betterment of both." It pools members' savings and applies them "to earth-friendly and socially responsible loans and investments." It operates like most credit unions by offering "share accounts" (savings) and making loans of various kinds with an "aggressive discount" for loans to sustainable businesses. It opened in 2000 and now has more than 1,000 members and $2.8 million in assets.

PO Box 29300, Santa Fe, NM 87592, (505) 954-3479, www.pcuonline.org

Rainbow/PUSH Wall Street Project. The Rev. Jesse L. Jackson organized the Wall Street Project to deal with corporate America on behalf of minority companies, consumers and workers. It stems directly from the Southern Christian Leadership Conference's Operation Breadbasket, which Reverend Jackson ran in Chicago during the Rev. Martin Luther King Jr.'s Poor People's Campaign in the early 1960s. Rainbow/PUSH's objectives are to persuade private industries to improve minority hiring and promotion, name more minorities to corporate boards, give more business to minority companies and increase the amount of business minority firms conduct with one another. It has been vocal in calling for federal action to help subprime borrowers, many of whom are black.

5 Hanover Square, 2nd floor, New York, NY 10004, (212) 425-7874, www.wallstreetproject.org

Social Investment Forum. Social Investment Forum is a national nonprofit membership organization that offers a guide to socially conscious investments for financial professionals and institutions. The *Socially Responsible Investing Guide* "gives you hands-on advice and information to help you put your dollars to work to build healthy communities, promote economic equity, and foster a clean environment."

1612 K Street NW, Suite 650, Washington, DC 20006, (202) 872-5361, www.socialinvest.org

Working Assets. Here's how it works. You sign up for long distance, credit card or wireless services and the company donates a portion of your monthly charges to the causes you select. It says it has apportioned more than $50 million among progressive nonprofits like Greenpeace, Amnesty International, Project Vote and others. The company also maintains a website Working for Change (www.credoaction.com), which aggregates Tom Tomorrow's cartoons and columns by Ellen Goodman, Robert Scheer, David Sirota, Joe Conason and other progressive journos; and ActForChange, which urges visitors to express their views on current political issues. (They were combined into the CREDOAction website. Members can sign up for text message alerts on their mobiles. The company claims it has generated thousands of calls on issues such as oil drilling in the Alaska National Wildlife Refuge and saving the Endangered Species Act. Members complain that Bank of America, which handles WA's credit cards, finances companies with values sharply hostile to the environment and contrary to what Working Assets professes to support. Michael Kieschnick, the company's president, told *Grist,* "Unfortunately, we've never come across a credit card provider that is in line with the Working Assets mission and philosophy." Business is business and they have to live "on the grid." Kieschnick points out they give to projects opposing the coal companies in which Bank of America owns shares, such as Rain Forest Action's Dirty Money Campaign (see page 245). WA joined the ACLU's suit to stop NSA's warrantless wiretapping and opposed amnesty for phone giants that cooperated.

101 Market Street, Suite 700, San Francisco, CA 94105, (800) 668-9253, www.workingassets.com

WORKER-OWNED COOPERATIVES

Network of Bay Area Worker Cooperatives. NoBAWC (pronounced "no boss!") is a grassroots organization representing co-ops and other workplaces in the Bay Area that "incorporate democratic principles." It helps interested workers develop new co-ops and promotes the worker cooperative movement, which is making a footprint in the Bay Area. Its website includes lists and maps of Bay Area co-ops. Clusters of cooperatives and worker collectives are cropping up in a few other parts in the country, in progressive enclaves like Portland and the Minneapolis–St. Paul area. Oakland and Berkeley have the highest concentration. Several of them are experiencing hard times, requiring worker pay concessions to stay afloat. Nevertheless, Innosanto Nagara, a member of the Oakland, California, Design Action Collective, believes that collectives are a viable business model. "Co-ops are more stable in the long run," he told an interviewer. "They move a little bit slower but as a result make better decisions." Among Berkeley successes is Design Action Collective (see page 22) a spin-off from Inkworks (see page 24).

2335 Valley Street, Oakland, CA 94612, (510) 835-0254, www.nobawc.org

United States Federation of Worker Cooperatives. Set up to assist worker-owned businesses, the USFWC estimates that there are more than 300 such establishments in the United States, employing more than 35,000 people. The majority of them are small businesses, mainly in the retail and service sectors. A number are printing firms, bookstores and restaurants. Cooperatives give workers power over their own jobs and working conditions and operate in a sustainable fashion. The USFWC's "seven principles" include voluntary and open membership, democratic member control, member economic participation, autonomy and independence, full economic participation, cooperation with other co-ops and concern for community.

PO Box 170701, San Francisco, CA 94117, (415) 379-9201, www.usworker.coop

TRAVEL AND TOUR GUIDANCE

Alaska Wildland Adventures. This organization offers ecofriendly tours of Alaska's parks and Arctic region. Tours are small (twelve to sixteen people) and the emphasis is educational, highlighting natural and cultural history. Tours include activities such as hiking, rafting, cycling and kayaking. Ten percent of the profits are donated to local conservation efforts.

PO Box 389, Girdwood, AK 99587, (800) 334-8730, www.alaskawildland.com

Alternative Tourism Group. This Palestinian NGO organizes tours to Palestine and Israel for people looking for a deeper understanding of the political situation in the

---

MY FAVORITE AMERICAN PLACE

Almost anywhere in Vermont. Probably there are ugly places in Vermont, but I have driven lots of back roads and not found them. Postcard Vermont is the antique villages and classic old churches with white steeples and I commend them to tourists. It's also tramping through the woods in May to commune with the rioting wildflowers or discovering an old stone wall lost in the deep forest, our American version of Roman ruins.

But what enthralls me and Linda is the Vermont that is an open history book—still alive and active in the people, the politics and culture. This is the America that might have been if we hadn't become a big and powerful industrial nation. Vermont missed out on that story, yet it seems oddly grateful for the differences. The state was settled last in New England, mostly by an eclectic mix of stubborn folks trying to make their way in the unpromising terrain. Two centuries later, those people are still here, still stubbornly proud of their differences. They do not intend to change.

This may be the only thing Vermonters agree on. The political combat is endlessly entertaining and defined by three sectors—Ben and Jerry's progressives, middle-middle business types and "Take Back Vermont" rustics who generally resist whatever the other two groups are promoting. The state disputes over volatile issues from marriage rights for gays to "ancient roads," whether to abandon the thousands of old township roads that still exist on official maps but are lost in the forest alongside the stone walls. Either way, the issue is about redefining Vermont while preserving it. These people seem to have figured out how to honor the past and move forward.

—**WILLIAM GREIDER** *is* The Nation*'s national affairs correspondent and author of* Secrets of the Temple, Who will Tell the People? *and* The Soul of Capitalism.

Middle East. The tours include visits to refugee camps and meetings with intellectuals from various Palestinian governmental and nongovernmental organizations. Based in Israeli-occupied Beit Sahour, it operates according to the tenets of "justice tourism," that is, "tourism that holds as its central goals the creation of economic opportunities for the local community, positive cultural exchange between guest and host through one-on-one interaction, the protection of the environment, and political/historical education." ATG has arranged tours for international solidarity groups, academic and fact-finding delegations, church groups concerned with issues of social justice, diplomats, journalists and researchers, NGOs and political organizations, tourists and pilgrims groups.

74 Star Street, PO Box 173, Beit Sahour, Palestine, 972-2-277-2151, www.atg.ps

Center on Ecotourism and Sustainable Development. "Ecotourism" is a buzzword in the tourism industry, but the center, a joint project of Stanford University and the Institute for Policy Studies (see page 199), views ecotourism as a development and conservation tool. It conducts serious research on ecotourism policies, publishes papers and a newsletter and offers courses in ecotourism at Stanford.

1333 H Street NW, Suite 300, East Tower, Washington, DC 20005, (202) 347-9203, www.ecotourismcesd.org

Hina Adventures. The company provides cultural tours of Oahu that include hiking, stargazing, Polynesian navigational theory, sightseeing and botanical and archaeological restoration projects. Hina Adventures works closely with environmentally based community organizations and grassroots cultural groups to protect the islands.

Honolulu, HI 96813, (888) 933-4462, www.hinaadventures.com

International Bike Fund. This nonprofit organization promotes "sustainable transport and international understanding" by way of bicycle tours. Their tour groups are small, no more than a maximum of twelve people. The idea is that bicycle travel uses no carbon products, only human leg power. Moreover, it's conducive to social tourism, letting you see a foreign culture at eye level. IBF guides take their charges to museums but also down rugged back roads, to meet and talk to the natives. These tours require some motor vehicles to get from here to there and on to your bike. IBF offers U.S. and Central American tours (including one in Cuba); Asian tours in Korea, Nepal and Vietnam and circuits in all parts of Africa.

4887 Columbia Drive S, Seattle, WA, 98108, (206) 767-0848, www.ibike.org

The Lower East Side Tenement Tours. The Lower East Side Tenement Museum offers guided tours (by appointment) of the area in New York City that is key to its immigrant, working-class and progressive history. The museum is an actual apartment building, with many of the original or contemporary furnishings, and memorabilia of the generations who made homes here. Many of the oral histories of those who lived here and are still living have been collected. Memories of families who lived and died here flit through these rooms like ghosts. One looks at the tiny airless cells with wonderment that so many survived them and moved on.

Lower East Side Tenement Museum, 108 Orchard Street, New York, NY 10002, (212) 431-0233, www.tenement.org

The Nation Cruise. *The Nation* offers a yearly seminar cruise (run by the Nation Institute) with discussion groups, receptions, guest speakers, informal chats with your favorite editors and columnists and the opportunity to meet and bond with like-minded *Nation* readers. Past cruises have plied the Caribbean and sailed to Alaska. Since 2006 in conjunction with EcoLogic, cruisers got an opportunity to offset carbon emissions of the cruise by contributing to reforest an area in Guatemala devastated by mud slides.

Cruise Authority, 1760 Powers Ferry Road, Suite 100, Marietta, GA 30067, (800) 707-1634, www.nationcruise.com

Purple Roofs. For the gay traveler, here's a useful website with listings of gay and lesbian hotels, inns, guesthouses, bed and breakfasts, travel agents and tour operators. The main criterion is that the host must be gay or gay friendly. One feature is Mi Casa Su

Casa, a membership deal that provides access to other gay people's private homes in return for opening yours.

www.purpleroofs.com

Reality Tours. Sponsored by the San Francisco–based antiglobalization organization Global Exchange (see page 199), the tours are excursions to more than thirty countries in Latin America, Africa, Asia and the Middle East. You might hear firsthand about women's rights in Afghanistan or discuss Palestinian-Israeli issues on the ground. Global Exchange will also design trips for groups (for example, schools and workplaces). They say "regardless of age." Search the website by country, date or issue. Or call Malía Everette.

2017 Mission Street, 2nd floor, San Francisco, CA 94110, (800) 497-1994, ext. 233,

www.globalexchange.org

The Sojourn Project. The Sojourn Project/Sojourn to the Past gives students and parents a ten-day tour of key sites from the civil rights movement across the South, as well as an opportunity to hear from eyewitnesses and participants. Stops include Atlanta, Montgomery, Selma, Birmingham, Hattiesburg, Jackson, Little Rock and Memphis. Says Rev. Billy Kyles, Sojourn allows participants to "touch history, and the people who made it."

300 Piedmont Avenue, Room 222, San Bruno, CA 94066, (650) 925-1510, www.sojournproject.org

Venceremos Brigade. This group, formed in 1969, arranges educational trips to Cuba by work brigades. By summer 2007 some thirty-eight such contingents had made the (illegal) journey. The brigades are composed of American citizens in search of what Bob Guild of the brigade describes as "a combined work and educational experience which brings together an incredibly diverse group of citizens to assert our constitutional rights to travel to the island and see it with our own eyes." He says that around 10,000 people have participated in the program, among them community, academic and trade union leaders; artists, poets, professors and elected officials, including mayors and congressional representatives. The groups often fly from Canada. Upon its

return in 2006, the thirty-seventh contingent came home via the International Peace Bridge from Fort Erie, Ontario, to Buffalo, New York. The Bush administration tightened restrictions on Cuban travel, making it impossible even for Cuban Americans to visit their families except with a special license and only every three years. Some brigadistas have received "requests to provide information" and threats of fines from the Office of Foreign Assets Control of the Treasury Department. Yet many of these "travel challengers" are unregenerate repeat offenders. The experiences of the thirty-seventh contingent are typical. They worked in the fields in Granma province for a week and went on to Havana to help in a construction project. They traveled by bus and visited towns and historical and cultural sites.

PO Box 5202, Englewood, NJ 07631, (212) 560-4360, www.venceremosbrigade.org

HOTELS AND B AND Bs

Charley Montana's Bed & Breakfast. This B and B run by Jim and Katherine Lee ("solid liberal Democrats," Jerry Navratil assures us)—is the 1907 well-restored Krug Mansion, which is on the National Register of Historic Places.

103 N. Douglas Street, Glendive, MT 59330, (406) 365-3207, www.charley-montana.com

Chelsea Hotel. Slightly louche, seedy, this genteel Victorian old lady has a wicked gleam in her eye and a past. Like an apparition from another time, it looms up suddenly, a red brick twelve-story structure with ironwork balconies. When the Chelsea was built in 1883 it was the tallest building in New York, an elegant cooperative apartment with three-foot thick outer walls, elegant suites with warrens of rooms, and a grand staircase. When the theater world moved uptown, the co-op went bankrupt, but the Chelsea survived as a hotel. It has sheltered artists, writers, old Bohemians and young radicals of all stripes. Literary lights like Edgar Lee Masters, Thomas Wolfe, Dylan Thomas, Arthur C. Clarke, Brendan Behan and Arthur Miller slept here. Thomas was staying here when he drank eighteen straight shots at the White Horse Tavern and died in the hospital of "acute alcoholic insult to the brain." (Ask for his old room.) Here, too, punk star Sid Vicious stabbed his girlfriend Nancy Spungen in 1978; Valerie

MY FAVORITE AMERICAN PLACE

Shelter Island, quietly floating between the twin forks of Long Island, New York, was always a wonderful place to visit, then to weekend, to summer, now live part-time, but it didn't become my favorite place until last year when—at my wife, Lois's, urging—I reluctantly made it my official address so I could vote there. I had never been involved in the politics of New York City, where I was born and raised, because they seemed distant. But on Shelter Island I know the guy running for town supervisor. The issues may be complicated, but they fit in my hand. My vote will make a difference. How can it not be my favorite place when suddenly I have a chance to make it better?

—ROBERT LIPSYTE has been a sportswriter with *The New York Times*. He has written award-winning young adult novels, including *The Contender, One Fat Summer, The Brave* and *The Chief*.

Solanas, founder of SCUM, hung out here before stalking and shooting Andy Warhol. The names reel on: Janis Joplin, Bob Dylan, Jimi Hendrix, Allen Ginsberg, Virgil Thompson, Gregory Corso and Charles Jackson wrote here; artists like Willem de Kooning and Larry Rivers painted here. Manager Stanley Bard was famous for his TLC of artists and the Felliniesque cast of geniuses, oddballs, weirdos and characters he tolerated as tenants, never pushing them on past-due bills. An outside corporation bought the hotel in 2007 and ousted Bard; tenants protested with window signs, and there were fears that the Shady Lady of 23rd Street would be dragged into the twenty-first century and turned into a bland boutique hotel.

222 W. 23rd Street, New York, NY 10011, (212) 243-3700, www.hotelchelsea.com

Hotel Bohème. Built by an Italian immigrant family, the original hotel was demolished to make a firebreak after the San Francisco quake of 1906. The current hotel replaced it and then, over time, was restored, upgraded and decorated to reflect the late-fifties North Beach Beat atmosphere when Allen Ginsberg and other Beats supposedly slept here. According to the *Los Angeles Times*, "Jerry Stoll's 1950's black and white photos lining the hallways recall Kerouac's smoky prose and double as windows on the city's old bohemian scene. . . . Hanging lampshades, which double as exquisite collages, are festooned with evocations of an era: bits and pieces of old Blue Note Records album sleeves, paperback covers from City Lights poetry books." Just a few steps away is the City Lights Bookstore itself (see page 59). Rooms have been state-of-the-art wired for the business traveler with fax, modem and computer hookups. What would Jack say?

444 Columbus Avenue, San Francisco, CA 94133, (415) 433-9111, www.hotelboheme.com

Hotel Tabard Inn. The Tabard Inn takes pride in being the classic small hotel in the age of chains. It is popular with politicos, reporters and in-the-know travelers. The inn, which occupies three adjacent Victorian row houses, has forty rooms, each uniquely designed and comfortably cluttered with antique furniture, unexpected color combinations and original touches. It has banished standard hotel accoutrements—elevators, televisions, room service—in favor of homey amenities such as sitting rooms scattered along labyrinthine hallways, laughing Buddha statues in wall nooks, live jazz in the bar, a restaurant serving organic food and a resident ghost. The Tabard takes its name from the inn in Chaucer's *Canterbury Tales*, which promised refuge from the road for weary pilgrims. As Irene Mayer, the hotel's in-house designer for more than twenty-five years, put it: "There are no surprises at the Marriott"—but surprises aplenty at the Tabard.

1739 N Street NW, Washington DC 20036, (202) 785-1277, www.tabardinn.com

Inn Serendipity Bed & Breakfast and Organic Farm. This lodge in Wisconsin is heated and lit by 100 percent renewable energy. Featured as one of the "Top 10 Eco-destinations in North America" by *Natural Home* magazine, it's an ecoretreat that's an ideal place to relax. Distinctive features include writing and music rooms to encourage guests to uncork their creativity.

7843 County P, Broomtown, WI 53522, (608) 329-7056, www.innserendipity.com

The Jenks House Bed and Breakfast. A 1925 Prairie School–style house that manages both to move with the times and resist them. It's ecoprimed to the top green living standards, while retaining the original furniture, the heart pine woodwork and oak flooring. In 2007 it became only the second Florida B and B to be certified by the state's Green Lodging Program, which cited owners Ila Rae and Tom Merten for "environmental feedback and suggestions from guests, a linen reuse program . . . low-flow faucets to save water and ENERGY STAR® air-conditioning equipment in guest rooms to conserve energy as well as high-efficiency compact fluorescent lighting, motion detector lighting outdoors and a solar water heater . . . recycling program, purchasing products with recycled content and composting." Merten says business went up after they earned the citation, with guests mentioning it as a reason for coming.

2804 Post Street, Jacksonville, FL 32205, (904) 387-2092, www.bbonline.com/fl/jenks/

Mountain Home Ranch Resort. Scenically located in the middle of California's wine country, Mountain Home has been run by the same family since 1913; the present owners are Suzanne and John Fouts, who wrote: "It has a long tradition of tolerance. During the 20s, 30s and 40s, it was a haven for local labor leaders such as Harry Bridges, founder of the ILWU, whom the government tried to deport for Communist connections. During and following World War II, it was virtually the only California resort that was integrated, allowing black families a place to vacation. The family has resisted the pressures to develop its 300-plus acres, maintaining it as a nature preserve and growing much of the produce used in their meals. The ranch hosts yoga, meditation and personal growth groups, but is always open to individuals or families wanting a mountain home getaway."

3400 Mountain Home Ranch Road, Calistoga, CA 94515, (707) 942-6616,
www.mountainhomeranch.com

Neahtawanta Inn. First opened as an inn in 1906, it's been the Neahtawanta since the early 1980s. Innkeepers Sally Van Vleck and her husband, Bob Russell, are longtime environmental and peace activists, and they pledged to be "ecologically sensitive, using products made from recycled content, providing recycling options and serving organic food. In addition most of our cleaning products are non-toxic and biodegradable." Don't miss the morning yoga classes, led by Sally. Check out the Neahtawanta

Research and Education Center, "a nonprofit organization working on peace, community, sustainable use of resources and personal growth issues," right there at the inn.

1308 Neahtawanta Road, Traverse City, MI 49686, (800) 220-1415, www.neahtawantainn.com

Pilgrim House Hostel and Retreat Center. Recommended by *Nation* associate David Ciscel: "In Memphis, this is the place where peace activists stay when passing through town. It is located in one wing of the First Congregational Church—on the first floor is the MidSouth Peace and Justice Center and Revolutions Bicycle Shop. There are a couple of vegetarian restaurants within a block or two—plus a locally owned bookstore. Finally, it is poorly served by Memphis's low-quality bus system."

1000 S. Cooper Street, Memphis, TN 38104, (901) 273-8341, www.pilgrimhouse.org

Rainbow Mountain Resort. This rural pleasure dome sits high atop the Pocono Mountains. It's gay owned and operated, specializing in an LGBT clientele since 1981. The resort covers twenty-six acres, including a two-acre pond. It's open year-round and features an Olympic-size pool, ten-person hot tub, tennis and volleyball courts, a nightclub in the barn and other diversions.

210 Mt. Nebo Road, East Stroudsburg, PA 18301, (570) 223-8484, www.rainbowmountain.com

Silver Jack Inn and 'Lectrolux Café. *Nation* associate and innkeeper Terry Marasco says: "I am a left-wing leftie—social activist, environmentalist, green innkeeper (developing gardens for the restaurant with locally recycled organic matter and water from our laundry and restaurant). I am an openly gay man in rural Nevada and fly the rainbow flag; the entire facility including the gardens is NONsmoking." The 'Lectrolux Gallery Café and Movie House serves "Nevada comfort food and drinks." On Wednesdays and Saturday evenings, American and foreign movies are shown in the café. "We are diversity and motorcycle friendly," adds Terry.

PO Box 69, Baker, NV 89311, (775) 234-7323, www.silverjackinn.com

Topia Inn and Café Topia. This adjunct of the Topia Arts Center is in the beautiful northern Berkshires. You might say that it's a profit-oriented caboose to the main engine, the nonprofit, taxpayer-supported Arts Center. The inn serves students and artists at the Arts Center "as well as guests looking for a conscious eco-experience tailored to the purest and most aesthetic environment for rest and relaxation." The inn is ecofriendly, powered by biodiesel and solar panels.

10 Pleasant Street, Adams, MA 01220, (413) 743-9605, http://topiainn.com

ULTIMATE DESTINATIONS

The fashionable color of mourning these days is not black but green. The way to go is via an ecologically correct, sustainable and emotionally honest nonsectarian funeral. Rather than the strain and expense of a standard funeral and burial (costing an average of $6,500 for a no-frills send-off), more and more people are choosing a home service, where friends and family gather for the ritual of their choice. Or no service at all. The body will be washed and packed in dry ice, placed in a coffin made of cardboard or some other biodegradable material and transported to a green preserve set aside for natural burials. Actually, green graveyards are still rare in the United States, but becoming more common in the twenty-first century if visionaries like Billy Campbell (see page 329) get their way. The Brits, who are not nearly as religious as Americans, seem to have quickly taken to greenyards as a better final resting place. England has more than 200 of these green and pleasant pieces of land. Such interments, of course, hold a strong appeal to environmentalists, who favor biodegradable coffins (cardboard, willow, pine, walnut, chipboard, instead of mahogany from the Third World or toxic lead covering); no embalming, avoiding the leaching of formaldehyde or other toxic fluids into the soil; green burial parks that hold land in trust, thus guaranteeing it will remain in its natural state in perpetuity. Also, in home funerals fewer vehicles are used, saving gas, and cremation in a cardboard coffin is less polluting than doing it the traditional way. In all states but five, home funerals are legal. In the five—New York, Connecticut, Indiana, Louisiana, Nebraska—the funeral industry has reserved for itself a piece of the action, such as embalming or transporting the dead. Still, an increasing number of morticians will provide professional help in a home funeral, such as preparing and/or transporting the body. (See page 318.) There's a widely recommended book on the subject: Caring for the Dead: Your Final Act of Love, *by Lisa Carlson (Upper Access, 1998, www.upperaccess.com).*

Ways to Go

Final Passages. This firm is in the home funeral trade and has participated in more than 150 of them. It takes charge of all of the funeral arrangements to "secure profound closure and healing without incurring alarming debt." The director and founder is Jerrigrace Lyons, who is an ordained minister and can conduct a home service if requested. She or assistants will also perform services such as washing the corpse and laying it out. Under California law, one family member needs Durable Power of Attorney for Health Care to take the place of the funeral director, making all the decisions and orchestrating all the funeral arrangements.

PO Box 1721, Sebastopol, CA 95473, (707) 824-0268, www.finalpassages.org

Glendale Memorial Nature Preserve. This green cemetery treats a burial as an opportunity to remove nonindigenous plants and replace them with native ones. Most of the burials take place in areas that were formerly farmed or logged. Families are allowed to take control of all aspects of the funeral, from the service to the digging of the grave. The cemetery also has an on-site sawmill that makes biodegradable caskets from trees on the site. You are not required to use one of these caskets.

297 Railroad Avenue, DeFuniak Springs, FL 32433, (850) 859-2141, www.glendalenatureperserve.org

Ramsey Creek Preserve. The nation's first fully green cemetery was opened and operated by Memorial Ecosystems, Inc., a company formed to "harness the funeral industry for land protection and restoration," in addition to providing affordable burials. Burials do not use vaults or embalming fluids, and all caskets are biodegradable and made from nonendangered woods. The cemetery itself uses only plants native to the area, so as not to unbalance the ecosystem with foreign species. The graves are scattered about; they are grassy hummocks marked by flat stones inscribed with the names of the deceased. Space is open for community use, and the organization works closely with local nonprofits. "We are committed to being the leaders in environmentally and socially responsible death care." This heavenly resting place was the down-to-earth idea of Billy Campbell, the only doctor in the small town of Westminster, South Carolina. An ardent environmentalist, in 1998 he conceived the idea of laying out a green cemetery near Westminster. He bought a patch of lovely woodland and started burying patients, friends and strangers among the pines and poplars. More than twenty people have been interred there in biodegradable coffins in graves Campbell dug himself. He regards "memorial preserves" like this one as a way of creating nature preserves and preserving naturally beautiful spots.

111 W. Main Street, Westminster, SC 29693, (864) 647-7798, www.memorialecosystems.com

Caskets

Bannock Pride. Skilled cabinet makers on Idaho's Fort Hall Shoshone Bannock Indian Reservation make ecofriendly caskets and defend the right of the bereaved to care for the dead in the manner they choose. The principals are David Robles and his wife, Marcia Racehorse-Robles, who turned their carpentry skills to casket making a few years ago. David designs and makes individualized caskets using alder or pine, and Marcia decorates them with buckskin and brass adornments. Members of the Native American Church, who take peyote in their rituals, may have symbols of the plant inscribed on their caskets. David and Marcia counsel all comers on home funerals. They work mostly with clients on the reservation but more non-Indians are utilizing their services.

Fort Hall Indian Reservation, RR2, Box 1586, Pocatello, ID 83202, (208) 241-3360, www.bannockpride.com

Trappist Caskets. Trappist monks at the New Melleray Abbey in Iowa make affordable caskets out of sustainable wood culled from the forests on the monastery's property. The profits go to the maintenance of the monastery. Caskets range in price from $975 for a plain pine box to $2,185 for a handsome walnut model that "applies the highest arts of the woodworker's craft; vintage dovetails, raised-panels on mortised stiles & rails." Comes with a free, engraved keepsake cross.

New Melleray Abbey, 16632 Monastery Road, Peosta, IA 52068, (888) 433-6934, www.trappistcaskets.com

People's Memorial Association. This nonprofit membership corporation, founded in 1939, is devoted to making it possible for people in western or central Washington to carry out ethical, affordable and informed funeral practices, through education, outreach, consumer advocacy and other forms of assistance. The association publishes annual reports on funeral costs at area funeral homes. Members receive discounted prices and may choose various-priced standard services knowing they will be available to survivors at the agreed-on price and free from pressure. They receive reciprocal benefits from Funeral Consumers Alliance (see below), which offers a home funeral service, including preparation of the body, preservation in dry ice for up to three days, delivery of a coffin or other container to the home and transportation to the cemetery, filing of a death certificate and notification of Social Security. A home funeral followed by cremation costs around $1,250.

801 12th Avenue, Suite A, Seattle, WA 98122, (866) 325-0489, www.peoplesmemorial.org

Funeral Consumers Alliance. This organization is a federation of nonprofit societies that provides information to consumers on end-of-life issues, affirming their right to choose a dignified and affordable funeral, without sales pressure or hidden costs. FCA is affiliated with more than 150 nonprofit funeral-planning groups across the country. These groups started out in the 1930s as a response to rising funeral costs resulting from the greater use of embalming techniques and manufactured coffins. The FCA is a clearinghouse that educates consumers about funeral choices, monitoring trends and abuses in the funeral industry, advocating reforms to serve consumers, working with other national organizations on increasing funeral choice and liaising with 115 funeral-planning societies. The FCA board of directors has adopted bylaws governing FCA's operations. Affiliates have investigated comparative prices of mortuaries in their cities and some function as buyers' clubs to negotiate lower prices.

3 Patchen Road, South Burlington, VT 05403, (800) 765-0107, www.funerals.org

Nature's Passage. Ahoy there, what could be more romantic than burial at sea? There's a firm specializing in this ancient rite. The proprietor and skipper is Lars Hedstrom, a captain in the United States Merchant Marine and a retired U.S. Army lieutenant colonel. For a fee that he says is less than the average funeral cost, he'll sail your loved one's remains into the sunset. The law specifies that a body must be buried at depths of more than 600 feet, so Cap'n Lars hauls the decedent a full eighty-five miles out (his/her ashes need only be dropped off beyond the three-mile limit). If you like, the body will be wrapped in "cotton sailcloth of standard width and about 4.5 meters in length, weighted with several Egyptian cotton-cloth bags containing about 150 pounds of sand, hand-sewn closed and then placed in a container for transportation to sea." The sailcloth-wrapped body is dumped smartly down the slide and into the drink to the tune of a bosun's whistle or suitable music. Captain Hedstrom is partial to veterans: there's a 25 percent discount for them; make that 50 percent for old salts who served during one of our wars. And they'll receive a fitting military send-off.

85 Shore Road, Amityville, NY 11701, (800) 407-8917, www.naturespassage.com

Neptune Society. This organization, with offices in eleven states, specializes in cheap, no-frills cremation services for those who want one-stop service, so to speak. The society's offices are listed on its website. They are available twenty-four hours a day. Services include removing the body, transporting it to a refrigerated storage facility, obtaining a copy of death certificate and cremation permit, overseeing cremation, disposing of ashes (if requested), and so on.

888 East Olas Boulevard, 3rd Floor, Ft. Lauderdale, FL 33301, 954-556-9400, www.neptunesociety.com

Left Heritage Trail

WASHINGTON

Anti-WTO Demonstrations. The Seattle protests against the World Trade Organization reflected the growing anger among poor and working-class people about the low-wage working conditions imposed by the corporate-dominated global economy. On November 29, 1999, representatives of the WTO convened in Seattle to unfetter global capital, draft very free trade agreements, underbid American workers' wages, whatever. But this time 20,000 citizens took a stand against the Darwinian world of globalization. Some 1,300 civil, social and trade

union groups were involved, along with environmental groups, radicals, anarchists. Although most marchers were peaceful, a few violent anarchists damaged downtown luxury stores. Police teargassed the crowd at 4th

and Pike Street and rounded up people in nearby West-lake Park. This event marked the birth of the antiglobalization movement, but no plaque marks the spot where enviros, vegetarians, Greens and pedestrians alike were teargassed in the melee.

Centralia Massacre. The town erected a statue of a World War I doughboy honoring the three American Legionnaires killed in an attack on the local headquarters of a band of IWW organizers. One of them, Wesley Everest, shot three vets as they closed in on him; that night vigilantes broke into the jail and took him away to be tortured, castrated and lynched. Eleven Wobblies were convicted of murder of the Legionnaires; no Legion member was ever implicated in Everest's death. *The Sentinel* looks the other way.

The Sentinel statue, George Washington Park, Centralia, WA.

Wesley Everest's Grave, Greenwood Memorial Park, Centralia, WA.

OREGON

PORTLAND'S RADICAL SITES AND SOUNDS

1. The only memorial to John Reed in the United States is a bench near his birthplace north of the entrance to Washington Park. A bronze plaque recognizes his contributions as a radical journalist and author of *Ten Days That Shook the World,* as well as his appreciation of Portland's natural beauty.

2. Two early leaders of the Communist Party have Portland ties: William Z. Foster worked here in the early 1900s and hung out at skid row bars such as Brazier Brothers and Erikson's East. Elizabeth Gurley Flynn lived with radical doctor Marie Equi for several years in Equi's home at 1423 SW Hall Street.

3. Woody Guthrie composed his Columbia River songs while living at 6111 SE 92nd Avenue. The Bonneville Power Authority headquarters has a Woody Guthrie Circle driveway with stone tablets containing passages from the songs. Woody was hired by BPA to write songs celebrating the construction of the Bonneville Dam. The best known is "Roll on Columbia."

4. The overpass overlooking the scene of "Bloody Wednesday" on which, during the 1934 longshoremen's strike, police fired on 500 strikers trying to prevent a trainload of scabs from getting through picket lines at Terminal 4 on the Willamette River, wounding four men.

5. The studio of Louise Bryant, feminist journalist who became the lover of John Reed, was in the Professional Building at 121 SW Yamhill Street. The movie *Reds* has her entertaining Reed there.

6. The House of Sound, a record store in a black neighborhood at 2343 N. Williams Avenue, braved hostile public opinion to sell tickets to a concert by the Red Paul Robeson during the McCarthy era.

—**MICHAEL MUNK,** author of *The Portland Red Guide: Sites and Stories from Our Radical Past* (Ooligan Press, 2007)

CALIFORNIA

Southern California Library for Social Studies and Research. Urban historian Mike Davis calls this Los Angeles library the "premier radical archive, especially good on Black history." Shelved here are some 30,000 books focusing on "labor, women, civil rights, civil liberties, people of color, left culture, peace, radicalism, socialism, Communism, Marxism, and other political theories and movements." It also houses 3,000 periodical titles, 25,000 pamphlets, 1,500 posters, 2,000 photographs. It's open to the public for browsing but membership is a condition for checking out material. It's a nonprofit organization and needs the money (donations gratefully accepted).

6120 S. Vermont Avenue, Los Angeles, CA 90044, (323) 759-6063, www.socallib.org

Bradbury Building. The Bradbury building is believed to have been patterned after one described by Edward Bellamy in his 1887 socialist utopian novel, *Looking Back-*

UTOPIAN VISIONS

It was the first interior of a twentieth-century public building that I had ever beheld, and the spectacle naturally impressed me deeply. I was in a vast hall full of light, received not alone from the windows on all sides, but from the dome, the point of which was a hundred feet above. Beneath it, in the centre of the hall, a magnificent fountain played, cooling the atmosphere to a delicious freshness with its spray. The walls and ceiling were frescoed in mellow tints, calculated to soften without absorbing the light which flooded the interior. Around the fountain was a space occupied with chairs and sofas, on which many persons were seated conversing.

—EDWARD BELLAMY, *Looking Backward*

---

ward. Completed in 1893, it's the oldest commercial office in the central city. It has appeared in noir films and TV shows including *D.O.A.*, *Blade Runner* and *Wolf.* It has a plain Romanesque exterior but inside Bellamy's vision leaps to the eye: a glass-ceilinged, fifty-foot high atrium with Victorian cast-iron railings, marble walls and stairs and cage elevators. The story is that a young draftsman named George Wyman designed it after the owner, mining tycoon Lewis Bradbury, fired architect Sumner P. Hunt for not understanding what he wanted.

304 S. Broadway, Los Angeles, CA 90013

Manzanar National Historic Site. Manzanar was one of ten detention centers where Japanese Americans were invited by Uncle Sam to spend World War II. The grim, arid 6,000-acre tract in Inyo County, 280 miles from Los Angeles, was home to some 110,000 internees from 1942 through 1945. It was described by *Life* magazine as "a concentration camp" filled with "potential enemies of the United States." There were no barbed wire fences, as at the other detention centers, but the roads were guarded and the desert was regarded as sufficient deterrence to flight. The camp buildings were tar paper sheds with colorful red roofs and walls of white plasterboard, unlike the raw-wood walls of the barracks in other sites,

making it a showcase camp. But in 1942 it was the site of a riot in which two internees were killed by U.S. troops. The trouble arose out of tensions between pro-Japanese and pro-U.S. inmates. Now run by the U.S. Park Service, several of the camp buildings and the graves of six inmates remain.

PO Box 426, Independence, CA 93526, (760) 878-2194, ext. 2710, www.nps.gov/manz/

Colonel Allensworth State Historic Park. Founded in 1908, Allensworth was the first settlement in California of, by and for African Americans escaping racism and violence in the South. The town took its name from its inspirational leader, Colonel Allen Allensworth, a U.S. Army chaplain who retired with the highest rank achieved by a black officer. Meticulously planned, the town thrived with a variety of economic and cultural facilities, but its growth was impeded by legal battles with the original white owners over water rights and the Santa Fe Railroad's refusal to stop at the depot. Then in the 1960s arsenic was found in the water supply, causing many residents to leave. By 1973 the town had to be abandoned, but a movement grew up to save it, and it is now a state historic site with costumed docents and tours. Allensworth's custom of holding a jubilee after the harvest has been revived, but in 2007 the park's environmental quality was threatened by plans to build a large, odiferous dairy farm nearby.

Seven miles west of Earlimart, CA, (661) 849-3433, www.parks.ca.gov/?page_id=24825

Llano del Rio. In 1914 a Utopian colony was founded in Antelope Valley, forty-five miles north of Los Angeles, by the lawyer and socialist leader Job Harriman. Harriman ran for vice president on the Socialist ticket with Eugene Debs in 1900 and later for mayor of Los Angeles. His defense of the McNamara brothers, trade unionists who confessed to blowing up the *Los Angeles*

Times building, queered his chances of becoming mayor. Disillusioned (or maybe *re*illusioned), he founded the Llano del Rio colony in the Mojave Desert. It thrived for several years as a laboratory of socialism, offering the minimum wage, Social Security, low-cost housing, welfare, universal health care. The population reached around 1,000, but the colonists had to abandon the place in 1917 because of a shortage of water. Llamo was moved to Louisiana, where it continued its utopian career.

Off Highway 138, Antelope Valley, CA

People's Park. This much contested 2.8-square-acre postage stamp of land in downtown Berkeley is owned by the University of California–Berkeley. In the late sixties, the university razed the public housing that occupied the land, planning to turn the space into an athletic field, but the community rose up in protest. In April 1968, egged on by the *Berkeley Barb*, the voice of the counterculture, students, professors, hippies, radicals, urban naturalists and an oddball or two took back the park. They planted and landscaped it and installed sandboxes for kids, creating a lovely community space. The university bided its time, then struck again, bulldozing every improvement. The "people" swarmed into the denuded land and police moved in with clubs and tear gas. The protesters threw things; there were many injuries and a demonstrator was killed. In December 2006, park lovers were alerted by the university's announcement of plans to level two gardening berms formed during the 1960s. The move was called an anti-crime measure against drug dealers and the homeless. The "people" mobilized to turn back another invasion of their space.

2556 Haste Street, half a block east of Telegraph Avenue between Haste Street and Dwight Way, southeast Berkeley

Jack London State Historic Park. In 1911, the wealthy and internationally famous Socialist author purchased this spectacular tract. He built a dream home, Wolf House, handcrafted of native rock to his every whim. It burned to the ground days after it was completed in 1913. London died a few years after that. He had told his wife, Charmian, "If I should beat you to it, I wouldn't mind if you laid my ashes on the knoll where the Greenlaw children [offspring of a pioneer family in the area] are buried. And roll over me a red boulder from the ruins of the Big House." In accordance with his wishes his ashes lie under a rugged, solitary rock near the ruins of Wolf House, high above the Valley of the Moon, to the west the trackless Pacific.

2400 London Ranch Road, Glen Ellen, CA 95442, (707) 938-5216, www.parks.ca.gov/?page_id=478; www.parks.sonoma.net/JLPark.html

MY FAVORITE AMERICAN PLACE

M & M Bar and Café in Butte, Montana, where on a quiet evening (most) you can hear the ghost ore cars rattling under the "richest hill on earth." Also the wonderful Unarius Academy of Science in El Cajon, California, where the followers of Nikola Tesla are still waiting patiently for the landing of the "33 Ships of the Federation" and the million-year reign of interplanetary peace.

—MIKE DAVIS is a journalist, activist and urban historian who teaches at the University of California–Irvine. He is author of *City of Quartz, Ecology of Fear* and other books.

Part V.

SOCIAL:

CONNECTING

Eat, Drink, Talk

BOOKSHOP CAFÉS

Busboys and Poets. This big, lofty and comfortable space is part café, part bookstore, part performance space, part meeting place. The guiding genius is Andy Shallal, an Iraqi-American peace activist who was against the Iraq war from the beginning. One of the most popular meeting places for progressives in the D.C. area, Busboys and Poets is a major center for antiwar activity. Says Shallal: "People that are in the peace movement are used to working out of church basements, you know, the environment isn't always the most beautiful, not always the most conducive to creativity and openness and thought provocation." In the Langston Room political and social meetings, performances and lectures and poetry slams happen daily. Sums up one regular: "A great place to hang out and meet up with other city activists. You can also have a great dinner at the café, or lunch, meet friends for a drink or coffee." A first-time visitor marveled at the 2006 election night festivities: "It was the most eclectic bunch of people! There were varying shades of funkiness—professors and Howard students and policy wonks, hipsters and cool guys in dreadlocks." Reported the Capital weekly *The Hill*: "Busboys and Poets oozes blue state cool. . . ."

2021 14th Street, Washington, DC 20009, (202) 387-7638, www.busboysandpoets.com

Hildegard's Café and Bookstore. Here is a combination "nonprofit coffee and tea lounge, free wireless internet provider, fresh deli, bookstore, performance space and art gallery." It's owned by Christ the King Episcopal Church. From Mark Kiyak: "Hildegard's Café here in Valdosta, Georgia, is like an oasis in a desert. Many of the locals here are aghast that a bookstore café (sponsored by the Episcopal church) stocks books on Islam. Evil! From what I understand, the city government has tried to make life difficult for them by charging them obscenely high property taxes, which unfortunately drains them of funds since they're always in court fighting it."

101 E. Central Avenue, Valdosta, GA 31601, (221) 247-6802, www.myspace.com/hildegards

The Lost Dog Café. This place was started by a couple who used to live in the East Village, Manhattan, and missed the coffeehouses where you could hang out and which served honest fare. So they started a place in a former garage on Main Street in Binghamton. It has thrived and they expanded to Ithaca. They serve up vegetarian food made with vegetable stock, no MSG or chemicals, and also nonvegetarian items. And of course coffee: *Nation* reader Laura Jones wrote in that she's particularly fond of a coffee called Mama's Racehorse, which the café describes as follows: "On your way to an all-nighter? Mama's Racehorse will do the trick . . . four (that's 4!) hits of espresso guaranteed to keep you shakin' from 8am to 2pm." That's a quote from the website, not from Laura Jones. This is a good thing to know if you plan on attending the Binghamton monthly dance off where they pit two bands (on CDs) against each other and the one that gets the most people out on the dance floor "wins." Yes, there actually is a dog, named Clarese, who is always running away. When that happens, the regulars form search parties, phone in sightings and suggest ways to lure her back. Eventually, she turns up.

222 Water Street, Binghamton, NY 13901, (607) 771-6063; 106–112 S. Cayuga Street, Ithaca, NY 14850, (607) 277-9143; www.lostdogcafe.net

Mercury Café. This Denver café specializes in "organic Colorado cuisine" and spiritual living. Says *Nation* associate Annette Walker: "The Mercury Café defies categories and is best defined as eclectic. Established 32 years ago by Marilyn Megenity and friends, 'The Merc' is at once Denver's premier alternative political and cultural space as well as a haven for organic dining and environmental consciousness." Windmills and solar panels grace the rooftop, and green climbing plants blanket one side of the two-storied building. Megenity calls it "the living wall." The café's organic coffee is prepared from beans grown in Chiapas, Mexico—center of the Zapatista rebels. In 2006 the café's resident theatrical group, the Motley Players, produced Howard Zinn's *Marx in Soho* to sold-out performances. The group created special theater pieces to coincide with the 2008 Democratic Convention in the Mile High City. The Mercury features weekly documentary film screenings and poetry readings and has become a center for a variety of dance and movement classes, such as belly dancing, cajun, tango, jitterbug and swing. A plethora of organizations and ad hoc groups meet and hold events at the Merc, and the bulletin board in the foyer is replete with notices of local events.

2199 California Street, Denver, CO 80205, (303) 294-9281, www.mercurycafe.com

COFFEE AND TEA SHOPS

Comma Coffee. Says our special Carson City rover, Marcia Bennett: "In Carson City, Nevada, the place to go for progressive fellowship is Comma Coffee. You can get great sandwiches, coffee and espresso drinks and sit on a couch, an overstuffed chair or around a number of tables. Comma Coffee is where MoveOn oriented us for the get-out-the-vote drive. They also bring in great music you won't find in the casinos. Comma Coffee takes you back to the atmosphere of the coffeehouse of old." Well, what do you expect when their philosophy is "If life were a sentence . . . Comma Coffee would be the comma . . . the pause . . . the breath . . . the break between thoughts"?

312 S. Carson Street, Carson City, NV 89701, (775) 883-2662, www.commacoffee.com

Gimme Coffee. Gimme Coffee is a small chain of coffeehouses with several locations in upstate New York and one in Manhattan and one in Williamsburg, Brooklyn, where it is generally acknowledged to be the best coffee in that borough. Their roastery is at the State Street location, but their first and still busiest location is Cayuga Street, a "home away from home for professionals, grad students and neighborhood anarchists," to quote their website. Our woman Laura Jones says: "Hardcore caffeination. Gimme features local artwork on its walls, and also carries a number of organic and fairly traded, locally roasted beans for purchase, as well as the very best and strongest cup I've had since I left Berkeley in the '80s." The first Gimme Coffee saw the light of day in 2000 in a tiny 240-square-foot space. But they knew their way to the twitchy neurons of caffeine maniacs.

506 W. State Street, Ithaca, NY 14850, (607) 272-8564; 430 N. Cayuga Street, Ithaca, NY 14850, (607) 277-8393; 7 E. Main Street, Trumansburg, NY 14850, (607) 387-3960; 495 Lorimer Street, Brooklyn, NY 11211, (718) 388-7771; 288 Mott Street, New York, NY 10012, (212) 226-4011; 2075 E. Shore Drive, Lansing, NY 14850, (607) 533-4852; www.gimmecoffee.com

Magdalena's Tea House. Magdalena's Tea House is not in it just for the tea. It wants to encourage original composers and promote art and community awareness and positive change and other good stuff. Its food comes from organic farms in the area, thus supporting family farmers. It serves self-certified whole food and fair trade down the line. Confirms *Nation* associate Dan Nortman: "Magdalena's is a progressive, smoke-free tea/coffee shop in Lansing serving organic and local drinks and food. They also host a number of local folk music groups and screen progressive-leaning movies." Other activities include raw dinners, anime film nights, monthly drum chants, open stage nights, jam sessions, poetry readings, plays, art receptions and exhibitions and so on.

2006 E. Michigan Avenue, Lansing, MI 48912, (517) 487-1822, www.magdalenasteahouse.com

The Old Creamery Grocery and Deli. Our New Rochelle correspondent Ken Weiss writes: "What's doing in New Rochelle? Nothing that I know of. But in Cummington, Massachusetts, on Route 9 (directly between Northampton and Pittsfield) there's a general store called The Old Creamery that serves great coffee and (mostly organic) food and acts as a weekend-morning meeting place for local progressives. There are tables to sit at, no one rushes you and, yes, there are even old copies of *The Nation* in the magazine rack. A little out of the way for most people, but if you happen to be in the neighborhood . . ."

445 Berkshire Trail (Route 9), Cummington, MA 01026, (413) 634-5560, www.hidden-hills.org/oldcreamery/

Vox Pop. A coffee shop, bookstore, publishing company and radical gathering spot in one, Vox Pop's motto is "Books, coffee, democracy." The place was started by Sander

Hicks, founder of Soft Skull Press (see page 41), a 9/11 truth-er and all-around activist-provocateur. Vox Pop boasts: "We are a community-empowering, retail-revolution, live-event-loving, info-shop dedicated to 'vox pop,' Latin shorthand for 'voice of the people.'... We offer fair-trade certified coffee drinks, and all-natural, healthy food. We offer books and newspapers that surpass the limits of information offered by the conglomerate media." Vox Pop also offers a Sunday barbecue, select wines and microbrews on tap, including Dogfish Head, Rehoboth, Delaware's finest. On Sunday nights there's an open mike for poets, comedians, artists and speakers. And for authors who want no truck with publishers they have an InstaBook press, with a print-on-demand option so you can have your book printed on the premises, and they'll throw you a publishing party for a nominal price. The operator is located next door at Publish Yourself.

1022 Cortelyou Road, Brooklyn, NY 11218, (718) 940-2084, www.voxpopnet.net

BARS, PUBS AND SALOONS

Artist's Café. This restaurant, formerly called Artist's Snack Shop, was recommended to us by Penelope Rosemont. It is located in the landmark Fine Arts Building, which was built in 1885 by the Studebaker Company and later became a warren of artists' studios and theaters, as it still is. The café is frequented by reporters, students, surrealists, actors and assorted radicals. Boldface names passing through Chicago have dined here; it's also a favorite of First Chicagoan Studs Terkel.

412 S. Michigan Avenue, Chicago, IL 60605, (312) 939-7855, www.artists-cafe.com

Blue Moon Tavern. One patron called the Blue Moon the "Platonic ideal" of a dive bar. When it opened in 1934 it was just over a mile from the University of Washington campus, which got it around a law saying no bars within a mile of the campus. The name came from a nearby café, whose sign founder Hank Reverman bought. Fastidious people can't see the charm, but the regulars like it precisely because of the grungy atmosphere and the fourteen brews on tap. Blue Moon is said to have been a hangout for Beat writers Ginsberg and Kerouac and the poet Theodore Roethke in the fifties and sixties. It was also a hangout of Joe Butterworth, a former UW English professor who was fired for flunking the "Are you or have you ever been a member of the Communist Party" question. In the 1980s developers wanted to demolish it and put up condos, but a group of literary and political celebrities—including Calvin Trillin, Governor Mike Lowry and Stanley Kunitz—rallied to save it. Says Petra Hellthaler, the owner's sister, "We worry the liquor board and piss off the city attorney's office when, in reality, we're all very nice people who love talking politics and religion and are somewhat active—many letters to the editor, marching, etc. . . . We try to think green; for example, instead of spraying nasty chemicals, we put a drosera [insect-eating plant] named Audrey on the payroll to get rid of beer-loving fruit flies, etc. She's so good at her job, she made employee of the month after being on the job for only three weeks."

712 NE 45th Street, Seattle, WA 98105, (206) 675-9116

The Bourgeois Pig. Not to be confused with other fine but completely different restaurants that go by the same name in Chicago, New York, Los Angeles and who knows where else, the Lawrence, Kansas BP represents a sanctuary of creativity or eccentricity in this Big 12 basketball-crazy university town. It's a coffeehouse bar that's evolved into a chosen rendezvous and talk shop for resident writers, filmmakers, painters, students and freelance intellectuals of all breeds. There's a back porch with a smoking area in winter. They also offer live music and monthly art shows of works created in local ateliers. Yes, we're really in Kansas, Toto.

6 E. Ninth Street, Lawrence, KS 66044, (785) 843-1001

Club Charles. This old-time bar used to be located where all the strip bars were clustered during the heyday of nightclubs in the 1940s and 1950s. Legend has it that after doing a gig here in 1951 the great comedian Lenny Bruce met his future wife, Honey Bruce Friedman, who stripped under the nom de guerre Hot Honey Harlowe. The current, refurbished version—replete with deep red walls and gothic murals—is a major hipster hangout, and you may see Baltimore native and indie filmmaker John (*Hairspray*) Waters holding court.

1724 N. Charles Street, Baltimore, MD 21201, (410) 727-8815

The Goose Hollow Inn. This is Bud Clark's bailiwick. He calls it "Portland's living room." The pub keeper and former mayor of Portland bought up Ann's Tavern in 1967 and renamed it. Habitués just call it "the Goose." Several kinds of microbrews are on tap, cheap imperial pints, specialty Reuben sandwiches and other bar fare. The Goose gets regular walk-ins from nearby government and media offices. (Legend has it that a state legislator enjoyed dancing so much after a few microbrews that he successfully pushed for repeal of a blue law banning dancing in saloons.) It's a venue for political talk and the TV's usually off. Bud says: "We are also dedicated to extremes of opinion, hoping that a livable marriage will result. If physical violence is your nature, either develop your verbal abilities or leave."

1927 SW Jefferson Street, Portland, OR 97201, (503) 228-7010, www.goosehollowinn.com

Hal & Mal's. This beloved restaurant pub, a Southern liberal hangout, was opened in 1986 in a former train depot by Hal and Malcolm White, Mississippi-born brothers. It features live jazz and rock, and Dizzy Gillespie and Snoop Dogg have performed there. It has hosted various progressive events, such as a funder for the Mississippi chapter of NOW in summer 2006 and an LGBT event organized by Unity Mississippi. The annual St. Paddy's Day Parade, which Mal kicked off some years ago, is a much anticipated challenge for Jackson's drinking class, even if the city does not have enough Irish to shake a shillelagh at. Malcolm White served as executive director of the Mississippi Arts Commission Board and is a member of the Mississippi Blues Commission.

200 S. Commerce Street, Jackson, MS 39201, (601) 948-0888, www.halandmals.com

Manuel's Tavern. In Atlanta everybody goes to Manuel's place. Manuel Maloof started his restaurant in 1956, taking over the space from Harry's Delicatessen. His inspiration was the English pubs he'd frequented as a GI during World War II, places where the neighbors

ATLANTA NIGHTS

Manuel's Tavern is the most prominent local watering hole for liberals, including artists and professors. It was the location of the famous "God is dead" conversation among Emory theologians in the sixties, or at least that's the local legend.

The Colonnade and its adjacent motel are legendary among gay people in Atlanta. Fifties gay culture centered around the restaurant, which is another place for Southern cooking. Men would meet for anonymous liaisons in the motel, come to Atlanta and party for the weekend and stay there, and take their meals in the restaurant. It's located on Cheshire Ridge Road.

There are a couple of diners that are significant, the Majestic on Ponce de Leon and Evans Fine Foods in Decatur. Majestic is famous for the waitresses and the varied clientele, and is in a part of town where the clientele would be left-leaning. Evans Fine Foods is located on N. Decatur Road in Decatur and is a hangout for Decatur and DeKalb county politicians.

—JIM GRIMSLEY is author of *The Ordinary* and *The Last Green Tree,* both science fiction, *Comfort & Joy, Winter Birds* and other books.

met and talked over a pint about current affairs. He furnished the place with a bar from his father's billiard parlor; the mountain granite stone front came with the deli. As the business grew, Manuel turned to politics, eventually being elected to the office of DeKalb County chief executive and using his place as a permanent floating focus group. His brother, Robert, ran the place while he was away. The tavern acquired a patina of political history mixed with the smoke of bygone cigars. It was the site of Jimmy Carter's announcement that he would run for governor; the place

where Atlanta mayors Andrew Young, Maynard Jackson and Shirley Franklin schmoozed with their friends. After Manuel Maloof died in 2006, his ashes were placed in an urn behind the bar, just under the big portrait of FDR. The Maloof family continues to own the place and old employees with thirty years under their belts run it.

602 North Highland Avenue, Atlanta, GA 30307, (404) 525-3447, www.manuelstavern.com

McMenamin Brothers. Mike and Brian McMenamin started their beer-selling careers in 1983 when they bought a dive in Portland called the Fat Little Rooster, cleaning it up, painting murals on the walls, installing neon lights and changing the name to the Barley Mill Pub (after the barley mill—actually a kitty litter grinder—they installed as a rather huge conversation piece). They tout themselves as part of the Good Pub movement, an alternative to dark, hard-drinking, men's bars—a place more like English pubs, to which the entire family could come. They also tied into the microbrew revolution that swept the Pacific Northwest and was given a great push by a law that allowed breweries to sell their product in attached pubs. The McMenamins' business philosophy worked, and the brothers now operate more than fifty-five (and counting) neighborhood gathering spots in Oregon and Washington. The pubs are very local neighborhood focused and offer live music, theater and other communal activities.

www.mcmenamins.com

Old Town Ale House. Chicago dive bar that gained its fame as the hangout in the seventies for the satirists from the Second City across the street and free speech advocates. There's a large mural depicting regulars from the 1970s era. The late Severn Darden, cofounder of Second City and a genuine eccentric, frequented the place. (Perhaps it was here that Allan Bloom, a formidable intellectual even then and future author of *The Closing of the American Mind,* asked Darden, "Severn, is the game worth the candle?" Darden promptly pulled a candle out of his pocket and lit it. Even the haughty

Bloom was impressed.) Dan Aykroyd and John Belushi also popped over from Second City, to shake up the pinball machine, and Chris Farley had some wild nights here before his too early demise.

219 W. North Avenue, Chicago, IL 60610, (312) 944-7020, www.oldtownalehouse.net

The Owl Bar. For almost one hundred years this saloon has been a famous Baltimore fixture. The Baltimore sage and critic H. L. Mencken celebrated the end of Prohibition there; a famous photo shows him downing a schooner, eyes popping with pleasure, epitomizing the end of an ignoble experiment in legislating morality. This Jazz Age hot spot has barely blinked since the twenties, so beautifully preserved is the woodwork, the stained glass and the soaring ceiling. The room was made for drinking and dancing— the Charleston.

Hotel Belvedere, 1 East Chasse Street, Baltimore, MD 21202, (410) 347-0888, www.theowlbar.com/owlbar

Scholz Garten. *Haben sie BBQ? Ja!* This landmark Tex-Deutsch restaurant, founded in the state capital by Confederate vet August Scholz in 1866, continues to be a key fueling stop for state pols, political buffs and members of the drawling class who cover the State House spectacle. In the fifties liberal Democratic legislators like Maury Maverick, Jr., and Bob Eckhardt and lefty journalists like Ronnie Dugger, Willie Morris, Bill Brammer (who celebrated it in his 1961 Texas political novel about LBJ *The Gay Place*), Robert Sherill, Jim Hightower, Geoffrey Rips, Molly Ivins and the staff of the *Texas Observer* (see page 130) hung out there. When Molly died in 2007, too young and too beautiful, they held a wake for her there. She would have loved it. Scholz Garten is no longer a Democratic redoubt despite the 2004 challenge of State Representative Glen Maxey, a Howard Dean supporter: "We're going to take back Scholz

---

SCHOLZ IN FICTION

The beer garden was shielded on three sides by the low yellow frame structure, a U-shaped Gothicism, scalloped and jigsawed and wonderfully grotesque. The bar, the kitchen and dining spaces were at the front; the one side and the back were club-rooms for the Germans who came to town once or twice a week to bowl and play cards. . . . During the hard times of the 1930's they had begun leasing out the front part as a public bar, an arrangement that had proved so profitable that it was continued through the war years and was now apparently destined for the ever-after.

—BILLY LEE BRAMMER, *The Gay Place* (1961)

Garten, we're going to take back the state of Texas, and then we're going to take back the White House!" With the gemütlichkeit you can get a decent bratwurst plate, wiener schnitzel, chicken fried steak or the Four Meat BBQ. There are German beers on tap, along with native brews like Lonestar and Shiner Light and Bock. Relax in the Biergarten at a picnic table under the cottonwood trees with a stein of Spaten Pilsner. It you're lucky the Wurst German Band will serenade you.

1607 San Jacinto, Austin, TX 78701, (512) 474-1958

Stoneleigh P. This bar and restaurant has been around since 1973 and is a hangout for creative people in design and advertising in generally conservative Dallas. The "P" stands for "pharmacy," which the place was before the present owners bought it. (It was also across the street from the Stoneleigh Terrace Hotel.) Anyhow, the new owners wanted to call it the Stoneleigh Pharmacy, but the bureaucrats pointed to a law saying that a full-time pharmacist would have to be on duty if they called it "pharmacy." So their lawyer simply whited out "harmacy" wherever it appeared on the application, leaving just the "p," and it went through. They kept the cabinets that were in the drugstore and other touches. The place has a singles scene and is home to the Dallas chapter of Drinking Liberally.

2926 Maple Avenue, Dallas, TX 75201, (214) 871-2346, www.stoneleighp.com

The Weary Traveler. We have two testimonials for this beloved lefty saloon. First from *Nation* Washington correspondent John Nichols, whose family goes way back in Madison:

A snapshot of the real Madison—circa 1903, or is it 1967?—can be found at the Weary Traveler on funky Williamson Street. Locals settle in to an old-world pub with wooden floors and a long bar, local beers on tap, comfort foods with just enough flair to keep them interesting, and a portrait of Walt Whitman overlooking a room that even on the coldest winter night radiates a warmth steeped in poetry and acoustic folk, blues and world-beat music. The talk here is of politics (Senator Russ Feingold has been known to drop by) and the outdoor pleasures of an isthmus neighborhood bounded by two large lakes and the river that connects them.

Nation reader Jan Levine Thal:

Located on Williamson Street, in the heart of Madison's alternative communities, across the street from Madison's Social Justice Center (and how many communities have one of those?), the Weary is always packed full of serious drinkers and serious politicos cheek by jowl. The bar offers a short, delicious and inexpensive menu of vegetarian and nonvegetarian food borrowed from ethnicities as varied as Thai and Hungarian. Wooden floors, wooden chairs and tables decorated with odd castoffs like old telephones are tucked into two cozy rooms, one of which offers a tiny stage where local musicians play on weekends. It's loud even with no music and you may have to shout to be heard by your companion so you may have to be content to play a board game, available from the great-looking overqualified staff that dresses with individual panache.

1201 Williamson Street, Madison, WI 53703, (608) 442-6207

RESTAURANTS OF PROGRESSIVE PROVENANCE

California

Big Kitchen Café. Here the emphasis is as much on community as it is on food. So testifies Michael Jonak: "I recently moved from a very progressive place (Minneapolis) to San Diego, a place where, umm, things are significantly less progressive. Fortunately, I found a friend at a little café in the South Park (no, not *that* South Park) neighborhood of S.D. It's called the Big Kitchen. The proprietor is Judy 'the Beauty' Forman, who is pretty much always on duty, greeting customers and spreading '*très biens!*' Her food and service have won a number of awards, and the Big Kitchen is also the epicenter of San Diego's progressive community. Any time there's a march, demonstration or meeting, you can bet that Judy is encouraging one and all to hit the streets (after finishing their meal, of course). And, although she is much too modest to talk about herself, she is known in the community for a lifetime of contributions to progressive causes—and for her personal efforts on behalf of the homeless, hungry and downtrodden. So if you're coming to San Diego, just remember that LA and San Francisco may be in the same state, but they are light-years away politically. So, thank goodness for our café."

3003 Grape Street, San Diego, CA 92102, (619) 234-5789, www.bigkitchencafe.com

Connecticut

Bloodroot. This feminist vegetarian restaurant and bookstore celebrated its thirtieth anniversary in 2007. It was founded by a collective of women of whom Selma Miriam and Noel Furie abide. This is a voluntary cooperative, with about fifteen women helping out part-time, preparing lunch and dinner with fresh organic produce. The drill is that you give your orders to Miriam at the front door and then you hand it off to the kitchen staff. When you're finished, you clear your table. " There aren't any chefs here. We're all cooks," said Miriam. Their dishes are inspired by many different cultures—

about thirty-three to be exact. The summer menu is inspired by Mediterranean cooking. Asian, Syrian, Russian and Polish cuisines get into the mix, too. Over the years, the collective has produced four cookbooks—the first was called *The Political Palate*—which offer seasonal vegetarian and vegan recipes that reflect Bloodroot's animal-free, local and organic culinary vision. A feminist bookstore next door to the restaurant is also part of the Bloodroot venture.

85 Ferris Street, Bridgeport, CT 06605, (203) 576-9168, www.bloodroot.com

Hawaii

Banana Joe's. The north shore of Kauai, Hawaii, a jungle paradise, has no fast food and no fast driving: a string of thirteen one-way bridges on the coast road makes everybody slow down. The road begins at Banana Joe's, a heavenly fruit stand. They've had as many as five varieties of bananas on sale, along with the sunrise papaya and the sweet white sugarloaf pineapple. And there are drinks: you can have a tropical fruit smoothie or a tropical fruit frostie. It's a tough choice.

Kauai, HI, www.bananajoekauai.com

Hamura Saimin Stand. Saimin is a noodle soup, apparently unique to Hawaii, that's based on a fish stock, with soft wheat egg noodles. Frommer's says that Hamura would belong in the saimin hall of fame (if there was one). The place has a screen door that slams, a U-shaped counter and a separate take-out window. The menu is simple: you can have a small, medium or large bowl of saimin; you can add vegetables, wontons and/or meat (pork). Also, it's open till midnight on weekends for late-night noodle lovers.

2956 Kress Street, Lihue, Kauai, HI 96766, (808) 245-3271

Illinois

First Slice. First Slice, a nonprofit restaurant/soup kitchen, is the brainchild of Mary Ellen Diaz, a former chef who decided to use her cooking skills to help Chicago's needy. First Slice operates as both a café and as a prepared-meal service; customers eat in the restaurant or they can sign up for the shareholder program, which, for a weekly fee, provides three triple-course take-home meals that will feed a family of three. That money, in turn, goes to providing the same nutritious meals to Chicago's homeless and hungry—one subscription to the program pays for the food of twenty needy people. Diaz's meals, which might include a spinach and butternut squash lasagna or cauliflower soup with pecans and rye croutons, are made with mostly local, organic ingredients. Says Diaz, "The farmers I work with are community based and a bit quirky and

Madison's L'Etoile, a Capital Square restaurant created by Odessa Piper in the 1970s, confirmed the then radical notion that fresh, local food was the stuff of a perfect meal. L'Etoile is still going strong, but it is no longer an island of innovation. Madison has become a foodie paradise of ethnic cuisine (perhaps best exemplified by State Street's Nepalese stalwart Himal Chuli) and innovative fusions (like that of Himal Chuli's offspring, Chautara on State Street and Dobhan near the grand old Barrymore Theater on the east side's Atwood Avenue). The choicest place in town is Restaurant Magnus, near the Frank Lloyd Wright–designed Monona Terrace Community and Convention Center, where co-owner Christopher Berge cannot help himself; he simply must insist that you try this wine he discovered while bicycling through eastern Europe.

—**JOHN NICHOLS**, Washington correspondent for *The Nation*

antiestablishment, like me." And, of course, there's pie: Diaz says, "Pie is a symbol of community, and giving the first slice is like giving the best. This organization gives the first slice to people who rarely get anything special." Part of First Slice's mission is also to make the homeless feel more at home: In 2005, Diaz cooked up batches of Cajun food for displaced victims of Hurricane Katrina.

4401 N. Ravenswood, Chicago, IL 60640, (773) 506-1719

Heartland Café. A Chicago spot that is frequented by much more than "activist green types." Its cofounder and co-owner Michael James was active in the Berkeley Free Speech Movement 1964, SDS, JOIN and Rising Up Angry. The café has had many leftist art shows, including several featuring historic IWW and other radical posters. A recent one was inspired by the revival of Students for a Democratic Society in 2006. The restaurant also hosts a weekly radio show with an activist focus, *Live from the Heartland* (WLUW, 88.7 FM). Once or twice a year, it publishes a decidedly leftist newspaper, *Heartland Journal*. It serves breakfast, lunch and dinner. There is also the nearby No Exit Café, a coffeehouse open for parties and special events like *Democracy Burlesque,* an every-Tuesday political satire review with songs and sketches, and Red Line Tap, a bar 'round the corner showcasing rock groups. The No Exit started in 1958, when intellectual phonies were still impressing girls by telling them that the name was the title of a play by Jean-Paul Sartre, that hip existentialist, and continued to display the latest manifestations of hip in various locations over the passing years.

7000 N. Glenwood, Chicago, IL 60626, (773) 465-8005, www.heartlandcafe.com; Red Line Tap, 7006 N. Glenwood, Chicago, IL 60626, (773) 274-5463; No Exit Café, 6970 N. Glenwood, Chicago, IL 60626, (773) 743-3355

Indiana

Roots. Roots is a 100 percent vegetarian restaurant, the only one of its kind in Bloomington, home of cosmopolitan Indiana University and a liberal city in a very red state. Roots is housed in a mid-nineteenth-century brick building that the owners renovated from the ground up, using mostly recycled and sustainable materials, like wood from a local mill. The cooks at Roots make an effort not to let any food go to waste, and any scraps left over are composted. Nearly all ingredients used in the restaurant are recyclable, including the cooking oil, which, after it has served its purpose, is recycled into fuel. Roots's clientele comes for fresh, vegetable-centered food that often comes from organic, local farms; the biggest crowd pleaser at Roots is the country fried seitan.

126 N. Walnut Street, Bloomington, IN 47404, (812) 336-7668

Iowa

Hamburg Inn. Founded in 1948, Hamburg Inn is Iowa City's oldest family-owned restaurant. In presidential campaign seasons, this restaurant has become a necessary stop for politicians campaigning for the Iowa presidential caucuses. Ronald Reagan, Bill Clinton and, in our own day, John Edwards, Barack Obama, Joe Biden and even President Bartlet of TV's *West Wing* have dropped by to press the flesh, kiss some babies and eat with the common folk. They sponsor a Coffee Bean Caucus (customers drop beans into their candidate's can).

214 N. Linn, Iowa City, IA 52245, (319) 337-5512, www.hamburginn.com

Simone's Plain and Simple. Not quite a restaurant, not quite a catering service, Simone's pretty much defines the notion of "slow food" as a revival of the social nature of dining. On the second Monday of each month, Simone Delaty, a native of France, hosts a table d'hôte dinner in her home on a farm in the rolling hills of Wellman, Iowa (population 1,400). Diners sit at a communal table on the screened-in porch and get to know one another as Simone serves them home-cooked meals made from locally grown, organic ingredients, along with French country bread made from scratch and baked in the wood-fired brick oven in her backyard. The other option is to reserve Simone's for a private group dinner (minimum eight people), with the choice of four different cuisines: French, Moroccan, Cajun/Creole or pizza. Each meal highlights the freshest in-season herbs and vegetables, and as Simone serves the food she explains the preparation and traditions of each dish, inviting diners to "reconnect with the source, flavor, and fellowship of food."

1478 470th Street SW, Wellman, IA 52356, (319) 683-2896, www.simoneplainandsimple.com

Minnesota

Amazing Grace Bakery & Café. Here's a discovery of our former *Nation* associates manager (and Duluth native) Peter Fifield, who alerted us during a visit to his hometown: "It's definitely a place for the *Nation Guide*. Granola flowing [!], strong coffee, organic this and that, live music every evening almost, progressives all around." Breakfast here earned a *New York Times* kudo: "Few places in Duluth do breakfast as well as the Amazing Grace Bakery. . . . Try the maple vanilla battered French toast with three strips of bacon, or one of the muffins or scones."

394 S. Lake Avenue, Duluth, MN 55802, (218) 723-0075, www.amazinggracebakery.com

Missouri

Riddles Penultimate Café and Wine Bar. Owner and chef Andy Ayers is certainly not afraid to speak his mind—the restaurant's website features information on the BENCH BUSH! Movement, which, when the president was slated to throw the first pitch at the 2004 Opening Day game at Busch Stadium, offered its followers helpful advice on how to sneak anti-Bush signs past security into the stadium (the secret: "bed sheet and/or pillowcase signs of your own design that fold up for easy and convenient concealment in one's underwear!") Ayers opened his restaurant in 1979, in a smaller location down the street from one of the last working farms in the area. One bite of a tomato from that farm (along with some prodding from his wife, Paula) convinced Ayers that his customers would appreciate fresh, locally grown produce. Twenty-eight years later, he has managed to cultivate relationships with a broad circle of St. Louis–area growers, who, he says, appreciate his "no-bullshit business practices." He knows who to go to for the earliest spinach of the season or the freshest sweet corn, and this knowledge is reflected in his menu, which changes with the seasons. The restaurant features live jazz and bluegrass music six nights a week. Whenever anyone voices a problem with Ayers's mixing his food with his politics, he takes the time to respond personally, since, as he puts it, "the fear of stating one's views is antithetical to everything it means to be an American citizen."

6307 Delmar Boulevard, St. Louis, MO 63130, (314) 725-6985, www.riddlescafe.com

New Mexico

Daily Pie Café. Pie Town, "America's friendliest little town," sits astride the Great Divide about 8,000 feet above sea level. It hosts the Annual Pie Town Festival on the second Saturday in September. The Toaster House is a hostel for hikers and bikers trekking the Continental Divide Trail. The Daily Pie Café was founded in the 1920s by Clyde Norman, a World War I vet who ran a gas station on U.S. 60 and sold homemade apple pies. The success of his pies encouraged him to open the Daily Pie Café, which serves meals. A *Nation* associate had this comment: "Whereas for 25 years I lived just off pre-1937 Route 66 and El Camino Real, the historic colonial route from Mexico City to Santa Fe, these days I am hanging out 7 miles north of Route 60—America's first transoceanic highway, right at Pie Town on the Continental Divide! For an early morning cup of joe or a Friday evening dress up dinner I go to the Daily Pie. The atmosphere is friendly to blue staters—a YEEHAW IS NOT A FOREIGN POLICY bumper sticker is prominently displayed over the counter!"

Pie Town, NM 87827, (505) 772-2700, www.dailypie.com

Food Not Bombs. This is a political kitchen rather than a restaurant. It was started by antinuke activists in Cambridge in 1980 and serves up free vegetarian meals to the hungry while protesting militarism, war economies and poverty. There are now Food Not Bombs chapters all over the world, and they are an active force in movements to

---

FORTY KINDS OF PIE

Michael Rawls, owner of Daily Pie, came out here from Baltimore to escape the rat race: "We serve lots of pie—forty kinds," he tells us, "about fifteen kinds on any given day. Our house pie is New Mexican apple, a provincial pie made with Granny Smith apples, green chilis and piñon (pine) nuts, all New Mexico grown. We also serve an eclectic menu of American and Continental cuisine from biscuits and gravy, omelets and steak and eggs for breakfast to burgers, BBQ, fresh salads and seafood for lunch and steaks, seafood, Thai, French and Italian; more dishes for Friday dinner. We serve lots of locals and highway travelers as well as hikers and bicyclists off the Continental Divide trail.

"Politics? Catron County, New Mexico, is a conservative but rebellious county. It was red in 2000, blue in 2004. I have a picture of Thomas Jefferson on my mantel and a sticker facing my diners that says, 'Someone else for president' that will stay there no matter who is in office. I believe in term limits even if we have to do it at the polls. Political office should be a service not a career."

address homelessness and poverty; encourage vegetarianism; fight war making, corporate globalization and imperialism; and bring about progressive social change. See the website for the directory of local chapters and hours that food is served. The New York chapter is affiliated with the Lower East Side radical mecca ABC No Rio (see page 364) and serves food every Sunday at 3:30 in Tompkins Square Park.

PO Box 424, Arroyo Seco, NM 87514, (505) 776-3880, (800) 884-1136, www.foodnotbombs.net

New York

The Donut Pub. Attention editor: Your hardworking assistants have a nomination for you in the restaurant, coffee shop or whatever category: the Donut Pub. What's the justification for a donut joint? Simply that without this place *The Nation Guide to the Nation* might not have been possible. This place has provided us with the sustenance, sugar rushes and satiety needed to finish our work. We are quite aware that debates rage over where to find New York's finest donuts, but the destination of choice for *The Nation Guide to the Nation* team will always be the Donut Pub. Located just across town from *The Nation* offices, this mom-and-pop shop has been Chelsea's premier donut emporium since the early 1960s, persevering despite an insidious move by corporate behemoth Dunkin' Donuts, which opened a store just down the street in late 2007. If you know anything finer in all creation than a glazed marble cruller from the Donut Pub, tell us where to find it.

203 W. 14th Street, New York, NY 10011, (212) 929-0126

Oregon

Sisters of the Road. Founded in Portland by two social service workers in 1979, Sisters was conceived as "a restaurant where wholesome meals would be affordable to very low-income people, and where those who lacked the price of the meal could trade work for food." *Nation* reader Stella Kopperud put us on to the place: "Sisters of the Road Café is located in Old Town Portland and provides low-cost (I think $1.25) hot meals to anyone who wishes to come in. The great thing is that if you don't have any money, you can work for your meal by washing dishes, serving food, etc. The staff is dedicated to interacting with all patrons in a respectful, positive manner, and encouraging the patrons to do the same. People can learn job skills as well. The organization also provides meal tickets to the public for a cost of around $2. These tickets can be given out to anyone asking for money on the street. I have used them and most people are very pleased to receive them. You can find out more from my friend Monica Beemer, who is the executive director there (monica@sistersoftheroad.org)."

133 NW Sixth Avenue, Portland, OR 97209, (503) 222-5694, www.sistersoftheroad.org

Sunnyside Up Café. Recommended by *Nation* associate Roberta Hall: "Sunnyside Up on 3rd Street in Corvallis, Oregon, is a comfortable hangout for progressive folks and is the site for many small meetings of artists, musicians, war protesters, politicos and their constituents, improvisation groups and just folks. Our group—Alternatives to War—puts on a monthly benefit concert there that features excellent local musicians. We call it Second Saturday for the day of the month that it is staged, and it started as a benefit for Lt. Ehren Watada [court-martialed for refusing to go to Iraq], which brought in around 150 people and more than $700.00. We have done benefits for our counterrecruitment committee, the campaign for a department of peace, Military Families Speak Out, Agustin Aguayo and others. We meet there for planning meetings of all sorts. Internet access is available, and some people do their office work from Sunnyside Up. The walls are a bright, sunny yellow, decorated with rotating art shows—it all works well for this community."

116 NW 3rd Street, Corvallis, OR 97330, (541) 758-3353, http://sunnyside-up-cafe.com

Pennsylvania

White Dog Café. One of the best (and best-known) activism-oriented restaurants in the United States, White Dog Café was started in 1983 by Judy Wicks. The café has become a hotbed of antiwar activism and is now connected to a nonprofit also run by Wicks. Among the many projects Wicks is involved in is a campaign to help minority-run restaurants in the Philadelphia area. We should definitely note, though, a not-so-pleasant side of the café's history: several of Wicks's employees once tried to unionize, and the maternalistic Wicks did everything she could to stop them.

3420 Sansom Street, Philadelphia, PA 19104, (215) 386-9224, www.whitedog.com

South Carolina

Bowen's Island Restaurant. A funky oyster shack right on Folly Beach in Charleston County, Bowen's Island Restaurant is a local tradition, having been in existence since 1946, and is reputed to have the best oysters in the state. The restaurant itself is very bare-bones, with only counter service and graffiti-covered walls. They shovel piles of roasted oysters on your table, or you can get shrimp and other seafood. Owner Robert Barber received the 2006 James Beard Foundation Award. He wore a tuxedo and white shrimping boots for the occasion. His grandparents May and Jimmy Bowen opened the place right after the war. Robert took over in 1990, then in 2006 the restaurant burned down. That actually didn't cause any great trouble since it was little more than

a cinder block cube and easily rebuilt. Barber's been very active in South Carolina's Democratic Party, serving in the state legislature and running unsuccessfully for Congress and for lieutenant governor of South Carolina.

1870 Bowens Island Road, Charleston, SC 29412, (843) 795-2757

Utah

Hell's Backbone Grill. As described by one customer, Hell's Backbone Grill is a "strange kind of cowboy cosmic crazy Buddha vortex." The restaurant, which dishes up a cosmic crazy mix of Western, Pueblo Indian and Southwestern fare, and uses mostly organic, local ingredients, is owned by two women, Jen Castle and Blake Spalding, who "operate their restaurant following Buddhist principles." Tibetan prayer flags hang from the entryway. The restaurant gets most of its vegetables from its two gardens and six-

MY FAVORITE AMERICAN PLACE

The enviro online magazine *Grist* had this to say of Salt Lake City's popular Democratic mayor Rocky Anderson, who completed his two-term stint in 2007: "A green mayor in a 'red' state, Salt Lake City's Rocky Anderson has remade his municipality during two terms in office. Anderson outlined a plan to lower the city government's carbon dioxide emissions 21 percent between 2001 and 2012, and met those targets six years ahead of schedule. Salt Lake now has an improved public transit system, including light rail, and requires that new and renovated city-owned or -managed buildings be certified under the U.S. Green Building Council's LEED program." Anderson is a Democrat, divorced and a lapsed Mormon.

NATION: How do you account for your political success in such a conservative state?

ROCKY: There's no way I'd have been elected mayor if Salt Lake City wasn't a more liberal place than the state. Before running for mayor I ran for Congress. I lost because I came out in favor of gay marriage. That was a pretty good indicator. The Mormon church used to dodge taking a stand on gay marriage, but the state GOP made it a wedge issue, so the vote for me was pretty much down religious lines.

The state is heavily Republican, but Salt Lake City is a liberal city. There have been major rallies against the Iraq War, which were organized by some local left groups. On the two occasions when President Bush came to town, 8,000 people turned out in protest of the war. That was a huge crowd for us. [Mayor Anderson was in the forefront of those rallies.]

Antiwar people have been working with Brigham Young University students about this issue. They're mostly political conservatives, and the church exercises strict control over the campus. It has fired professors who made controversial speeches contrary to Mormon ideas. A professor who wrote a paper on gay-lesbian issues was fired immediately. But the students came out in opposition to Vice President Cheney speaking on campus. They invited Ralph Nader to come and speak to them at an alternative facility.

NATION: So SLC sounds like a friendly place for liberals.

ROCKY: People who move here find it an easy community to get into. There are some wonderful places to socialize, including bars. I've spoken to the Drinking Liberally group. There was a large crowd. Groups like that foster a sense of community. People on the left who are hungry for community can join progressive organizations with a socializing aspect like the American Humanist Association and the Universalist Church.

Note: The SLC Drinking Liberally group meets every Friday at the Piper Down Pub, 1492 S. State Street. Its signature drink is the Shock and Awe, made of vodka (Russian), Frangelico, Kahlua, Malibu rum and heavy cream.

acre farm, and its fruit comes from its heirloom orchard. What makes it interesting is its location: Boulder, Utah, one of the most remote towns in the United States—population: 180 people, mostly Mormon. There was a law against serving alcohol in restaurants. Jen and Blake brought the issue up with the town council, explaining that wine and beer were the only way to make a profit, and got the okay. On St. Patrick's Day in 2002, Hell's Backbone became the first restaurant in Boulder's history to serve a glass of beer with a meal. Now the restaurant has a full wine and beer list, including one beer called Polygamy Porter.

20 North Highway 12, PO Box 1428, Boulder, UT 84716, (435) 335-7464, www.hellsbackbonegrill.com

One World Café. A cafeteria-style restaurant opened by Denise Cerreta in 2003, One World is unusual in many ways, most notably its pricing system—there isn't one. Diners choose their own portion sizes and, at the end of their meal, are asked to deposit however much money they think is fair in a basket as they leave. There is no menu, as the food changes daily based on what Cerreta feels like cooking—the one constant is fresh, organic ingredients. In addition to providing healthy food to people who might otherwise not be able to afford it, One World's strange system allows people to take only as much as they want, reducing waste (any leftovers at the end of the day are donated to the needy). As the website puts it, "Ms. Cerreta is attempting to help people see the value of food as more than a mere consumable but rather as a glue and a catalyst for healthy people, relationships and communities." One World doesn't advertise, preferring to rely on word-of-mouth recommendations from its loyal customers. That the café has lasted this long is a testament to that loyalty, since the premise of the place doesn't exactly seem like a sustainable business model. Anyone who can't afford to pay for food is welcome to pay in labor by volunteering in the kitchen or garden, where Cerreta grows organic herbs, spices and vegetables.

41 S. 300 East, Salt Lake City, UT 84111, (801) 519-2002, www.oneworldeverybodyeats.com

Wyoming

Harvest Café. Wyoming overwhelmingly supported Bush, and Dick and Lynne Cheney own a summer place in Jackson. Consequently, between Republican steak houses and fast food for the plebeians, there isn't much foodwise—except the Harvest Café, a cheerfully defiant counterculture spot. Memorable homemade pie, good organic salads and strong espresso, plus couches to sit on, New Age magazines to read and live music at night. If it can happen here, it can happen anywhere.

130 West Broadway, Jackson, WY 83001, (307) 733-5418

Places to Grow In

READING CLUBS AND DISCUSSION GROUPS

People interested in joining meetup.com clubs should sign up on each group's website, which has information about meeting times and places. Also check out Progressive Book Clubs, a list-serv that functions as an umbrella meeting room where people from different progressive book clubs can share their opinions on what they're reading.

> http://progressivebookclubs.blogspot.com

California

Breakthrough. This new group, based in California, is one of the Breakthrough Institute's reading groups. Organized by Americans "creating a new politics," it's committed to progressive politics that speak to "core needs and values, not issues and interests." The first book read was *Break Through: From the Death of Environmentalism to the Politics of Possibility* by Michael Shellenberger and Ted Nordhaus.

> http://bookclub.meetup.com/947/

The Los Angeles Philosophy Meetup Group. "Those with an ax to grind, please bore elsewhere" is the watchword of this group, which refuses to limit its philosophical dialogue to someone's obsessive agenda. What's on the list? Religion, politics, ethics, classic philosophy models—the usual suspects. Members are invited to bring munchies as discussions tend to go on for a bit.

http://philosophy.meetup.com/195/

The San Diego GLTB Christians Meetup Group. Gay or gay-friendly Christians, or people with the values of morality, kindness, spirituality and love: welcome.

http://gaychristians.meetup.com/197/

SFDebate Political Discussion Meetup. This San Francisco debate club is intended to moderate extreme viewpoints, find common ground and share and expand perspectives. According to its web page, "If you want to be able to convince others of your ideas, if you want to change the world we live in, SFdebate is the forum for you." But it's not all hard politics; debating sessions are followed by a drink and a bite to eat at a local bar or restaurant.

http://politicalcafe.meetup.com/50/

District of Columbia

DC Progressive Book Club. Apart from the usual rules—respectful discussion of books, not hogging all the time—the DC Club adds a new one: discussion of an "action item" for each member. This could mean conversing with and listening to someone else with an opposing viewpoint, bringing someone new to the next meeting and so on. At subsequent meetings, members expect feedback on these action items.

http://progressivebooksdc.blogspot.com

Georgia

Atlanta Beyond Oil. For the past three and a half years, this Georgia group has been engaged in discussing issues such as peak oil, global warming, sustainable communities, alternative energy and more.

http://oilawareness.meetup.com/67/

Iowa

Iowa Democratic Veterans' Caucus. Members should consider participation in this group a second call to arms. Rules include not speaking ill of another Democrat and not posting divisive messages. The group aims to "establish a network of county veterans' caucuses and a veterans' liaison in every Iowa county as a function of their Democratic Central Committee."

http://vets.meetup.com/39/

Maryland

The Progressive-Action Book Discussion Group. These readers foregather in a used, rare and out-of-print bookstore in Kensington, Maryland, on the evening of the third Monday of every month to discuss books with fellow liberals—no arguments, please—and brainstorm on how to bring about change.

http://members.verizon.net/~vze4nbyt/

Michigan

Detroit Democracy for America Book Club. Join this group and meet other Detroit members to read and discuss a new book every month. Topics range from sociology to politics to history and more; most of the books have a progressive agenda.

http://bookclub.meetup.com/215/

Progressive Women's Alliance Book Club. The book club of the Progressive Women's Alliance of West Michigan meets on the fourth Wednesday evening of every month. One month the book read was Jane Goodall's *Harvest for Hope: A Guide to Mindful Eating.* Examples of others: *Screwed: The Undeclared War Against the Middle Class—and What We Can Do About It* by Thom Hartmann; *Moral Politics: How Liberals and Conservatives Think,* 2nd edition, by George Lakoff; *The Audacity of Hope: Thoughts on Reclaiming the American Dream* by Barack Obama.

http://progressivewomensalliance.org

New York

Hudson Valley Humanists Book Club. Typical fare for these left-minded folk: Tariq Ali's *Pirates of the Caribbean: Axis of Hope* and *Hugo Chavez: The Bolivarian Revolution* by Richard Gott. The talk's good, start to finish.

http://hudsonvalley.humanists.net/

Progressive Gay Men. New York City gay or bisexual men with progressive values meet over fair-trade coffee or a beer in a bar, restaurant or park to discuss topics that are left of center. If you're a Republican, wear Armani, are a born-again Christian and support Bush, this group isn't for you—unless you really want to check it out, says the group organizer, in which case, what the heck, come anyway.

http://lgbtfriends.meetup.com/94/

16 Beaver Group. The name comes from the New York City address where this group holds its meetings. This book-film-everything club was chosen by *The Village Voice* as New York City's best Marxist group. On Monday evenings, it organizes events that include readings and book discussions. Check before going however, because they also screen films, organize exhibitions and more.

www.16beavergroup.org

Ohio

Ohio Democratic Party Watch Blogspot. This is an active group of people who meet in cyberspace to discuss ways to keep a close watch on the Ohio Democratic Party. Why? So that they can take it to task if it doesn't get it together after fifteen years of failure in statewide elections.

http://20millionloud.meetup.com/101/

http://watchodp.blogspot.com

Oregon

Liberal Book Club Meetup Group. This Portland group calls for more democracy, less propaganda in its reading matter. Therefore, favorite authors not surprisingly include Noam Chomsky, Howard Zinn, Greg Palast, Amy Goodman and works such as *The Federalist Papers* and Tom Paine's *Common Sense*.

http://bookclub.meetup.com/803/

Pennsylvania

Secular Book Club—Willow Grove. This Pennsylvania reading club aims to build a community of atheists, freethinkers, humanists and other nontheists by reading books around this theme. Their events—which include luncheons, readings, lectures, movie nights and a biannual antisuperstition party—are sponsored by the Humanist Association of Greater Philadelphia (www.hagp.org) and Freethought Society of Greater Philadelphia (www.fsgp.org).

http://bookclub.meetup.com/435/

Texas

Dallas Progressive Book Club—Dallas Air America Group. This is how Democrats, liberals and progressives in Dallas get together to share books on progressive topics. Members are also interested in swapping and lending videos.

> http://bookclub.meetup.com/342/; www.dallasairamerica.org

The Other Mothers: A Progressive Playgroup. This is a north Austin, Texas, playgroup for mothers who venture from the straight and narrow when it comes to parenting. They could be vegetarian/vegan, have an organic lifestyle, subscribe to alternative parenting techniques or be simply "liberal awesomely open-minded mamas looking for diversity and a little something different." Some meetings take place in members' homes; before a new mama can attend one of these, she has to have already attended a public event and have met one of the other moms. There's a $5 annual membership fee.

> http://playgroup.meetup.com/780/

Washington

Book Readings—Local, Independent Authors. As the name indicates, this Seattle book club supports homegrown literary figures, that is, writers who live in the Pacific Northwest. Independent authors are those "who retain the rights to their work rather than allowing the publisher to edit or trim the content." The books selected focus on politics, activism and political opinion, history and historical novels, poetry, gay and lesbian issues and more.

> http://book-swap.meetup.com/158/

Progressive Book Club. On the fourth Sunday afternoon of every month, a group of hardcore readers meets at the Vashon Tea Shop to socialize and chat about progressive books. Although the book club is organized by the Vashon–Maury Island Green Party, membership in the party is not necessary. Some of the books chosen were *American Fascists: The Christian Right and the War on America* by Chris Hedges and *Peace Is the Way* by Deepak Chopra.

> www.vashongreen.org/Projects/ProgressiveBookClub/tabid/56/

Nation Discussion Groups. Where smart, well-informed, curious *Nation*-reading progressives talk it out. To learn how to join one of these groups, or to find out how to start your own, call Nation Associates at (212) 209-5400. As of press time, there were active groups in seventy-two cities. For the latest listings see:
www.thenation.com/associates/discussion.mhtm

ACLU Handbook: The Rights of Students. Eve Cary, Norman Dorsen, and Alan H. Levine

The Activist's Handbook: A Primer. Randy Shaw

Banishing Bureaucracy: The Five Strategies for Reinventing Government. David Osborne and Peter Plastrik

The Better World Handbook: From Good Intentions to Everyday Actions. Ellis Jones and Ross Haenfler

Beyond Identity Politics: Emerging Social Justice Movements in Communities of Color. John Annerm, editor

Bridging the Class Divide and Other Lessons for Grassroots Organizing. Linda Stout and Howard Zinn

Bridging the Global Gap: A Handbook to Linking Citizens of the First and Third Worlds. Medea Benjamin and Andrea Freedman

Doing Democracy: The MAP [Movement Action Plan] Model for Organizing Social Movements. Bill Moyers

Earth First! Direct Action Manual (2nd ed.). DAM Collective

Fundraising for Social Change. Kim Klein

The Global Activists Manual: Local Ways to Change the World. Mike Prokosch and Laura Raymond, editors

Globalizing Civil Society: Reclaiming Our Right to Power. David Korten

Goodworks: A Guide to Careers in Social Change. Donna Colvin

Grassroots and Nonprofit Leadership: A Guide for Organizations in Changing Times. Berit Lakey, George Lakey and Rod Napier

Grassroots Grants: An Activist's Guide to Proposal Writing. Andy Robinson

Grassroots Journalism: A Practical Manual. Eesha Williams

How People Get Power. Si Kahn

Moving Forward: Program for a Participatory Economy. Michael Albert

Organizing: A Guide for Grass Roots Leaders. Si Kahn

Organizing for Community Action. Steve Burghardt

Organizing for Social Change: Midwest Academy Manual for Activists. Kim Bobo, Jackie Kenoall and Steve Max

Ralph Nader Presents Practicing Democracy: A Guide to Student Action. Katherine Isaac and Ralph Nader

Reclaiming America. Randy Shaw

Roots of Justice: Stories of Organizing in Communities of Color. Larry Salomon

Roots to Power: A Manual for Grassroots Organizing. W. Collette

Rules for Radicals. Saul Alinsky

The Snarling Citizen. Barbara Ehrenreich

Soul of a Citizen: Living with Conviction in a Cynical Time. Paul Rogat Loeb

Statistics for Social Change. Lucy Horwitz and Lou Ferleger

The Trajectory of Change: Activist Strategies for Social Transformation. Michael Albert

Transforming the Revolution: Social Movements and the World System. Samir Amin and Giovanni Arrighi

War Resisters League, Organizer's Manual. Ed Hedemann

Women Activists: Challenging The Abuse of Power. Anne Witte Garland

Why Bother? Getting a Life in a Locked-down Land. Sam Smith

The Zinn Reader: Writings on Disobedience and Democracy. Howard Zinn

CAMPS FOR LEFTY KIDS AND GROWN-UPS, TOO

Camp Inquiry. This annual week-long summer assembly is run by the Center for Inquiry (see page 219) and cosponsored by its affiliates, the Council for Secular

Humanism and the Committee for the Scientific Investigation of Claims of the Paranormal. In 2007 the camp was held at Camp Seven Hills in Holland, New York. The organizers offered, in addition to sports and outdoor activities, classes teaching young people about the virtues of skepticism and science and reason over faith.

www.campinquiry.org

Camp Kinderland is etched in the memories of many Jewish red-diaper babies. Founded in 1923 by the socialist Workmen's Circle (see page 140), it provided fresh air and fun, along with lessons in socialism, secular Jewish culture and Yiddish for the tenement-dwelling campers. It was situated on Sylvan Lake, Hopewell Junction, New York. A few years after its founding, the camp owners sided with a dissident faction of the Workmen's Circle called the International Workers Order, which was militantly pro-Soviet. Throughout the early 1930s, Camp Kinderland remained staunchly Stalinist. (In a memorable 1936 game of capture the flag, the "Fascist" team beat the "Loyalists." By the 1950s the games always ended in a sportsmanlike "Kinderland tie.") The coming of World War II changed the politics to anti-Fascism and patriotism. A rival camp for anticommunist socialist kids operated on the other side of Sylvan Lake, and was the subject of much ideological condemnation (its aluminum rowboats were "fascist"). Camp Kinderland survived the competition as well as McCarthyism, the dissolution of the International Workers Order as "subversive," moves to new sites and changes in ownership. Today the emphasis is on discussions of political issues, activism in behalf of peace and social justice, multiculturalism and "group living cooperative decision making, and a strong sense of community," according to *Jewish Currents* (see page 140). Above all, there's *hemshekh*—continuity.

1543 Colebrook River Road, Tolland, MA 01934, (413) 258-4463, www.campkinderland.org

People Camp. This all-ages retreat, run by Minnesota-based Friends for a Non-Violent World, is dedicated to opening up people's minds to the philosophy and techniques of nonviolence. There are no counselors shepherding the kids, who do assigned tasks. Mornings are devoted to workshops on subjects like Compassionate Communication. The afternoons are free for the usual camp activities—sports, games, hiking, handicraft, nature study and the like. The camp is located in Northern Pines, Minnesota, and is open every summer. Friends for a Non-Violent World "draw from Quaker traditions and affirm the dignity and self-determination of each person, promoting nonviolence as a powerful means to accomplish all just ends."

1050 Selby Avenue, St. Paul, MN 55104, (651) 917-0383, www.fnvw.org/contact/peoplecamp

Radical Encuentro. Radical Encuentro holds a biannual retreat where radical activists from across Texas can share ideas, strategies, successes and failures, as well as receive training in social justice and environmental issues. The slogan is: "educate to liberate." The weekend-long affairs held twice a year regularly draw 150 to 300 people. The idea gestated in 1999 at the Radical Education Community in Houston that such a facility was needed to inculcate grassroots organizing skills. The leaders, Rene Feltz and Scott Crow, changed the name to Radical Encuentro ("radical encounter," inspired by the encounters held by the Zapatista movement in Chiapas, Mexico). They also wanted to set up gatherings of social justice people that would connect them to others like them. Campers pay $15 but no one is turned away. The group sometimes focuses discussions around a theme that leads to a day of action, such as attending the ExxonMobil shareholders meeting in Houston in 2002.

www.radicalencuentro.org

Camp Quest. "It's beyond belief" is the motto of the first summer camp for children of atheists and freethinkers. Edwin Kagin, a well-known freethinker, and his wife founded it in 1996 because they were fed up with seeing kids pressured to believe in one religious doctrine or another. Kagin and his wife served as directors for the camp's first ten years. The original Camp Quest is near Clarksville, Ohio; now there are a total of six in California, Michigan, Minnesota and Ontario. The Ohio camp borrows the Clarksville 4H Club facilities for the one-week sessions. Activities include all the usual things but they do some things a bit differently, such as talking about famous freethinkers or discussing evolution. You need not be an atheist to apply, but obviously the idea is to give support to kids brought up without religion. The camp is supported by the Institute for Humanist Studies.

48 Howard Street, Albany, NY 12207, www.camp-quest.org

World Fellowship Center. Summer in the White Mountains of New Hampshire awaits. There are cabins and campsites for rent, woods for walking and a pond for canoeing. There's a main lodge, several homes and campsites and space for more than one hundred campers. Accommodations are rustic—shared bathrooms, bunks, cafeteria-style dining—but attendees say they don't want a bed and breakfast inn. Homemade bread and vegetables grown in the organic garden are served; the food is primarily vegetarian. Activities are unstructured; campers are of all ages, races and backgrounds. In addition to relaxing activities like yoga and boating, WFC offers panels and activities that revolve around politics and social justice. Activists, writers and university professors come to deliver talks with titles like "Empire's Workshop: Latin America, the US and the Rise of the New Imperialism," "A Look at the Welfare State in Europe and the US" and "Broken Promises, Broken Dreams: Stories of Jewish & Palestinian Trauma and Resilience," as well as workshops on community organizing. Also lighter fare like Yiddish sing-alongs and English country dances.

PO Box 2280, Conway, NH 03818, (603) 447-2280, www.worldfellowship.org

SCHOOLS, ACADEMIES AND ACTIVIST TRAINING

Highlander Research and Education Center. In 2007 this training ground and school for activists celebrated seventy-five years of catalyzing social change. It was born in 1932 as the Highlander Folk School. The founders were a labor activist, Myles Horton, and a teacher, Don West. Their objectives were "to provide an educational center in the South for the training of rural and industrial leaders, and for the conservation and enrichment of the indigenous cultural values of the mountains." But they would concentrate on training organizers for the reviving union movement, which was confronting rampant joblessness; its staff supported organizing drives of the Committee for Industrial Organization. In the 1950s Highlander switched to training leaders of the nascent civil rights movement. A student named Rosa Parks sparked the SCLC's Montgomery bus boycott. Amid the civil rights unrest, Highlander was condemned by segregationists for "race mixing." Workshops at Highlander shared inspirational songs, from which emerged "We Shall Overcome," adapted by Pete Seeger from an African-American hymn. (Highlander continues to administer the We Shall Overcome Fund, which receives royalties from the song.) In the seventies, Highlander moved beyond civil rights and voting rights to training community organizers to challenge corporate-dominated state governments in the South. Recently, it has opposed plant closings and NAFTA, fought for more representative local government and helped immigrant workers organize and stand up for their rights.

1959 Highlander Way, New Market, TN 37820, (865) 933-3443, www.highlandercenter.org

Midwest Academy. The Midwest Academy has been around since 1973 and has prepped more than 25,000 activists affiliated with change-seeking organizations and coalitions all over the country. It aims to teach ordinary folks the skills that will enable them to harness the power of many. The school's founder was Heather Booth, who was a leader in the labor, women's and civil rights movements. She started the new organization using money she received in a back-pay lawsuit settlement and drew on her own experiences in writing a curriculum that emphasized forming networks of many kinds of organizations. The academy started out by training feminist organizers and went on to train multi-issue statewide organizations of students, senior citizens, neighborhood and other constituencies.

28 E. Jackson Street, #605, Chicago, IL 60604, (312) 427-2304, www.midwestacademy.com

Wellstone Action. A political training course started by the children of Paul and Sheila Wellstone and friends and supporters of the couple interested in carrying on the political commitment of the Minnesota senator whose career, along with his wife's, was tragically cut short in a plane crash while campaigning. Wellstone, one of the most progressive legislators in Congress, emerged from a background of wide-ranging political activism and teaching political science at Carleton. The courses in his name, covering two and a half days, are given all over the country on college campuses, high schools, in cities. Students choose one of three tracks: how to run a winning electoral campaign, how to be an effective citizen activist or how to be a candidate for public office. Wellstone Action also offers a labor training program for unionists and a Native American leadership program.

2446 University Ave. W, Suite 170, St. Paul, MN 55114, (651) 645-3939, www.wellstone.org

POLITICAL TRAINER

Julie Lewin. Connecticut-based Julie Lewin is an animal rights activist, political trainer, consultant and lecturer whose theory is that progressives could wield far more power in the lawmaking arena at every level of government by organizing voting blocs. She says: "A politically organized minority issue group drives laws and public policies on its issue, because every lawmaker knows that even a tiny group can threaten his or her winning vote margin on Election Day." Her strong personal cause is animal rights and she founded the National Institute for Animal Advocacy in 2002 and in 2008 published *Get Political for Animals and Win the Laws They Need: Why and How to Launch a Voting Bloc for Animals in Your Town, City, County or State.*

6 Long Hill Farm, Guilford, CT, jlewin@igc.org

FARMS, WORK CAMPS AND COMMUNES

Alpha Farm. "Compared to that of mainstream America, life at Alpha is simple," they like to say here; "all are welcome who are interested in this kind of cooperative living." Visitors flock to Alpha Farm, an intentional community, meaning a group of people living cooperatively and sharing a common political or spiritual vision. Initial stays are usually limited to three days, though they can be longer. Normally fifteen to twenty people of all ages are in residence. The farm is twenty-five miles from the Pacific Ocean and fifty-five from Eugene, Oregon. The buildings on the property include a large old farmhouse, a new five-bedroom house and several cottages, cabins, yurts and trailers. "At Alpha, the value of commitment runs deep. A good number of the people who have lived as residents for a year-long introductory period have stayed to become members. Our bylaws define the membership commitment as 'for the foreseeable future' and for the average member, this has been five to ten years or more. Many people, too, have come for shorter periods, staying for a summer or perhaps a year, a welcome addition to the diversity of the whole."

92819 Deadwood Creek Road, Deadwood, OR 97430, (541) 964-5102, www.pioneer.net/~alpha/index.htm

The Farm. The Farm was founded by hippies in 1971 near the town of Summertown, Tennessee. It's known for its communal living, ecovillage training center and development of permaculture and alternative technologies. The best times to visit are on the farm experience weekends, after which visitors can make longer-term commitments.

Summertown, TN 38483, (913) 964-3574, www.thefarm.org

Pumpkin Hollow Community. Here we have a recently settled habitat catering to rural radicals and anarchists. (See *Fifth Estate*, page 124, which publishes out of Pumpkin Hollow.) It was planned as a haven for sustainable agriculture, communal living, art, education and left-wing politics. It's governed (or not governed) according to anarchist principles under the precept, " 'Harming none, do as you will' shall be the whole of the law." The fine print: "You take full responsibility for yourself when visiting our land." Pumpkin Hollow welcomes visitors if they let the community know in advance that they're coming.

1467 Pumpkin Hollow Road, Liberty, TN 37095, (615) 536-5022, www.pumpkinhollow.net

Red Earth Farms. Red Earth Farms is "dedicated to developing sustainable lifestyle choices," as well as "nonviolence, permaculture, feminism, and our personal spiritual paths." Its guiding principle: "Love the land; love your neighbors." Red Earth produces most of its own food, as well as supplying other needs. "We are in the beginning stages of our quest for a sustainable lifestyle, but as we learn from our experiences, we hope to share our knowledge with others and inspire them to also live in a gentler, more sustainable way." Visitors can help Red Earth folk do their thing for however long they want.

1 Smith Road, Rutledge, MO 63563, (660) 883-5330, http://redearthfarms.org

Twin Oaks. This intentional community in rural Virginia has been around since 1967. According to Twin Oaks, "Our way of life has reflected our values of cooperation, sharing, nonviolence, equality, and ecology." They welcome visitors for a three-week stay, which involves forty-two hours of weekly work and is a "structured program designed to give the visitor some general education and experience in living at Twin Oaks."

138 Twin Oaks Road, #W, Louisa, VA 23093, (540) 894-5126, www.twinoaks.org

Wildroots. A back-to-nature collective, "Wildroots is a 30-acre radical homestead adjacent to the Pisgah [National Forest] in Madison County, Western, North Carolina (about 45 minutes from Asheville). Our focus is on experiential learning and living, while practicing, developing and sharing skills for rewilding and reconnection. . . . Our interests include permaculture, gardening by the moon, natural and primitive shelter building, hide tanning, herbal medicine, nature crafts, and wild food foraging." The collective holds events on Wildroots Homestead and welcomes long-term residents as well as short-term visitors and day-trippers "interested in experiential learning."

PO Box 1485, Asheville, NC 28801, www.wildroots.org

PARKS AND PRESERVES

Mesaba Co-op Park. A member-owned land and facilities co-op near Hibbing, Minnesota, Mesaba Park occupies 240 acres of woodlands surrounding a lake. It was started in 1929, and is considered the best surviving example of the socialist communities and cooperatives that Finnish settlers set up around that time. A group of co-ops acquired the land for the purpose of a "common festival and camping grounds." During the Depression the Minnesota Farmer-Labor Party and the Communist Party were active in Minnesota. During the McCarthy era, FBI agents parked outside the gates and copied incoming lefties' license plate numbers. In the 1970s Mesaba welcomed antiwar, feminist and environmental activists, who found common ground with the older lefties. The park continues to be inspired by the Left and the progressive ideals of its founders.

3827 Mesaba Park Road, Hibbing, MN 55746, (218) 262-1350, www.mesabapark.us

Up on the far northern cusp of the United States, along the shore of Lake Superior, you'll find the old timber town of Ashland, Wisconsin. Settled by radical Finns and Norwegians who erected great brownstone buildings to protect themselves against the harsh winters, Ashland is a ruggedly handsome city—both physically and politically—where socialists still celebrate May Day in a lakefront park, members of the Northland Anti-War Coalition rally at the old-fashioned band shell and students enroll in Northland College's Sigurd Olson Environmental Institute to learn a green citizenship that is practiced daily in a region where walking to work on a January morning is an extreme sport. It can snow in May, but an Ashland summer is about as close as you'll get to heaven on earth. For me, the heart of Ashland is the 200 block of historic Chapple Avenue, where locals shop the Chequamegon Food Co-op for

wild rice, gather fresh corn and berries at a seasonal farmers' market, pick up artisan breads from the Ashland Baking Company shop and then settle at the remarkable Black Cat Coffee House for espresso in the morning and microbrews at night. . . . If the Black Cat were located in Manhattan or San Francisco it would be hailed by food and design critics as an archetype, a pristine relic of a disappearing Europe or a Beat generation gathering spot. But the folks in Ashland would laugh off such pretenses and steer the conversation toward the more immediate concerns of upsetting the global economic order or identifying the best stretch of shoreline for kayaking.

—JOHN NICHOLS, Washington correspondent of *The Nation*

Orient Land Trust. Orient is dedicated to the "preservation . . . of the northern San Luis Valley for the enjoyment of current and future generations." Writes *Nation* associate Karen Hunter: "Here in Colorado there is a very left-leaning and wonderful place to spend a few days. It used to be called Valley View Hot Springs and is now the Orient Land Trust and Valley View Hot Springs. . . . A few miles past Villa Grove south on

Highway 285. Several years ago the owners turned the property into a land trust so that it will always be the way it has always been. Clothing optional and a great way to give back to Colorado. Check it out. I've never met a Republican there." Camping and lodgings available.

PO Box 65, Valley View Hot Springs, Villa Grove, CO 81155, (719) 256-4315, www.olt.org

ACTING LOCALLY

ABC No Rio. This is a community center for art and activism on New York's Lower East Side—"The culture of opposition since 1980." The whole thing started on New Year's Day 1980 at the Real Estate Show, an exhibition of art attacking New York's real estate market and landlords mounted by more than thirty artists who had taken over an abandoned building. The cops shut them down, but they persisted; and the city gave them their present space, originally a storefront. They epitomized the political and artistic ferment on the Lower East Side (see Bread & Puppet Theater, page 65) and continue that tradition of "artistic expression dealing with war, homelessness, drugs, sex, violence, and the politics of housing and real estate." In the eighties they were at the center of the Lower East Side performance art, poetry and hardcore music scene (though ABC No Rio refused to book racist, sexist or homophobic bands). Now they are open to all sorts of forums and meetings, workshops and benefits. Credo: "We believe that art and activism should be for everyone, not just the professionals, experts, and cognoscenti. . . . Our community includes . . . punks who embrace the Do-It-Yourself ethos, express positive outrage, and reject corporate commercialism. It includes nomads, squatters, fringe dwellers, and those among society's disenfranchised who find at ABC No Rio a place to be heard and valued." (See website for events, information on facilities and affiliated groups/projects.)

156 Rivington Street, New York, NY 10002, (212) 254-3697, www.abcnorio.org

Ella Baker Center for Human Rights. In a tiny office in 1996 with a computer belonging to a colleague, a young attorney named Van Jones started Bay Area Police Watch to monitor police brutality. From a hotline and a small staff documenting brutality it steadily expanded its scope and soon outgrew that early space, raised some seed money and became the Ella Baker Center, named after the legendary civil rights pioneer who mentored the young students in SNCC in the early 1960s. The new center launched its first human rights campaign against a cop who had killed an unarmed African-American man without justification. As a result, the cop was fired. Next came the Books Not Bars campaign, to stop Oakland's Alameda County from building an enormous jail for young people. The center agitated for other reforms in the California youth

programs as well. And then came Silence the Violence, a youth-led campaign to cool the gang-ridden streets of Oakland. That effort kicked off with the Summer of Non-Violence and a compilation hip-hop CD featuring "some of the Bay Area's hottest rappers talking about neighborhood violence." The latest initiative is the Green-Collar Jobs Campaign. Jones preaches that the ultimate remedy is more jobs and specifically proenvironment "green collar" jobs in Oakland: "Quite simply, Oakland is underemployed and over-polluted. We can solve both of these problems by making sure that the emerging 'clean and green' economy comes to Oakland, and that the jobs go to people coming out of prison or at risk of going in." Van Jones and the Ella Baker Center believe that the safest communities are not the ones with the most cops on the streets but the ones with the most and best-paying jobs. (See Apollo Alliance, page 232.)

344 40th Street, Oakland, CA 94609, (510) 428-3939, www.ellabakercenter.org

Esperanza Peace and Justice Center. This community arts and cultural center involves itself in progressive activism, cultural activity and creative work, including art exhibitions, craft programs, educational projects and an environmental justice project. Members have led protests against U.S. military intervention in Central America and Iraq, celebrated International Women's Day, organized counterprotests to the Ku Klux Klan, exposed gay bashing and demonstrated against the closure of a major local newspaper. They were also involved in a controversial lawsuit against the city over censorship issues, resolved in the center's favor in 2001. (See page 33.)

922 San Pedro, San Antonio, TX 78212, (210) 228-0201, www.esperanzacenter.org

Labor Community Strategy Center. Guiding light here is Eric Mann, who emerged from the socialist student movements of the sixties and had been a UAW activist at the Van Nuys General Motors plant. The center grew out of a movement to keep the GM plant open. Working with Barry Commoner, Mann says he realized that a fundamental question was involved: "We want to keep the GM plant open but do we want to keep the internal combustion machine with all its pollution?" His priorities shifted to organizing the grossly underserved public transit riders. It was a class issue: the riders were mostly black and Hispanic working poor who had great difficulty getting to their jobs because the LA public transportation system was so bad. The Bus Riders Union demanded more routes and more buses. In 1999 the BRU won court decisions ordering the Los Angeles MTA to provide hundreds of new buses, but the city kept stalling and raising fares. Today the Strategy Center calls itself a multiracial "think tank/act tank." It melds grassroots organizing such as the Bus Riders Union and community rights projects with education, policy development and artistic productions. It sponsors the Center for Transportation Strategies, the National School for Strategic Organizing, *Voices from the Frontlines* radio show and a magazine, *AhoraNow*.

3780 Wilshire Boulevard, Suite 1200, Los Angeles, CA 90010, (213) 387-2800,
www.thestrategycenter.org

PARADES AND FESTIVALS

Fighting Bob Fest. We received the following communication from *Nation* associate Chuck Kalina:

> Every year, in September, the "Fighting Bob Fest" is held in Baraboo, Wisconsin. [That's "Fighting Bob" La Follette, the Progressive senator from Wisconsin and presidential candidate in the twenties.] My wife and I attend every year, and it affords a chance for a small piece of the progressive community to come together, exchange ideas, check out what's new and recharge the batteries of activism. [In 2007] September 8 was the date.... Some featured speakers in attendance were Gwen Moore, Cindy Sheehan, Jim Hightower, Jeremy Scahill, and the Raging Grannies.

> This progressive happening was organized by ten activists in 2001, who gathered at a restaurant; all were veterans of the fight to stop water giant Perrier from taking over the state's prime springs. They felt they should talk about the lessons learned from the Perrier campaign and decide how to arm themselves for the next crisis. At the end of the day they coalesced around the idea of a "Chautauqua on citizen action" named after "Fighting Bob" La Follette (see *The Progressive*, page 121). At the first Fest, in 2002, they talked about the best tactics to use to stop a new Wal-Mart and how to file a Freedom of Information Act request. The fests continued to grow; 6,000 showed up at the 2006 event. "That is at least 10 times the number of people who show up for the state's annual Democratic and Republican party conventions," observes the Fighting Bob Fest site.

PO Box 2131, Madison, WI 53701, (608) 256-1339, www.fightingbobfest.org

"How Berkeley Can You Be!?" Maybe it's just the title that intrigues us—how Berkeley do you want to be? This parade in the heart of free speech land is touted as "an annual cel-

ebration of the uniquely wild, wonderful spirit of Berkeley!" It was organized in 1996 to promote a depressed downtown and have fun. The event draws more than 1,000 participants and 15,000 spectators. It's organized by Epic Arts, a community arts non-profit, and features live music and dance, food and drink, crafts, children's activities and funny hats.

www.howberkeleycanyoube.com

SEX . . . ROMANCE . . . LOVE?

Act for Love. An online matchmaking site for progressives. Its motto is: "Activist? Leftist? Take action, get action!"

www.actforlove.org

Earth Wise Singles. This is an online dating service for "green-living and environmentally responsible adults; friends of Mother Earth; organic gardeners, farmers and ranchers; lovers of nature and the outdoors; concerned about human rights and world peace; interested in alternative and holistic medicine; looking for long-term friendship and romance." If you meet those requirements, you may go to the website, though they insist: "We are NOT another on-line classified ad service."

www.ewsingles.com

Exotic Fever Records. This record company released a CD called *This Is a Care Package: A Compilation Benefiting Helping Individual Prostitutes Survive.* Proceeds from the CD go to Helping Individual Prostitutes Survive, a D.C.-based organization that aims to provide health services for prostitutes.

PO Box 297, College Park, MD 20741, www.exoticfever.com

Good Vibrations. In 1977, Joani Blank, sex therapist, educator and founder of Down There Press, opened an adult bookstore, Good Vibrations, in San Francisco. She wanted her store to be a friendly, well-lit alternative to the usual places for furtive guys in raincoats. A decade later, Blank became the lone board member and stockholder in the newly incorporated Open Enterprises, which launched a mail-order video and book catalog. In 1990, employees bought Open Enterprises Inc. from Blank and restructured it into a worker-owned cooperative. New stores have opened in Berkeley and San Francisco, California, and Brookline, Massachusetts. In 2005, the board of directors decided to restructure as a corporation rather than remain a co-op to meet changing customer needs and to address market demands. In 2006, the change was complete, but worker policies remain the same. The store has received positive press as a woman-focused adult retail store with knowledgeable and friendly staff. It also sells a wide variety of sex products on its website.

603 Valencia Street, San Francisco, CA 94110, (415) 522-5460; 1620 Polk Street, San Francisco, CA 94109, (415) 345-0400; 2504 San Pablo Avenue, Berkeley, CA 94702, (510) 841-8987; 308-A Harvard Street, Brookline, MA 02446, (617) 264-4400; www.goodvibes.com

Lusty Lady Theatre. "The world's only unionized, worker-owned peep show co-op!" Years ago, this place operated only as a peep show, with private movie booths. Then the owners decided to hire live acts. The introduction of women who thought for themselves onto the premises  led to trouble. When the owners foisted some unfair sex work practices on the girls, they rebelled and went to SEIU Local 790. Negotiations were joined and an election called on whether to unionize. The bosses resisted with union-busting lawyers, but the gals held firm. They picketed and were locked out, but in April 1997 the union won the election 57 to 15. Thus was the Exotic Dancers Union formed, said to be the only sex workers' union of its kind. In 2003 employees bought the club, which was on the verge of going under. Revived, it won Best Strip Club Award in 2006 in readers' polls conducted by rival alternative weeklies, *SF Weekly* and the *San Francisco Bay Guardian*. For the sex workers the deal is "No contact, no hustling, and a guaranteed hourly wage." The shows go from 11 A.M. to 3 A.M. daily. There are private fantasy booths that feature "a rotating schedule of naughty show-offs."

1033 Kearney Street, San Francisco, CA 94133, (416) 391-3991, www.lustyladysf.com

National Coalition for Sexual Freedom. They are dedicated to "alternative sexual expression," primarily for the "leather-fetish, swing, and polyamory communities." NCSF was formed in 1997 by a small group led by Susan Wright under the auspices of the New York SM Activists. Other groups joined: the National Leather Association—International, Gay Male S/M Activists, the Eulenspiegel Society, Black Rose and Society of Janus. Today the NCSF claims more than fifty coalition partners and annual meetings. They also work with other organizations that defend sexual freedom rights: Free Speech Coalition; the ACLU; American Association of Sex Educators, Councilors and Therapists; Society for the Scientific Study of Sexuality; National Gay and Lesbian Task Force and the Gay and Lesbian Activist Alliance, among others.

822 Guilford Avenue, Box 127, Baltimore, MD 21202, (410) 539-4824, www.ncsfreedom.org

The New York Liberal Singles Meetup Group. A real, as opposed to online, social group where single progressives can meet other single progressives in the flesh. You should go to the website to find out the time and location of the next meeting.

http://singles.meetup.com/1273/

Sex Workers Outreach Project USA. This self-help organization to combat violence against men and women in the sex trade started in San Francisco in 2003. One of the first projects was proclaiming and sustaining an International Day to End Violence Against Sex Workers, each December 17. SWOP works to achieve its main objective by decriminalizing prostitution and ending police harassment of prostitutes. There are now chapters in Alabama, Arizona, Chicago, Las Vegas, Los Angeles/UCLA, Michigan, Northern California and Texas. The SWOP at UCLA is recognized as an official student organization and is eligible for school aid. The Tucson chapter put on a sex workers' art festival, using art to communicate with the square populace. SWOP publishes a free manual on organizing a chapter. They also cosponsored a conference on prostitution, sex work and the commercial sex industry and set up the National Sex Worker Leadership Training Institute. SWOP has introduced a measure in the Berkeley city council to make prostitution legal.

912 Cole Street, #202, San Francisco, CA 94117, (877) 776-2004, www.swopusa.org

Smitten Kitten. This vendor of "progressive adult sex toys" operates a 2,400-square-foot store for a "boutique style shopping experience complete with complimentary coffee or tea," staffed by "sex educators" who will match you with the appropriate products. Candidates for the job must have a background in sex education and sexual health and also women's studies or gender studies. (Ahem.) Smitten Kitten calls itself "a truly feminist sex toy store." The co-owners are Jessica Giordani and Jennifer Pritchett, and their concept is that it's a woman-friendly sex store that offers hygienic, nontoxic, hypoallergenic sex toys.

3010 Lyndale Avenue South, Minneapolis, MN 55408, (888) 751-0523, www.smittenkittenonline.com

$pread. A magazine by and for present or former sex workers and the johns who love them. *$pread* gives its readers honest reporting on the sex workplace, porn personalities and health and legal matters and hazards peculiar to the Life. A typical issue features a scatological description of a phone-sex session, a profile of a husband-and-wife team that makes X-rated films and the story of another adult film figure who is female-to-male transgendered. But the same issue also crusades to improve the pay, health and legal rights of sex workers all over the world. *Spread* ran an interview with Leslie Cagan, national coordinator of United for Peace and Justice, mainly pressing her on the organization's failure to stand up for sex workers. (Cagan, a

veteran lefty, politely agreed UPJ should do more but pointed out that the coalition's constituents were necessarily focused on ending the Iraq War.) The magazine reported on the health risks of sex toys, in an article that could have come from the pages of *Consumer Reports* if it were not a family magazine.

PO Box 305, Cooper Station, New York, NY 10276, www.spreadmagazine.org

VeganErotica.com. An online store run by Reach Out Publications, VeganErotica bills itself as "passion for the compassionate," and manufactures and sells all kinds of vegan (no animals used) bondage gear, whips, belts, harnesses and other pleather items. There are also bondage bracelets, an "intimate lubricant and personal moisturizer" and bondage collars. Managed by Camilla Taylor, who is "dedicated to veganism, sex positive politics, and hand crafts."

PO Box 2762, Salt Lake City, UT 84110, (801) 560-8238, www.veganerotica.com

Veggiedate. Alienated from the regular dating and meet-up sites? Perhaps this one is for you. It's a "dating service for vegetarians, raw foodists, macrobiotics, adventists, Baha'is, Taoists, Scientologists, Buddhists, Hindus. . . ." and also "assists with sharing of vegetarian recipes and vegetarian meals, meetings at vegetarian restaurants and enjoyment of a vegetarian lifestyle."

www.veggiedate.com

COMMUNITY CENTERS

C-Space. A combined community center, activist hub and political site, C-Space aims to bring together activists and progressive social justice groups "in a way that fosters the ideas of cooperation, equality, and grassroots community action." It offers space, technology, programming, educational material and assistance and other resources to community members and activists on Cleveland's West Side. It's volunteer-run, donation driven.

4323 Clark Avenue, Cleveland, OH 44109, (216) 631-2233, www.clevelandspace.org

Tacoma Friends Meeting House. This place comes highly recommended by *Nation* associate Susan Donaldson:

In Tacoma, Washington, a prime gathering place for progressives has been Hillside Community Church/Tacoma Friends Meeting House. The church was first founded in 1953 as a spin-off from St. Paul's Methodist Church when the then-pastor, Harold Bass, began criticizing the Korean War from the pulpit and in letters to the editor of the local newspaper and was encouraged to leave St. Paul's—taking about half the congregation with him. In the 1980s and early 1990s, Sixth Sense, a local peace/justice network (so-named because of our being in Washington State's sixth congressional district) met there. As did the local PFLAG chapter under the leadership of Rev. Milton Andrews (long Washington State's representative for the War Resisters League). The church congregation is smaller now (and the property has been sold to the Quakers), but the building and grounds are still often used for peace-group gatherings. (See Progressive Protestants, page 217.)

2508 S. 39th Street, Tacoma, WA 98409, (253) 759-1910, http://tacoma.quaker.org

The Unitarian Church of Staten Island. We'll include this particular one out of many progressive churches of this denomination because of Dan Icolari's e-mail, which read in the subject line: "Where lefties commune on Staten Island." Dan goes on:

Dear *Nation Guide*:

Now that you've picked yourself up off the floor, having fallen out of your chairs at the startling news that there actually *are* lefties on Staten Island, I'll tell you where we (or many of us, at any rate) hang out, and that's the Unitarian Church. During the 30 years we've lived here, I can't think of a single issue, a single movement, a single progressive event local, national or global, where the Unitarian Church and many of its members weren't involved, and usually in a significant way. While, yes, it is a church (founded originally by freethinkers, followers of Emerson, etc.), I and my wife have always considered it a forum for progressive social and cultural ideas—as well as a magnet for people interested in those ideas—a uniquely active church and which in many different locations is a major focal point for social activism and activist culture. And not only Staten Island. . . .

Doesn't surprise us, Dan, that the Unitarians on ultraconservative Staten Island hold to their liberal principles. That's what they've been doing for many years. In the course of our researches for this guide we've heard from Boston, Massachusetts; Bellevue, Washington; Delaware County, Pennsylvania; Idyllwild, California; Austin, Texas and a number of other cities that credit the Unitarian Universalist church with being a haven for progressive action and community. (See Beacon Press, page 35.) And this just in from our Chicago correspondent, Penelope Rosemont: "Third Unitarian Church was probably the only church to defend the Haymarket Riot defendants. It is still highly activist and sponsors radical speakers." And don't forget the United Church of Christ!

312 Fillmore Street, Staten Island, NY 10301, (718) 447-2204, www.unitarianchurchofstatenisland; Third Unitarian Church, 301 N. Mayfield Street, Chicago, IL, 60644, (773) 626-9385, www.thirdunitarianchurch.org

Workmen's Circle/Arbeiter Ring. This fraternal organization and mutual-aid society was created by Jewish immigrants in the early twentieth century. Like many New York Jewish organizations at the time, it embraced avowedly socialist politics in its early years. The group organizes Yiddish cultural events, still runs a summer retreat/lodge and summer camp founded in 1927 and provides elder services. (See *Jewish Currents*, page 140.)

45 E. 33rd Street, New York, NY 10016, (212) 889-6800 (with regional branches), www.circle.org

HOW TO BUILD COMMUNITY

TURN OFF YOUR TV

LEAVE YOUR HOUSE

KNOW YOUR NEIGHBORS

LOOK UP WHEN YOU ARE TALKING

GREET PEOPLE

SIT ON YOUR STOOP

PLANT FLOWERS

USE YOUR LIBRARY

PLAN TOGETHER

BUY FROM LOCAL MERCHANTS

SHARE WHAT YOU HAVE

HELP A LOST DOG

TAKE CHILDREN TO THE PLAY GARDEN TOGETHER

SUPPORT NEIGHBORHOOD SCHOOLS

FIX IT EVEN IF YOU DIDN'T BREAK IT

HAVE POT LUCKS

HONOR ELDERS

PICK UP LITTER

READ STORIES ALOUD

DANCE IN THE STREET . . .

—Poster inside the front door of the Mercury Café, Denver, CO (see page 331)

Acknowledgments

My thanks to many friends of *The Nation* who helped with the compiling of this *Guide*. Peter Rothberg and Peter Fifield of the *Nation* and Nation Associates, respectively, launched flotillas of emails to readers and supporters asking for recommendations of favorite "Progressive Places." We are grateful to the readers and friends who responded, thereby endowing the *Guide* with added political and geographical reach. Editors, contributors and supporters of the magazine also offered expertise, ideas, suggestions and words (e.g., for the "My Favorite American Place" series). The following contributors qualify as above and beyond the call of duty: Stuart Klawans, Phil Green, Danny Goldberg, Eric Alterman, Rabbi Arthur Waskow, Studs Terkel, Penelope Rosemont, Marcus Raskin, William Greider, Rocky Anderson, Marjorie Cohn, Howard Zinn. (To those inadvertently unthanked—your time will come.) Maggie Berkvist and Bob Hammond rounded up the illustrations that enliven these pages. Jim Silberman provided sage editorial counsel.

And this book wouldn't be what it is without artist Ed Koren's lovable liberals. Chris Calhoun of Sterling Lord Literistic was our literary agent. Our editors at Vintage Books—Andrew Miller (now with Knopf), Lisa Weinert, (a former *Nation* intern) and Andrea Robinson—gave essential guidance at successive stages of the project. Finally, gracias to Numero Uno Nationistas Katrina vanden Heuvel, Victor Navasky and Teresa Stack for their continuing encouragement and support to this writer, who had a ball.

—RICHARD LINGEMAN

Photographic Credits

Page 8—Sacco and Vanzetti, Getty Images. Page 10—Socialist Labor Party Hall, Barre Historical Society. Page 11—Wesleyan Chapel, Women's Rights Historical Park, US Park Service. Page 11—John Brown's Grave, Getty Images. Page 13—Union Square Park, Tamiment Library, NYU. Page 14—Paterson Strike Poster, Tamiment Library, NYU. Page 30—"The Parks, the Circus, the Klan, the Press" by Thomas Hart Benton, Indiana University Archives. Page 65—Bread & Puppet Theater, Jack Sumberg. Page 109—"Great Battle of Homestead," Rivers of Steel National Heritage Area. Page 110—Funeral Procession for Victims of the Ludlow Massacre, Denver Public Library. Page 114—"Free the Catonsville 9," Dean Papas, Enoch Pratt Free Library. Page 182—Congo Square dancers, Hogan Jazz Archive, Tulane University. Page 183—Mme. C.J. Walker and friends in Model T ca 1912, Walker Family Collection/madamcjwalker.com (see also A'Lelia Bundles, *On Her Own Ground: The Life and Times of Madam C. J. Walker*). Page 184—Haymarket Martyrs Monument, Forest Park Cemetery, photograph by Max Hucke www.graveyards.com. Page 204—Honk! Festival band, Davind Chin. Page 235—Step It Up in snow, photograph by Chris Pilaro/Working Films; Step It Up Congress, gazebo, photograph by Tim Calabro/The Herald of Randolph; Step It Up Congress, underwater, photograph by Craig Quirolo/Reef Relief. Page 242—"No New Coal," photograph by Ronnie Blakeney/Spectral Q. Page 261—Pete Seeger by the Guthrie Tree, photograph by D. Jones. Page 262—Joe Hill's corpse, University of Utah Library, Special Collections. Pages 269, 272, 275—Greenmarket patrons, photographs by Maggie Berkvist. Page 332—"Global Injustice" protesters, photograph by Al Crespo, author of *Protest in the Land of Plenty*. Page 333—Marker at John Reed Bench, photograph by David Milholland.

Page 334—Japanese-American detainees at Manzanar station, Bancroft Library, University of California, Berkeley. Page 386—Lusty Lady chalk, Thomas Hawk; Page 386—Lusty Lady signs, photographs by Nick Gripton.

Other photographs and images provided by listed organizations. Our thanks to them.

Index